Research Guide
for Studies in
Infancy and Childhood

RESEARCH GUIDE FOR STUDIES IN INFANCY AND CHILDHOOD

Enid E. Haag

Reference Sources for the Social Sciences and Humanities,
Number 8

GREENWOOD PRESS
New York • Westport, Connecticut • London

Library of Congress Cataloging-in-Publication Data

Haag, Enid E.
  Research guide for studies in infancy and childhood.

  (Reference sources for the social sciences and humanities, ISSN
0730-3335 ; no. 8)
  Bibliography: p.
  Includes index.
  1. Children—Bibliography. 2. Reference books—Children—
Bibliography. I. Title. II. Series.
Z7164.C5H3   1988   [HQ767.85]   016.3052 '3   88-5690
ISBN 0-313-24763-3 (lib. bdg. : alk. paper)

British Library Cataloguing in Publication Data is available.

Library of Congress Catalog Card Number: 88-5690
ISBN: 0-313-24763-3
ISSN: 0730-3335

First published in 1988

Greenwood Press, Inc.
88 Post Road West, Westport, Connecticut 06881

Printed in the United States of America

The paper used in this book complies with the
Permanent Paper Standard issued by the National
Information Standards Organization (Z39.48-1984).

10 9 8 7 6 5 4 3 2 1

To my daughter Vikki

Contents

Series Foreword

Discipline by discipline, research is a process that includes locating information that helps us understand and explain unexplored areas of study. The information we seek, whether factual evidence or theoretical concepts, is needed to support the arguments we use for interpreting our own data. Research can, in addition, help us revise or expand our understanding of topics investigated by others.

Whatever the subject, our search for information often requires that we examine materials on library shelves. The sheer quantity, the indeterminate content of these materials causes most people to approach this task apprehensively. One is well advised to seek assistance. Wherever possible, of course, utilize the skilled services of librarians; they can assist you in immeasurable ways. Often, however, places to look for the "answers" to your research problems are difficult to specify concretely or directly. If this is indeed the case, librarians give you a set of helpful instructions about what sources you can consult and hope that you find the specific information you need.

If this approach does not prove successful, what do you do? Patricia Knapp, a librarian who helped us develop a theory of library research instruction, observed that "high-level library competence calls upon a wide range of knowledge and skills, and probably involves a particular kind of mental activity." "This type of mental activity," Knapp argues, "is not just picked up." "Instead," she stresses, "it must be taught."

This is the third research guide in this series. Like the first two and subsequent research guides, it is designed to help you develop library search strategies in the manner to which Knapp refers.

Written by an experienced education librarian, with assistance from colleagues with other specialties, this research guide introduces the major reference sources in infancy and childhood as well as references for special subject areas. Skillfully organized, it is intended to meet the needs of undergraduates, graduates, scholars, and professionals in the field.

This research guide fills a long-standing need. It makes more accessible the extensive, scattered references and related sources necessary for developing effective research strategies. To have helped in its creation is very rewarding.

Raymond G. McInnis,
Series Editor

Preface

This guide is an outgrowth of thirteen years of reference work with university students, researchers, and faculty from the many disciplines concerned with infancy and childhood including psychology, social work, education, sociology, medicine, law, home economics, and the arts. The book falls naturally into two sections. The first section, made up of three chapters, is a general guide to the literature in the field. The second section is a compilation of special subject bibliographies which serves to draw attention to available resources or tools on a particular topic not fully covered in the general guide to the literature.

A diverse collection of entries, the volume brings together approximately 1,400 entries. Initially I began with a number of individual subject bibliographies developed as in-house publications. Other subject sections were added to fill gaps in the published literature. Noteworthy of these are the sections on reading, exceptional children, communication disorders, music (compiled by Marian Ritter), sport, and child study guides. As the book took form, I added other subject sections. I have made a special effort to include resources which are often requested but extremely difficult to locate. A good example of these is the ORACLE project, usually referred to in the literature by the acronym, but seldom indexed under it. This also explains why individual reports of research and chapters from particular books are cited. To locate other possible entries, I searched a variety of databases and library collections, and checked book reviews from *Child Development Abstracts*, *Young Children, Early Child Development and Care, Choice*, and *Contemporary Psychology*, to name a few. I also perused publisher's catalogs. Materials which I could not personally review were not included.

My philosophy and experience suggest that research guides are used if people can glean information quickly and easily. This made me reject writing a prose style "how to" guide. I also wanted to write a research guide which would introduce researchers to the advantages of combining both traditional literature searching and the new technologies. My grand plan soon faded as I struggled to create a format which would allow the integration of the two. The inclusion of Chapter 2 by Dana Johnson along with the introduction of an annotated list of suggested databases to search became a viable alternative. Thus the book evolved into an annotated bibliography with suggested databases for each broad topic given a prominent place at the beginning of each chapter. To satisfy the need for some direction about literature searching, the first section of the book was written. It briefly introduces methodology as well as resources to facilitate literature searching. A special feature of Chapter 1 is a list of general research guides to the various disciplines.

This book and its corresponding database were compiled through the use of SCIMATE and MICROSOFT WORD software. Bibliographic entries and their annotations were entered into a field searchable database using SCIMATE MANAGER. Records were then sorted to conform to the chapter divisions presented in the book. Once sorted, the records were proofread and corrected.

Following the editing of the database, records selected for inclusion in the book were formatted to the bibliographic style used throughout the book with SCIMATE EDITOR. The resulting files were then converted into ASCII format which allowed for more final editing and production using MICROSOFT WORD. At this point, chapter headings and titles were added, spelling checked, and page formatting completed. The manuscript went to the publisher as camera-ready copy.

Acknowledgments

I would like to thank all those people who contributed to making this book possible. First, I want to express my gratitude to Dr. Bearnice Skeen, Professor Emeritus, who advised on the book's scope and content and who proofread the early chapters. And I thank Dr. Roberta Bouverat for keeping me appraised of developments in the field as I focused on the book.

A very special thanks goes to Greg Ballog, graduate student in science education who orchestrated the computer program used in developing the database from which the manuscript evolved. For the superlative service of Wilson Library's interlibrary loan services, especially Evelyn Darrow, Jo Dereske, Leslie Hall, and Susan Bannerstrom, I am thankful. I also wish to express my gratitude to Diane Parker for her making time and resources available so that the project could be brought to completion.

Also I wish to thank the staff of the Bureau for Faculty Research at Western Washington University and Joy Dabney of Media Services who prepared the camera-ready manuscript.

SECTION I
GENERAL INTRODUCTORY MATERIAL

1

Researching Infancy and Childhood

Introduction

This guide is for anyone studying children who wishes to search the literature effectively. It is for students just beginning to seek answers to questions concerning children, as well as professionals with years of experience and the practitioner seeking answers to problems. It will be helpful for anyone wishing to learn about using databases in the literature searching process. This volume is not designed to answer particular questions but it will assist in the gathering of information necessary to make decisions or arrive at informed conclusions to problems regarding children.

The need for information about children is great. Recently, public awareness has been focused upon such topics as latchkey children, child abuse and neglect, child care, one-parent families, hyperactive children, attention deficit syndrome, child abduction, and fathers as primary care givers. A quick perusal of recent issues of the *Report on Preschool Programs* will give some idea of the enormous governmental concern, both federal and state, for the welfare of our children. Among the items highlighted on the agenda of the annual meeting of the National Association for the Education of Young Children (NAEYC) in the fall of 1987 was the new national child care bill, the academic development of young children, and a new child care outreach campaign. This last is a campaign initiated with the Public Broadcasting Outreach Alliance to present a nationwide documentary on child care during NAEYC's Week of the Young Child in April 1988. It is time for us all to recognize that the world's greatest treasure and resource, our children, is in danger. Children need help to develop fully their potential talents and intellect so that they too can become mature citizens ready to shoulder the responsibilities of society.

Now that the government and public are concerned about the importance of a child's early years, answers to current problems are being sought. As students and professionals in the field, we can help document the needs of developing children at the close of the twentieth century. Through research and study we need to generate new information on how best to meet these needs.

Childhood

People usually define "childhood" according to an age range. What "childhood" is varies among cultures, socioeconomic groups, and historical periods. In general, it is thought of as that period of life between infancy and youth. At one end of the spectrum we find some children whose "childhood" ends at age four or five when they, as youths, begin working to supplement the family income. At the other end we have individuals who remain children all their lives. There is no universally agreed upon definition of the years which encompass childhood, let alone infancy. For the purposes of this guide, the period of infancy and childhood is defined as the period from birth to age thirteen.

Literature Searching: Finding What You Want

The goal of literature searching is to locate information and data on a chosen topic. There are three common methods used in the location of needed information: (1) trial and error, (2) happenstance, and (3) use of a search strategy. Any one of the three may eventually result in the collection of items containing the knowledge sought. Of the three methods, however, one is more expeditious than the others. Using a carefully organized search strategy in the initial stages of the research process places the emphasis on the reading and synthesizing of knowledge rather than the task of location. When, at the beginning of a project, the researcher locates a review of research, a bibliography, or a research study on the chosen topic, access is gained quickly to a network of literature via the cited works. Locating the same literature piece by piece might entail considerable time and effort. This annotated research guide to the literature of infancy and childhood is intended to alert the user to the existence of these materials which will assist in the initial stages of the literature search process.

Planning a Research Strategy

Searching the literature involves a five-step process:

1.   Determine from reference tools which materials look promising. Some books are published to alert users to the existence of specific reference tools. They are called guides to the literature. Working either from such a guide produced by the academic/research library where the research is conducted or a published guide to the literature such as you have in hand will expedite the research process. The bibliography is a location tool, providing exact titles of reference tools in a particular subject area. From consulting the guide the user becomes aware of titles of references which will be helpful in locating information on the chosen topic. Literature guides may be general or specialized in their subject coverage. Titles to recommended general guides to the literature which might be helpful are listed at the end of Chapter 1. Specialized guides to the literature cover in depth the literature of a discipline. This guide to infancy and childhood resources is a good example of a subject specialized guide. Chapter 3, Part I annotates "core references" in the area of childhood under reference type (such as abstract, bibliography, directory, encyclopedia, child study guide, reviews of research, or statistics) to assist in locating appropriate reference tools which should be consulted in the initial stages of the search process.

Chapter 3, Part II annotates general anthologies on child development that do not fall into the type of reference usually included in this sort of research guide yet are rich sources of information. These anthologies also do not fall into the subject-oriented chapters because their coverage is diverse. Other general subjects covered in this part include the areas of law, history, and curriculum. The latter topic includes nursery, preschool, and elementary school subjects up to grade 9.

Chapters 4 through 12 cover specific subject areas each of which is further subdivided into four areas by the type of information the entry provides: bibliographies, reviews of literature, reports of research, and other references. In some cases a "general" subcategory is included for entries which do not fall neatly into any one subject area.

     2.   Determine databases to be searched. Once a determination has been made of the appropriate reference tools to be consulted, a division should be made of those which must be searched through traditional methods (manually searching paper indexes and abstracts), and those that may be searched using new technologies such as databases, laser disks, optical disks, and CD-ROM. Chapter 2 discusses how to incorporate database searching in the literature search process, and all the factors affecting such a search. The databases are annotated in Part II of Chapter 2.

     3.   Gather and peruse monographs, journal articles, and documents located in steps one and two. The references consulted in step one and the database search done in step two provide a core of exact titles of books, monographs, journal articles, and documents which possibly contain needed information on the research topic. These should be gathered and read or skimmed to determine whether they will be of value in furthering the knowledge base of the chosen topic.

     4.   Read bibliographies of materials gathered in step three and identify key publications of the subject. If necessary repeat step two. While reading the materials, the researcher needs to become an avid and astute reader of bibliographies and footnotes. These form a network of literature themselves. The citing of the same individual's work in numerous studies points to the possibility that he or she could be a key source and that his or her published research or paper could be a key source. Once the determination is made that a certain individual is in fact a key authority in a given area and that a particular report is a landmark or classic, step 2 may be repeated in one of the Citation Index databases mentioned on page 14. Consulting the proper Index will help answer any or all of the following questions:

        Has this paper been cited?
        Has there been a review of this subject?
        Who else is working in this field?
        Was this "to be published" paper published and where?
        What other works has this person written?

     5.   Repeat steps three and four if necessary. As literature is read and the cited entries scrutinized for potentially fruitful information, the steps of gathering and reading continue until the researcher has gathered all the necessary literature to complete the research of the chosen topic. For most researchers the end becomes very apparent when it is discovered that all the pertinent as well as remotely pertinent entries in a bibliography have already been gathered and read. At this point the search of the literature ends.

Limitations of this Guide

Because of the interdisciplinary nature of infancy and childhood, this work is not all encompassing. Some areas such as medical aspects of a topic are only briefly covered because other specialized guides already cover these materials. Users should consult one or more appropriate literature guides depending on the nature of their research topic. Titles of recommended guides are listed in the bibliography at the end of this chapter. These are selective and users should not hesitate to consult other guides to the literature which they consider helpful. Keep in mind that this guide is intended to complement already existing guides to the literature.

In addition, this guide is selective in that references which may be readily retrieved via a database, either online or optical disks, are not included unless the reference is considered a landmark or classic publication. Two excellent examples of publications or references excluded are government documents and ERIC documents. Both are rich sources of materials on all topics covered in this book.

Explanation of Entries

Entries are alphabetical by title under each of the subcategories. This style was carefully selected because current cataloging practice favors title entries more than author entries. Many works are the result of multiple or joint authorship where assignment of primary responsibility for the intellectual content is difficult. With this title entry style, it is thought that users will be able to locate entries in card catalogs more easily. Following the title is the date of publication in parenthesis, then the author's name or names, preceding the place of publication and publisher. Last of all, again in parenthesis, is the series title if the book is part of a series.

Organizing the references which focus on infancy and childhood has been a "hair splitting" task. Nine specialized topics are used in the book as chapters: families, child care, communication, cognition, behavior development, social/cultural development, physical development, atypical development, and creativity. The order of the chapters is intentional. There is a natural overlap between each chapter. For instance, there is a linkage between families and child care; between communication and cognition; between behavior and social/cultural development; between physical development and atypical development; and between atypical development and creativity. Even within these ten subject categories, questionable areas exist; for example, entries on death and dying are placed in behavior development rather than families. Therefore, users are urged to make use of both the table of contents and the subject index in locating entries on topics.

GENERAL GUIDES TO THE LITERATURE

Bibliography

Art Research Methods and Resources: A Guide to Finding Art Information. Second edition, revised and enlarged. (1984). Lois Swan Jones. Dubuque, IA: Kendall/Hunt.

A comprehensive guide to methods of research and reference tools useful in locating art information. Of the four parts, the first provides definitions and discusses how to begin to locate art information. Part II gives a step-by-step approach to carrying out a search of the literature. Part III consists of the individually annotated entries. Indexed.

A Guide to Research in Music Education. Third edition. (1986). Roger P. Phelps. Metuchen, NJ: Scarecrow.

One of two guides to music research and the most recent. The majority of the guide is in essay form with brief bibliographies concluding the chapters. The well chosen references cited are gems in locating sources difficult to locate through other literature in this area.

A Guide to Sources of Educational Information. Second edition. (1982). Marda Woodbury. Arlington, VA: Information Resources.

Although outdated, this annotated bibliography alerts users to general educational references published in the United States.

How to Find Out in Psychology: A Guide to the Literature and Methods of Research. (1984). D. H. Borchardt, R. D. Francis. Oxford: Pergamon.

This guide emphasizes basic international titles published since the early 1970s.

How to Find the Law. Eighth edition. (1983). Morris L. Cohen, Robert C. Berry. St. Paul, MN: West.

A classic guide to finding legal literature.

Legal Research in a Nutshell. Fourth edition. (1985). Morris L. Cohen. St. Paul, MN: West.

Concise and readable guide to legal literature.

Reference Sources in Social Work: An Annotated Bibliography. (1982). James H. Conrad. Metuchen, NJ: Scarecrow.

A guide focusing on works published between 1970 and 1981.

Research Guide for Psychology. (1982).   Raymond G. McInnis.   Westport, CT: Greenwood.

A critical guide to the literature.   Entries are introduced in essay form. Indexed.

Research Guide to the Health Sciences: Medical, Nutritional, and Environmental. (1987). Kathy Haselbauer. Westport, CT: Greenwood.

Cites and annotates over 2,000 references in the many disciplines making up health sciences. Indexed.

Sociology: A Guide to References and Information Sources. (1987).   Stephen H. Aby.   Littleton, CO: Libraries Unlimited.

A bibliography of 659 entries divided into three parts: general references, individual disciplines, and sociology.

Sources of Information in the Social Sciences, a Guide to the Literature.   Third edition. (1986).   William H. Webb.   Chicago and London: American Library Association.

A comprehensive guide to reference works in the many disciplines included in the social sciences. Indexed.

The Student Sociologist's Handbook. Third edition. (1981).   Pauline Bart, Linda Frankel.   Glenview, IL: Scott, Foresman.

Includes reference tools, research and other resource materials on the topic. Concise and readable.

2

Using the New Technologies by Dana Johnson

PART I. INTRODUCTION

Database Searching: Getting Started

Researchers today must sift through a huge and mounting array of publications to find pertinent materials. To do this most efficiently, it is necessary to determine early in the search process which reference tools can be searched as databases. A database, broadly defined, is any collection of information systematically organized for retrieval by computer. Many databases are computer-readable versions of printed indexes, abstracts, or directories. Because these databases cumulate, the records of many years can be searched at the same time.

Benefits

The advantages of database searching over the use of print publications can be summed up in three words: speed, power, and availability. Database searching is much faster than searching of print resources, so researchers can spend more time reading and synthesizing the materials. In the time it takes to locate a few citations in one volume of an index, a computer can quickly scan an entire database and produce a list of citations matching the search specifications.

Because more of the information can be searched, database searching offers users greater power. Individual words in the titles, abstracts, and texts can be searched using "natural language" (also called free text or keyword) searching. More subject terms (called descriptors) are provided for each entry, as are access points (fields) such as journal name, type of publication, or language. It is possible to search a database looking for a single word or descriptor, or any number of these access points in combination.

Some resources are available only as databases, some combine several publications into a single file, and many databases include more information than their print versions. In addition, database searching offers users access to many more resources than are available in any single library. Finally, databases are updated frequently and their records are immediately searchable.

Limitations

Despite the obvious advantages of database searching, its limitations should be considered. First of all, many important resources are not available online, and this will be true for a long time to come. Most databases' retrospective coverage goes back only to the 1960s, and many interdisciplinary topics are widely scattered. For a complete literature search, therefore, both manual and automated sources should be consulted.

Databases and search software are complex and constantly changing. Effective database searching requires training, ongoing experience, and an understanding of the database content and structure. Many libraries designate subject specialist librarians, who execute the actual searches for patrons. These specialists translate research questions into terminology appropriate to particular databases, and often anticipate the kinds of problems that search requests might encounter. Unfortunately, patrons must nearly always wait for searches to be performed, and problems with communication and interpretation are sometimes unavoidable.

Users often endow computer technologies with supernatural powers, and assume that a database search will find everything. It is important to remember that computers are quite stupid, or at least mindless, and operate totally on the basis of character matching. If a word is misspelled, or the correct indexing terms and important synonyms are not used, all records which contain those terms will be missed. If, on the other hand, a common word with several meanings is used as a search term, all records, however irrelevant, which contain that term in any context will be retrieved. Thus it is extremely important to understand the chosen topic thoroughly, and to explore its vocabulary, the printed literature and indexes, and any available database documentation before beginning a search.

Lastly, database searching costs money. Libraries manage their database services differently, but in many cases, online users are charged for searches, whether or not useful information is generated. The development of after-hours search services (which offer access to some databases at reduced rates) and databases on laser disc and CD-ROM (which allow unlimited use at a fixed subscription rate) have helped to lessen this problem, but user charges have not, and probably will not, disappear.

Database Types

Databases may be bibliographic, directory, numeric, or full text. Bibliographic databases, such as ERIC and PSYCINFO (PSYCHOLOGICAL ABSTRACTS), are by far the most common and familiar. The entries contain citation information such as: author, title, source, publication year; and index/descriptor terms, and often will have abstracts or summaries of the cited work.

Directory databases do not contain citations to other works, but are listings of people, associations, businesses, or products, and information about them. Numeric/Statistical databases contain primarily statistical data, such as census figures. Full text databases include all the citation information and the entire text of the cited work is available and searchable. At present, most full text databases are in the fields of law, medicine, and business, but their numbers and use are growing.

Accessing Databases

Databases are made available to the public in several ways. The most common form of access is online, using a personal computer and modem to communicate with much larger computers operated by online vendors such as Bibliographic Retrieval Services (BRS), Dialog Information Services, and the National Library of Medicine (NLM). These vendors provide access to many databases, and they generally charge on the basis of connect time, telecommunications use, and records printed. For individual databases, costs vary. BRS and Dialog also offer access to some databases at lower rates on evenings and weekends through their after-hours services, After Dark and Knowledge Index.

Databases stored on CD-ROM and laser discs and searched with microcomputers are becoming more widely used. Though the number of databases available in this format is a small fraction of those available through online vendors, it is growing fast and includes classics such as ERIC, MEDLINE, and PSYCINFO. Searching capabilities are similar to those available through online vendors, and libraries which own such databases usually offer them to users without charge.

Most academic and many public libraries offer database search services, but these vary widely. Important questions to ask when investigating services include:

1. Who can use the services?
2. What databases are available?
3. Do librarians, patrons, or both, do the searching?
4. If librarians do, can the requester be present for the search?
5. Are there any charges? If so, what is the average cost and how are the charges computed?
6. Are after-hours searches (at lower cost) available?
7. When will the results of the search be available?

It is also possible to access online services independently, and the availability of after-hours search services and simplified search protocols make this a reasonable option. The costs of initial subscription, equipment, training, and search fees should be weighed against the advantages of doing one's own searching. For readers interested in learning more about online searching options, there is a bibliography of useful sources and a list of vendors at the end of this chapter.

Search Considerations

When needed resources are accessible as databases, the next step is to explore the local database services. If CD-ROM versions of these databases are available, or online searching is free, it will save time to use databases, even for simple research questions.

If database searching is not free, cost effectiveness becomes an issue. Factors which increase the cost effectiveness of database searches are the same ones which make manual searches difficult or tedious, including:

1.   Are the needed resources unavailable or difficult to use in print form?
2.   Is the chosen topic interdisciplinary, and thus covered in a number of resources?
3.   Will two or more terms need to be combined?
4.   Is the terminology of the topic new or highly specific, and therefore unlikely to be indexed in print?
5.   Is an exhaustive search required?
6.   How much time do you have, and how much is it worth?

Search Preparation

Search planning is vital, and usually will take longer than the search itself. No matter who is going to perform the search, the researcher should carefully explore the search topic beforehand using all available resources (described below) and the core resources (discussed in Chapter 3). Planning tasks include:

1.   describing the search topic clearly;
2.   finding useful descriptors and synonyms;
3.   anticipating related terms which should be eliminated from the search;
4.   locating "classic" or "key" publications which can be used for citation searches;
5.   deciding whether the search should be limited by publication date, language, type of material, or cost.

Choosing databases to search can be an extremely straightforward task, especially if the chosen topic's broad subject area is clear and the researcher is familiar with that discipline's print resources. However, for researchers working outside their areas of expertise or with an interdisciplinary topic, the array of available databases can be overwhelming. The resources described below can help researchers determine the best databases for their topic, and assist them in planning an appropriate and flexible search strategy. For additional information about search strategy development, there is a bibliography of helpful sources at the end of this chapter.

Database directories can help to identify the major databases in a field and provide the most comprehensive view of the available resources. Database information is constantly changing as new databases are created, names change, mergers occur, and some are eliminated, so it is important to use the latest print editions or the online versions whenever possible. Vendors will provide catalogs of their database offerings. Listed below are two useful comprehensive directories and regularly featured table of available databases.

Computer-Readable Databases: A Directory and Data Sourcebook. Edited by Martha E. Williams. (1985). Chicago: American Library Association. Vol. 1: Science, Technology, Medicine. Vol. 2: Business, Law, Humanities, Social Sciences.
Available through Dialog (#230).

Data Base Directory. (1984 -). White Plains, NY: Knowledge Industry Publications. Published in cooperation with the American Society for Information Science.
Available through BRS (KIPD).

Online Review: The International Journal of Online & Videotex Information Systems. (1977 -). Medford, NJ: Learned Information.

"Databases Online," a regular feature of this journal, provides information in tabular form about available databases, subject coverage, vendors, and current charges.

Another useful group of database selection resources are the crossfiles, such as BRS's CROS and Dialog's DialIndex. In these files, a searcher first selects either individual databases of interest or a group of databases under broad headings like "Education" or "Medicine/Pharmacology," and then enters the search term(s). The search is run in all of the databases in the group selected, and the system reports the number of records which match the search specifications (called postings) available in each database. The search must then be executed in the appropriate file(s). Dialog recently introduced another feature, called OneSearch, which allows searchers to specify up to 20 files to search at the same time. OneSearch reports the number of postings for each search and each file, and allows the searcher to immediately download or print the retrieved records. Such services are especially useful for because they are search-specific, but remember that they are also vendor-specific, and thus will not reveal sources which are not available through their services.

Probably the most useful source of database information, when available, is the printed version of the database. By scanning the records associated with the main subject headings of a topic in just a few volumes, it is possible to get an idea of the types of information available in the database and also to assess the amount and depth of its coverage in that area. One can quickly develop a list of potential search terms by looking at both the subject headings and the natural language used in the titles and abstracts. If such a search is not immediately successful, try synonyms and more general terms, or consult a database thesaurus. Research topics can be faddish, so if there isn't must recent material, check a few of the older volumes before giving up on the resource.

A huge variety of database documentation is available from both database producers and vendors, and such resources are useful both for choosing a database and planning a search. Database vendors offer information sheets for each database which contain directory-type information (subject coverage, size, years of coverage, producer, update frequency, and available user aids), diagram the structure of the database, and show a sample record. Vendors also provide database chapters, which discuss the database in greater detail and include searching instructions and advice, as well as general search guides which assist in the use of the system's search language.

Documentation available from the database producers is usually more specific.   Database thersauri provide detailed information about the indexing structure and language used to produce the database, and are vital resources which should be consulted whenever possible. A well-constructed thesaurus will have an alphabetical list of authorized subject terms, or descriptors. Under each term the broader, narrower, and related terms will be listed, along with scope notes, which provide a definition or further description of when the term is applied. Thesauri may also include: "used for" references, which indicate synonyms for the authorized term; posting notes, which indicate the number of records which had been indexed under the term (as of publication); and other displays of the descriptors in hierarchical order or keyword-in-context. Sometimes database users' guides also are available. These will usually provide in-depth information, step-by-step search examples, and searching advice specific to a database or group of related databases.

PART II. DATABASES USEFUL IN INFANCY AND CHILDHOOD RESEARCH

The following section consists of an annotated list of the major databases useful in infancy and childhood research. It is by no means an exhaustive one; instead it is intended to alert readers to the best and most widely available databases in the main disciplines associated with infancy and childhood research. Notably absent are some of the extremely general sources, such as BOOKS IN PRINT or NATIONAL NEWSPAPER INDEX, and databases which are not available through the vendors discussed.

Explanation of Entries

Each of the resources listed is available through at least one of the online vendors (BRS, Dialog, or NLM). For each entry, the vendors and their names or numbers for the file are indicated. An asterisk after the file name/number means that the database can be accessed through the vendor's less expensive, after-hours search service. The date following each database's title indicates the starting date of coverage. In the description the main access points (fields) are given, but others may be available. The list is organized by subject or format into the broad categories of: interdisciplinary resources, citation indexes, education, law and government documents, medicine, psychology, sociology, and social work. Within each category the databases are listed alphabetically.

Interdisciplinary Databases

General Sources

Many familiar general indexes, such as *Reader's Guide to Periodical Literature, Education Index,* and *Social Sciences Index,* are now available as online and CD-ROM databases through Wilsonline. The advantages of these databases over their print versions are not as dramatic because the indexes' coverage did not begin until the early 1980s, but their power and usefulness as databases will increase as they cumulate.

Other general-interest databases produced by Information Access Corporation, such as *General Periodicals Index, Magazine Index,* and *Government Publications Index,* are found in many libraries. These too are useful for getting started on a topic, and their coverage of academic and research-oriented publications is increasing.

Dissertation Abstracts Online (1861 -). Ann Arbor, MI: University Microfilms International.
Available through BRS (DISS*), Dialog (#35*).

A comprehensive index of the majority of dissertations produced in the United States and selected international institutions as well. Access points such as author, corporate source (issuing institution), and descriptors (broad subject areas such as education, early childhood) can be useful, but because most dissertation searches are extremely specific, natural language searches of the title and abstract fields are recommended.

Linguistics and Language Behavior Abstracts. (1973 -). San Diego, CA: Sociological Abstracts.
Available through BRS (LLBA*), Dialog (#36).

LLBA is the online version of the printed index with the same name and is a vital source for language development and communication disorders research. The main searchable fields are abstract, descriptor, section heading, title, author, document type, journal name, language, and corporate source. As with *Sociological Abstracts* (which is produced by the same organization), a mixture of natural language and descriptor terms is usually the best strategy for complete retrieval.

Public Affairs Information Service (PAIS). (1976 -). New York: Public Affairs Information Service.
Available through BRS (PAIS*), Dialog (#44).

To produce this index of national and international public policy resources in all formats, PAIS scans academic, governmental and professional publications, and the general press, emphasizing factual and statistical information. Availability information for most of the entries is provided. PAIS covers a wide variety of public policy and law regarding children, and its international scope makes it an excellent source of comparative policy information.

Access points include title, descriptor, abstract (for about 15% of the records), author, corporate source, document type, journal name, and publication year. One caution: there is quite a bit of non-English language material, so consider limiting searches.

Citation Indexes

Arts and Humanities Search. (1980 -). Philadelphia, PA: The Institute for Scientific Information.
Available through BRS (AHCI*), Dialog (#439).

Scisearch. (1974 -). Philadelphia, PA: The Institute for Scientific Information.
Available through Dialog (#34, #87).

Social Scisearch. (1972 -).   Philadelphia, PA: The Institute for Scientific Information.
Available through BRS (SSCI*), Dialog (#7).

The online version of the *Arts and Humanities Citation Index,* AHCI indexes the international literature of the arts and humanities, including areas such as dance, art, television and radio, language, folklore, music, theater, and religion. It contains more than 500,000 records.

Scisearch, a multidisciplinary, international database of literature in science and technology, contains all entries from the printed *Science Citation Index* and records from the *Current Contents* series. Documents subsequently included in the cumulative indexes are not covered. The database contains more than 5,500,000 records, and is divided into several files by year ranges.

Social Scisearch corresponds to the printed *Social Science Citation Index,* and is an international, multidisciplinary index of the social and behavioral sciences containing more than 1,500,000 records.

The distinctive and useful feature common to all these files is that citations function as subject headings. The citation of a known publication can be used as a search term in order to locate other publications which have cited it. Each database can also be searched by author, title, corporate source, document type, journal name, availability, language, publication year, and update. **Social Scisearch** has additional access points such as journal subject category, geographic location, and zip code of corporate source. The files are updated biweekly and the full texts of most documents cited are available through the producer's document delivery service.   There is no subject indexing in these large files, so natural language searching of the title field is the only subject-searching option. Searchers should also note that authors' names and citations are taken directly from the documents and so may vary.

Education Databases

Educational Resources Information Center (1966 -).   Bethesda, MD: ERIC Processing and Reference Facility.
Available through BRS (ERIC*), Dialog (#1*).

ERIC is the most important and comprehensive database of education-related research reports, journal articles, theses, curricula, and project reports. It corresponds to the printed indexes, *Current Journals in Education* (CIJE), which indexes published journal articles, and *Resources in Education* (RIE), which indexes unpublished documents. ERIC is an excellent resource for education-related topics at all levels; it also contains a wealth of information from fields applicable to education, such as psychology, business, and sociology. ERIC was one of the first databases on CD-ROM, so it is often available without charge even in smaller college and university libraries.

ERIC is a large file (over 600,000 records) and has a highly developed index vocabulary. Consult the Thesaurus of ERIC Descriptors before beginning a search. Records are indexed as specifically as possible, so carefully explore broader, narrower, and related terms in order to make a complete list of descriptors for a search. The main searchable fields are: author, title, abstract, source, document type, language, publication year, identifier and descriptor. Access points such as clearinghouse codes, target audience, subfile, project number, and report number are also available.

Exceptional Child Education Resources. (1966 -).   Reston, VA: The Council for Exceptional Children.
Available through BRS (ECER*), Dialog (#54).

A comprehensive database of literature and research related to gifted and handicapped children, ECER is also one of the ERIC clearinghouses. About half of the records found in ECER are also found in ERIC, and ECER uses the same thesaurus and database structure. When searching both databases, search first in ERIC, then ECER, and use the clearinghouse codes to eliminate duplicates.

Law and Government Documents Databases

American Statistics Index. (1973 -).   Washington, DC: Congressional Information Service.
Available through Dialog (#102).

ASI provides indexing and detailed abstracts of all statistical publications of the U.S. government.   It covers periodicals, annuals, biennials, series and special publications, and corresponds to the printed index with the same name. A wide range of statistical material is available: social and demographic data; medical, health and educational data; and statistics and reports about families, labor, and crime.

The primary searchable fields are: author, category, corporate source, document type, publication number, title, descriptor, abstract, and the Superintendent of Documents' classification number. Because each entry has a descriptive abstract, a search of ASI will often turn up publications missed in a search of the *GPO Monthly Catalog*.

Congressional Information Service. (1970 -). Washington, DC: Congressional Information Service.
Available through Dialog (#101).

CIS abstracts and cites all publications of the nearly 300 United States House, Senate and joint committees and subcommittees. Child-related topics covered include all levels of education, child and family welfare, drug abuse, infant mortality and medical care, and juvenile justice.

The main searchable fields are abstract, descriptor, title, document type, and publication year. Unique access points are committee code, witness affiliation and witness name, and the annual legislative history bibliographies. CIS is more expensive to search, but has informative abstracts that provide more access points for Congressional documents than *GPO Monthly Catalog*.

GPO Monthly Catalog. (1976 -). Washington, DC: Superintendent of Documents, U.S. Government Printing Office.
Available through BRS (GPOM*), Dialog (#66).

This online version of the *Monthly Catalog of United States Government Publications* covers the full range of public documents produced by the executive branch, including publications from cabinet level departments such as Health and Human Services, Education, Commerce, and Justice, and publications of the legislative branch, such as bills, hearings, reports, committee and subcommittee documents, and laws from Congress. Some documents of the judicial branch are also indexed.

GPO Monthly Catalog is usually the first place to search for government documents because it casts the widest net, is very systematic and accurate in its entries, and is cheap by comparison to privately produced databases. The main searchable fields are author, corporate source, conference title, journal name, language, document type, abstract, descriptor, named person, title, and note. Additional fields include Government Printing Office number, item number, series, International Standard Serial Number, and Library of Congress or Dewey call number, some of which can be useful for subject retrieval.

Legal Resource Index. (1980 -). Belmont, CA: Information Access.
   Available through BRS (LAWS*), Dialog (#150*).

   The legal world has many online services of its own, such as LEXIS and WESTLAW, but for the researcher merely seeking the legal perspective, such systems can be both overwhelmingly specific and expensive. For such users, LRI provides indexing of the secondary legal literature of English-speaking, common law countries, covering more than 700 journals, including law reviews, commercially published journals, bar association journals, and seven legal newspapers. It also includes entries from other Information Access Company databases such as *Magazine Index* and *National Newspaper Index*. It is analytical in scope and does not cover case digests or the primary legal literature.

   There are a large number of searchable fields, including title, product name, case name, article type, geographic location, author, source, jurisdiction, statute name, ticker symbol, and some abstracts. LRI contains over 250,000 entries from a variety of sources; thus, a natural language search strategy with use of synonyms and truncation is advised.

National Technical Information Service (NTIS). (1964 -). Springfield, VA: National Technical Information Service, U.S. Department of Commerce.
   Available through BRS (NTIS*), Dialog (#6*).

   The online version of *Government Reports Announcements and Index* and twenty-six abstract newsletters, NTIS is the main source of data about government-sponsored research of all types.   Document availability information is also included.

   The principal searchable fields are author, title, abstract, descriptor, identifier, publication year, sponsoring agency, language, sponsoring organization, and update.

Medical and Health Sciences Databases

EMBASE. (1974 -). Amsterdam, The Netherlands: Excerpta Medica.
   Available through BRS (EMED), Dialog (#72, #172, #173).

   EMBASE is a comprehensive international file of medical literature which contains over 3,000,000 records.   The 46 printed indexes and bibliographies produced by Excerpta Medica are made from this file, and many additional records not found in any of these sources are also included. Its overlap with MEDLINE is significant, but it contains many unique records in areas such as sports medicine and kinesiology, physical education, speech pathology, and drug research, and its international coverage is superior.   It is also more expensive than MEDLINE but should be considered as a primary source in these areas.

Searchable fields include author, source author affiliation, country of publication, publication year, language, trade name (for drugs and other products), descriptors and tags, title, and abstract. Records are indexed by professionals in specific fields, and the indexing policy allows them to create new descriptors when needed. The terminology is less controlled than MEDLINE's subject heading structure, but more responsive to changing vocabulary, so a combination of natural language and descriptor searching is most effective.

Medline (Medlars-on-Line). (1966 -). Bethesda, MD: National Library of Medicine.
Available through BRS (MESZ*, MESH*, MS81*, MS76, MS71*), Dialog (#154*, #155*), NLM.

MEDLINE is the primary resource for biomedical literature, covering medical science and practice, and also public health and related fields. It is international in scope, and covers journal articles, substantive editorials, letters, biographies, and newsletters. It contains the records of three printed indexes: *Index Medicus, Index to Dental Literature,* and *International Nursing Index,* and also some materials not available in print, such as those pertaining to communication disorders. Though a range of sources is covered, MEDLINE's primary emphasis is clinical and most of the material included is technical.

MEDLINE's file and indexing structure is complex and powerful, and the online version contains more than twice as many descriptors per record as the printed form. Use of the Medical Subject Headings (MeSH) documentation (available from NTIS) is vital; particularly useful are the subject heading subheadings or qualifiers (such as *therapy* or *etiology*) and the tree (hierarchical) structure's alphanumeric codes for searching related terms. MEDLINE is available from several vendors. Each vendor has loaded the file of more than 5,000,000 records differently and provides different features and year-range breakdowns. Searchable fields will vary, but include author, title, language, registry number, personal name, year of publication, document type, journal name, descriptor, abstract, and checktag. Because MEDLINE is a government-sponsored project, it is relatively inexpensive to search.

Sport. (1949 -). Ottawa, Ontario: Sport Information Resource Center.
Available through BRS (SFDB*), Dialog (#48*).

SPORT is an index to the serial and monographic literature of all areas of sport, including motor learning, exercise physiology, physical education, sports for the handicapped, recreation, coaching, and sport history and psychology. It covers both the research and popular sports literature, and corresponds to the printed *Sport Bibliography.*

SPORT has a large number of searchable fields, including author, corporate source, document type, journal name, language, audience level, publication year, series, update, title, descriptor, and abstract (for about 30% of the records). A *Sport Thesaurus* is available from the producer. For full retrieval a combination of natural language and descriptor searching is advised.

Psychology, Sociology, and Social Work Databases

Child Abuse and Neglect. (1965 -). Washington, DC: National Center on Child
  Abuse and Neglect.
  Available through Dialog (#64).

An authoritative source of information on all aspects of child abuse, this file is divided into five subfiles: ongoing research project descriptions; audiovisual material abstracts; service program descriptions; current state statute excerpts; and bibliographic references to current documents and legal decisions. It is limited to English language materials and U.S. research and service projects. There is no direct print counterpart, but the center's three major publications: *Child Abuse and Neglect: Projects and Publications*; *Child Abuse and Neglect Programs*; and *Child Abuse and Neglect Audiovisual Materials*, are made from this file.

The more than 15,000 records are searchable by author, title, decriptors, and abstract, and it is possible to limit searches by subfile, state, or federal region. Since the file is small and vocabulary used in this area varies over time and across disciplines, searching broadly using free-text methods is advised.

Criminal Justice Periodical Index. (1975 -). Ann Arbor, MI: University
  Microfilms International.
  Available through Dialog (#171).

An index to leading criminal justice journals, this database contains more than 100,000 records covering all aspects of criminal justice, including child abuse, juvenile justice, victim issues, and drug abuse and control.

Though this is a larger file than NCJRS, it is more expensive to search and has fewer access points. Searchable fields include title, descriptor, author, journal name, publication year, and update. Abstracts are not available.

Family Resources. (1970 -). Minneapolis, MN: National Council on Family
Relations, Family Resource and Referral Center.
Available through BRS (NCFR*), Dialog (#291).

This file provides bibliographic references to a wide variety of family-
related literature in the fields of medicine, education, sociology, and
psychology. It also contains directory files: the Human Resources Bank (a
directory of people who are resources in their specialties); the Idea Bank (a
file of works-in-progress); and the Family Study Centers (a directory of
family life reserach organizations).

The author, title, abstract, journal name, language, document type,
and publication year fields all are searchable. Some other useful fields
include the section heading and the source (publisher). The index
vocabulary is limited to section headings, so natural language searches are
advised.

Mental Health Abstracts. (1969 -). Rockville, MD: National Clearinghouse,
National Institute of Mental Health, 1969 - 1982.   Alexandria, VA:
IFI/Plenum Data, 1983 - .
Available through Dialog (#86*).

This service scans books, research and technical reports, dissertations,
and more than 1,000 periodicals to provide comprehensive international
coverage of mental health and mental illness literature. It is a good source of
information on the legal, social and policy aspects of mental health, but its
coverage of theoretical and philosophical aspects of psychological topics is
less complete than PSYCINFO.

Searchable fields include author, title, corporate source, descriptor,
identifier, document type, publication year, update, language, source, and
contractor code. Searching this database can be confusing as the change of
producers in 1983 resulted in changes in the indexing language and database
structure. Both former and present forms of descriptor terms and fields must
be searched for full retrieval.

Mental Measurements Yearbook. (1977 -). Lincoln, NB: Buros Institute of Mental
Measurements.
Available through BRS (MMYD*).

This is the standard source of factual information, critical reviews, and
reliability-validity information on published tests used in education, social
sciences, and business. The printed yearbook is irregularly published. The
online version offers the considerable advantages of currency (it is updated
monthly) and the ability to search the full text of the test summary or
commentary contained in the print form. It does not contain the tests
themselves, since most of them are for sale, but it does have availability and

price information, and the critical information is invaluable in selecting appropriate and affordable measures.

Searchable elements include test name, classification, author, publisher, population, publication date, type of reliability and validity data, manual information, reviewer(s), comments, and text. Combining terms will yield precise retrieval of usable test options. Other helpful data such as price, availability of scoring services, time requirements, and reviews will display but are not searchable.

National Criminal Justice Reference Service. (1972 -). Rockville, MD: National Criminal Justice Reference Service.
Available through Dialog (#21).

NCJRS indexes more than 200 periodicals, all publications of the U.S. Department of Justice, and related dissertations, books, and audiovisual materials. The database is useful for criminal justice topics such as juvenile delinquency, child abuse and neglect, runaways, and family law.

Searchable fields include title, abstract, descriptor, corporate source, document type, note, publication year, language, sponsor, grant and report number, and country of origin. Though NCJRS is a smaller database than CRIMINAL JUSTICE PERIODICAL INDEX, its entries contain abstracts and more detailed information, it covers a wider range of sources, and because it is publicly owned it costs about half as much to search. Thus it is a good database in which to develop a search on a criminal justice-related topic, but both files should be searched for full retrieval.

PsycINFO. (1967 -). Washington, DC: American Psychological Association.
PsycALERT. (current). Washington, DC: American Psychological Association.
Available through BRS (PSYC*, PSAL*), Dialog (#11, #140).

PSYCINFO, the online version of *Psychological Abstracts*, provides the most comprehensive indexing of the international literature of psychology and related behavioral and social sciences. In 1980, the print version dropped its coverage of dissertations and book chapters, and as of 1988 contains only English language materials, but these can still be located on PSYCINFO.

The main searchable fields in PSYCINFO are author, title, source, language, author affiliation, publication year, document type, abstract, and descriptor. Because the file contains a significant amount (8% - 10%) of non-English language material and also many dissertations (about 20%), search limiters should be considered. Subject descriptors can be found in the *Thesaurus of Psychological Index Terms*, which has been used by the database producers since 1973. Records produced in preceding years were not indexed using this vocabulary and there are still many inconsistencies in the indexing structure and language, so search strategies using a combination of available descriptors and natural language terms are advised. Descriptors applied to literature dealing with children will differ depending upon context (educational or noneducational); for full retrieval, use all available terms for specific age groups and also terms for more general age ranges.

PSYCALERT, the in-process file of PSYCINFO, indexes the most current psychology literature. Within two weeks of receipt by the American Psychological Association, items are searchable on PSYCALERT. The file is updated weekly, and records transferred each month to PSYCINFO. Searchable fields include author, title, corporate source, document type, language, journal name, update, publication year, and descriptor. The abstract field is not available, so natural language searches will search the title only. Because the file is so small, fairly general descriptor searches will usually yield a manageable number of records.

Social Work Abstracts. (1977 -). Silver Springs, MD: National Association of Social Workers.
Available through BRS (SWAB*).

SOCIAL WORK ABSTRACTS is a smaller database (16,000 records) which focuses on indexing and abstracting articles published in over 150 social work journals and some journals in related fields such as economics, psychology and psychiatry, and sociology. The bulk of the documents are from the United States, but some foreign articles are included. In early childhood research the database is useful for its coverage of family and child welfare issues and services, education, substance abuse, and mental health as they relate to and impact social work.

It is a classic bibliographic database searchable by author, title, source, language, descriptor, and abstract. The descriptors are sometimes long and awkwardly phrased, and each item may be given several which are very similar.

Sociological Abstracts. (1963 -). San Diego, CA: Sociological Abstracts.
Available through BRS (SOCA*, SPDA*, SOCZ*), Dialog (#37*).

An international index of sociological theory, research, and practice, it covers all types of publications including books, journal articles, technical reports, case studies, and conference proceedings. Two files are actually produced: SOCIOLOGICAL ABSTRACTS, which is theoretical and academic in its focus, and SOCIAL PLANNING/POLICY AND DEVELOPMENT ABSTRACTS (SOPODA), which focuses on action and policy aimed at problem solving. On Dialog, they are available as a single file, but on BRS they are available both individually and in combination.

The principal searchable fields are author, title, corporate source, journal name, publication year, subfile, language, update, document type, abstract, and descriptor. Subject indexing is sometimes inconsistent, so search strategies which use both descriptors found in *Thesaurus of Sociological Indexing Terms* and natural language terms are strongly advised.

Database Searching and Systems: A Bibliography

At Home with ERIC: Online Searching from Your Home Computer. (1986). Emma Gonzalez-Stupp, Barbara M. Wildemuth. Princeton, NJ: ERIC Clearinghouse on Tests, Educational Testing Service.

Available in both BRS After Dark and Dialog Knowledge Index editions, this guide provides specific instruction in online searching of ERIC. No online knowledge is assumed and explanations of database structure and searching techniques are thorough. Some discussion of searching techniques for other after hours databases, such as PSYCINFO and MENTAL MEASUREMENTS YEARBOOK, is also included.

BRS/SEARCH Service Video Course. (1986 - 1987). Latham, NY: BRS Information Technologies.

The three-part BRS Training Video and accompanying workbooks are designed to teach viewers how to search using the BRS system and search protocols. Part I covers the basic system commands and features, Part II covers search strategy and refinements, and Part III discusses more complex search features such as multi-database and full text searching, saved searches, printing options, and troubleshooting.

Database: The Magazine of Database Reference and Review. (1978 -). Weston, CT: Database.

This is a journal for online searchers and provides database reviews, search strategy discussion, and a special section devoted to end-user searching.

Databases: A Primer for Retrieving Information by Computer. (1986). Susanne M. Humphrey, Biagio John Melloni. Englewood Cliffs, NJ: Prentice-Hall.

The most general of the books discussed here, *Databases*, discusses the principles and possibilities of online searching with little mention of specific services. There is an excellent chapter on selecting vendors, and cartoons and illustrations grace the text.

Effective Online Searching: A Basic Text. (1984). Christine L. Borgman and others. New York: Dekker.

Intended for search intermediaries and library school students, this book provides a solid basic foundation without instructing in any one system, and is particularly useful for search strategy development and understanding search vocabulary.

Going Online: An Introduction to the World of Online Information.   (1986). Medford, NJ: Learned Information.

> This video introduces viewers to the power and potential of online searching. It provides a basic introduction to how databases are made, sold, and used, but does not instruct in online searching techniques.

An Introduction to Online Searching. (1986). Tze-Chung Li. Westport, CT: Greenwood.

> This book provides a general overview of online searching and also gives instruction in the search protocols of BRS, Dialog, and Orbit. It is an excellent starting point, but since system features change frequently, it should be used in combination with vendor documentation.

Introduction to Searching Dialog. (1987). Palo Alto, CA: Dialog Information Services.

> This video and its accompanying workbook provide a basic explanation and demonstration of techniques of online searching using the Dialog system. Instructions and practice exercises are included.

Online: The Magazine of Online Information Systems. (1977 -). Weston, CT: Online.

> ONLINE's focus in on practical articles related to database searching and systems. Its coverage is broader than its sister publication DATABASE; it also covers library automation and microcomputer use strategies.

Online Database Vendors

BRS and After Dark Search Services:

BRS Information Technologies
1200 Route 7
Latham, NY 12110
(800) 345-4277

Dialog and Knowledge Index Search Services:

Dialog Information Services
3460 Hillview Avenue
Palo Alto, CA 93404
(800) 334-2564

National Library of Medicine Search Services:

Medlars Management Section
Bibliographic Services Division
National Library of Medicine
8600 Rockville Pike
Bethesda, MD 20894
(800) 638-8480

Wilsonline Search Services:

The H. W. Wilson Company
950 University Avenue
Bronx, NY 10452
(800) 367-6770

3

General Introductory References

	Citation Indexes	ASI
DATABASES	Dissertation Abstracts	CIS
TO CONSIDER	Education Index	ERIC
	GPO Monthly Catalog	NTIS
	Legal Resources Index	PAIS
		LLBA

PART I: COMPREHENSIVE REFERENCES

ABSTRACTS

Child Development Abstracts and Bibliography, Vol. 1 - . (1927 -). Chicago, IL: Univ. of Chicago Press for the Society for Research in Child Development.

Abstracts about 160 periodicals and reviews books in the area of child development. Published three times per year; coverage is international in scope. Provides a subject and author index. Abstracts of articles are divided into the general areas of: biology, health, medicine; cognition, learning, perception; social, psychological, cultural, and personality studies; educational processes; psychiatry, clinical psychology; and general theory and methodology.

Exceptional Child Education Abstracts, Vols. 1 - 8. (1969 - 1977). The Council for Exceptional Children. Reston, VA: Council for Exceptional Children.

Became *Exceptional Child Education Resources.* See annotation under that title.

Exceptional Child Education Resources, Vol. 9 - . (1977 -). The Council for Exceptional Children. Reston, VA: Council for Exceptional Children.

Published four times a year by the council, the publication is designed as a resource for those concerned with handicapped and gifted children. There are title, subject, and author indexes which refer the researcher into the abstract section by number. From the abstract, the researcher is referred either by ED number to the ERIC microfiche or to a particular periodical.

Computer searchable through Dialog or BRS. Formerly Exceptional Child Education Abstracts.

Language and Language Behavior Abstracts (LLBA), Vols. 1 - 18. (1967 - 1984). Ann Arbor, MI: Center for Research on Language and Language Behavior.

Became *Linguistics and Language Behavior Abstracts*. See annotation under that title.

Linguistics and Language Behavior Abstracts (LLBA), Vol. 19 - . (1985 -). Ann Arbor, MI: Center for Research on Language and Language Behavior.

Formerly *Language and Language Behavior Abstracts*, Vols. 1 - 18. (1967 - 1984). A collection of nonevaluative abstracts of the world's literature covering language behavior, linguistics, and related disciplines. Entries are arranged under headings: linguistics; psychology; communication sciences; and hearing. Published quarterly with annual cumulative indexes (author, subject, book review, and publication source). LLBA is computer searchable through BRS and Dialog.

The Psychoanalytic Study of the Child: Abstracts and Index. (1975). New Haven, CT: Yale Univ. Press.

Volume is divided into three parts. The first section is the contents of volumes 1 - 25 of the yearbooks by the same name in alphabetical order by author, with each entry assigned a number. The second section is the abstracts of the articles listed in the first section. The abstracts have the same numbers as the contents. The third section is a subject index to the abstracting volume. Each entry, both in the contents and the abstract section, refers to the volume and pages where the article may be located.

Reading Abstracts. Vol. 1 - . (April 1975 -). La Jolla, CA: Essay.

This periodical, published twice yearly in June and October, indexes and abstracts scholarly articles selected from international journals pertaining to reading and related topics. The Basic Books outline of the abstract is similar to *Psychological Abstracts*. Aspects of reading related to the following are included: linguistics, orthography, lexicography, hearing pathology, language pathology, learning disabilities, and special education. Through use of the subject, author, or source indexes users may get at the specific abstract on a particular topic.

Social Work Research and Abstracts, Vol. 13 - . (1977 -). Silver Springs, MD: National Association of Social Workers.

Published four times a year, this abstract combines publication of research in the field of social welfare with the previous journal *Abstracts for Social Workers* (Vols. 1 - 12, 1965 - 1976). The expanded quarterly includes both original research papers and abstracts of articles previously published in social work and related fields. The entries are divided into six broad categories. Users will find the subject index the most useful in retrieving information. Subjects such as adoption, child abuse, behavioral disorders, day care, birth order, child care, child custody, child neglect, and child welfare are a few that may be found.

Bibliographies

Bibliographic Guide to Psychology. (1975 -). Boston, MA: G. K. Hall. (Bibliographic Guides).

Published yearly, this bibliography lists publications catalogued during the year by the Library of Congress and the Research Libraries of the New York Public Library. Of the fifteen major subject areas in psychology covered, several will be of interest to the child development specialist: sensation; cognition; perception; intelligence; emotion; personality; child psychology; and temperament. Access is by main entry (personal author, corporate body, names of conferences, etc.), added entries, titles, series titles, and subject headings. All entries are integrated into one alphabetical sequence. Full bibliographic information is provided.

A Bibliography of State Bibliographies, 1970 - 1982. (1985). David W. Parish. Littleton, CO: Libraries Unlimited.

This volume lists and annotates over 1,000 titles of state documents published between 1970 and 1982 with some important pre-1970 imprints included. The book is arranged alphabetically by state and then alphabetically by subject. A few interesting areas covered include: drug use and abuse; education and training; health; language and linguistics; law and legislation; minority groups; and social conditions.

Black Child Development in America, 1927 - 1977, an Annotated Bibliography. (1979). Hector F. Myers, G. Rana Phyllis, Marcia Harris. Westport, CT: Greenwood.

This annotated bibliography is a compilation of published articles found in the major social science journals and periodicals during the five decades. ERIC documents are also cited. Omitted are published articles in the popular literature. The bibliography is divided into five broad subject areas: language development; physical development; cognitive development; personality development; and social development. The subject index will be of some help in locating subsubjects within these broad categories but is by no means extensive.

Childbirth: An Annotated Bibliography and Guide. (1987).   Rosemary Cline Diulio.   NY: Garland.

This annotated bibliography comprehensively covers recently published books and revised editions of classical publications on topics involving childbirth.   Topics included are: pregnancy; prenatal and postnatal exercise; the expectant father; childbirth options; nutrition; Cesarean birth; breastfeeding; sibling preparation; postpartum adjustment; premature birth; multiple birth; single parenting; and infant care and development.

Chinese Education and Society; A Bibliographic Guide: The Cultural Revolution and Its Aftermath. (1972).   Stewart E. Fraser, Kuang-liang Hsu.   White Plains, NY: International Arts and Sciences.

Included in this bibliography are resources derived from English and Chinese language sources, as well as from Japanese, French, German, and Italian publications.   The majority of the references are available in English or translations.   Those only in Chinese are listed in romanized form with a concurrent English title.   Included are bibliographies, biographical dictionaries, yearbooks, dictionaries, and other standard reference works. The bibliography is divided into fourteen sections.   The first fourteen sections are under grade level headings such as elementary education, secondary education, etc.   Cross references are provided for almost half of the items which could be classified under more than one heading.

Fifty Years of Research, 1917 - 1967. (1967).   Institute of Child Behavior and Development. Iowa City, IA: Univ. of Iowa Press.

A bibliography of about two thousand entries divided into 12 subject categories: intellectual development; language development; learning and motivation; perception and sensory processes; motor development; child psychology;   child somatology;   psychophysiological and physiological processes; nutrition; preschool education; parent education; and teacher education.   Student theses and dissertations are also listed.   Only an author index is provided.

Group Work in the Helping Professions; A Bibliography. Second edition. (1984). David G. Zimpfer. Muncie, IN: Accelerated Development.

A continuation of the first 1975 edition, the bibliography includes books published mid-1975 to June 1983 in the human and helping services.   The bibliography is organized into two main sections: a topical listing and an author listing. Section six will be of particular interest to the early childhood specialist because the section includes group procedures for children, underachievement, and academic problems.   Section seven focuses on outcomes and evaluation of effectiveness and contains sections on counseling elementary school pupils, play therapy, movement, physical exercise, and family counseling.

Keeping Current in Child Care Research: An Annotated Bibliography. (1986). Carolle Howes. Washington, DC: National Association for the Education of Young Children.

This unannotated bibliography includes articles from peer-reviewed journals, books or portions of books, and conference papers. The bibliography is divided into 12 sections: attachment; social development; cognitive development; experiences in child care; child care as early intervention; specific indicators of child care quality; effects of overall child care quality; effects of age of entry; effects of child's total experience in child care; effects of length of day; relations between family and child care; and review articles and books.

The Kibbutz: A Bibliography of Scientific and Professional Publications in English. (1982). Simon Shur, Benjamin Biet-Hallahmi, Joseph R. Blasi, Albert I. Rabin. Darbey, PA: Norwood Editors. (Kibbutz, Communal Society, and Alternative Social Policy Series, Vol. 4).

This unannotated bibliography on the Kibbutz contains a subject index which will assist users in locating materials relevant to children, infants, schools, parent-child relationships, parental roles, and child rearing.

New Zealand Early Childhood Care and Education Bibliography, 1979 - 1982, with ERIC Descriptors. (1984). Compiled by Anne Meade, Elaine Marland. Wellington, NZ: New Zealand Council for Educational Research. (ED 250 081).

This bibliography is grouped under eighteen headings: abuse; advocacy; development; language and reading; disabilities; early childhood education; educational facilities; educational personnel; ethnic studies; family life; infant behavior; media research; parent education; parent participation; parent programs; research; safety; and training. Under each heading items are listed alphabetically by the author's last name.

Normal Child Development: An Annotated Bibliography of Articles and Books Published 1950 - 1969. (1971). Janice B. Schulman, Robert C. Prall. NY: Grune and Stratton.

An annotated bibliography of research on children ages 3 to 18 from 1950 through 1969 with a few pertinent sources in the 1940s. Most entries are nonexperimental. Summaries or compilation of other research are not included except when the original search was applicable to the subject being covered. Entries are arranged and categorized under eighteen subject headings.

Resources for Early Childhood: An Annotated Bibliography and Guide for Educators, Librarians, Health Care Professionals and Parents. (1983). Hannah Nuba Scheffler. NY: Garland. (Garland Reference Library of Social Science, No. 118).

> An overview of reference works written during the past five years. Organized by subject into 16 chapters covering different stages of childhood. Topical sections are introduced with very brief essays and followed with annotated and evaluative bibliographies. The essays give an overview, summary of patterns, trends and problems.

Work and Family: An Annotated Bibliography, 1978 - 1980. (1981). Compiled by Clifford Baden. Boston, MA: Wheelock College Center for Parenting Studies.

> Bibliography includes 269 books, reports in professional journals, magazine articles, and dissertations appearing in the literature between 1978 - 1980. Inclusion in the bibliography was based on relevance to the topic and availability.

DIRECTORIES

Biographical Directory of the American Academy of Pediatrics. (1980). Jaques Cattell. NY: R. R. Bowker.

> This is the first edition of the directory of fellows of the Academy of Pediatrics. Arrangement is by state and then city. Entries are abbreviated and give educational background, licensure information, experience, professional activities, membership and activities, mailing address, and phone numbers for each of the fellows listed. An alphabetical name index is provided.

Directory of Child Day Care Centers. (1986). Phoenix, AZ: Oryx.

> A series of directories covering the United States which list day care centers regulated by the state, the city, or the county in which they are located.

The National Children's Directory: An Organizational Directory and Reference Guide for Changing Conditions for Children and Youth. (1977). Edited by Mary L. Bundy, Rebecca Glenn Whaley. College Park, MD: Urban Information Interpreters.

> A directory of groups organized to improve conditions of children and youth in the United States. Groups included are those actively seeking institutional reform or change to benefit children. Included in the directory are essays on children's rights issues, descriptions of alternative programs for children, and a section on the federal involvement in children's affairs. A bibliography of

sources for citizen action is included along with a list of periodicals pertinent to the area.

Who's Who Biographical Record--Child Development Professionals. (1976). Chicago, IL: Marquis Who's Who.

An alphabetical list of professionals working in the field of child development. Pertinent biographical information about each professional is given.

Youth-Serving Organizations Directory. (1978). Detroit, MI: Gale Research.

Although a decade old, the directory serves to refer users to the existence of a particular organization. Users should always cross check with the *Encyclopedia of Association* to ascertain currency of information. Included in the directory are organizations that are directly or indirectly concerned with young people. "Youth" in the work generally refers to children between the ages of 12 to 20. The entries are arranged in alphabetical order by the first word of the organizational name. Each organization is indexed by its name and one or two key words. The user is referred by number to the entry. Entries provide addresses and phone numbers for the organization along with goals or missions of the group, membership requirements, and publications.

ENCYCLOPEDIAS

Encyclopedia of Pediatric Psychology. (1979). Logan Wright, Arlene B. Schaefer, Gerald Solomons. Baltimore, MD: Univ. Park Press.

The encyclopedia provides a comprehensive but succinct treatment of the behavioral and psychological aspects of pediatrics. Reviews of literature are supplemented with clinical tips on diagnosis and psychotherapeutic intervention. Topics selected are those most relevant to the field of medical psychology for children including 114 medical/psychological problems that tend to present themselves in the health care setting. Sections related to diagnosis and treatment, but not focusing on any particular pediatric disorder, have been included: parent consultation; developmental assessment; developmental intervention; and the use of behavior therapy. The entries are arranged alphabetically. A term glossary and a test glossary are located at the end of the encyclopedia.

Encyclopedia of Psychology. 4 vols. (1984). Edited by Raymond J. Corsini. NY: John Wiley & Sons.

This four volume encyclopedia was written for the psychologists, psychiatrists, social workers, counselors, sociologists, anthropologists, and other professionals practicing or researching in the area of human behavior. The encyclopedia provides succinct information and data on topics within the field.   The editor used the *Thesaurus of Psychological Index Terms*, the *Psychological Abstracts*, and a number of other dictionaries, encyclopedias and recent textbooks to develop the subject entries.   Biographical entries include both living and deceased.   Volume 4 contains the bibliographies of entries cited in the text.   A subject and name index is also provided in the last volume.   Entries provide concise summaries of the topic, citing pertinent studies.   At the end of entries, suggestions of related topics to look under are given.   Suggested further readings may be given.

GUIDES TO THE LITERATURE

Childhood Information Resources.   (1985).   Marda Woodbury.   Arlington, VA: Information Resources.

This guide annotates most of the general reference works which touch on any aspect of the topic.   It is not limited to research and therefore very useful for the undergraduate or general public.   Indexed.

Infancy, a Guide to Research and Resources.   (1986).   Hannah Nuba-Scheffler, Deborah Lovitky Sheiman, Kathleen Pullen Watkins.   NY: Garland.

Cites works, books, and chapters dealing with infant development beginning at the prenatal period through age two.   Entries are divided into eleven chapters: physical development; nutrition and health concerns; social-emotional development; cognitive development; language development; exceptional infant; infant-family interaction; play; education; books and babies; and resources for infancy.

Reference Sources in Social Work, an Annotated Bibliography.   (1982).   James H. Conrad.   Metuchen, NJ: Scarecrow.

A guide to the literature of social work.   Useful in locating reference tools and information on programs, organizations, individuals, services, laws, legislation, readings, concepts and treatment techniques.   With the exceptions of historical monographs the author has limited himself to reference works only.   Divided into six parts, the fourth part will be of considerable interest since it covers adoption, child abuse, child welfare, day care, family and family planning, and health care.   Annotations are brief but adequate to decide whether the tool will be of use.

The Troubled Family: Source of Information.   (1982).   Theodore P. Peck. Jefferson, NC: McFarland.

A guide to information sources on the various problems encountered by the family today.   The first three parts of the volume give government, private, and other types of organizations pertinent to the topic.   The bibliography starts with Part 4 and is further subdivided into categories: adolescence; chemical dependency; child abuse; child care services; children general;

education for family living; handicaps; parent/child relations; and teen-age pregnancy, etc. Part 5 provides the user with additional information sources. A dictionary type index is provided at the end of the volume.

HANDBOOKS

Basic Books Handbook of Child Psychiatry. 4 vols. (1979). Edited by Joseph D. Noshpitz. NY: Basic Books.

This four volume set gives comprehensive coverage of the subject of child psychiatry. Volume 1 covers the areas of normal child development and the different varieties of child development. The last section of Volume 1 deals with the nature of assessment. Volume 2 covers the topic of child psychopathology. Volume 3 covers the area of therapeutics and Volume 4 covers the area of prevention and contains a series of studies concerning the impact of current cultural issues on children and child psychiatry. References.

Child Welfare: A Source Book of Knowledge and Practice. (1984). Edited by Frank Maidman. NY: Child Welfare League of America.

This encyclopedic-like reference covers virtually all areas of child welfare delivery. The book integrates real-life welfare practices with theoretical knowledge in concise, accurate, and practical terms. A sample of the numerous topics covered includes: child protection issues and practice; day care; child neglect; physical child abuse; sexual child abuse; foster child placement and foster family selection; services to foster families; residential child care; adoption; and working with unmarried parents.

The Competent Infant: Research and Commentary. (1973). Edited by L. Joseph Stone, Henrietta T. Smith, Lois B. Murphy. NY: Basic Books.

This anthology covers all aspects of infancy. The volume is divided into six chapters covering development of the individual, prenatal and perinatal development, capabilities of the newborn, development during the first year, early experience, and socialization. Although over a decade old, this anthology remains quite useful for researchers, undergraduates, and graduate students embarking on a literature search in an unfamiliar area within the topic of infancy. References.

Developmental-Behavioral Pediatrics. (1983). Edited by Melvin D. Levine, William B. Carey, Allen C. Crocker, Ruth T. Gross. Philadelphia, PA: W. B. Saunders.

Synthesizes the knowledge concerning developmental normalcy, variation, and deviation in infancy. Each of the entries provides "key" references or suggested readings focusing on the theory and research findings of clinical relevance. The handbook is divided into eight parts. The first reviews development and behavior. The eight chapters in Part II are concerned with "patterns of variation over time," or common themes and influences that characterize normal development change from the prenatal period until the end of adolescence. Part III, seven chapters, covers environmental, family, and cultural aspects affecting development. Part IV's eight chapters cover biological influences and development: heredity, perinatal stress, nutrition, environmental toxins, and illness. Part V, comprising 15 chapters, covers problematic outcomes, difficult states, variations, dysfunctions, and clinical disorders. Part VI concerns assessment. Part VII concentrates on treatment. Part VIII covers relevant legal issues, research and methodology, professional training, and ethical considerations. Bibliographies accompany each article. The volume is indexed.

The Developmental Resource, Behavioral Sequences for Assessment and Program Planning. 2 vols. (1979). Marilyn A. Cohen, Pamela J. Gross. NY: Grune and Stratton.

This two-volume overview of child growth from birth to six years old reviews the literature. The arrangement of the information is unique. The sequence of behavioral development has been traced as if it occurs individually within each of the major areas (sensorimotor/early cognitive, gross and fine motor, language, later cognitive/preacademic, social, self-help/adaptive living skills, creative activities, and response to reinforcement). Development within each area has been broken down functionally, in terms of behavioral milestones and critical environmental variables. The format emphasizes the sequential growth of behavior in individual areas and provides a comprehensive summary of information sought by practitioners. Volume 1 covers motor, self-help, and early cognitive development. Volume 2 covers creative activities and reinforcement. Lengthy bibliographies are included with each section in both volumes.

The Education of the Young Child; A Handbook for Nursery and Infant Teachers, Second edition. (1984). Edited by David Fontana. London: Basil Blackwell.

A synthesis of information on practical topics of interest to professionals working with young children. Section I of the handbook covers social and psychological aspects of child development including: physical, cognitive, language, personality, social behavior, and assessment. Section II covers topics on learning including: mathematical skills, readings skills, writing skills, movement education, music, arts and crafts skills, play, and parent-teacher cooperation. References.

Handbook for the Practice of Pediatric Psychology. (1982). June M. Tuma. NY: John Wiley & Sons. (Wiley Series on Personality Processes).

Volume's nine chapters cover pediatric psychology and its role in the health care of children. Reviews of the literature are broken into the categories of: conceptualization and definition; psychological effects of physical illness; assessment techniques; intervention techniques; the psychologist's role in catastrophic illness; pediatric outpatient and inpatient settings; cooperation between psychologist and pediatrician; pediatric psychology as an area of scientific research; and training in pediatric psychology. References.

Handbook of Child Psychiatry and Psychology. Second edition. (1980). Edited and translated by Julian de Ajuriaguerra, Raymond P. Lorion. NY: Masson Publishing USA.

An overview of topics in child psychiatry and psychology along with lengthy bibliographies. Research methodology and therapy approaches are not discussed in detail in the handbook. Part I covers major developmental issues: history and sources of child psychiatry, the genetic psychologist's view of child development, general developmental problems, and general problems of psychobiological disorganization in children. Part II covers major functional disorders in children: sleep disorders; oral-alimentary system; psychomotor functioning; sphincteral control and disorders; language, disorders of body and self-awareness. and sexuality; and psychosexual disorders of childhood. Part III covers major syndromes: emotional, social, and sensory deprivation; epilepsy, retardation, childhood neurosis; childhood depressed and manic states; psychoses; child and the family; child and school; illness and physical handicaps; and abused children. References.

Handbook of Child Psychology. Fourth edition, 4 vols. (1983). Edited by Paul H. Mussen. NY: John Wiley & Sons.

Formerly *Carmichael's Manual of Child Psychology*, the handbook gives a comprehensive overview to all aspects of early development including social, psychological, and educational. Each chapter is written by a specialist and provides a comprehensive review of the topic along with a lengthy list of resources. Volume I covers history, theory and methods. Volume 2 covers developmental psychobiology of infancy. Volume 3 covers cognitive development. Volume 4 covers socialization, personality, and other aspects of social development. Each volume contains its own index. References.

Handbook of Clinical Child Psychology. (1983). C. Eugene Walker, Michael C. Roberts. NY: John Wiley & Sons.

One chapter reviews the theories of child development. Four chapters deal with cross-cultural research with children and families. Section II has six chapters on diagnostics and assessment of children. Sections III, IV, and V cover problems at various stages of growth. Section VI deals with intervention strategies including: sex education; television watching and children; effects of divorce on children; grief and loss; and ethical and legal issues in the treatment of children. References.

Handbook of Cross-Cultural Human Development. (1981). Ruth H. Munroe, Robert L. Munroe, Beatrice B. Whiting. NY: Garland STPM. (Garland Anthropology and Human Development Series).

Contributors review studies considered important and indicative of areas where, based on existing cross-cultural work, future research looks promising. Coverage of comparative cognitive development is limited in the volume since other reviews exist. References.

Handbook of Pediatrics Primary Care. Second edition. (1984). Marilyn P. Chow, Barbara A. Durand, Marie N. Feldman, Marion A. Mills. NY: John Wiley & Sons.

Provides essential and current information on comprehensive pediatric primary care for health care professionals. Chapters 1 - 4 cover general topics of assessment, immunizations, nutrition, and parent-child interaction assessment. Chapters 5 - 7 contain essential information for providing comprehensive health maintenance care for specific age groups: infant, toddler, preschooler, and school-age children. Part II covers assessment and common clinical problems. References.

The Psychosocial Development of Minority Group Children. (1983). Edited by Gloria Johnson Powell. NY: Brunner/Mazel.

An overview of psychosocial development of minority group children. Authors of each chapter are mostly minority group professionals. Each group is integrated into the conceptual framework of the six general parts of the volume: health status; psychosocial development; family life patterns; mental health issues; educational issues; and research and social policy issues. Not every section contains a chapter on every racial or ethnic group; however, there are chapters on Afro-American, Mexican American, American Indian, and Alaskan natives, Filipino-American, Korean American, Chinese American and Japanese American children. Chapter 32 presents a model of how to conduct mental health research with Mexican American children. The epilogue deals with problems of poverty faced by minority children. References.

Young People with Problems; A Guide to Bibliotherapy. (1984). Jean A. Pardeck, John Pardeck. Westport, CT: Greenwood.

This volume provides information about bibliotherapy for children along with annotated lists of recommended books to use. The book is designed to be used by counselors, psychologists, psychiatrists, social workers, and others working with children. Special sections cover: alcohol and drug abuse; divorce; emotional and behavioral problems; moving to a new location; physical handicaps; pregnancy and abortion; serious illness and death; sexual awareness; sibling relationships; and stepparents. A title, author, and subject index is provided.

MEASUREMENT AND EVALUATION

Accreditation Criteria and Procedures: Position Statement of the National Academy of Early Childhood Programs. A Division of the National Association for the Education of Young Children. (1984). Washington, DC: National Association for the Education of Young Children.

Book sets forth the academy's criteria and procedures for accreditation for early childhood personnel and programs. The first part covers the policies and procedures for accreditation. The second part outlines the criteria for high quality early childhood programs including such items as: curriculum; staff-parent relations; staff qualification and development; administration; staffing; environment; health and safety; nutrition and food service; interactions among staff and children; and evaluation. Four appendixes, a bibliography, an index, and information regarding NYAEC conclude the book. References.

Behavioral Assessment of Childhood Disorders. (1981). Eric J. Mash, Leif G. Terdal. NY: Guilford. (Guilford Behavioral Assessment Series).

After an introduction to the general topic of behavioral assessment, the disorders covered are: (1) self-management problems, (2) hyperactivity, (3) conduct disorders, (4) child abuse, (5) fears and anxieties, (6) childhood depression, (7) social skills deficits, (8) autism, (9) learning disabilities, (10) psychosexual and gender problems, (11) asthma and juvenile diabetes, (12) childhood obesity, (13) seizure disorders, (14) sleep disturbances, and (15) encopresis/enuresis. Chapters frequently contain examples from different assessment devices. References to more than one hundred articles and books follow each of the 16 chapters.

Children's Psychological Testing: A Guide for Nonpsychologists. (1984). David L. Wodrich. Baltimore, MD: Brookes.

A summary of the general procedures and principles involved in the use of psychological tests with children. Coverage starts with the formulation of the referral problem, proceeds to the selection of the appropriate psychometric instrument, discusses the various scoring systems used to quantify the results, and concludes with a psychometric report focused on the referral problem. Over 50 of the most commonly used tests for children are briefly described. Major tests and the functions they assess are covered in the following four areas: infant scales--diagnosing early development delays; preschool tests-- diagnosing mental retardation and learning disabilities; school-age tests--

diagnosing mental retardation and learning disabilities; and personality measures--diagnosing children's emotional problems. The final chapter presents tips on judging the usefulness and validity of psychometric reports.

The Clinical Interview of the Child. (1981). Stanley I. Greenspan. NY: McGraw-Hill.

Provides guidelines, illustrations, and methods of conducting the interview for child study. Chapter 3 provides an illustrated age and phase appropriate difference in the categories of fine and gross motor coordination as well as moods of children from birth to ten years of age. Chapter 7 covers the topic of parent interviews. Users learning the craft of writing up interviews and observations of children will find the book extremely useful. References.

Developmental Screening in Early Childhood: A Guide, Revised edition. (1985). Samuel J. Meisels. Washington, DC: National Association for the Education of Young Children.

Discusses critical issues and practical aspects that play a role in the design of effective screening programs and in the selection of valid and reliable screening instruments. The 1985 edition includes new information about three valid screening instruments published since 1978 when the first edition was published. These may be found in the first appendix. Appendix 3 includes a sample parent questionnaire. Appendix 4 covers communicating with parents following screening. Appendix 5 discusses screening for vision and hearing. Appendix 6 gives a sample flow chart for conducting physical examinations.

Developmental Tasks for Kindergarten Readiness: An Assessment of Abilities and Skills in Preschool Children to Determine Kindergarten Readiness. (1978). Walter J. Lesiak. Brandon, VT: Clinical Psychology Publishers. (Archives of Behavioral Science Monograph No. 52).

Chapter 1 gives a brief review of preschool screening. The body of the monograph concerns the DTKR (Developmental Tasks for Kindergarten Readiness). Chapter 5 is a lengthy bibliography of resources.

Explorations into Patterns of Mental Development and Prediction from the Bayley Scales of Infant Development. (1971). Jane V. Hunt, Nancy Bayley. In *Minnesota Symposia on Child Psychology*. Vol. 5. Edited by John Hill. Minneapolis, MN: Univ. of Minnesota Press.

The paper discusses investigations employing the Bayley Scales of Infant Development and their predecessors. The paper mentions preliminary findings that suggest that test items may discriminate at eight months between infants judged neurologically impaired and those normal at birth. References.

Handbook for Measurement and Evaluation in Early Childhood Education. (1980). William L. Goodwin, Laura A. Driscoll. San Francisco, CA: Jossey-Bass.

In twelve chapters the author covers everything from the general topic of measurement and evaluation in early childhood education through a comprehensive survey of the literature to special measures of cognitive, affective, and psychomotor domains. References.

Infant Performance and Experience: New Findings with the Ordinal Scales. (1987). Ina C. Uzgiris, J. McVicker Hunt. Urbana and Chicago, IL: Univ. of Illinois Press.

Chapter 1 by Hunt looks at different kinds of experience in early rearing conditions. He suggests that it is not the situations themselves which influence development but rather which sensorimotor organizations are most activated by the situations, material or social. Chapter 2 focuses on stages of sensorimotor development. Chapter 3 concerns sequential order in cognitive development. Chapter 4 is an account of the famous debate in Royaumont, France between Chomsky and Piaget concerning language acquisition. Chapter 5 looks at early experience and early cognitive development. Chapter 6 reviews studies relating interpersonal relationships and measures of the rate of habituation in early infancy to later measures of advancement on the various scales, and of early assessment of performance on the scales with measures of later cognitive functioning. Chapter 7 reviews studies employing the Uzgisir-Hunt Scales with the mentally retarded persons. Chapter 8 reports a study comparing use of the scales with normal infants and Down's syndrome infants. Chapter 9 differentiates developmental assessment from traditional assessment with sensorimotor development in impaired infants. Chapter 10 is a review of studies using the scale in early intervention settings. References.

Kindergarten Screening, Early Identification of Potential High Risk Learners. (1976). Shirley Zeitlin. Springfield, IL: Charles C. Thomas.

Explores the process of identifying potential high-risk learners at the kindergarten level. Chapter 4 reviews tools for screening. Appendix E lists diagnostic tests suitable for prekindergarten and kindergarten children. Includes a lengthy bibliography.

Manual of Developmental Diagnosis: The Administration and Interpretation of the Revised Gesell and Amatruda Developmental and Neurologic Examination. (1980). Hilda Knobloch. NY: Harper and Row.

Presents the revised developmental stages for assessment of children. Chapters 1 and 2 discuss assessment and evaluation procedures. Chapter 3 outlines typical behavior expected at each age level along with a picture of assessment techniques, birth to 36 months. Chapter 4 discusses examination techniques. Chapter 5 investigates differential diagnosis. Chapter 6 covers recording data and appraisal. Chapter 7 looks at screening. The appendixes give procedures for the revised developmental schedules, materials, and audio-visual aids. This manual is intended for the professional evaluator.

Measures of Maturation: An Anthology of Early Childhood Observation Instruments. 3 vols. (1973). Edited by E. Gil Boyer, Anita Simon, Gail Karafin. Philadelphia, PA: Research for Better Schools.

This set contains observation systems useful with infants and young children. The seventy-three systems covered are designed for research. Some of the systems assist in the study of behavior, psychomotor traits, activities, feelings and personality. Other systems look at how children interact with peers, how they work and play, how they express roles of leadership and followership, how they communicate with others, the interaction involved in caretaking activities, reinforcement patterns, and how information is processed and exchanged.

Mirrors for Behavior III: An Anthology of Observation Instruments. (1974). Anita E. Simon, Gil Boyer. Wyncote, PA: Communication Materials Center. Philadelphia, PA: Humanizing Learning Program, Research for Better Schools.

An anthology of observational instruments from a wide variety of disciplines which describe verbal and nonverbal behavior. An extensive bibliography may be found on pages 685 - 747. In Section V is an index to systems and authors by system numbers. Users of these volumes are urged to read the overview section before trying to use the body of the text.

Pediatric Assessment of Self-Care Activities. (1978). Ida Lou Coley. Saint Louis, MO: C. V. Mosby.

Describes how a child attains independence in self-care. Presents assessment measures of the child's sufficiency in activities of daily living appropriate to his development status. Author looks at socialization, play, and tasks mastered, along with sensory awareness to arrive at assessing independence in self-care. The arrangement of the material throughout the handbook parallels a reader's professional growth from observer and recorder to participator-activator, interpreter, and consultant.

Pediatric Usefulness of Home Assessment. (1981). Robert H. Bradley, Betty M. Caldwell. In *Advances in Behavioral Pediatrics, A Research Annual,* Vol. 2. Edited by Bonnie Camp. Greenwich, CT: JAI.

The chapter describes the history leading up to the development of environmental process measures. The Caldwell HOME Inventory is discussed along with some of the research carried out with the instruments. Uses of the instrument also are covered. Appendixes A and B provide home observation measures of ages birth to three, as well as preschool. References.

Piagetian Tests for the Primary School. (1970). K. R. Fogelman. England and Wales: National Foundation for Educational Research in England and Wales.

Fogelman extracted from the best-known studies of Piaget's information on test performances of children in particular age groups. Brief descriptions of the materials are given, along with an outline of the procedure followed, in enough detail to enable the reader to use the tests. The researcher as well as the teacher should find this information of value. References.

Predicting Later Mental Performance for Normal, At-Risk, and Handicapped Infants. (1982). Claire B. Kopp, Robert B. McCall. In *Life-Span Development and Behavior*. Vol. 4. Edited by Paul Baltes and Orville Brim, Jr. NY: Academic.

The literature on developmental patterns of stability in mental test scores from infancy to childhood is reviewed for normal, at-risk, and handicapped children in this chapter. Clinically, useful predictions are not available for normal groups before age two. While the correlations are higher and appear earlier for at-risk and handicapped groups, they are not always very much higher. Possible statistical and theoretical explanations for these differences are offered. References.

Preschool Screening: The Measurement and Prediction of Children At-Risk. (1982). Keith E. Barnes. Springfield, IL: Charles C. Thomas.

Book focuses on those objective screening measures which appear to have the greatest potential for preschool assessment on a low-cost large-scale screening basis. Part I is a general introduction and overview of the developmental screening field. The second and third parts are more technically focused on the essential requirements for the development and construction of good predictive screening instruments. The book does not cover preschool diagnostic tests requiring professional administration.

Preschool Test Descriptions: Test Matrix and Correlated Test Descriptors. (1979). H. Wayne Johnson. Springfield, IL: Charles C. Thomas.

A compilation of preschool test information, the references consist of two basic resources: a test matrix, and a test descriptor form. The test matrix may be used as a quick reference tool when selecting devices for a specific need. Across the top of each matrix are six test descriptor terms (administrative, response mode, reference, content, emphasis, and category) that are in turn broken down into forty subdimensions (age/grade, criterion, time required, etc.). The descriptor dimension terms are to be used as identifiers of specific information about the nature of each assessment device listed. Each test listed on the test matrix may be located on the individual test descriptor sheets, which provide more information about each of the tests. The book is arranged sequentially. Users are urged to read the introduction prior to using the volume.

Psychological and Behavioral Assessment: Impact on Pediatric Care. (1984). Edited by Phyllis R. Magrab. NY: Plenum.

Book assists in the development of adequate assessment strategies for children with chronic diseases and potentially handicapping conditions. Chapter 1 provides a developmental framework for assessment procedures. The next three chapters address infant, neuropsychological, and behavioral assessment. The first chapters in the second section cover development disorders, learning disorders, cognitive effects of acute and chronic conditions, psychosocial assessment in chronic and fatal illness, and child abuse.

Psychological Methods of Child Assessment. (1983). Jacquelin Goldman, Claudia L'Engle Stein, Shirley Guerry. NY: Brunner/Mazel.

Reviews easily obtainable and adequately standardized instruments. General background information is given to assist in determining the appropriate instrument. In most cases information on reliability and validity is included. The purpose of the instrument, its administration and scoring, and data on its standardization are also included. Part I covers psychological considerations in child assessment. Part II covers six areas of child assessment including: intelligence, achievement, developmental, projective assessment, and behaviorally-based and neuropsychological assessment techniques. Part III covers applications of principles and methods.

Questionnaires Design and Use. Second edition. (1986). Doug R. Berdie, John F. Anderson, Marsha A. Niebuhr. Metuchen, NJ: Scarecrow.

The first six chapters or 66 pages of this volume provide the user with an overview of developing and using questionnaires effectively in doing research projects. The annotated bibliography section, pages 67 - 204, lists and describes 494 publications related to survey research on the topic. The last section of the book is made up of four appendixes giving sample questionnaires, a case history of a study using questionnaires, a sample of follow-up letters, and a sample check-off list. This is a good tool for researchers planning to make use of a questionnaire in their research projects.

Screening Growth and Development of Preschool Children: A Guide for Test Selection. (1980).   Sharon R. Stangler, Cathee J. Huber, Donald K. Routh. NY: McGraw-Hill.

Presents a systematic approach to the assessment of developmental screening tests.   Chapter 1 gives an overview of the concept of screening.   Chapters 2 and 3 cover the application of the screening test assessment process. Chapters 4 through 8 demonstrate the application of the assessment process to screening tests in five categories: physical growth, general development, hearing, speech and language, and vision.   References.

Socioemotional Measures for Preschool and Kindergarten Children.   (1973). Deborah Klein Walker.   San Francisco, CA: Jossey-Bass.   (Jossey-Bass Behavioral Science Series).

A guide to all socioemotional measures available at the time of publication of the book to use with children ages three to six.   The measures were compiled from Buros as well as other published sources from 1956 to 1972. An index by instrument name is provided as well as a bibliography of references.

Tests and Measurements in Child Development: A Handbook. (1971).   Orval G. Johnson. San Francisco, CA: Jossey-Bass.

Brings together information about several hundred instruments useful to researchers and practitioners.   Descriptions of tests include such information as: what the tests measure; how constructed; and how administered.   Test instruments measuring variables in the following areas are included: cognition; personality; emotional characteristics; children's perceptions of the environment; skills; brain injury; sensory perception; physical attributes; attitudes and interests not otherwise classified; and social behavior.

Tests and Measurements in Child Development: Handbook II. (1976).   San Francisco, CA: Jossey-Bass.

An extension of the 1971 handbook and covering the literature from 1966 through 1974.   Age coverage includes children up to 18.   Behavior rating scales, behavior checklists, and certain classroom observation procedures have been excluded from the two volumes.   Handbook II includes measures dealing with various aspects of the child's environment and measures of attitudes toward children.   Sufficient information is given about each measure so that the reader may decide whether or not to pursue the measure further.   The two volumes are divided into several general categories and then subdivided where appropriate.

REVIEWS OF RESEARCH

ANNUALS

Advances in Applied Developmental Psychology. Vol. 1 - . (1985 -). Edited by Irving E. Sigel. Norwood, NJ: Ablex. (Advances in Applied Developmental Psychology).

> Series is not thematic but publishes research or policy papers on a variety of topics of interest to the child development specialists such as effects of preschool, continuity between home and day care, or early motor development. References.

Advances in Child Development and Behavior. Vol. 1 - . (1957 -). NY: Academic.

> Publishes papers dealing with research and theoretical discussions in the field of child development. Volumes do not focus on any particular subject but cover a variety of topics. Extensive bibliographies usually are included with each paper.

Advances in Clinical Child Psychology. Vol. 1 - . (1977 -). Edited by Benjamin B. Lahey, Alan E. Kazdin. NY: Plenum.

> A serial publication designed to bring together original summaries of the most important research findings during the previous year. Each chapter is written by a noted specialist in the field who presents their own research. Chapters conclude with references.

Advances in Developmental and Behavioral Pediatrics, a Research Annual. Vol. 1 - . (1980 -). Edited by Mark Wolraich, Donald K. Routh. Greenwich, CT: JAI.

> Reviews research on topics loosely related to behavioral pediatrics. The topics are chosen to cover research concerned with the psychosocial, biomedical/physiological, developmental, ecological, and experiential influences on the health and welfare of children from infancy to adolescence. References.

Advances in Early Education and Day Care: A Research Annual. Vol. 1 - . (1980 -). Edited by Sally Kilmer. Greenwich, CT: JAI.

> Reviews and analyzes research on the care of young children. No general theme is carried out in any one volume. The papers vary in areas covered. For example the fourth volume contains: papers on the history of infant schools in North America, 1825 - 1940; a report of experimental studies of preschool environment, the Sheffield Project; learning to read and write; a naturalistic study of two first-year teachers; and language environments of family day care. References.

Advances in Infancy Research. Vol. 1 - . (1981 -). Edited by Lewis P. Lipsitt, Carolyn K. Rovee-Collier. Norwood, NJ: Ablex.

Series reports recent advances in infancy research. Volumes do not focus on any particular topic. Both human and animal infancy studies are included in the yearbooks. References.

Advances in Learning and Behavior Disabilities: A Research Annual. Vol. 1 - . (1982 -). Kenneth D. Gadow, Irv Bialer. Greenwich, CT: JAI.

Reports recent research and theory formation in the areas of learning disabilities and behavior. Papers conclude with bibliographies. Each annual contains separate author and subject indexes.

Advances in Pediatrics. Vol. 1 - . (1942 -). Chicago, IL: Year Book Medical.

This yearbook contains scholarly reviews of pediatric medical research and investigations. The chapters are extremely technical and conclude with sizeable references. Each volume is indexed.

Advances in the Behavioral Measurement of Children, a Research Annual. Vol. 1 - . (1984 -). Edited by Roslyn A. Glow, Ronald J. Prinz. Greenwich, CT: JAI.

An annual devoted to behavioral assessment. Contributions include comprehensive empirical studies, papers on individual programs of research, and a few selective reviews of literature. The first half of each volume covers general topics on a variety of child assessment topics. The second half of each volume covers a special topic or theme.

Annals of Child Development: A Research Annual. Vol. 1 - . (1984 -). Greenwich, CT: JAI.

A series devoted to providing surveys of the field of psychology in the style provided by the *Annual Review of Psychology*. Each yearbook is "weighted" toward a particular topic area with at least one chapter relating to child development as a profession. References.

Annual Progress in Child Psychiatry and Child Development. (1968 -). Edited by Stella Chess, Alexander Thomas. NY: Brunner/Mazel.

These volumes review research on current topics in the area of early childhood through adolescence. Subjects range from developmental patterns, reading disability, autism, child abuse, drug abuse, adolescent violence, etc. Lengthy bibliographies included at the end of each subject.

Child Development Research and Social Policy. Vol. 1 - . (1984 -). Harold W. Stevenson, Alberta E. Siegel. Chicago, IL: Univ. of Chicago Press.

A review series under the auspices of the Society for Research in Child Development intended to link research and theory. The references cited for each chapter are authoritative rather than comprehensive. The eight chapters in Volume 1 cover: social policies toward bilingual, multi-cultured people; child health policy; divorce; children and social policy; the Early and Periodic Screening Diagnosis and Treatment program (EPSDT); institutions and mental retardation; sex roles, socialization and occupational behavior; nutrition and public policy; and political socialization and policy.

Current Topics in Early Childhood Education. Vol. 1 - . (1977 -). Edited by Lilian G. Katz. Norwood, NJ: Ablex. (Current Topics in Early Childhood Education).

Series published regularly, usually annually, covering a variety of current topics in research and theory. References.

Early Childhood Education, the Year in Review. (1975 -). James L. Hymes. Carman, CA: Hacienda.

A yearly report on the happenings in early childhood education. Usually not more than 25 pages.

The Minnesota Symposia on Child Psychology. Vol. 1 - . (1967 -). Edited by Andrew Collins. Hillsdale, NJ: Lawrence Erlbaum.

In each of the volumes an invited group of scholars presents current research significant to the topic of child psychology. Each chapter concludes with a lengthy bibliography.

The Psychoanalytic Study of the Child. Vol. 1 - . (1945 - 1972, 1973 -). New Haven, CT: Yale Univ. Press. NY: International Universities Press, Vols. 1 - 27. New Haven, CT: Yale Univ. Press, Vol. 28 - .

An annual begun in 1945 covering various topics on psychoanalysis and the study of the child. Subject index to the first 25 volumes in the abstract and index supplement published in 1975. Beginning with Volume 26, a subject index is included with each annual.

Review of Child Development Research. Vol. 1 - . (Vol. 1 [1964], Vol. 2 [1966], Vol. 3 [1973] -). Society for Research in Child Development. Chicago, IL: Univ. of Chicago Press.

A series begun in 1964 which presents a sample of reviews of research on important issues in child development. References.

Society for Research in Child Development Monographs. (1935 -). Chicago, IL: Univ. of Chicago Press.

A quarterly publication indexed in *Child Development Abstracts* and *Psychological Abstracts*. Each issue deals with a single topic such as learning disorders in children, sibling studies, growth of primary-age children, and interactions between mothers and their young children. References.

Sociological Studies of Child Development. Vol. 1 - . (1986 -). Peter Adler, Patricia Adler. Greenwich, CT: JAI.

This is the first volume of an intended series which will present current concepts and research in child development from the sociological perspective. Subject coverage includes: conservation, play, relationships; friendships, instinctual versus environmental influences on development, families, education, day care, schooling; and religion, and mass media. References

The Young Child, Reviews of Research. Vol. 1 - . (1967 -). Willard W. Hartup, Nancy L. Smothergill. Washington, DC: National Association for the Education of Young Children.

Published regularly, this series is a collection of reviews on a variety of topics pertaining to children. In the latest volume, chapters were clustered under socioemotional, language, social relationship, biological development, and exceptional children. References.

MONOGRAPHS

Aspects of Early Childhood Education: Theory to Research to Practice. (1980). Dale Range, James R. Layton, Darrell L. Roubineck. NY: Academic.

Chapter 1 traces the historical origins of early childhood education from Plato and Aristotle through contemporary practices. Chapter 2 presents relevant research findings related to the effects of Project Follow Through and the positive and negative effects of television, play and formal reading instruction for young children. Chapter 3 details specific methods that may be used by teachers and parents in modifying and controlling the behavior of young children. Chapter 5 discusses parental influences and parent education programs. Chapter 6 presents research findings and expert opinion related to teacher effectiveness. References.

Cultural Perspectives on Child Development. (1982). Daniel A. Wagner, Harold W. Stevenson. San Francisco, CA: W. H. Freeman. (A Series of Books in Psychology).

Provides a sampling of cross-cultural studies on child development for the non-professional. Chapter 1 addresses emotional development during infancy and early childhood. Chapter 2 integrates research from several cultures on neonatal behavior. Chapter 3 describes prominent components of parental language crucial for the acquisition of language skills comparing English- and Spanish-speaking parents. Chapter 4 describes children's perception of representation of objects and depth in pictures. Chapter 5 discusses ontogenetic or developmental research in formulating theories of cognition. Chapter 6 is an overview of the effects of nutrition on mental development. Chapter 7 reports a comparison of Canadian children from English-speaking and Micmac Indian families using Piaget's "conservation" tasks. Chapter 8 looks at the phenomenon of "animism," the tendency to attribute "life" and "will" to objects, among Pidgin-speaking children in Hawaii. Chapter 10 looks at transfer of learning in Quechua Indians. Chapter 11 discusses a personality study of Mexican and American youths. Chapter 12 summarizes work on moral judgment among Kenyon children. References.

Development During Middle Childhood: The Years from Six to Twelve. (1984). Edited by W. Andrew Collins. Washington, DC: National Academy.

A selective review of research, Chapters 2, 3, and 4 focus on physical and cognitive growth and the fundamental psychological processes of developing a sense of self and capabilities for self-regulation during middle childhood. Chapters 5, 6, and 7 look at the impact of shifting social relations with parents to more extensive involvement with peers. Chapter 8 looks at the influence of a cross cultural environment. Chapter 9 discusses research related to psychopathology. A list of cited sources ends each chapter. The books contains a subject index.

Early Childhood Curriculum: A Review of Current Research. (1987). Edited by Carol Seefeldt. NY: Teachers College Press. Columbia Univ.

This volume is a compilation of the research and theory in the curriculum content areas. Each chapter presents an overview of the theory, research, and implications for practice in a specific curriculum content area. The book is for use by any professional or graduate student interested in early childhood education and needing an overview of the topic.

Early Childhood Education: The Seventy-First Yearbook of the National Society for the Study of Education. Part II. (1972). Edited by Ira J. Gordon. Chicago, IL: Univ. of Chicago Press. (Yearbook of the National Society for the Study of Education).

The sixteen chapters synthesize the topics covered, including pertinent research and theory. A wide variety of topics is covered in the chapters: health of the preschool child; malnutrition and behavioral development; early identification of at-risk children; sociolinguistic competence and dialect diversity; media and development; an empirical analysis of selected follow-through programs; research strategies; cross-cultural views of early education; and staff requirements in early childhood educators. Each chapter contains a bibliography of references. Includes a subject index.

Early Education and Psychological Development. (1984). Barbara Biber. New Haven, CT: Yale Univ. Press.

A collection of Barbara Biber's selected papers published between 1934 and 1977. Topics covered include: thought processes, language, feelings, play, creativity, the environment, self-worth, socialization, and public responsibility toward the child. A bibliography and index are included.

Early Education: Current Theory, Research, and Action. (1968). Edited by Robert D. Hess, Roberta Meyer Bear. Chicago, IL: Aldine.

Initial versions of the papers in this volume were presented at the Conference on Pre-School Education, held in Chicago in February, 1966. Seventeen papers are included in the volume covering a wide variety of research: cognitive, social, and language development. A lengthy bibliography concludes the volume.

Early Experience and Human Development. (1982). Theodore D. Wachs, Gerald E. Gruen. NY: Plenum.

Provides a detailed review of effects of early experience on the development of the young child, including relationships between cognitive-intellectual development and the physical, social, and emotional-attitudinal environment. Additional chapters cover early social experience as a factor in social development and child socialization, as well as relations between social and cognitive development. A limitation of the material reviewed is the deliberate omission of comparative research. The final chapter points out the implications for and applications of the evidence to institutional and preschool environments and the planning of intervention programs. References.

Handbook of Infant Development. Second edition. (1987). Edited by Joy D. Osofsky. NY: John Wiley & Sons. (Wiley Series on Personality Processes).

A compilation of ideas, conceptualizations, and research in the area of infancy for teachers, researchers, and scholars. Part 1 deals with newborn and early infant behavior. Part 2 deals with developmental perspectives in infancy. Part 3 deals with parent-infant relationships and infant-infant relationships. Part 4 deals with the general issue of continuity and change and the relationship of early and later behavior. Part 5 reviews the research, theory, and application of work in the area of infancy. References.

Handbook of Research in Early Childhood Education. (1982). Edited by Bernard Spodek. NY: Free Press.

The first four sections of the handbook present reviews of research and theory within the various areas of early childhood education: child development, developmental theories, classroom processes, and public policy. The last section addresses methods of research data collection and concerns of the field. Lengthy references are provided at the end of each chapter.

The Middle Years of Childhood. (1977). Patricia P. Minuchin. Monterey, CA: Brooks/Cole. (Life-Span Human Development Series).

Summarizes theory and relevant research on four major aspects of childhood from six to twelve. The book is divided into five chapters: introductory concepts and theories; cognitive development; social development; individual development, self-concept and sex-role formation; and the school. A lengthy bibliography follows the last chapter.

Piagetian Research: A Handbook of Recent Studies. (1974). Sohan Modgil. NY: Humanities.

A comprehensive book of readings containing published and unpublished research from the work of Jean Piaget. The book is organized to include traditional categories of research on the various developmental levels from sensorimotor to formal operations as well as research on atypical children. The book finishes with a review of tests. The second half of the section includes detailed abstracts of individual studies. Because many of these studies are European or English in origin, this book provides a useful adjunct to a more traditional North American literature search through *Psychological Abstracts*. Includes a comprehensive bibliography of over 1,500 references appearing up to August 1973.

Piagetian Research: Compilation and Commentary. (1976). Sohan Modgil, Celia Modgil. Windsor, Berks: NFER.

Designed to make available a substantial number of Piaget-oriented researches, each volume deals with a single topic. A review of the Piaget-oriented research is presented along with abstracts of the cited research. A bibliography and author index are provided.

Potentials of Childhood. 2 vols. (1983). William Fowler. Lexington, MA: Lexington Books, D. C. Heath.

Reviews the experimental data on early stimulation. Volume 1 is a historical survey and critical analysis of perspectives and research on early education and early experience. Volume 2 includes studies on early developmental learning. The first four chapters in Volume 1 review the literature on a cultural and group basis. An early chapter in Volume 2 summarizes studies on early reading, and general cognitive, motor, and language simulation. References.

A Primer of Infant Development. (1977). T. G. R. Bower. San Francisco, CA: W. H. Freeman. (A Series of Books in Psychology).

Summarizes information on the needs and abilities of infants. Chapter 2 looks at infancy, its significance, current methods of study, and a description of the abilities of a newborn. Chapters 3 and 4 review social-emotional developments (the smile, separation anxiety, and fear of strangers). Chapter 4 discusses the role which communication plays in attachment behaviors. Chapters 5, 6, and 7 cover topics on perceptual, motor, and cognitive development. Some of the authors own work is introduced. Chapter 8 looks at language development including the infant's nonverbal communication. Bower concludes the book with a discussion of the long-term impact which experience or the lack of it during the first two years has on personality development and, to a lesser degree, on the development of cognitive and perceptual motor abilities.

Psychobiology of the Human Newborn. (1982). Edited by Peter Stratton. NY: John Wiley & Sons. (Wiley Series in Developmental Psychology).

A brief guide to infancy research, primarily in the areas of capacities of the neonate, the types of environmental interactions in which they participate, and the methodologies used in studying these concerns. A chapter on learning, adaptation, and memory is included. One chapter briefly reviews the structure of the neonatal nervous system while another is a synthesis of rhythmic functions. A chapter on sensory and perceptual capacities is included. One paper appraises neonatal assessment instruments. Important data on nonhuman primate newborns is missing. A chapter on neonatal social interchanges will be of interest to developmentalists. References.

Psychological Development in the Elementary Years. (1982). Edited by Judith Worell. NY: Academic. (Educational Psychology).

Reviews current theory and research on psychological development relating to educational practice and focuses on school entrance until early adolescence, ages five through twelve. The book is divided into four parts: social interaction processes, cognitive processes, social influences, and developmental problems. Included under social interaction are chapters on sex roles, peer relations, aggression in young children, and self control. In Part II, under cognition, chapters cover learning, cognitive development, and achievement. Part III, on social influences, includes a chapter on family influences on language and cognitive development and one on personal and social causation in the school context. The latter includes learned helplessness and teacher expectancy. Part IV, about developmental problems, covers learning and behavioral problems. Lengthy bibliographies follow each chapter.

Research on Early Childhood and Elementary School Teaching Programs. (1986). Jane A. Stallings, Deborah Stipik. In *Handbook of Research on Teaching*. Third edition. Edited by Merlin Wittrock. NY: Macmillan.

A concise but comprehensive synthesis of research on the topic. Reviews longitudinal studies of day care programs, and well-known programs developed for the early elementary school years. Substantial bibliography.

Understanding Infancy. (1979). Eleanor Willemsen. San Francisco, CA: W. H. Freeman.

Reviews research and theories regarding infant development in nontechnical terms. The book starts chronologically in the first two chapters and traces development from conception through prenatal development and pregnancy, childbirth, and the newborn period. In chapters 3-6 emphasis is on topics such as learning and perception, cognition, attachment and first social relations, and infant personality. An extensive appendix is presented on techniques for studying infants. References.

Young Children's Academic Expectations. (1983). Doris R. Entwisle, Leslie Alec Hayduk. In *Research in Sociology of Education and Socialization*. Vol. 4. Greenwich, CT: JAI.

The chapter synthesizes the research from 1962 to 1980 dealing with the transition of the young child from home to school. References.

STATISTICS

American Children in Poverty. (1984). Washington, DC: Children's Defense Fund.

Provides statistical data, state by state, of the needs of America's poor children. Part I covers the major findings of investigators. Part II is a portrait of child poverty. Part III lays out the costs to the nation of this poverty. An appendix of detailed state tables is included.

American Statistics Index: A Comprehensive Guide and Index to Statistical Publications of the U.S. Government. (1973 -). Washington, DC: Congressional Information Service.

This annual, with monthly supplements, lists and indexes federal government publications "which contain statistical data of research significance, whether published periodically, irregularly, or as monographs." The ASI Microfiche publications are cited in ASI.

A Children's Defense Budget: An Analysis of the FY 1988 Budget and Children. (1987). Washington, DC: Children's Defense Fund.

Published yearly, the monograph analyzes and discusses the federal budget priorities and their effect on the nation's poor children. In separate sections, issues analyzed include: health; family income; housing; food assistance; education; youth employment; abused and neglected children; runaways; child care; Head Start; and civil rights. In the various appendixes may be found individual state statistics. No index is provided.

PART II: SPECIALIZED INFORMATIONAL REFERENCES

CHILD DEVELOPMENT

The Challenge of Child Welfare. (1985). Edited by Kenneth L. Levitt, Brian Wharf. Vancouver, BC: Univ. of British Columbia Press.

First Canadian text to examine issues representing the state-of-the-art of child welfare. The eighteen chapters cover a wide range of topics: abuse, poverty, native child welfare, subsidized adoption, family treatment, day care, children's rights, and preventive approaches to child welfare. Chapter 11 by David A. Cruickshank covers the "Berger Commission Report on the Protection of Children: The Impact on Prevention of Child Abuse and Neglect." Each chapter ends with a sizeable bibliography.

The Inner World of Childhood. (1978). Frances Gillespy Wickes. Englewood Cliffs, NJ: Prentice-Hall.

A classic in psychiatric literature, the book explores the intricacies of the parent-child relationship. Chapter 1 discusses the scope and methods of analytical psychology. Chapter 2 looks at the influence of parental difficulties. Chapter 3 discusses the power of the projected image. Chapter 4 delves into the effects of early relationships. Chapter 5 examines the adolescent. Chapter 6 looks at the child's desire for remaining unconscious, and acceptance of consciousness. Chapter 7 looks at types of personalities. Chapter 8 discusses imaginary companions. Chapter 9 delves into children's fears. Chapter 10 covers the topic of sex. Chapter 11 discusses dreams. Footnotes are provided.

Life and Ways of the Seven- to Eight-Year-Old. (1942). Barbara Biber, Lois B. Murphy, Louise P. Woodcock, Irma S. Black. NY: Basic Books.

Although published over forty years ago, this landmark study describes stages in growth and maturing during the middle childhood years as seen by a psychologist, a sociologist, and an educator. The bibliography will be of particular interest to scholars and researchers of historical or retrospective literature on the topic.

Mind in Society: The Development of Higher Psychological Process. (1978). L. S. Vygotsky. Cambridge, MA: Harvard Univ. Press.

A carefully edited and organized collection of some of Vygotsky's major works which have been unavailable previously in English. Several of the chapters are derived from unpublished notes and manuscripts obtained from his student, A. R. Luria. Chapter titles are: tool and symbol in child development; the development of perception and attention; mastery of memory and thinking; internalization of higher psychological functions; problems of method; interaction between learning and development; the role of play in development; and the prehistory of written language. A list of Vygotsky's works by year, 1915 - 1935, is included.

Piaget Systematized. (1982). Gilbert E. Voyat. Hillsdale, NJ: Lawrence Erlbaum.

A compendium of Piaget's tasks, 152 in all, drawn from eight areas: geometry, space, number, time, movement and speed, physical causality, early logic, and formal logic. First there is a description of each task, including the types of materials used and the general line of questioning. Finally a series of protocols is given that is representative of the stages of development for each task as these stages are delineated by Piaget. Norms are given for each task. References.

Psychopathology and Adaptation in Infancy and Early Childhood: Principles of Clinical Diagnosis and Preventive Intervention. (1981). Stanley I. Greenspan. NY: International Universities Press. (Clinical Infant Reports: Series of the National Center for Clinical Infant Programs).

Analyses of the development of children in the first four years of life. An integration of several theories, including Piagetian and psychoanalytic, is used to identify stages of early intervention, assessment, and evaluation of children. Criteria for the level, depth, resiliency, and personal uniqueness of the activities at each of these stages are presented. The author also examines the relationship between the child's developmental stage and parental functioning and discusses the environmental characteristics that are growth-promoting and growth-inhibiting. Principles of intervention are reviewed and clinical examples are given. References.

The Structuring of Experience. (1977). Edited by Ina C. Uzgiris, Frederich Weizmann. NY: Plenum.

Sixteen chapters summarize J. McVicker Hunt's contributions to psychology. Intelligence, intrinsic motivation, the construction of schemata, the role of experience, and the factors that underline cognitive growth are covered. In the introductory chapter, Weizmann presents a summary of Hunt's principal interests and ideas as developed over his long career. A good summary of research and thinking on early development of infant visual attention and its determinants makes up one chapter. References.

Theory and Problems of Child Development. Second edition. (1970). David P. Ausubel, Edmund V. Sullivan. NY: Grune and Stratten.

An overview of the generalizations and empirical findings on human development. Part II deals with the general theoretical and methodological issues in child development. Part II discusses the origins, raw materials, and beginning status of behavior and capacity. Part III deals with the general theory of personality development. Part IV covers various special aspects of development such as development of language, perceptual and cognitive development, and the growth of intelligence. Part V looks at physical and motor development. References.

Three Theories of Child Development. Revised edition. (1969). Henry W. Maier. NY: Harper and Row.

Maier's book presents the theories of Erik H. Erikson, Jean Piaget, and Robert R. Sears together with some implications of these theories in practice. The presentation of these three theories is based upon research in the primary literature of all three writers. A bibliography and suggested further readings may be found at the end of the volume. In the appendix is a partial bibliography of works of the three men.

CHILD STUDY GUIDES

Applied Child Study, a Developmental Approach. (1987). Anthony D. Pellegrini. Hillsdale, NJ: Lawrence Erlbaum.

The book outlines ways in which children may be studied. This includes a number of current theories of child development (Piaget, Vygotsky, Bandura, Fillmore, Kempler, Wang, and Kogan). Several different methodologies of child study also are presented. Readable and concise, those studying children will find it helpful during the research planning stage. References.

Approaches to Child Study. (1983). John Touliatos, Norma Compton. Minneapolis, MN: Burgess.

Discusses methods of child observation and recording behavior in naturalistic settings. Chapter 1 provides a framework for the scientific study of children, including a review of the historical development of the field. Chapter 2 discusses direct observation of behavior including language behavior, paralinguistic behavior, gestures, posture, facial expressions, eye behavior, spatial behavior, touching behavior, personal appearance, and environment. Chapter 3 talks about anecdotal records, specimen records, running records, time sampling, event sampling, and environmental analysis. Chapter 4 discusses choosing observational methods. Chapters 5 and 6 describe the use of various observational aids (rating scales, checklists, and mechanical aids). Scientific approaches to child study are discussed in Chapters 7, 8, and 9. Chapter 10 delves into studying the family. The case study method is covered in Chapter 11. The final chapter looks at ethics of child study. References.

Child Study and Observation Guide. (1976). Gene R. Medinnus. NY: John Wiley & Sons.

Part I discusses the various methods of observation ranging from hand-written recording of a child's behavior in an unstructured situation through precise methods of recording observational data focusing on specific aspects of behavior. Part II focuses on important areas of the child behavior and development field. References.

Longitudinal Research: Methods and Uses in Behavioral Science. (1981). Fini Schulsinger, Sarnoff A. Mednick, J. Knop. The Hague: Martinus Nijhoff. (Longitudinal Research in the Behavioral, Social, and Medical Sciences).

Volume discusses methods, techniques, and practices of carrying out longitudinal research in the behavioral sciences. Part I outlines some of the problems and strategies in mental health research. Parts II and III are papers concerning design problems, and tools of long-term research. Part IV includes chapters describing experiences and results of a number of ongoing and well-known longitudinal projects using different types of samples. Part VI considers the implications of long-term research and offers recommendations for designing and conducting such investigations. References.

Observing and Recording the Behavior of Young Children. Third Collection. (1983). Dorothy H. Cohen, Virginia Stern, Nancy Balaban. NY: Teachers College Press, Columbia Univ.

This guide outlines how to objectively observe and record children's classroom behavior. Considered a classic.

The Psychotherapeutic Process: A Research Handbook. (1986). Edited by Leslie S. Greenberg, William M. Pinsof. NY: Guilford.

This is a comprehensive handbook of process research systems. The first chapter provides an overview of the current state of process research. The book is divided into two major sections. The first part presents the major instruments in the field. The second section delves into methodological issues, illustrating how psychotherapy works. This volume is already recognized as a landmark publication. References.

Seeing Young Children: A Guide to Observing and Recording Behavior. (1985). W. R. Bentzen. Albany, NY: Delmar.

Discusses different methods of observing and recording behavior. These include specimen records, time sampling, event sampling, diary description, anecdotal records, frequency counts or duration records, and checklists.

Studying Children: An Introduction to Research Methods. (1979). Ross Vasta. San Francisco, CA: W. H. Freeman. (A Series of Books in Psychology).

Describes aspects of psychological research common to all disciplines and indicates some of the unique characteristics of research with children. The text progresses from general approaches to specific procedures. Numerous examples of research with children may be found throughout the chapters. References.

A Teachers' Guide to Action Research: Evaluation, Enquiry and Development in the Classroom. (1981). Edited by Jon Nixon. London: Grant McIntyre.

This book through discussion and sample case studies guides the classroom teacher in the areas of observational/action research. Twelve chapters divided into three parts make up the guide. The book parts correspond to the different settings of action research: the classroom, the school, and the wider educational context. Brief references are supplied at the end of chapters.

Ways of Studying Children; A Manual for Teachers. (1959). Millie Almy, Ruth Cunningham. NY: Teachers College Press, Columbia Univ.

A classic, the book is broken into eight chapters covering topics such as what is child study, the basics of studying children, studying children in groups, asking children about themselves, studying the ways children express themselves, studying children through others, and using existing records on the child in a study. A summary, along with suggested readings, concludes each chapter.

Curriculum

The Bilingual Child: Research and Analysis of Existing Educational Themes. (1976). Edited by Antonio Simoes. NY: Academic. (Educational Psychology Series).

The focus of the book is on trends in research on bilingual children and their educational needs. Subjects covered in the fourteen chapters include: developing cultural attitudes scales; continuing literacy in the home language; cognitive style of the bilingual; controversy over the immersion philosophy; examination of submersion programs; the American Indian population; bilingualism and reading; classroom management; interaction analysis; and bilingual education in the future.

Bilingual Education, a Sourcebook. (1985). Alba N. Ambert, Sarah E. Melendez. NY: Garland.

This book, intended for teachers, teacher aides, teacher trainers, supervisors, administrators, parents, child advocates, and others interested in bilingual education issues, contains eleven chapters which discuss program models, legal issues, English as a second language, reading, assessment, bilingual special education, bilingual vocational education, program evaluation, parental involvement and participation, teachers and teacher training, and antibilingualism. Each chapter contains a general analysis of the topic followed by an extensive annotated bibliography in the area. Three appendixes offer further resources and bibliographies in bilingual education.

Bilingual Education for Hispanic Students in the United States. (1982). Edited by Joshua A. Fishman, Gary D. Keller. NY: Teachers College Press, Columbia Univ. (Bilingual Education Series).

Part I provides a concise chronology of bilingual education in the United States. Part II, made up of five chapters, defines the goals of bilingual education. Part III, containing six chapters, looks at the issues in language diversity and language standardization in U.S. Spanish. Part IV covers attitudes toward Spanish and bilingual education. Part V, entitled Research on Bilingual Instruction and Assessment, encompasses six chapters. The last and seventh part of the book looks at how young children become bilingual. Pertinent references and studies are cited throughout the book.

Bilingualism in Education: Aspects of Theory, Research, and Practice. (1986). Jim Cummins, Merrill Swain. London: Longman. (Applied Linguistics and Language Study Series).

This book provides a guide to the research in bilingual education taking place currently in Canada. The volume contains a synthesis of recent work relating to the educational development of bilingual children. References.

The Child's Political World: A Longitudinal Perspective. (1985). A. Stanley Moore, James Lare, Kenneth A. Wagner. NY: Praeger.

This book is a major longitudinal study of political knowledge and attitudes in kindergarten through fourth grade. At one year intervals 243 Southern California children were interviewed using structured questions. These children showed strong positive feeling for the unifying symbols of government and ambivalent feelings about political conflict. Forty percent of the kindergartners had a theocratic orientation, believing that either God or Jesus appoints political leaders. Strong partisan identification was lacking.

There are also some interesting findings on the child's view of law. The book includes many detailed tables illustrating the data gathered. References.

Civic Education in Ten Countries: An Empirical Study. (1975). Judith V. Torney, A. N. Oppenheim, Russell F. Farnen. NY: John Wiley & Sons.

The International Association of Educational Achievement (IEA) began the Civic Education Project in 1967 to study the cross-national achievement in civics. This is the final report of its findings. Several issues are addressed in the report. First, it defines the subject area of cross-nationality. Second, it deals with methodological problems encountered in cross-national assessment of civic achievement and attitudes among students. Third, it conveys a detailed picture of student knowledge in civics and of attitudes such as support of the national government, and interest/participation in civic affairs at three age levels. Fourth, it attempts to assess the relative impact of home and school on the acquisition of civic knowledge and attitudes. Fifth, it relates selected characteristics of the schools and the national political systems to the affective and cognitive outcomes of civic education. Findings of the committee show that there were few differences between responses, on the average, between girls and boys, or by children from different social backgrounds. Traditional schools with a strong emphasis on memorizing facts produced students who tended to be less knowledgeable and informed about politics. Students who reported frequent participation in patriotic rituals were both less knowledgeable and less democratic in their outlook. Findings indicate that classroom climate is very important in fostering democratic learning.

Continuity and Connection: Curriculum in Five Open Classrooms. (1979). Beth Alberty, Lillian Weber. NY: City College Workshop Center for Open Education.

This paper reports a study focusing on documentation of curriculum themes around which many Open Corridor teachers organize their presentation of content. The study sheds light on curriculum continuity in open educational settings. Part I provides the rationale for the study. Part II describes the study. Part III looks at the study setting. Part IV covers emerging aspects of continuity and connection in curriculum. Part V presents the conclusions. An annotated interview is located in the appendix. References.

Creative Writing in the Classroom: An Annotated Bibliography of Selected Resources (K - 12). (1978). Edited by Robert Day. Urbana, IL: National Council of Teachers of English and ERIC Clearinghouse on Reading and Communication Skills.

The annotated bibliography provides a list of resources dealing with techniques of teaching writing and the study of teaching creative writing, kindergarten through grade 12. Journal articles, ERIC documents, and books are included in the bibliography.

Cross-Cultural Longitudinal Research on Child Development: Studies of American and Mexican School Children. (1969). Wayne H. Holtzman, Rogelio Diaz-Guerrero, Jon D. Swartz, Luis Lara Tapia. In *Minnesota Symposia on Child Psychology.* Vol. 2. Edited by John Hill. Minneapolis, MN: Univ. of Minnesota Press.

In this paper the authors present the results of the first two years of a large-scale, cross-cultural longitudinal study of cognitive, perceptual, and personality development. They found that at this stage, American children approach assessment situations actively. The Austin, Texas children were direct and forthright in their approach to problem solving. They were risk takers. The Mexico City children approached the assessment situation passively, responding more to immediate sensory experiences and giving evidence of less highly differentiated cognitive and perceptual structure. Thirty-seven references are provided at the end of the chapter.

Curriculum for the Preschool-Primary Child: A Review of the Research. (1976). Edited by Carol Seefeldt. Columbus, OH: C. E. Merrill.

This volume is a compilation of the theoretical foundations and current research in the content areas of curriculum for early childhood education. Past and current theory is examined and conclusions are presented. Each chapter reviews a different content area and ends with a lengthy bibliography. An author and subject index is provided.

Early Childhood Bilingual Education. (1971). Vera P. John, Vivian M. Horner. NY: Modern Language Association of America.

Considered a classic on the topic, the book is written from the perspective of both the immigrant and the native born. The book not only provides practical information to help individuals, professionals, and communities in presenting their demands for early bilingual programs but also provides demographic characteristics of target populations, information on teacher recruitment and training, and review of research in bilingual education. Programs, curriculum, and models of bilingual education are also covered. References.

Early Childhood Bilingual Education: A Hispanic Perspective. (1983). Edited by Theresa Herrera Escobedo. NY: Teachers College Press, Columbia Univ. (Bilingual Education Series).

A collection of research studies in bilingual education. The general categories into which the studies are divided include: language, culture, and classroom strategies. Four studies are provided under language and culture and six studies in the last category. References.

Early Childhood Education: An Alternative Perspective. (1976). Gilbert R. Austin. NY: Academic.

Summarizes the results of a five-year cross-cultural survey of early childhood education in the Western world. References.

Early Childhood Education: An International Perspective. (1982). Nechama Nir-Janiv, Bernard Spodek, Doreen Steg. NY: Plenum.

Includes reports of research studies, programs, practices, and policies. The volume is organized in sections according to broad categories: educational foundations; children's development; teacher education; parents, family, and home intervention; children's learning; social environment of children; educational programs; test and testing; and evaluation. References.

Effective Reading Programs: Summaries of 222 Selected Programs. (1975). National Right to Read Effort. Urbana, IL: National Council of Teachers of English.

A directory of programs around the United States which were started under the Right to Read program. Under each program information is given on: program size and target population, year started, staff, major feature; facilities, materials, equipment; cost; and addresses to write to for further information. There is a geographical ERIC index of programs along with Clearinghouse accession numbers which means each number must be converted to the ED number in order to locate the microfiche.

Estimation and Mental Computation: 1986 Yearbook, National Council of Teachers of Mathematics. (1986). Edited by Harold L. Schoen, Marilyn J. Zweng. Reston, VA: National Council of Teachers of Mathematics.

This 1986 yearbook focuses on the theme of the importance of teaching and learning estimation. The yearbook is divided into five sections with brief "benchmarks" between sections. The benchmarks contain topical teaching ideas or interesting information concerning estimation or mental computation. The first section containing five chapters provides a framework for the yearbook. Part II contains eight chapters which present specific instructional activities. Part III, chapters 15 - 21, stresses the remarkable variety of types of estimation and uses for estimation. Part IV has three chapters, all focusing on estimation in measurement. Part V, two chapters, comprises a review of research on teaching and learning estimation and discusses recent attempts to test students' abilities to estimate. The chapters in this section include references.

First Lessons: A Report on Elementary Education in America. (1986). U.S. Secretary of Education, William J. Bennett. Washington, DC: Government Printing Office.

A detailed report by the Secretary of Education on the condition of elementary education in America today. Suggestions are given for future direction of the elementary education program. Chapter 1 covers children, parents, and the community. Chapter 2 covers the various subject areas in the curriculum including art, foreign language, health, and physical education. Noticeably absent is music. Chapter 3 covers elementary school professionals. Chapter 4 delves into school policy. A bibliography of references ends the government document.

Improving Children's Competence. (1982). Edited by Paul Karoly, John J. Steffen. Lexington, MA: Lexington Books. (Advances in Child Behavioral Analysis and Therapy, Vol. 1).

This book presents research and practice on the topic of how social and/or intellectual skills are taught. Chapter 1 is an introduction to the field of social competence. Chapter 2 delves into the topic of socially-isolated children and reviews varied clinical interventions. Chapter 3 focuses on retarded or developmentally disabled children. Chapter 4 examines the Direct Instruction model or program. Chapter 5 examines memory. Chapter 6 summarizes the discussions throughout the book and discusses self-regulation as a means to children achieving competence.

Inside the Primary Classroom. (1980). Maurice J. Galton, Brian Simon, Paul Croll. London: Routledge & Kegan Paul.

This volume reports the findings of the first large-scale observational study of primary school classrooms undertaken in England. It presents an analysis of pupil and teacher activity, identifying different patterns of teacher and pupil behavior. This volume forms part of a larger research program, Observational Research and Classroom Learning Evaluation (ORACLE), funded by the Social Science Research Council from 1975 - 1980. The goal of ORACLE was to study the effectiveness of different teaching approaches across subject areas of primary school teaching. References.

International Research in Early Childhood Education. (1978). Edited by Maurice Chazan. Windsor, Berks: NFER.

This volume reviews research in the area of early childhood education from the countries of Australia, Belgium, the Federal Republic of Germany, Israel, the Netherlands, Scandinavia, and the USSR. References.

Language Teaching: The International Abstracting Journal for Language Teachers and Applied Linguists. Vol. 15 - . (1981 -). Cambridge: Cambridge Univ. Press.

Formerly *Language Teaching and Linguistic Abstracts* (1968 - 1981), this journal is published quarterly in January, April, July, and October. Although coverage is from infancy to adulthood, child development people will find numerous indexed journal articles of interest, especially those researching in the area of language arts.

Learning to Read in American Schools: Basal Readers and Content Texts. (1984). Richard C. Anderson, Jean Osborn, Robert J. Turney. Hillsdale, NJ: Lawrence Erlbaum (Psychology of Reading and Reading Instruction).

Five topics are covered in the volume: reading comprehension instruction; stories in basal readers and trade books, appraising text difficulty; content area textbooks; and teachers' guides and workbooks. Each chapter discusses what is known about the topic and summarizes recent research. Most chapters are followed by critiques written by authorities in the field. References.

Mathematics for the Middle Grades (5 - 9): 1982 Yearbook, National Council of Teachers of Mathematics. (1982). Linda Silvey, James R. Smart. Reston, VA: National Council of Teachers of Mathematics.

This 1982 yearbook focuses on topics dealing with teaching and learning mathematics in grades five to nine. The volume has three major sections. The first section deals with critical issues in mathematics for the middle grades. The second section focuses on learning activities including indoor, outdoors, and community type activities. The last section discusses games, contests, and student presentations. Three articles offer ideas for game strategies and game development. Some chapters end with references.

Mathematics Learning in Early Childhood: Thirty-seventh Yearbook, National Council of Teachers of Mathematics. (1985). Edited by Joseph N. Payne. Reston, VA: National Council of Teachers of Mathematics.

The twelve chapters in the yearbook cover various aspects of teaching and learning mathematics with children ages three to eight. Knowledge about children's cognitive development, the way they learn mathematics, and curriculum design is discussed in chapters 1 - 3. Knowledge about learning and teaching specific mathematical content is covered in chapters 4 - 11. Special curriculum projects and directions for change are outlined in Chapter 12. References are included with each chapter.

Measurement in School Mathematics: 1976 Yearbook, National Council of Teachers of Mathematics. (1976). Doyal Nelson, Robert E. Reys. Reston, VA: National Council of Teachers of Mathematics.

This is the first NCTM yearbook developed around a central theme, measurement systems in the United States and Canada. Part I of the yearbook addresses issues of learning and teaching measurement. Part II delves into some of the unusual and novel activities used to teach measurement. Part III contains two chapters. Chapter 14 introduces readers to manipulative devices which may be purchased to teach measurement to elementary school children. Chapter 15 is a bibliography of materials available for the teaching of measurement. It includes books and workbooks. Scholars working in the area of curriculum resource history will find this chapter helpful. References.

The Measurement of Children's Civic Attitudes in Different Nations. (1974). Abraham Naftali Oppenheim, Judith Torney. NY: John Wiley & Sons. (IEA Monograph Studies, No. 2. International Association for the Evaluation of Educational Achievement).

This notable study describes the means for assessing children's achievements in civic education. The study involved seven countries and 200 - 300 pupils. Measures used included perceptions of the community, egalitarianism, citizenship values, and other precepts.

Moving from the Primary Classroom. (1983). Edited by Maurice Galton, John Willcocks. London: Routledge & Kegan Paul.

This volume describes the ORACLE (Observational Research and Classroom Learning Evaluation) investigations teams' observations of the effects of school transfer upon students. Part I of the book looks at the background of the transfer problem. Part II compares students' reactions to new teachers upon transfer versus reactions to new teachers after a period of time had passed. Part III looks at students' performances before and after transfer. The findings suggest that performance drops upon transfer. Part IV describes some of the students' experiences upon transfer. The final section of the book attempts to integrate all the findings of the ORACLE research. References.

Organizing for Mathematics Instruction: 1977 Yearbook, National Council of Teachers of Mathematics. (1977). F. Joe Crosswhite, Robert E. Reys. Reston, VA: National Council of Teachers of Mathematics.

This is the second NCTM yearbook in which the entire volume is developed around a single theme, classroom practices. The first eleven chapters contribute to that topic. Chapter 12 reviews the literature of self pacing and discusses the implications of it on instruction in mathematics. Chapter 13 includes four reports on hand-held calculators and the teaching of mathematics. References.

A Place Called Kindergarten. (1987). Lilian G. Katz, James D. Raths, Rosalie T. Torres. Urbana, IL: Clearinghouse on Elementary Education and Early Childhood. (ED 280 595).

This report chronicles the district's progress in arriving at goals and problems related to kindergarten education. Section I summarizes information obtained from parents, school board members, central district staff, teachers, and principals. Section II addresses questions concerning developmental readiness, optional and regular kindergarten programs, and needed changes. Section III discusses: (1) the practice of "red-shirting," or parental withholding of six-year-old children from first grade; (2) community competitiveness and parents' concern with their children "making it"; (3) curriculum issues, particularly the importance of appropriate methods of instruction; and (4) the cycle of blame allocation among interested groups. Appended are a nearly verbatim record of participants' comments and an extensive ERIC ready search of 1985 and 1986 journal articles and documents about kindergarten and kindergarten children.

The Psychological Impact of School Experience: A Comparative Study of Nine-Year-Old Children in Contrasting Schools. (1969). Patricia Minuchin, Biber Shapiro, Herbert Zimiles. NY: Basic Books. (Psychological Studies in Education).

An intensive study of nine-year-olds who were attending very different types of schools. The study looks at how these different experiences affected the children's self-awareness, interpersonal skills, problem-solving patterns, group behavior, and other aspects of psychological functioning relating to human development. References.

The Religious Effects of Parochial Education. (1971). Andrew M. Greeley, Galen L. Gockel. In *Research on Religious Development, A Comprehensive Handbook.* NY: Hawthorn Books.

An analysis of three studies of parochial school education. Indications are that parochial school education is a secondary though positive factor in the educational process. References and an annotated bibliography conclude the chapter.

Research and Practice in the Primary Classroom. (1981). Edited by Brian Simon, John Willcocks. London and Boston: Routledge & Kegan Paul.

This volume covers major contemporary problems in the general area of the primary classroom in England. Chapters within the three parts address issues such as goals of primary education, implications of the ORACLE studies, influence of teachers on student social interactions, teachers' perceptions of students' abilities, teachers' perceptions of student anxiety, and assessment of teachers. Substantial references.

Research in the Language Arts: Language and Schooling. (1981). Edited by Victor Froese, Stanley B. Straw. Baltimore, MD: Univ. Park Press.

The book provides summaries of research and classroom practices in the major areas of language arts. The volume is organized generally into two parts. The first seven chapters on oralcy fall into the first part. Chapters 8 - 16 are in Part II and fall into the general category of literacy. Each chapter is followed by a bibliography of varying length.

Review of Research in Social Studies Education: 1976 - 1983. (1985). William B. Stanley et al. Boulder, CO and Washington, DC: ERIC Clearinghouse for Social Studies; National Council for the Social Studies; Social Science Education Consortium.

Reviews literature related to: critical thinking and cognitive processes; curriculum and instruction; ethnographic research; foundations of social education; and social education. Chapter 3 by Richard K. Jantz and Kenneth Klawitter reviews the literature of "early childhood/elementary social studies." A substantial number of references are provided at the end of each chapter.

Review of Research in the Social Studies Education, 1970 - 1975. (1977). Francis Hunkins, Lee H. Ehman, Carole L. Hahn, Peter H. Martarella, Jan L. Tucker. Washington DC: National Council for the Social Studies.

Reviews the literature related to cognitive learning and instruction, values education, teacher education, and diffusion of innovations in the social studies. Each of the chapters contains lengthy bibliographies. No index is provided.

Science Education. (1986). Edited by Eileen E. Schroeder, David A. Tyckoson. Phoenix, AZ: Oryx. (Oryx Science Bibliographies, Vol. 6).

Annotated bibliography of books and journal articles. Entries are organized under categories such as research reviews, elementary school science, teaching method, achievement test scores, major studies, and science education for special populations.

The Strangelove Legacy: Children, Parents and Teachers in the Nuclear Age. (1987). Phyllis La Farge. NY: Harper and Row.

A cogent discussion of various aspects of teaching children about their future during a century of a heightened arms race. The author delves into the child's feelings about the environment and other world issues.   The notes/bibliography at the end of the book is excellent and worth looking at whether the text is read or not.

The Study of Primary Education: A Source Book. 3 vols. (1984). Colin Richards. London: Falmer.

The three volumes provide users with extracts from "official" publications and from academic materials that put primary education in context and provide insight into important theoretical issues that British practitioners must consider. Most of the extracts would be impossible for U.S. researchers to obtain other than through these source books. Intended to be used by British students taking education courses and by teachers in service, the material will give the U.S. user insight into current primary education and about primary-aged children in Britain. Volume 1 comprises extracts that examine primary education from the historical, ideological, philosophical, sociological and psychological perspective. Volume 2 deals with curriculum studies. Volume 3 examines classroom and teaching studies, roles, and relationships. With each extract the source of the material is given in detail. Unfortunately the compilers, in the interest of space, deleted all cross-references in the original text. Through use of the author and subject index the user will easily access extracts of hard-to-locate materials on such topics as: Hadow Reports; Plowden Report; National Child Development Study; Education Acts; William Tyndal "affair"; Assessment of Performance Unit Act (APU); Black Papers; Bullock Report or Committee; Cockcroft Committee; Evaluation of Testing in Schools Project (ETSP); Ford T project; ORACLE project; Taylor Report; Central Advisory Council for Education (CACE); and Department of Education and Science (DES). References.

Teaching Science to Children: A Resource Book. (1986). Mary D. Iatridis, with a chapter by Phyllis Morrison. NY: Garland.

Part I lists books on how to teach science. Part II lists books on science activities. Part III lists and reviews science books for children. All entries are annotated.

Urban Education, a Guide to Information Sources. (1978). George E. Spear, Donald W. Mocker. Detroit, MI: Gale Research. (Urban Studies Information Guide Series, Vol. 3).

The editors of this work address the urban character of the United States in terms of the educational process. They have divided their work into three categories: adult education; urban higher education; and preschool, elementary, and secondary schools. The last of these deserves notice because of its content: It considers the future of education in the urban environment focusing on the preschool, elementary, and secondary areas of instruction. One beneficial aspect of the work is that many of the listings are available through ERIC.

Using Children's Books in Social Studies: Early Childhood through Primary Grades. (1984). Edited by J. E. Schreiber. Washington, DC: National Council for the Social Studies. (National Council for the Social Studies Bulletin No. 71).

This book, along with discussing the use of children's books to support and enhance the study of social studies, provides an annotated bibliography of books for each of the critical areas of early social studies education, world cultures, geography, and history. References.

Young Children and Science: The Oxford Primary Project. (1983). Stewart Redman and others. In *The Teaching of Primary Science: Policy and Practice.* Colin Richards, Derek Holford. NY: Falmer.

The research reported suggests that in teaching science to primary age children it is not enough for the teacher to decide what to teach. The teacher must be aware of the child's limitations in thinking and conceptualizing so that advantage may be taken when the child reaches the stage of readiness to learn a particular concept. Furthermore, it is suggested that the child's primary years should not be wasted. Science should be an integral part of the curriculum. References.

History

American Childhood: A Research Guide and Historical Handbook. (1985). Edited by Joseph M. Hawes, N. Ray Hiner. Westport, CT: Greenwood.

Reviews available literature, from the seventeenth century to present, of American childhood. Most of the book is organized in chronological order; however, some chapters treat specialized topics such as Native American children, ethnicity, or children's literature. An index to the volume is provided. References.

The Baby Boom: A Selective Annotated Bibliography. (1985). Greg Byerly, Richard E. Rubin. Lexington, MA: D. C. Heath. (Lexington Books Special Series in Libraries and Librarianship).

A selected, annotated bibliography on the American baby boom. Includes 702 references from business publications and scholarly journals in the social sciences. The eight chapters cover demographic, economic, marketing, managerial, sociological, and popular aspects of the topic. The index lists the periodicals cited separately from the author and subject index.

Centuries of Childhood: A Social History of Family Life. (1962). Philippe Aries. NY: Alfred A. Knopf.

Translated from the French by Robert Baldick, this illustrated classic is a historical account of childhood from the medieval period to 1960s. The chapters are broken into three parts: idea of childhood, scholastic life, and the family. A bibliography according to the subjects covered in the chapters is located at the end of the text. Index to the entire text concludes the book.

Child Development and Education in Japan. (1986). Edited by Harold Stevenson, Hiroshi Azuma, Kenji Hakuta. NY: W. H. Freeman.

The volume contrasts Japanese and American child socialization practices. The nineteen chapters are divided into three sections: background, empirical studies, and conceptual issues. A comprehensive review of the historical, social, cultural, and political developments regarding child rearing in Japan is given. The last section looks at cross-cultural research: linguistic comparisons, cultural influences on socioemotional development, and a comparison between American and Japanese children. References.

Childhood and Family in Canadian History. (1982). Edited by Joy Parr. Toronto: McClelland and Stewart.

"This book is about the families of seigneurs, fur traders, moccasin-makers, pioneer farmers, loggers, maritime shipbuilders, Montreal factory workers, seamstresses, and doctors, and about families recently arrived in Canada, those preparing to leave Canada, and those whose households were changed by the pressures of trying to stay in one place." References.

A Crosscultural Analysis of the Child Care System. (1977). Sarane Spence Boocock. In *Current Topics in Early Childhood*, Vol. 1, edited by Lilian Katz. Norwood, NJ: Ablex. (Current Topics in Early Childhood Education).

This chapter reviews and discusses the various historical views in America regarding the place of children in society and child care philosophies.

Education and Anthropology, an Annotated Bibliography. (1977). Annette Rosenstiel. NY: Garland.

This volume contains 3,435 entries linking the fields of education and anthropology. Coverage attempts to reflect historical influences, trends, theoretical concerns, and practical methodology. Coverage is from 1689 to 1976. Entries are listed alphabetically. The most useful method of locating materials is by consulting the topical index beginning on page 617. A regional index is also provided starting on page 631. The bibliography will be helpful to those studying multicultural topics, bilingualism, subculturals and children, and urbanization of children, among other topics.

Education Under Six. (1978). Denison Deasey. London: Croom Helm.

Reviews historical efforts at educating children under six. Part I introduces Oberlin, Froebel, Owen, and Madame de Pastoret. The second part reviews the development of preschool education in contemporary times and covers France, Britain, and the United States. Three chapters integrate historical and theoretical material giving an overview of the current issues. The last section is a short description of the author's visit to a British and a French nursery school.

Federal Involvement in Early Education (1933 - 1973): The Need for Historical Perspectives. (1977). Ruby Takanishi. In *Current Topics in Early Childhood Education*, Vol. 1, edited by Lilian Katz. Norwood, NJ: Ablex.

This chapter identifies the incidents of federal involvement in early education and discusses the recurring themes which emerge from a historical inquiry into the federal government's role. Fifty-eight references.

Forgotten Children: Parent-Child Relations from 1500 to 1900. (1984). Linda A. Pollock. NY: Cambridge Univ. Press.

Reviews past histories on children. The author then presents her own interpretation of childhood history from an analysis of British and American family diaries and autobiographies dating from 1500 to 1900. References.

Growing Up in America: Children in Historical Perspective. (1985). Edited by N. Ray Hiner, Joseph M. Hawes. Urbana and Chicago, IL: Univ. of Illinois Press.

An anthology of previously published articles giving insight into growing up in America. The book is divided into four parts: Colonial America; Nineteenth Century; Twentieth Century; and Indians and blacks.

History and Research in Child Development. (1985). Edited by Alice Boardman Smuts, John W. Hagen. In *Monographs of the Society for Research in Child Development No. 211*, Vol. 50, Nos. 4 - 5. Chicago, IL: Univ. of Chicago Press.

The eight chapters in the monograph are divided into three parts. Part I covers the history of the family and childhood. Chapters in Part II deal with historical approaches to child development. Part III is devoted to describing the history of the Society for Research in Child Development. References.

The Lost Children: A Study of Charity Children in Ireland, 1700 - 1900. (1980). Joseph Robins. Dublin: Institute of Public Administration.

Describes the plight of orphaned, illegitimate, and abandoned children in Ireland from 1700 - 1900. Individual chapters cover such institutions as foundling hospitals, charter schools, houses of industry and gaols, orphanages, and several chapters on workhouses. Chapter 6 discusses the efforts of various Bible societies. Chapter 7 describes the development of the Poor Law system in Ireland. A lengthy bibliography and index are included.

Past, Present, and Personal: The Family and Life Course in American History. (1986). John Demos. Oxford: Oxford Univ. Press.

Contains eight essays illustrating a new research area called family history. Chapter 2 presents a sketch of the American family. Chapter 3 traces fatherhood history. Chapter 4 is a social history of child abuse. Chapter 5 covers the adolescent. Chapters 6 and 7 looks at the history of mid-life and old age. Chapter 8 gives the history of the Carnegie Council on Children in retrospect by the council's resident historian.

The Rise and Fall of Childhood. (1982). C. John Sommerville. Beverly Hills, CA: Sage. (Sage Library of Social Research, Vol. 140).

Discusses ways children have been important to adults throughout history and the reasons for changes in their status down through time. The twenty chapters are chronological and cover all topics related to childhood. Bibliographical information of sources cited in the twenty chapters may be found in the chapter notes at the end of the text.

Saving the Waifs, Reformers, and Dependent Children, 1890 - 1971. (1984). LeRoy Ashby. Philadelphia, PA: Temple Univ. Press. (American Civilization).

The book examines the diversity and complexity of child rescue campaigns carried on in the late 1800s and early 1900s. Chapter 1 describes how Edward L. Bradley started with Allendale Farm in Illinois and enumerates various other homes founded through 1925 by various individuals. Chapter 2 concerns E. P. Savage and the Children's Home Society of Minnesota. Chapter 3 covers the orphanages of the National Benevolent Association. Chapter 4 discusses John Gunckel and the Toledo Newsboys' Association. Chapter 5 talks about the Ford Republic for delinquent and homeless boys. Chapter 6 covers the history of G.W. Hinckley and Good Will Farm. Bibliographic notes at the end of the text cite both primary and secondary sources of information.

Speaking Out for America's Children. (1977). Milton J. E. Senn. New Haven, CT: Yale Univ. Press.

A brief introduction to the literature and history of policy making in child welfare based on interviews with 90 leaders in the field. References.

200 Years of Children. (1976). Edited by Edith J. Grotberg. Washington, DC: Government Printing Office.

This book looks at the major events, the ideas, and the forces which prompted changes in life styles and changes in social institutions which in turn affected the child growing up. Chapters 1 and 2 present critical information on immigration and migration patterns of families over the past 200 years. Chapters 3, 4, and 5 address the three major administrative structures at the federal and state levels that are concerned with the well-being and learning of children. Chapters 6 and 7 focus on sources of pleasure for children. Chapters 8 and 9 are concerned with child development. Pages 480 - 486 contain the bibliography.

Law

Advances in Law and Child Development, a Research Annual. Vol. 1 - . (1982 -). Edited by Robert L. Sprague. Greenwich, CT: JAI.

The stated aim of this annual is to "focus specifically on the interaction of data from behavioral science and theories of child development with the making of social policy." The first of the series includes six chapters in four major areas including theory of moral and legal conscience development, mental health policy and administration, federal regulation of child development research, and state regulation of public schools. Three chapters deal with federal regulation of child development research.

Beyond the Best Interests of the Child. (1973). Joseph Goldstein, Anna Freud, Albert J. Solnit. NY: Free Press.

A critique of laws and policies of child placement in the United States. A collaborative work by a lawyer and two psychoanalysts, this examines child placement policy in the light of two premises: the importance to society that the child's needs, both physical and psychological, be paramount, and the right to privacy of the parent once the decision is made concerning who will be his parent. Guidelines are proposed determining placement and process of placement which safeguard the child's continuity of relationships. The book presents a model child placement statute which has as main feature: granting party status and court representation to the child, final and unconditional placement, and timely hearing and appeal. The text is supported by excerpts from actual court decisions, a fictional rewriting of one typical decision in accord with the proposed guidelines, and 48 pages of very pertinent notes.

Child Advocacy: Psychological Issues and Interventions. (1983). G. S. Melton. NY: Plenum.

This volume is a comprehensive review of child advocacy. In nine chapters, diverse topics ranging from the role of therapy as an intervention to tactics used in legislative lobbying are discussed. Chapter 1 examines children's rights as a foundation for child advocacy and focuses on such critical issues as the definition of children's rights and the social scientist's role in child advocacy. Chapter 2 summarizes Melton's dissertation and answers the question of what children think about their own rights. Chapters 3 and 4 offer case studies involving individual children. Each of the next four chapters of the book examine advocacy from a general perspective (The Nature of Advocacy); an administrative chapter including an emphasis on the nature and strategies to deal with bureaucracies (Administrative Advocacy: Changing Bureaucracies); the legislative component of advocacy represented best by the who and how of lobbying (Legislative Advocacy: Lobbying on Behalf of Children); and finally, the legal component, including children and the courts, and more (Legal Advocacy: Social Change and the Law).

Children, Families, and Government: Perspectives on American Social Policy. (1983). Edited by Edward Zigler, Sharon L. Kagan, Edgar Klugman. NY: Cambridge Univ. Press.

This volume is a comprehensive review of the relationship between social policy and social problems. The book is arranged in six parts. The introduction provides an overview of current policy practices. Part II focuses on the use of policy to foster understanding between various constituencies. Part III covers the policy-making process as well, but also focuses on state, local, and federal perspectives and concerns. Part IV reviews the factors that can influence the policy-making process such as the media and advocacy movements. Part V guides the reader through the transition from the identification of a social problem to the design and implementation of a policy. This is the most content focused part of the book, with chapters on drug use, child abuse, public law 84 - 142, Head Start, and other current topics. The book offers practical illustrations of certain child and family policies both from a policy as well as from a substantive perspective.

Children's Competence to Consent. (1983). Edited by Gary B. Melton, Gerald P. Koocher, Michael J. Saks. NY: Plenum. (Critical Issues in Social Justice).

This anthology focuses on a problem most researchers, clinicians, educators, and other human service professionals encounter daily but confront rarely: children's competence to consent in decisions affecting their own welfare. The chapters in this book explore legal, psychological, sociological, and ethical perspectives concerning children's competence to consent. The first section confronts generally psychological issues that are related to increasing children's self-determination. Melton reviews the conditions under which some children become better decision makers than others; Saks presents a social-psychological perspective demonstrating how education in self-determination can be considered advocacy by some but manipulation by others. The second section of the volume presents specific legal, medical, and psychological perspectives on consent. Lewis reports data from several training studies designed to teach children decision-making; Grodin and Alpert recommend the primary care setting as the best model for medical consent. Koocher discusses the problem of the "doubly incompetent": those who legally are minors and who psychologically or intellectually have diminished abilities. The third section explores consent in delinquency proceedings. Finally, Tapp and Melton discuss the implications of legal socialization research, and Weithorn presents guidelines for professionals concerned with increasing children's self-determination. All of the chapters are clearly written and suggest a range of research possibilities.

Children's Rights: A Philosophical Study. (1981). C. A. Wringe. London: Routledge & Kegan Paul. (International Library of the Philosophy of Education).

This study looked at the broad questions regarding the "rights" of children which have become popular during the "children's rights movement." Those looked at include: legal rights, rights of freedom, rights of participation, special rights, welfare rights, and the right to an education. References.

Legal Directory of Children's Rights. Vol. 1 (Federal Statutes). (1985). Thomas A. Jacobs. Frederick, MD: University Publications of America.

A complete collection of federal laws regarding children. The collection was taken from the *U.S. Code* and *U.S. Code Annotated*. Included are adult and parental responsibilities to children. This is the first of an intended four-volume set.

Making Policies for Children: A Study of the Federal Process. (1982). Edited by Cheryl D. Hayes. Washington, DC: National Academy.

This report is the product of a thirty-month study sponsored by the Administration for children, youth, and families of the U.S. Department of Health and Human Services. Three objectives were set for the study: (1) to understand the process by which federal policy is formulated; (2) to identify factors likely to influence child and family policy; and (3) to offer suggestions to those concerned with influencing child and family policy. To achieve these objectives, the authors identify and define six components of the federal policy formation process, offer a three-tiered framework of federal decision making, provide an overview of prospects for future policy formation affecting children and families, and present three case studies. Though bearing only a thin relationship with the concepts developed in the first part of the book, the case studies are lively, interesting, and well documented and demonstrate, among other things, the fortuitous and haphazard nature of policy making for children and families. References.

Models for Analysis of Social Policy: An Introduction. (1981). Edited by Ron Haskins, James Gallagher. Norwood, NJ: Ablex. (Advances in Child and Family Policy).

This volume explores the various methods by which social policy analysis has been pursued. In Chapter 1 background information on the growth of policy analysis as a discipline is provided. Chapters 2, 3, and 4 present three distinct approaches or models to social policy analysis (James Gallagher, Robert Maroney, and Duncan MacRae). The chapter by Turnbull, an attorney, focuses on law and the U.S. Constitution as they effect social policy. The chapters in the volume will give a good overview to the topic. The extensive references provide convenient access to the standard literature on the public policy process and its narrow component policy analysis.

The Rights of Children. (1986). Edited by Bob Franklin. Oxford: Basil Blackwell.

This book covers a wide range of issues regarding the legal rights of children. Previous research studies are reviewed in full. Topics covered include: political rights, rights at school, rights while being cared for, rights at work, sexual rights, girls' rights, black children's rights, and children's rights according to the Scottish perspective. References.

The Role of the Juvenile Court. (1987). Edited by Francis X. Hartmann. NY: Springer-Verlag. (From Children to Citizens, Vol. 2).

In 21 chapters this book looks at all aspects of the juvenile justice system in the United States. Family matters, child abuse, violent offenders, courts, detention, and jurisdiction are just a few of the topics covered. Some references.

A Source Book of Royal Commissions and Other Major Governmental Inquiries in Canadian Education, 1787 - 1978. (1981). Carey F. Goulson. Toronto: Univ. of Toronto Press.

This volume presents 367 inquiries by royal commissions into Canadian education up to about 1979. These are presented chronologically by province beginning with the Eastern Seaboard. Each entry gives the type of commission or committee for the inquiry, dates of appointment, size of the commission, name of chairperson, purpose, and primary reference sources. In addition major conclusions or recommendations are given. In the appendix may be found very early provincial public inquiries, acts, and a chronological tabulation of forty-seven Royal Commissions in Canadian Education. The lack of an index makes this reference extremely difficult to use.

SECTION II

SPECIAL SUBJECT AREA BIBLIOGRAPHIES

4

Families

DATABASES
TO CONSIDER

Child Abuse and Neglect
Family Resources
Sociological Abstracts

ERIC
PsycINFO

GENERAL

Bibliographies

American Family History: A Historical Bibliography. (1984). Santa Barbara, CA:
ABC-Clio Information Services. (ABC Clio Research Guides, 12).

Contains 1,167 abstracts and citations of journal articles covering over 2,000
countries. Coverage is from 1973-1982. Citations are arranged
alphabetically by author in four chapters. The Family in Historical
Perspective focuses on the colonial period through the last decade. The
Family and Other Social Institutions focuses on the interaction between
socioeconomic forces and the family. The Familial Roles and Relationships
focuses on internal family dynamics. The Chapter entitled Individual Family
Histories focuses on individual genealogical studies. Entries were drawn
from the history database of the ABC-Clio Information Services.

**The Family Law Decision-Making Process: An Annotated Law, Psychiatry, and
Policy Science Bibliography.** (1979). John William James Batt. Buffalo,
NY: William S. Hein.

Entries are annotated and divided among seven broad categories: marriage
and the legally constituted family; reproduction, contraception, and family
planning; divorce and dissolution; child custody conflicts; adoption; paternity;
and illegitimacy.

Family Life and Child Development: A Selective, Annotated Bibliography. Cumulative through June 1979. (1979). Jewish Board of Family and Children's Services. NY: Jewish Board of Family and Children's Services.

This annotated bibliography lists 362 books and pamphlets published since 1969 through June 1979. The bibliography is intended for parents; however, professionals planning parenting programs or undergraduate students seeking materials on child development topics may find this bibliography helpful.

Family Life and Child Development: A Selective Annotated Bibliography through 1975. (1976). Child Study Association of America. NY: Child Study.

An annotated list of 320 books and pamphlets published through 1975 of interest to parents and those working with parents and children in the area of child development and family life. Entries are arranged alphabetically by title under seven broad topics, and then subdivided under each. An author and title index is provided.

History of the Family and Kinship: A Select International Bibliography. (1980). Edited by Gerald L. Soliday. Millwood, NY: Kraus International.

This volume provides users with a select group of important scholarly materials on the history of kinship and the family. Coverage is worldwide. Organization is by geographical areas and individual countries and then subdivided into time periods.

Inventory of Marriage and Family Literature. Vol. 1 - . (1973 -). Beverly Hills, CA: Sage.

This index provides an annual listing of all pertinent articles published in professional literature on marriage and the family. Each annual volume contains three indexes: author, subject, and key word in title. Interesting subject categories on child development include: single-parent families; step families; mother-child relationship; father-child relationship; sibling relationship; birth order differences; custody and child support; child abuse; runaways; children and divorce; achievement and the family; and parent education.

The Literature on Military Families. (1980). Edna J. Hunter, Donald de Dulk, John W. Williams. Washington, DC: Government Printing Office.

Research compiled contains over 400 references covering adjustment to separation, family reunion and reintegration, adjustment to loss, families in transition, and services to families under stress, single-parent families, dual career families, and changing roles of men and women. Entries are alphabetical by author's last name. Previous edition was entitled *Families in the Military System*. (Beverly Hills, CA: Sage, 1976).

Men's Studies: A Selected and Annotated Interdisciplinary Bibliography. (1985). Eugene R. August. Littleton, CO: Libraries Unlimited.

Contains both scholarly and popular works. Examples of entries are: single parenting, househusbands, fathers and children, divorce and custody, men in families, and growing up to be a man. Cross-references are given between sections. Subject index provided.

Reviews of Literature

The Child and Its Family: Genesis of Behavior. (1979). Edited by Michael Lewis, Leonard Rosenblum. NY: Plenum.

Synthesizes current research on factors which influence social development. Thirteen papers focus on the social world into which the child is born. Brazelton offers a description of reciprocity and effect in the mother-father-infant triad, followed by a strongly theoretical paper on paternal influences in the infancy period. Falbo provides a critical review of research on only children. Greenbaum and Landau examine the importance of older siblings as a source of verbal stimulation. Dunn and Kendrick emphasize the importance of observing young siblings at home to obtain a true picture of interaction patterns. Mueller focuses on the development of toddler-peer relations in a play group. The last paper provides a framework for describing how the infant's social relationships may be affected by maternal employment. References.

The Child in His Family. Vol. 1. (1970). Edited by E. James Anthony and Cyrille Koupernick. NY: Wiley-Interscience. (The International Yearbook for Child Psychiatry and Allied Disciplines, Vol. 1).

The 22 papers in the volume are categorized into four main sections: family dynamics, family crisis, chronic family pathology, and family variation and mental health. Subjects covered by individual chapters include: atypical behavior, bonding, temperament, sex differences, stress, eating disorders, black African family, and child rearing in various foreign countries. Each section is preceded by an editorial comment and most papers include an extensive bibliography.

The Child in His Family: Preventive Child Psychiatry in an Age of Transitions. Vol. 6. (1980). Edited by E. James Anthony, Colette Chiland. NY: John Wiley & Sons. (Child in His Family).

The general theme of this volume deals with the pains of transition from one developmental stage to another, from one mode of living to another, from one country to another, and from one culture to another. In the first section of the volume, a number of papers discuss parental bonding or attachment from the perspective of the mother and the father. The second section includes five papers addressing early detachment behavior of the child, interplay of twins, and development of moral judgment in Indian children. The third section includes nine papers on child-rearing practices in various cultures. The section entitled Discomforts and Disorders Symptomatic of Our Times of Transition contains eight papers dealing with the child's response to adverse circumstances such as paranoia, environmental uprooting, and child abuse. In the section entitled Prevention, Intervention and Improved Service Delivery, twelve papers cover various aspects of preventive mental health measures. The last section contains five reports from international study groups of problems of change and transition in the field of child psychiatry. Not all papers provide bibliographies.

Child Care in the Family: A Review of Research and Some Propositions for Policy. (1977). Alison Clarke-Stewart. NY: Academic.

The volume examines research on how children's psychological development is influenced by characteristics and behavior of family members. It focuses on "normal" children in "typical" families and does not include data from clinical, biographical, and cross-cultural sources. Analysis is psychological and behavioral and not sociological and economic. Research on children's development of physical-motor skills, intellectual and language development, and social relations, as they relate to family size, structure, and socioeconomic status and to behavior and attitudes of parents toward children is examined. A brief outline of the history of research on early child care is provided in the introduction. References.

Children and Families in Australia: Contemporary Issues and Problems. (1979). Ailsa Burns, Jacqueline Goodnow. Sydney: George Allen & Unwin. (Studies in Society: Sidney: 5, edited by Colin Bell).

Discusses the different ideologies regarded as crucial determinants of social issues that concern people and communities along with proposed solutions. Special issues included are: television; disadvantaged; violence against children; and children and the law. A sizable bibliography concludes the volume.

Children of Handicapped Parents: Research and Clinical Perspectives. (1985). Edited by S. Kenneth Thurman. NY: Academic.

This volume reviews research and clinical problems relating to families with handicapped parents. At the same time it discusses research models and strategies that can be applied to this population. Each chapter approaches the topic from a different perspective. Chapter 2 looks at the legal and public policy issues. Chapter 3 discusses how families with handicapped parents might be studied using an ecological model. Chapter 4 reviews research on the effects of parental emotional handicap on early development. Chapter 5 outlines qualitative research approaches useful in the study of mentally retarded parents. Chapter 6 looks at the family environment of children with diabetic parents. Chapter 7 looks at deaf families. Chapters 8 and 9 discuss physical disability and how it can affect parenting and family functioning. Chapter 10 discusses and analyzes methodological issues regarding the study of children of disabled parents. The last chapter is a synthesis of the research regarding the handicapped parent in the community. References.

Children of Working Parents: Experiences and Outcomes. (1983).   Cheryl D. Hayes, Sheila B. Kamerman. Washington, DC: National Academy.

This volume is a review of the research on the effects of changing parental employment patterns, particularly the increase in maternal employment, on children's growth and development. It is the second report of the Panel on Work, Family, and Community. One section covers the research on the effects of parental employment on peer relationships, television viewing, and the family school relationship. The material in the second section concerns a survey conducted by the panel of existing data set with variables pertaining to the relationship between work and family life. References.

Families As Learning Environments for Children. (1982). Luis M. Laosa, Irving E. Sigel. NY: Plenum.

This book is a collection of 11 readings presenting data generated by current research projects.   Individual chapters review such topics as: teaching strategies of parents; literacy in the family context; family social systems; play; working mothers; differences of interactions between infant and parents; family day care; and child behavior theories held by parents and siblings. References.

Family Development and the Child. (April 1985). Edited by Kenneth Kaye, Frank F. Furstenberg, Jr. In *Child Development*, Special Issue 56 (2).

The fifteen manuscripts included in this issue are mainly research. Of particular interest is the article by Rob Palkovitz, "Fathers' Birth Attendance,

Early contact, and Extended Contact with Their Newborns: A Critical Review." References.

Family Policy: Government and Families in Fourteen Countries. (1978). Sheila B. Kamerman, Alfred J. Kahn. NY: Columbia Univ. Press.

A landmark publication providing the first systematic, comparative survey of family policy among Western, industrialized nations. The collection of papers offers an assessment of family policy, reflecting the perspectives of economics, sociology, psychology, medicine, social work, political science, and public administration. References.

Home Environment and Intellectual Performance. (1981). Ronald W. Henderson. In *Parent-Child Interaction, Research Theory, and Prospects*, edited by Ronald W. Henderson. NY: Academic. (Educational Psychology).

The chapter synthesized the research investigating the relationship between family background and the intellectual, occupational, and economic attainments of individuals as adults. Family constellation variables addressed include: birth order, family size, sibling sex and spacing, and confluence theory. Separate sections review the research of socioeconomic status and home environmental variables such as family culture. References.

In Support of Families. (1986). Michael W. Yogman, T. Berry Brazelton. Cambridge, MA: Harvard Univ. Press.

The book reviews research in the area of a mother-father-infant triad and the mutual influences of three subsystems: mother-father, mother-infant, father-infant and stress. The authors look at the benefits to child development and family equilibrium, disruption of the system and its effect on the child, and restoration of equilibrium in nontraditional familial systems. Section 3 covers four areas of current family patterns, work, and family life. Chapter 9 discusses child care outside the home. Included in the book is a chapter on the effects of a child's chronic illness on the family. References.

Mothering and Teaching--Some Significant Distinctions. (1980). Lilian G. Katz. In *Current Topics in Early Childhood and Education,* Vol. 3, edited by Lilian G. Katz. Norwood, NJ: Ablex.

This chapter looks at the differences between mothering and teaching and draws distinctions between the two so that each role is properly understood. Twenty-one references.

Newborns and Parents: Parent-Infant Contact and Newborn Sensory Stimulation. (1981). Edited by Vincent L. Smerglio. Hillsdale, NJ: Lawrence Erlbaum.

This book discusses two categories of environmental experiences: newborn sensory stimulation by equipment or hospital personnel, and parent-infant contact. Studies in the second category focus on mothers and newborns relating primarily to mother-infant bonding and mother-infant separation. Effects studied include maternal behavior, maternal attitudes, and indices of infant and child development. References.

Non-Traditional Families: Parenting and Child Development. (1982). Edited by Michael E. Lamb. Hillsdale, NJ: Lawrence Erlbaum.

This volume reviews the effects of creative family styles on parenting and child development. The eleven chapters cover topics such as: two-paycheck families; fathers share child-rearing responsibilities; single parent families headed by both men and women; alternative family styles in which mothers avoid legal marriage; and extrafamilial child care. Three of the chapters provide reviews and the rest present unpublished results from various studies conducted in the United States, Sweden, Israel, and Australia. The Family Styles Project results are reported and discussed in the chapter by Eiduson, Kornfein, Simmerman, and Weisner. References.

Parent-Child Interaction: Theory, Research, and Prospects. (1981). Edited by Ronald W. Henderson. NY: Academic. (Educational Psychology).

Chapter 1 discusses research related to family influences on intellectual development. Chapter 2 examines the impact of divorce on family functioning and the effect on children. Chapter 3 looks at literature on cognitive development and learning theory. Chapter 4 examines the theoretical bases of moral development and provides a synthesis of research. Chapter 5 synthesizes the literature on mother-child interaction. Chapter 6 looks at the family and child abuse. The two chapters in Part II examine the methods employed in research and measurement in family research. Part III of the book contains two chapters which provide perspective on the application of psychological knowledge to the socialization process. References.

Parenting in Dual-Career Families. (1985). Lucia Albino Gilbert with Sue Wich Lucas. In *Man in Dual-Career Families: Current Realities and Future Prospects*, by Lucia Albino Gilbert. Hillsdale, NJ: Lawrence Erlbaum. (Vocational Psychology).

This chapter has a very brief section on "How adjusted are the children?" A number of studies are cited suggesting that children in families where the mother works are more independent, more resourceful, and more able to draw on a wide repertoire of role models than children raised in a traditional home where the mother is a housewife only. References.

Philosophy, Children, and Family. (1982). Edited by Albert C. Cafagna, Richard T. Peterson, Craig A. Staudenbaur. NY: Plenum. (Child Nurturance, Vol. 1).

Contains essays or reviews organized into five sections: (1) Conceptualizing the family, (2) Women and family life, (3) Children's rights, (4) Moral education, and (5) Medical decisions affecting children. References.

Review of Child Development Research: The Family. Vol. 7. (1984). Edited by Ross D. Parke. Chicago, IL: Univ. of Chicago Press.

The volume gives an overview of theory and research pertinent to the topic. Approaches to family study are provided by biologists, comparative psychologists, developmental psychologists, and sociologists. One chapter covers the social history of the family. Three chapters consider various contexts within which families are influenced by family dynamics, the school, the workplace, and the community. The final three chapters focus on families within minority subcultures, on issues concerning expectant and new parenthood, and on divorce and dissolution. References.

Social Systems and Family Patterns: A Propositional Inventory. (1971). William J. Goode, Elizabeth Hopkins, Helen M. McClure. NY: Bobbs-Merrill.

This compilation contains most of the major correlations among factors internal to the family as well as most of the major propositions relating family variables to other institutions. This inventory has four main areas of usefulness within social science research: (1) social engineering, such as family counseling and community planning, (2) family research, (3) sociology theory, and (4) social science, the strategy of development. If the research report asserted that there is a correlation or association between a family variable and another variable, whether or not related to the family, it is recorded twice, once under each variable. The book is in alphabetical order by the subject of the variable with numbers corresponding to the bibliographic entry of the item given at the end of each brief abstract of the variable. Subcategories abound. For example, under the topic of conformity, the subcategories are: age of child, child-rearing attitudes, child-rearing practices, and father-daughter relations. Although dated, this is a very remarkable index to studies carried out prior to 1970. References.

They Love Me, They Love Me Not: A Worldwide Study of the Effects of Parental Acceptance and Rejection. (1975). Ronald P. Rohner. New Haven, CT: Human Relations Area File Press.

This volume reports the findings of a study of the effects of acceptance and rejection by caretakers on children. Research evidence from a variety of sources is reviewed, for example, maternal deprivation, child abuse, and adult personality problems resulting from rejection. This introduces the author's cross-cultural survey of 101 societies. Each culture was rated as either an accepting or rejecting society. Personality dispositions of children and adults in each of these cultures were assessed, as were aspects of societal maintenance systems, worship, games, and art form. Rejecting societies tended to produce higher levels of less-than-optimal functioning in children. Adults in the rejecting societies exhibited conflicts over nurturance. Substantial bibliography.

Toward a Theory of Family Influence in the Socialization of Children. (1983). Sheldon Stryker, Richard T. Serpe. In *Research in Sociology of Education and Socialization: A Research Annual,* Vol. 4. Greenwich, CT: JAI.

The chapter reviews the various theories set forth regarding how families exercise influence on their children in the socialization process. References include works from 1902 to 1981.

Young Children and Their Families: Needs and the Nineties. (1982). Shirley Hill, B. J. Varnes. Lexington, MA: D. C. Heath.

Chapter 1 raises issues and concerns about current national political climate threatening the well-being of young children and their families. Chapters 2 - 5 cover topics related to families: parent education, child abuse, minority children, and adaptations of mothers and toddlers to multiple social roles. Chapters 6 - 11 address specific needs: language development, quality child care, public policy and special education, sex-role development, representational play, and transformational knowledge. Each chapter concludes with a substantial bibliography. The volume is indexed.

Reports of Research

Anxiety and Ego Formation in Infancy. (1971). Sylvia Brody, Sidney Axelrad. NY: International Universities Press.

The first volume of two reporting the findings of a longitudinal investigation of the relationship between forms of parental care during the child's first year and the subsequent psychological development of the child through age seven. This first volume describes the construction of the typology of maternal behavior with infants, and presents findings about infant development according to the types of mothering the infants received. The methodology, the significance of the maternal classification, and certain issues regarding mother-infant interaction are discussed. Sensing that the quality of mothering did result in smoother and better development during the first year of the infants' lives, the researchers continued their study, called the Infant Development Research Project. The continuation of the study is reported in another book entitled *Mothers, Fathers and Children* (1978).

Experience and Environment: Major Influences on the Development of the Young Child. Vol. 1. (1973). Burton L. White, J. C. Watts. Englewood Cliffs, NJ: Prentice-Hall.

The first report on the research of the Harvard Preschool Project. Describes the origins, methods, and preliminary results of the study. Contains only the "first" generation hypotheses about effects of child rearing practices. Vol. 2, *Experience and Environment*, contains considerably more data on the development of the 39 children involved in the longitudinal study. References.

Experience and Environment: Major Influences on the Development of the Young Child. Vol. 2. (1978). Burton L. White. Englewood Cliffs, NJ: Prentice-Hall.

This book is the second report on the research of the Harvard Preschool Project. The text relates a longitudinal study of 39 children from birth to six years of age, concerning eight dimensions of social competence: gaining adult attention; using adults as a resource; expressing affection and hostility to adults; engaging in role play; expressing pride in achievement; showing competition with peers; expressing affection and hostility to peers; and leading and following peers. One interesting finding was that blue-collar families are just as capable of educating young children as are families from higher classes of American society. Findings suggest that effective parents perform three major functions better than less competent parents: designing the child's world, consulting for the child, and controlling the child. This book contains individual subject data and a full manual of measurement techniques and reliability studies. References.

Identification and Child Rearing. (1965). Robert Sears, Lucy Rau, Richard Alpert. Stanford, CA: Stanford Univ. Press. (Stanford Studies in Psychology).

This volume reports a study of the interrelationships and child-rearing antecedents of several types of child behavior in four-year-olds, including dependency, aggression, adult role, gender role, guilt, and resistance to temptation. The research was conducted at the Stanford Village Nursery School using forty children and their parents as subjects during the summer session of 1958. References.

Mother, Grandmothers, and Daughters: Personality and Childcare in Three-Generation Families. (1981). Bertram J. Cohler and Henry U. Grunebaum with assistance of Donna and Moran Robbins. NY: John Wiley & Sons. (Wiley Series on Personality Processes).

Using four families, the authors studied intergenerational relations seeking empirical data regarding human behavior patterns within families. Chapter 1 places the study in the context of other work. Chapter 2 reviews empirical findings of past studies. Chapters 3 through 6 describe the individual families studied and characterize the personalities of the mothers and grandmothers involved, especially attitudes toward child care. Chapter 7 provides a framework for cross case comparisons of the families. Chapter 8 looks at the four families in terms of common ethnic heritage. Chapter 9 summarizes the findings from the study. Chapter 10 is a follow-up four years later. The appendixes provide the questionnaires, interview questions, and pictures used by the researchers in the study. References.

Mothers and Fathers. (1982). Kathryn C. Backett. NY: St. Martin's.

A study carried on in England from mid-1971 to mid-1973 which studied 22 middle class couples, each with two children, one approximately three years old and the other either older or younger. Backett sought to further the sociological knowledge of family life. Some of the conclusions drawn from the study add a great deal to what is known about fatherhood. References.

Mothers, Fathers, and Children: Explorations in the Formation of Character in the First Seven Years. (1978). Sylvia Brody, Sidney Axelrad. NY: International Univ. Press.

The second volume of two, this work reports the findings of a longitudinal investigation of the relationship between forms of parental care and the psychological development of the child. Their previous book, *Anxiety and Ego Formation in Infancy*, reported findings on assessing varying influences of maternal behavior on the infant's behavior and development. This second phase of the study, known as the Child Development Research Project, began when the first infants studied reached the age of four and the last infants studied reached the age of two. Using observational techniques, the authors looked for systematic evidence for connections between the behavior and attitudes of parents, both mothers and fathers, and the character formation of their young children up to the age of seven. References.

Handbooks

The Troubled Family: Source of Information. (1982). Theodore Peck. Jefferson, NC: McFarland.

A guide to sources of information on problems faced by families today. Information in the volume is arranged in three basic categories: organizations, individual authorities in the fields covered, and current literature. These categories are in turn divided into separate parts: federal, state government, private national and community organizations; other research oriented organizations; and a selected, annotated, current bibliography of journal articles, books, documents, reports, and special studies. Topics covered include child abuse, counseling, divorce, mental health, runaways, single-parent families, and family violence.

ADOPTION

Bibliographies

Adoption: An Annotated Bibliography and Guide. (1987). R. L. Melina. NY: Garland.

This bibliography brings together from such fields as medicine, psychiatry, psychology, sociology, social work, child development, and law selected references from books, journals, audiovisual materials, and unpublished documents.

Special Adoptions: An Annotated Bibliography on Transracial, Transcultural, and Nonconventional Adoption and Minority Children. (1981). S. Peter Kim and the American Academy of Child Psychiatry. Rockville, MD: National Institute of Mental Health.

The book is in two parts: transracial, transcultural, and nonconventional adoption and related issues; and minority children. An author and subject index concludes the volume.

Reviews of Literature

The Adopted Child's IQ: A Critical Review. (1975). Harry Munsinger. In *Psychological Bulletin*, 825, 623-659.

A synthesis of research on adopted children's IQs and the relative importance of heredity and environment on children's mental development. References.

Large Sibling Groups. (1986). Dorothy W. La Pere, Lloyd E. Davis, James Conve, Mona McDonald. Washington, DC: Child Welfare League of America.

Reviews the literature on sibling adoptive placement. Contains an example of the questionnaire used in the study, discussion of the problems of large sibling placement, and some conclusions. In the several appendixes may be found lists of family strengths, family motivations, and post-placement services. References.

Transracial Adoption. (1977). Rita James Simon, Howard Altstein. NY: John Wiley & Sons.

Section 1 describes the history, prevalence, and types of transracial adoption in the United States. Section 2 contains three chapters which review prior studies dealing with transracial adoptions, including one study on the child's racial awareness and identity. Section 3 discusses subsidized and single parent adoptions. Chapter notes are provided along with a comprehensive index.

Reports of Research

Adoption: A Second Chance. (1977). Barbara Tizard. NY: Open Books.

This volume reports a study made of a group of children adopted from institutions after the age of two. Adoption social policy is discussed. Chapter 1 provides a concise history of adoption itself. Within the eighteen chapters of the book, subjects covered include: effects of institutions on children; early adopted children; attachment and adopted children; mixed-race adoptions; and fostering versus adopting. References.

Adoptions without Agencies: A Study of Independent Adoptions. (1978). William Meezan, Sanford Katz, Eva Manoff Russo, NY: Child Welfare League of America.

"A comprehensive national research study of the actual conditions under which independent, nonagency adoptions are carried out." Included is a review and analysis of state law related to independent adoptions. Not all chapters provide references.

Black Children-White Parents: A Study of Transracial Adoption. (1974). Lucille J. Grow, Deborah Shapiro. Washington, DC: Child Welfare League of America.

This monograph relates a study of transracial adoption. The authors sampled 125 black or part-black children of at least six years of age who had lived with their white adoptive parents at least three years. Grow and Shapiro looked at the children's adjustment at home, in school, and in the community as well as the children's awareness of their racial heritage. Footnoted.

Growing Up Adopted: A Long-Term National Study of Adopted Children and Their Families. (1972). Jean Mia Seglow, Kellmer Pringle, Peter Wedge. Windsor, Berks: National Foundation for Educational Research in England and Wales.

This is a sequel and companion to *Born Illegitimate*. The volume reports a study of how adopted British children adapted to adoption. There is a discussion of data gathered regarding adoption as seen by the adoptive parents. Contains a valuable summary of research findings from Britain, Europe and North America. References.

Mixed Families: Adopting across Racial Boundaries. (1977). Joyce A. Ladner. NY: Anchor/Doubleday.

Addresses various aspects of adoption across racial and ethnic lines. The author interviewed 136 white families geographically dispersed who adopted predominantly black, but also native American and Asian children. The volume provides insight into the American parent's attitude toward natural and adopted children. References.

Mother-Infant Attachment in Adoptive Families. (1985). Leslie M. Singer, David M. Brodzinsky, and Douglas Ramsay. In *Child Development*, 56 (6), 1543 - 1551.

This study compared the attachment relationship in adoptive and nonadoptive mother-infant pairs. Results indicated no difference between nonadopted nor intraracial adoptions. Fifty-three references.

Origins of Individual Differences in Infancy. (1985). Robert Plomin, John C. DeFries. Orlando, FL: Academic. (Developmental Psychology Series).

Summarizes the first comprehensive report of the Colorado Adoption Project (CAP), a longitudinal adoption study initiated in 1975 and conceived from a sophisticated behavioral genetic framework concerned with individual differences in infancy. This report is based on comprehensive data from 182 adopted and 165 matched nonadopted infants one to two years of age and their urban, middle-class biological and adoptive parents. CAP studied individual differences in the domains of physical and motor development, cognitive abilities, language, personality-temperament, and behavior problems. References.

A Study of Black Adoption Families: A Comparison of a Traditional and a Quasi-Adoption Program. (1971). Elizabeth A. Lawder, Janet L. Hoopes, Roberta G. Andrews, Katherine D. Lower, Susan Y. Perry. NY: Child Welfare League of America.

A study of a small group of black families, half of whom adopted through traditional means and half through an innovative and subsidized program. Parents in the latter group would have been classified as "undesirable" under traditional guide lines. There was no statistically significant difference found between the two groups. References.

Transracial Adoption Today: Views of Adoptive Parents and Social Workers. (1975). Lucille J. Grow, Deborah Shapiro. NY: Child Welfare League of America.

This volume reports a study made of white families with whom black children were placed for adoption in 1972 - 1973. In general the study indicated that transracial adoption is an acceptable practice and a better alternative to long term foster care. This monograph will be particularly useful to personnel in adoption agencies and public officials who demand empirical data before implementing changes in their adoption practices, pre- and post-placement. References.

Guides and Directory

Child Welfare League of America Standards for Adoption Service. (1978). Child Welfare League of America. NY: Child Welfare League of America.

This volume provides the standards for adoption service established by the League after surveying the professional literature, looking at standards set by other groups or state social service agencies, and studying scientific findings in the field of social work.

Intercountry Adoption Guidelines. (1980). Department of Health, Education and Welfare, Office of Human Services, et al., Washington, DC: Government Printing Office.

This guide, prepared by the American Public Welfare Association, provides information on the scope of intercountry adoptions as well as materials to assess the quality of services provided to families adopting internationally. The guide also outlines guidelines which specifically relate to the provision of services by public authorities and the private sector, and to the administrative mechanisms that facilitate the processing of intercountry adoptions.

National Directory of Intercountry Adoption Services Resources. (1980). U.S. Department of Health, Education and Welfare, Office of Human Development Services. Washington, DC: Government Printing Office.

The directory is organized into state sections with listings of agencies and organizations, contact personnel, and descriptive service resource information within each state. Subsections under each state include: public welfare agencies, United States-based international child placing agencies, domestic child placing agencies, and adoptive parent groups involved with intercountry adoptions. United States-based international child-placing agencies and specialized service resources are indicated in their individual listings as well as in the alphabetical index at the end of the directory.

CHILD ABUSE

Bibliographies

Child Abuse: An Annotated Bibliography. (1980). Compiled by Dorothy P. Wells. Metuchen, NJ: Scarecrow.

Included are nonbook materials, reference materials, books, chapters, journal articles, pamphlets, dissertations, and government documents. Foreign language materials are also included. The majority of the entries date from 1962 to December 1976. Entries are organized by subject: etiology, case studies, laws, medical aspects, etc. An author index is included.

Child Abuse and Neglect: An Annotated Bibliography. (1978). Beatrice J. Kalisch. Westport, CT: Greenwood. (Contemporary Problems of Childhood).

Covers the literature from the late 1800s to 1977 with the majority of the citations from the 1960s and 1970s. Literature covers the areas of sociology, psychology, nursing, social work, medicine, education, law, and child development. Entries are arranged under broad subject areas: causative factors, manifestations, treatment, sexual abuse, and legal issues. The first introductory section gives a historical overview, definitions, and demographic characteristics.

Child Abuse and Neglect Publication. (1986). National Advisory Board on Child Abuse and Neglect. Washington, DC: Clearinghouse on Child Abuse and Neglect.

The 38-page annotated bibliography lists 100 books and pamphlets. Citations are divided into seven categories: general child abuse and neglect; sexual abuse; parenting; books for adolescents; books for children;

community resources and kits; and legal issues/court appearances. About 70 percent of the titles cited are less than fifty pages in length.

Child Molestation, an Annotated Bibliography. (1987). Mary de Young. Jefferson, NC: McFarland.

Contains references from the social sciences, medical, and legal literature focusing on the clinical aspects of the topic. Chapter 2 provides references to statistical studies. Chapter 3 delves into the historical considerations. Chapter 6 covers entries dealing with the effects of molestation. Chapter 8 covers treatment. Chapter 9 looks at the legal issues. Chapter 10 is on child pornography and sex rings. Chapter 13 lists literature reviews. This bibliography is intended for lawyers, policy makers, researchers, and health care professionals.

How and Where to Research and Find Information about Child Abuse. (1983). Robert D. Reed. Saratoga, CA: R & E.

Guide to the location of information. After an introduction, the volume is divided into general sources, agencies, directories, publications, bibliographies, and glossary of terms. Entries are not annotated.

Incest Annotated Bibliography: Offenders, Victims, Families, Treatment Programs (Strategies). (1983). Melodye L. F. Dabney. Eugene, OR: Melodye L. F. Dabney.

Volume is divided into four sections: victims, family, offender treatment programs, and psychological counseling. Each of the sections contains references from journals, magazines, research projects, dissertations, government documents, other documents, and books. Coverage is from 1972 to 1982. The author used BRS and Dialog for compiling the references.

Incest: The Last Taboo: An Annotated Bibliography. (1983). Rick Rubin, Greg Byerly. NY: Garland.

Includes topics encompassing psychological, sociological, anthropological, medical, scientific, legal, popular, and literary perspectives. Limited to American society. Entries located through Psychological Abstracts, Sociological Abstracts, Index Medicus, BIP, NUC, and Comprehensive Dissertation Index. Subject index included.

Reviews of Literature

Child Abuse: A Community Concern. (1984). Edited by Kim Oates. NY: Brunner/Mazel.

Examines child abuse in a broad perspective as a problem concerning the whole community. Eight chapters are devoted to primary prevention, focusing on attachment and bonding. The other chapters deal with a variety of issues, including the hospital child-abuse team, sexual abuse, the child life protection team, community involvement in protection strategies, the role of the media in prevention, cross-cultural considerations of child rearing, and the question of societal violence. Of special significance in the book is Siegel's critical examination of studies of maternal infant bonding; Cohn's review of the 1976 media campaign by the National Committee for Prevention of Child Abuse; and Oates' chapter on Management--The Myth and Reality, a criticism of simplistic answers too often given by professionals as well as the public press. References.

Child Abuse and Neglect: Cross-Cultural Perspectives. (1981). Edited by J. E. Korbin. Berkeley, CA: Univ. of California Press.

Countries discussed include: New Guinea, Sub-Saharan Africa, Native South America, Rural India, Turkey, Japan, Taiwan, China, and Polenesia. Each contribution covers child rearing and maltreatment in the specified culture, and related issues. Issues covered include: controlling maltreatment in a given culture; child care and support by extended family or community; and cultural beliefs and abuse. Other factors minimizing maltreatment included the acceptance of abortion, marriage at an older age, regular physical exams of children. References.

The Common Secret: Sexual Abuse of Children and Adolescents. (1984). Ruth Kempe, Henry Kempe. NY: W. H. Freeman.

A comprehensive discussion of both intrafamilial (incest) and extrafamilial abuse. The book consists of nine chapters organized into three main parts, and concludes with three appendixes. Part I presents epidemiological data regarding the incidence and prevalence of reported sexual abuse. Part II examines the legal aspects of sexual abuse. The last section contains three appendixes: a description of a criminal diversion program, a format for case evaluation, and a listing of educational resources and materials. The case studies are informative, give a human texture to the problem, and illustrate the complexity and multiplicity of interacting variables that need to be addressed when working with the sexually abused child. The text is written on a level that is comprehensible to the layman yet is informative to the professional. References.

Exploring the Relationship between Child Abuse and Delinquency. (1981). Edited by Robert J. Hunner, Yvonne Elder Walker. Montclair, NJ: Allenheld, Osmun.

A collection of 19 chapters written largely by sociologists and social workers associated with educational institutions or social agencies. Chapters range from the theoretical to reports of large scale, statistical studies of abused and/or delinquent children and their families who have come to the attention of authorities. The book is divided into three parts: Policy Issues, Treatment Issues, and Research/Theoretical Issues. A number of the chapters link abuse and delinquency directly to sociological factors: large families, inadequate income, lack of education, minority group membership, early pregnancy, single parenthood, alcohol abuse, parental emotional distress, subnormal intelligence, etc. References.

Incest as Child Abuse: Research and Applications. (1986). Brenda J. Vander Mey, Ronald L. Neff. NY: Praeger.

A critical evaluation and synthesis of the research findings regarding incest and children. In eight chapters the authors cover not only a brief history of child abuse but review theory and research on the topic. Chapter 8 discusses methods of treatment, intervention, and assessment of treatment of victims and their families. A lengthy bibliography ends the book. A short but adequate subject index is included.

Reports of Research

At Risk: An Account of the Work of the Battered Child Research Department, NSPCC. (1976). Edwina Baher, Clare Hyman, Carolyn Jones, Ronald Jones, Anna Kerr, Ruth Mitchell. London: Routledge & Kegan Paul.

A landmark study, this book reports on a research-treatment project conducted under the auspices of the British National Society for the Prevention of Cruelty to Children. The study looked at twenty-five abusing families. Part I is a good introduction to the phenomenon of child abuse since it illustrates the research of others with specific examples from the National Society for the Prevention of Cruelty to Children files. Part II deals with the treatment program. Part III considers the psychological aspects of parents who batter. References.

Guides

Family Violence Prevention Resource Guide for Air Force Helping Professionals. 2 vols. (1987). Washington, DC: Air Force Family Matters Branch.

A guide to preventive programs in the areas of parenting, sexual abuse, child abuse, alcohol abuse, stress management, and growing up skills. Volume 1 covers program development issues. Volume 2 contains the course outlines for workshops. In Volume 1 users will find a list of national organizations involved in areas of interest to child development specialists. The workshops for parenting in Volume 2 will be of interest to those conducting parenting classes.

DIVORCE

Bibliographies

Children and Divorce, an Annotated Bibliography and Guide. (1983). Evelyn B. Hausslein. NY: Garland.

Contains references to books, magazines, and journals published between 1975 - 1980, useful to researchers, human services personnel, and counseling professionals working with children and their families experiencing divorce. The major part of the book is a basic bibliographic list, alphabetized by author's name. Each entry has a brief annotation and indicates the categories of professionals who may find the article most useful. Four other reference lists are included: materials for professions to refer parents; materials appropriate for children; and a list of organizations, and their addresses, that work with children.

The One-Parent Family: Perspectives and Annotated Bibliography. Third edition. (1975). Benjamin Schlesinger. Toronto and Buffalo, NY: Univ. of Toronto Press.

The first part consists of four essays dealing with one parent families in Canada, Australia, and Great Britain. The second part contains 535 annotated entries published prior to January 1975. The appendix contains now outdated census data on one-parent families in the countries covered in the text.

Stepfamilies: A Guide to the Sources and Resources. (1986). Ellen J. Gruber. NY: Garland.

An annotated list of books, newspaper articles, journal articles, and some dissertations covering 1980 - 1984. Sections cover resources for professionals, parents, and children as well as listing audiovisuals, support organizations, and newsletter resources.

Reviews of Literature

Children and Divorce. (1981). E. Mavis Hetherton. In *Parent-Child Interaction, Research Theory, and Prospects*, edited by Ronald W. Henderson. NY: Academic. (Educational Psychology).

This chapter reviews research findings involving the process of divorce and life in the one-parent household as experienced by the child. Subsections in the chapter include: temperament of the child of divorce, developmental status, stress, parent-child relationships, and extrafamiliar systems. References.

Children in Contemporary American Families: Divorce and Remarriage. (1984). Robert D. Cox, Martha J. Cox. In *Advances in Developmental and Behavioral Pediatrics*, Vol. 5. Greenwich, CT: JAI. (Advances in Developmental and Behavioral Pediatrics).

Discusses common questions and problems affecting children in families of divorce and/or remarriage. Research studies are reviewed and analyzed. Practical recommendations are suggested on the basis of the studies synthesized. Fifty-eight references.

Childhood in Sociodemographic Perspective. (1986). Donald J. Hernandez. In *Annual Review of Sociology*, Vol. 12, edited by Ralph H. Turner. Palo Alto, CA: Annual Reviews. (Annual Review of Sociology).

Reviews the literature on the relationship of children and their families to: (1) short-term implications for children; (2) short-term implications for parents of a number of children, ages, or spacing; (3) long-term implications of childhood family experiences with divorce; and (4) probable family circumstances of children in the future. Seventy-one references.

Divorced Parents and Their Children: A Guide for Mental Health Professionals. (1983). Dorothy W. Cantor, Ellen A. Drake. NY: Springer.

This volume provides a bibliography and, in the appendix, a recommended reading list which can serve as an up-to-date review of the literature on divorce. The text portion serves to instruct and assist the mental health professional deal with the most common problems confronting divorced parents and their children. Appendix A provides a sample lesson from the Post-Divorce Parenting Program. Appendix B contains three bibliographies: one for professionals, one for parents, and one for children. A separate reference section to the volume follows the appendix section. The book contains an index.

Joint Custody: A Critical Analysis and Appraisal. (1985). Andre P. Derdeyn. In *Annual Progress in Psychiatry and Child Development*, edited by Stella Chess, Alexander Thomas. NY: Brunner/Mazel. (Annual Progress in Child Psychiatry and Child Development).

This chapter looks at the literature of joint custody and its effects upon the child. Seventy-three references.

Reports of Research

Contemporary Single Mothers. (1980). Bernice T. Eiduson. In *Current Topics in Early Childhood Education*, Vol. 3, edited by Lilian G. Katz. Norwood, NJ: Ablex.

This chapter describes a longitudinal study made of the child-rearing practices of single mother families. Focus is given not only to her role as parent, but her values, attitudes and behaviors. Sixteen references.

Long-Term Effects of Divorce and Remarriage on the Adjustment of Children. (1986). E. Mavis Hetherington, Martha Cox, Roger Cox. In *Annual Progress in Child Psychiatry and Child Development*, edited by Stella Chess, Alexander Thomas. NY: Brunner/Mazel. (Annual Progress in Child Psychiatry and Child Development).

This paper presents the results of a six year follow-up of a longitudinal study of the effects of divorce on parents and children. Findings suggest that divorce has more adverse effects on boys. Remarriage was more disruptive for girls. Twenty-six references.

FATHERS

Reviews of Literature

The Changing Role of Fathers. (1982). Graeme Russell. NY and St. Lucia: Univ. of Queensland Press.

After looking at traditional patterns of father and mother involvement in child care, the book examines why some men become more involved than others in fathering. Chapter 6 looks at whether mothers are more competent than fathers in child care. Three chapters examine the likely consequences of fathers sharing in child care. The final chapter summarizes current knowledge about fathers and divisions of child care and points out the implications for changes in the family. References.

Competence and Performance of Fathers and Infants. (1984). Michael W. Yogman. In *Progress in Child Health*, Vol. 1, edited by J. A. MacFarlane. NY: Churchill Livingstone.

The chapter reviews studies of father and infant involvement as it affects infant personality development. Considerable consistency is noted with the studies. The research shows that fathers are more likely to develop a heightened, arousing, and playful relationship with their infants and to provide a more novel and complex environment than mothers. Substantial bibliography.

Dimensions of Fatherhood. (1985). Shirley M. H. Hanson, Frederick W. Bozett. Beverly Hills, CA: Sage.

A scholarly report of the state of knowledge about fathers as well as a call for further research on certain topics. Part I, Roles throughout the Life Cycle, looks at fatherhood throughout the father's life course. The section begins with men and family planning and progresses through pregnancy, infancy and childhood, and on into grandfatherhood. Part II, Variations of Fatherhood, discusses traditional fatherhood as well as nontraditional fatherhood: househusbands, gay fathers, and single custodial fathers. Tables of data are provided where necessary. References.

Father and Child: Developmental and Clinical Perspectives. (1982). Edited by Stanley H. Cathy, Alan R. Gurwitt, John Munder Ross. Boston, MA: Little, Brown.

The first two chapters review the psychoanalytic contributions on child-rearing fantasies and attitudes in boys and men. The fourth chapter is a selected critical review of psychological investigations of the early father-infant relationship. Part II of the volume explores the father's role in early development. The first chapter in this section by Greenberg and Morris has become a classic in the area of father research. The second chapter reviews the research on father-infant interaction. The chapter by Greenspan discusses the father's role in early personality formation with a special focus on the "dyadic-phallic" stage of early childhood. The next chapter looks at the mother's role in presenting and portraying the father to the young child. Chapter 9 by Galenson and Roiphe discusses their well known work on the "early genital phase" and what they believe is the preoedipal origin of castration anxiety. Chapter 10 looks at the father's role in development by examining the fantasy, play, and dreams at different developmental stages. Chapter 11 by Tyson discusses how the mother as well as the father influence gender identity in boys. Chapter 13 defines what is essential to a paternal identity and then traces it through a boy's development. Chapter 14 looks at the father's contribution to a daughter's way of loving and working. Part III examines the influences fathers have on children during middle childhood. Part V covers divorce, abuse, incest, homosexuality, death, and foster fathers. References.

Father, Child, and Sex Role: Paternal Determinants of Personality Development. (1971). Henry B. Biller. Lexington, MA: D. C. Heath. (Heath Lexington Books in Psychology).

This volume integrates the theory and research of what is known about the effects of parents, both mother and father, on the development of the child's personality. The seven chapters cover material published from 1967 - 1970: masculine personality development; paternal influence on personality, sociocultural, and constitutional factors; mother-son relationship; and fathering and the female personality development. References.

The Father Figure. (1982). Edited by Lorna McKee, Margaret O'Brien. NY: Tavistack.

The chapters in this volume are categorized under three major divisions; history and ideologies of fatherhood; becoming a father and fathers; and some alternative family patterns. Chapters cover approaches to studying fathers; the literature on men's experiences during pregnancy and childbirth; the father's participation in infant care; the literature on father-infant relationships; and explore types of fatherhood. References.

The Father: His Role in Child Development. (1974). David B. Lynn. Monterey, CA: Brooks/Cole.

The first major publication to summarize the research on the impact of fathers on child development. Part I looks at the history of fatherhood, paternal behavior in animals and early man, cultural experiments in restructuring the family (Soviet, Swedish, Kibbutz, communal living), and fathers in American society. Part II treats the nuances of the father-child relationship more directly. Theories of the father's role are explored. The significance of the mother-father relationship in child development is examined. Sex role development and the father is examined. Father's role in play is addressed. Moral development, the father's child-rearing influences, mental health and father's absence are discussed in Chapters 11 through 14. Substantial references.

Fatherless Children. (1984). Paul L. Adams, Judith R. Milner, Nancy A. Schrepf. NY: John Wiley & Sons. (Wiley Series in Child Mental Health).

A synthesis of theories, research, and numerous other sources concerning the influence fathers have on child development and how absence affects that development. The volume is organized into nine chapters according to broad topical areas of concern: father's meaning, father's place, sociological views of fatherhood; types of fatherlessness, effects on the offspring; school and sex role, delinquency, and mental disorders. The authors also discuss methodology for study in the area, suggest public policy needed, and advocate specific treatment strategies. References.

Father's Birth Attendance, Early Contact, and Extended Contact with Their Newborns: A Critical Review. (April 1985). Rob Palkovitz. *Child Development* 56 (2), 392 - 406.

Research concerning fathers' birth attendance, and early and extended contact with newborn infants is reviewed. Evidence seems to suggest that the earlier the contact the firmer the bonding. References.

The Father's Role: Applied Perspectives. (1986). Edited by Michael E. Lamb. NY: Wiley.

The 16 separately authored chapters cover what is known about the father's role as well as what is not known. Most of the chapters highlight gaps in our research knowledge as well as the lack of application of well-established findings. This is a valuable and provocative addition to the literature about fatherhood. References.

The Father's Role in Infancy: Determinants of Involvement in Caregiving and Play. (1981). Ross D. Parke, Barbara R. Tensley. In *The Role of the Father in Child Development,* 2nd edition, edited by Michael Lamb. NY: John Wiley & Sons.

The chapter provides an overview of research covering three areas of fathering: studies indicating fathers are capable and interested in both caregiving and noncaregiving contexts; reviews of studies covering stylistic differences in mother and father patterns; and studies indicating differences in traditional father-mother caregiving and play. References.

Paternal Deprivation: Family, School, Sexuality and Society. (1974). Henry B. Biller. Toronto: D. C. Heath.

A sequel to *Father, Child, and Sex Role* published in 1971 by the author, this volume differs from the previous book in its concentration on paternal deprivation. Chapters address such issues as: a boy's identification with his father; father-infant attachment; impact of father's behavior on the sex role functioning; effect of father absence, surrogate models, and sociocultural background on masculine development; impact of quality of fathering on personal and social adjustment; influence of the mother-child relationship on personality development of the paternally deprived boy; effect of the father-daughter relationship on emotional and interpersonal functioning; and impact of the father-child relationship on cognitive functioning and academic adjustment. References.

The Role of the Father in Child Development. Second edition. Completely revised and updated. (1981). Edited by Michael E. Lamb. NY: John Wiley & Sons. (Wiley Series on Personality Processes).

Provides an overview of the effects of the father's relationship or lack of relationship on the development of the child. Chapter 1 reviews the literature on psychoanalysis, attachment theory, Parson's theory, and social learning theory. Literature dealing with how the father-child relationship forms as well as aspects of personality development that father's influence is reviewed. Chapter 3 reviews the literature between 1975 and 1980 dealing with the role and functions of the father from the psychoanalytic viewpoint. Chapter 7 reviews the literature of the mother as care giver, including studies on attachment, and then reviews studies comparing the father's and mother's role and child's behavior toward the parents. Chapter 8 examines variation in paternal adaptation patterns and the interrelations of different family subsystems. Chapters 9 and 14 review the literature on the effects of father separation. Chapter 10 reviews the effect of the father on moral norms. Chapter 11 examines the role of the father in cognitive, academic, and intellectual development. Chapters 12 and 13 present an overview of research on the effect of father-infant interaction. References.

Reports of Research

The Nurturing Father: Discovering the Complete Man. (1987). Kyle D. Pruett. NY: Warner Books.

Discusses findings of a five-year study of 17 two-parent families whose primary care giver was the father. The book is extremely readable, intelligent, but not completely objectively reported. The author concludes that fathers nurture well but differently. The book focuses on three families, discussing their problems and coping strategies. Over half the material in the book relates to subjects like competition between parents, continued paternal nurturing after divorce, gender role confusions, and long-term fathering solutions. References.

Handbooks

Fatherhood U.S.A.: The First National Guide to Programs, Services, and Resources for and about Fathers. (1984). Debra G. Klinman, Rhiana Kohl. NY: Garland.

This concise catalog, written by the staff of the Fatherhood Project at Bank Street College of Education, focuses on the relationships between fathers and family health care, education, social and supportive services, family law, and employment. Extensive bibliographies, appendixes, and indexes are included. The section on books and publications by, for, and about fathers is especially informative. The volume will assist parents, teachers, helping professionals, resource centers, policy makers, funding agencies, researchers, and writers. References.

FOSTER CARE

Reviews of Literature

Foster Care: Current Issues, Policies, and Practices. (1985). Edited by Martha J. Cox, Roger D. Cox. Norwood, NJ: Ablex. (Child and Family Policy, edited by James L. Gallagher, Ron Haskins. Vol. 4.)

Each of the nine chapters first introduces the reader to a particular topic within a broad area: judicial standards; computerized information systems; cultural realities; obstacles to foster care; foster parent training; and permanency planning. The problems of foster care are then discussed citing studies, surveys, etc. on the topic. Where possible conclusions are provided at the end of the text along with a lengthy bibliography.

Foster Home Care, Facts and Fallacies: A Review of Research in the United States, Western Europe, Israel, and Great Britain between 1948 - 1966. (1967). Rosemary Dinnage, M. L. Kellmer Pringle. London: Longmans, Green. (Series in Child Development).

Chapter 2 is a review of research. Chapter 4 gives an overview of foster home care. Chapter 5 abstracts completed research projects. Chapter 6 is an annotated bibliography. Chapters 7 and 8 list research projects underway at the time of publications but not yet complete. References.

Reports of Research

Agencies and Foster Children. (1976). Deborah Shapiro. NY: Columbia Univ. Press.

This book presents the results of a longitudinal study of the foster care system in New York City from 1966 to 1971. Part I of the book presents an overview of the study population and worker perceptions of the placement process and its effects on children and families. Part II analyzes various agency investment strategies in relation to the course and outcomes to children in the system. Part III presents a substudy of child welfare workers, including data on the course of their careers and the impact of their perceptions of their work on the clients they serve. The book outlines many of the strengths and weaknesses of the foster care system. References.

Children in Foster Care: A Longitudinal Investigation. (1978). David Fanshel, Eugene B. Shinn. NY: Columbia Univ. Press.

The publication of this volume makes available the results from a large longitudinal assessment of status changes, intelligence, behavior, emotional problems, and school performance of 624 foster children. The book contains a complex, multidimensional assessment of 624 black, white, and Puerto Rican children ranging in age from birth to twelve years who were separated from their biological parents during 1966 and who spent varying intervals in foster care in New York City. The book contains so many tables, analyses, and results that it is impossible to give the reader a complete outline of the topics covered. References.

Children in Foster Care: Destitute, Neglected . . . Betrayed. (1978). Alan R. Gruber. NY: Human Sciences.

This book reports on a one-day study (in November 1971), through questionnaires completed by social workers, of almost all of the 5,933 children in foster home care in Massachusetts on that date. Interviews with some of the parents and foster parents of the children studied augmented findings. The study gathered data on a variety of issues: length of stay; amount of parent contact; social worker's case loads; and adoption difficulties. References.

Foster Care and Nonprofit Agencies. Dennis R. Young, Stephen J. Finch. (1977). Lexington, MA: D. C. Heath.

This volume describes and explains New York City's system of foster care for children. The emphasis is on the performance of the social service delivery system. Chapter notes are provided at the end of the text along with an index to the book.

Long-Term Foster Care. (1984). Jane Rowe, Hilary Cain, Marion Hundleby, Anne Kane. NY: St. Martin's.

Reports the findings of a five-year study of foster care and its effects. Extensive interviews with foster children, their foster parents, natural parents, and social workers were made to collect the data. The information collected was analyzed in relation to all aspects of foster care, the caregiver, and the child. The evidence suggests that children flourish in foster care situations but long-term fostering does not provide sufficient stability. References.

New Foster Parents, the First Experience. (1980). Patricia Woodward Cautley. NY: Human Science.

The study looks at factors in selection of successful foster parents and their adaptation to the parenting role. References conclude the study.

Other References

Five Models of Foster Family Group Homes: A Systematic View of Foster Care. (1974). Elizabeth A. Lawder, Roberta G. Andrews, Jon R. Parsons. NY: Child Welfare League of America.

Describes several different models of care: agency owned by group home; agency rented group home; group home for low functioning children; visiting foster home program; and medical foster homes.

GROUP EXPERIENCES

Bibliographies

Bibliography on Missionary Kids. (1987). Wheaton, IL: Billy Graham Center Library.

An extensive annotated bibliography of books, journal articles, graduate theses and studies, and miscellaneous unpublished documents related to all aspects, social-psychological-educational, of being the child of a missionary. Containing over 250 entries, the bibliography dates from 1908 to the present. Stephen Van Rooy, Wycliffe Bible Translators began the bibliography and in 1981 turned it over, along with the documents to the Billy Graham Center Library where the project is being continued. In November 1981 an unannotated version of the bibliography appeared in *Emissary*, 12 (3-4), entitled A Working 'MK' Bibliography. Copies of the bibliography may be requested from Mary Schimmels, Billy Graham Center Library, Wheaton College, Wheaton, IL 60187; (312) 260-2529.

Perspectives on Residential Child Care: An Annotated Bibliography: Research and Other Literature in the United States, Canada, and Great Britain, 1966 - 1974. (1976). Hilary Prosser. Windsor, Berks: NFER.

An annotated bibliography of research dealing with residential child care from 1966 to 1974, excluding the care of children, handicapped both physically and mentally. Those wishing to review the literature up to 1966 should use *Residential Child Care--Facts and Fallacies* (Dinnage and Pringle, 1967). Part I of the bibliography covers the topics of who the children are, consequences of residential care, what kind of care works, and the residential staff. Part II covers policy and practice and the history of residential child care.

Reviews of Literature

Child Care: Kith, Kin, and Hired Hands. (1984). Emmy E. Werner. Baltimore, MD: Univ. Park Press.

This book presents a scholarly, comparative review and analysis of alternative forms of child care. The coverage is broad, ranging from a look at care among primates, through shared child care in various historical and present domestic groupings, to nurses, nannies, family daycare, and foster parenting. Separate chapters are provided for "invisible" care givers, grandparents, and television. Each chapter is based on past and current research and identifies areas very ripe for research. The author draws from the literature of anthropology, child development, psychology, sociology, and social welfare. Each topic is presented cross-culturally and cross-nationally. References.

Nontraditional Families: Parenting and Child Development. (1982). Edited by Michael Lamb. Hillsdale, NJ: Lawrence Erlbaum.

This volume reviews studies dealing with families in which both parents are employed; families in which fathers share child-rearing responsibilities; single-parent families; alternative family styles in which mothers avoid legal marriage; and the effects of extrafamilial child care on child development. References.

Reports of Research

Children of the Dream. (1969). Bruno Bettelheim. NY: Avon.

A classic study of communal child rearing in the Kibbutz. The author focuses on the differences in personality formation which may be attributed to the group experience as opposed to the nuclear family. References.

Infants in Institutions: A Comparison of Their Development with Family-Reared Infants during the First Year of Life. (c. 1962, 1978). Sally A. Provence, Rose C. Lipton. NY: International Universities.

This volume reports a landmark longitudinal study comparing development of institutionalized infants with that of infants living in traditional family settings. Provence and Lipton analyze the infant's behavioral responses in detail: motor behavior; reactions to people; language; reactions to inanimate objects; discovery of self; and sleep behavior, just to mention a few. References.

ILLEGITIMACY

Reviews of Literature

Bastardy and Its Comparative History: Studies in the History of Illegitimacy and Nonconformism in Britain, France, Germany, Sweden, North America, Jamaica and Japan. (1980). Edited by Peter Laslett, Karla Oosterveen, Richard M. Smith. Cambridge, MA: Harvard Univ. Press.

Compares the history of the last several centuries of illegitimacy worldwide. The 19 chapters are divided among the categories of Britain, North America, Jamaica and Japan, and Western Europe. Focus is on the sociological aspects of illegitimacy in the various cultures. Substantial references. Indexed.

Illegitimacy. (1975). Shirley Foster Hartley. Berkeley, CA: Univ. of California Press.

A comprehensive, cross-cultural analysis of all aspects of the topic. A lengthy bibliography as well as a detailed index is provided.

Reports of Research

Born Illegitimate: Social and Educational Implications. (1971). Eileen Crellin, M. L. Kellmer Pringle, Patrick West. London: National Foundation for Educational Research in England and Wales.

This study looked at all aspects of development (physical, educational, social, and psychological) of the illegitimate child to the age of seven compared with other groups of children. References.

Study of Discrimination against Persons Born out of Wedlock. (1967). Vieno Voitto Saario. NY: United Nations. (Study of Discrimination in Education).

Reports the findings of a global study made of the status (socially, legally, and politically) of illegitimate children and adults. Rights of the child, of the mothers, and of the fathers were investigated. Solutions such as adoption were investigated in various cultures. Parental authority was explored. Legal aspects of proof of birth are discussed. Laws or codes from various countries are reprinted in the appendix.

MINORITIES

Bibliographies

Black Children and Their Families: A Bibliography. (1976). Charlotte J. Dunmore. San Francisco, CA: R & E Research.

Entries are predominantly post-1960 and include some classic works on black children. Regrettably the bibliography is not annotated and some racist works are included.

Reviews of Literature

Family Life and School Achievement: Why Poor Black Children Succeed or Fail. (1983). R. M. Clark. Chicago, IL: Univ. of Chicago Press.

This volume provides case studies of achievement-related functioning processes in low income black families. The studies highlight both single- and two-parent families. Family themes, early child-rearing practices, mental health, home living patterns, and intellectuality patterns were combined through taped interviews with ten urban school students. References.

PARENT-CHILD INTERACTION

Reviews of Literature

Attachment and Dependency. (1972). Edited by Jacob L. Gewirtz. Washington, DC: V. H. Winston & Sons.

This book provides an overview of the wide range of positions taken by authorities on the topic of attachment and dependency. An attempt is made to distinguish between the two concepts, attachment and dependency. The chapters also show a wide difference in the thinking of authorities and in their approaches to the level and mode of analysis in selected studies. References.

Attachment and Loss. 3 vols. (1969, 1973, 1980). John Bowlby. NY: Basic Books.

These three volumes summarize studies of the effect of maternal attachment and loss on the developing infant. Volume 1 on Attachment contains chapters on the effect bonding between mother and child has on the child's behavior and development. Volume 2 deals with problems of separation anxiety, grief, and mourning, and contains a critical review of the literature. Volume 3 about Loss, Sadness and Depression explores the implications for the psychology and psychopathology of personality of the ways in which young children respond to a temporary or permanent loss of the mother-figure. Each volume provides references as well as separate author and subject indexes.

The Development of Attachment and Affiliative Systems. (1982). Robert N. Emde, Robert J. Harman. NY: Plenum. (Topics in Developmental Psychology).

This volume, referred to as a storehouse of information by one reviewer, includes a wide array of empirical studies, varying from hormonal and other studies of primates to investigations of abused/neglected and Down's syndrome human infants. In fact, the most striking thing about the volume is the heuristic value of a theoretical construct like "attachment" in guiding research that is interdisciplinary. Part II, made up of chapters 8 - 18, covers topics on bonding having to do with the normal as well as the special child. Included in Part III are two commentaries on attachment research. References.

The Effect of the Infant on Its Caregiver. (1974). Edited by Michael Lewis, Leonard Rosenblum. NY: John Wiley. (The Origins of Behavior).

This volume reports a diversity of human and animal studies on the effect that the infant may have on its care giver. Four of the eleven chapters in the book are reviews, four are studies of mother-infant interaction in human dyads, and three are based on studies of adult-young interaction in monkeys. Stern's chapter presents data on dyadic gaze sequences along with subjective impressions on other aspects of mother-infant play. Chapters by Tanner on physical development and Drefus-Brisac on sleep in prematures suggest that the infant's body is something to be considered in the studies of interaction, but the tie between physical characteristics and care giving is not made explicit in either chapter. Kroner reviews the work relating state, sex, arousal, and maturity to care giving. Bell speculates as to how the infant can initiate, maintain, and terminate physical care and more sociable responses from the care giver. References.

The First Relationship: Infant and Mother. (1977). Daniel Stern. Cambridge, MA: Harvard Univ. Press. (Developing Child Series).

This volume presents a picture of how social interaction develops during the first six months of the child's life. In Chapter 2 Stern discusses the care giver's repertoire in detail and how mothers act differently with infants than they do with adults and older children. In Chapter 3 the infant's repertoire is discussed, showing how the infant has behavior to elicit and terminate social interactions. Chapters 4 and 5 take the laboratory findings and apply them to mother-infant interactions in natural settings. Chapter 6 is a detailed analysis of the structure and timing of play periods. Chapter 7 outlines how the discrete, short-lived periods of interaction are summed up to become an ongoing relationship. Chapter 8 discusses what happens when either the mother or the infant fails to learn cues. Chapter 9 provides arguments showing the necessity for understanding the social interactions of infants. References.

The Mental and Social Life of Babies: How Parents Create Persons. (1982). Kenneth Kaye. Chicago, IL: Univ. of Chicago Press.

Chapters 2 - 6 of the book explore what is known about human action at the level of two humans functioning together as a system (mother and child). Chapters 7 - 12 look at the symbolic basis of socialization, attachment, individual, and self-consciousness of the infant and parent. References.

Methodological Review of Research on Mother-Infant Bonding. (1981). Linda J. Morgan. In *Advances in Behavioral Pediatrics: A Research Annual*, Vol. 2, edited by Bonnie Camp. Greenwich, CT: JAI.

The chapter reviews studies on mother-infant bonding looking critically at the methodology and interpretation of the data. The author points out the need for further study in the area along with improved methods of carrying out the studies. References.

Mother-Infant Interaction. (1975). Edited by C. Etta Walters. NY: Behavioral Publications.

This series of nine review papers by the editor and others relates the psychoanalytic perspective on the mother-infant relationship to various studies, including some of the editor's own research on infant security. One paper of the nine deals with day care. There are 374 references.

Mother-Infant Interactions in Various Cultural Settings. (1986). Navaz Bhavnagri. In *Current Topics in Early Childhood Education*, Vol. 6, edited by Lilian G. Katz. Norwood, NJ: Ablex.

This chapter reviews the theoretical literature as well as the empirical research of infant-mother interaction in a cross-cultural setting. References.

Mothering. (1977). Rudolph Schaffer. Cambridge, MA: Harvard Univ. Press. (Developing Child Series).

This volume of the Developing Child Series reviews the research on early socialization of the infant. The book first looks at the topic of mothering from the traditional theoretical viewpoints, then from the viewpoint of writers of practical handbooks for parents, and finally the author summarizes the literature published in this area for the past ten years. Developing mothering skills are discussed as well as mothering beyond the biological mother. The book is extremely well written. References.

The Myth of Bonding. (1984). M. P. M. Richards. In *Progress in Child Health*, Vol. 1, edited by J. A. MacFarlane. NY: Churchill Livingstone.

Richards re-evaluates Klaus and Kennell's study on infant bonding and briefly reviews other studies. His premise is that there is insufficient evidence to substantiate the present acceptance of the bonding theory. References.

Object Relations, Dependency, and Attachment: A Theoretical Review of the Infant-Mother Relationship. (1969). Mary D. Salter Ainsworth. In *Child Development*, 40 (4), 969 - 1025.

A review of the three theories of mother-child relationship: object relations, dependency, and attachment. 120 references.

Parent-Baby Attachment in Premature Infants. (1983). Edited by J. A. Davis, M. P. M. Richards, N. R. C. Roberton. NY: St. Martin's.

Focus of the 22 chapters involves the parent-infant relationship within the context of the birth, early separation, and subsequent hospital course and handling of prematurity. The volume is organized into three major sections, with a final chapter discussing future directions in the care and handling of prematures and their families. The first section provides a general overview and background regarding prematurity and early parent-infant relationships. The following two sections provide a holistic discussion of the practical issues in managing the parent-infant relationship during the hospital course, and descriptions of six specific hospital programs are provided in separate chapters as examples of particular intervention strategies and issues. One appendix provides a specific social work protocol detailing social work functions within such a setting. References.

Parent-Child Interaction and Parent-Child Relations in Child Development. (1984). Edited by Marion Perlmutter. Hillsdale, NJ: (Minnesota Symposia on Child Psychology, Vol. 17).

One chapter presents research on parent-child interactions with infants, while another presents work on parent-child interactions between adults. Chapter 3 by Clarke-Stewart discusses an effort to document and understand day care effects on children two to four years of age. Chapter 4 by Lois Hoffman looks at maternal employment and the young child. References.

Parent-Child Interaction: The Socialization Process Observed in Twin and Singleton Families. (1980). Hugh Lytton. NY: Plenum.

The families of 46 male twin-pairs and 44 male singletons (with one sibling) about 32 months of age participated in this observational study investigating mother-son and father-son interaction during the toddler period. Findings indicate that mothers function as the main disciplinarian, even when the father is present; fathers attempt far less often than mothers to change sons' behavior; mothers who repeat their commands tend to have more disobedient children; mothers tend to respond warmly to their toddler's attachment behavior even in situations where it is the mother's negative behavior that initially precipitated the attachment behavior. References.

Parent-Infant Bonding. Second Edition. (1982).   Marshall H. Klaus, John H. Kennell. St. Louis, MO: C. V. Mosby.

The book reviews studies focusing on the exploration of birth, interaction and attachment between parent and child. The material is divided into seven chapters: the family during pregnancy; labor, birth, and bonding; care of the sibling; maternal behavior in mammals; caring for the parents of premature or sick infants; caring for the parents of infants with a congenital malformation; caring for the parents of a stillborn, or infant who dies. References.

Parent-Infant Bonding: Another Look. (1984). Susan Goldberg. In *Annual Progress in Child Psychiatry and Child and Development,* edited by Stella Chess, Alexander Thomas. NY: Brunner/Mazel.

This reviewer of the early parent-infant relationship literature asserts that the sensitive period hypothesis has not been tested on three counts: (1) there are no systematic studies of initial mother-infant contacts; (2) the majority of the studies confound timing and amount of contact; and (3) failure to consider underlying mechanics results in the omission of designs and dependent measures that could address appropriate questions. References.

Parent-Infant Relationships. (1980). Paul M. Taylor. NY: Grune and Stratton. (Monographs in Neonatology).

Written by authorities from several disciplines, the chapters address issues of parent-infant relationships and their effect on child development (behavioral, psychological, and emotional aspects). The chapters are categorized into three areas: basic developmental processes; influences of professional practices; and relationships at risk or approaches to intervention. References.

The Reproduction of Mothering: Psychoanalysis and the Sociology of Gender. (1978). Nancy Chodorow. Berkely, CA: UCLA Press.

This volume looks at the reproduction of women's mothering across generations. Research findings from genetic, sociological, and psychoanalytic literature are considered in support of the hypothesis that women's mothering perpetuates itself through socially structured induced psychological mechanisms. The book offers a provocative approach to understanding sex differences in parenting and offers some alternatives for the future. References.

The Role of Adults in Infant Development: Implications for Early Childhood Educators. (1986). Alan Fogel. In *Current Topics in Early Childhood Education*, Vol. 6, edited by Lilian G. Katz. Norwood, NJ: Ablex.

The first part presents research on the parent-infant relationship including topics such as bonding and fear of strangers. The next part examines the role of the nonfamilial care giver especially in a group setting. Lastly, the chapter looks at issues related to the lasting effects of the infant's early experience with adults. References.

Social-Emotional Consequences of Day Care for Preschool Children. (1982). Michael Rutter. In *Day Care Scientific and Social Policy Issues*, edited by Edward F. Zigler, Edmund W. Gordon. Boston, MA: Auburn House.

This volume reviews studies showing that quality day care does not impinge on the emotional bonding between child and parent. Studies show children continue to prefer parents over other care givers. Indications are that placing very young children in day care does not usually result in serious emotional disturbance. Day care does to some extent help form the child's social behavior. References.

Social Interchange in Infancy: Affect, Cognition, and Communication. (1982). Edited by Edward Z. Tronick. Baltimore, MD: Univ. Park Press.

Brazelton reviews data that support his belief that the mother-infant joint regulation starts before the baby is born. Cohn and Tronick present data on how mothers' "depressed" interactions with their three-month old infants can affect both the infants' concurrent and subsequent behavior. Fogel indicates that two-month-old infants have the capacity to remember and anticipate and to act in ways that reveal emotional involvement. Demos presents data that suggest that the affective relationship of one-year-olds to their mothers is related to the child's linguistic competence. References.

Reports of Research

Attachment Behavior of Deaf Children with Deaf Parents. (1984). Kathryn P. Keadow, Mark T. Greenberg, Carol Erting. In *Annual Progress in Child Psychiatry and Child Development*, edited by Stell Chess, Alexander Thomas. NY: Brunner/Mazel.

This chapter reports on a study made of 17 deaf children, all with two deaf parents. Most of the children were between ages three and five. The authors concluded that deaf children of deaf parents may follow a variety of developmental patterns. These depend on parental characteristics, history, and environment more than the developmental course of non-hearing-impaired children. Thirty-eight references.

Attachment Behavior Out-of-Doors. (1972). J. W. Anderson. In *Ethological Studies of Child Behavior*, edited by N. Blurton Jones. London: Cambridge Univ. Press.

The chapter reports the result of a study of attachment in human infants to their mothers by ascertaining the distances they maintain from the mother when at liberty in a familiar environment. The findings suggest that infants whose ages range from beginning-to-walk until two and one-half years kept within sight or sound of the mother. References.

Behaviour of Children and Their Mothers at Separation and Greeting. (1972). N. Blurton Jones, Gill M. Leach. In *Ethological Studies of Child Behavior*, edited by N. Blurton Jones. London: Cambridge Univ. Press.

The chapter reports an observational study of 35 mothers and their two- to four-year-old children during separation at the beginning of a playgroup and during greeting at the end of separation. Gestures or facial expressions were observed and counted up for each individual so that a factor analysis could be done. Ready departure from the mother went with greetings in which play continued or objects were shown or given to the mother. Smiling by mother and child was separate from these but went with smiling to the teacher. The child's approach and arm raising were both shown to increase the chance of the mother's touching the child. Mothers of criers at separation were found to behave no differently than mothers of children who did not cry. However, mothers of younger criers tended to be more responsive than mothers of noncriers. References.

A Longitudinal Study of the Consequences of Early Mother-Infant Interaction: A Microanalytic Approach. (1981). John A. Martin. Chicago, IL: Society for Research in Child Development (Monographs of the Society for Research in Child Development. Serial No. 190. Vol. 46, No. 3).

This monograph reports the results of a longitudinal study of the development of dyadic relations in mother-child pairs. The research traces the development of the relationship between mother, child, and dyadic characteristics measured during early interactions between them and changes over time. References.

Preschool Children with Working Parents: An Analysis of Attachment Relationships. (1984). Nancy Boyd Webb. New York and London: Lanham (University Press of America).

This book analyzes the daily lives of a group of preschoolers with working parents. It focuses on the children's relationships with their parents and nonfamily caretakers. It highlights advantages for the children resulting from their multiple caretaking experiences. References.

The Skills of Mothering: A Study of Parent Child Development Centers. (1982). Susan Ring Andrews, Janet B. Blumenthal, Dale L. Johnson, Alfred J. Kahn, Carol J. Ferguson, Thomas M. Lasater, Paul E. Malone, Doris B. Kahn, Doris B. Wallace. Chicago, IL: Society for Research in Child Development (Monographs of the Society for Research in Child Development. Serial No. 198. Vol. 47, No. 6).

This monograph reports the results of the Parent Child Development Center (PCDC) experiment begun in 1970 by the U.S. Office of Economic Opportunity. The project endeavored to promote development of children from low-income families. References.

PARENT EDUCATION

Bibliographies

Parenting: An Annotated Bibliography. (1980). Jane Morgan. Toronto, Ontario: Ontario Institute for Studies in Education. (Current Bibliography Series No. 13).

Contains a classified selection of noteworthy books of interest to parents, professionals and researchers published within the last decade. The bibliography is organized into topical sections which incorporate both major research results and practical advice. Twelve topical sections included are: general works; parents; infancy; child care and development; management; communication and discipline; play groups, nursery school and day care; educational concerns; reading; adolescence; sexuality; children and death; children with special needs.

Reviews of Literature

Enhancing the Effectiveness of Parent Education: An Analysis of Program Assumptions. (1984). Douglas Powell. In *Current Topics in Early Childhood Education*, Vol. 5, edited by Lilian G. Katz. Norwood, NJ: Ablex.

Dimensions of parent programs examined include: role of the professional in working with the parent; development of programs; and conceptions of how parents change. Forty-seven references.

Parent Education and Public Policy. (1983). Ron Haskins, Diane Adams. Norwood, NJ: Ablex. (Child and Family Policy, Vol. 3).

The book is divided into four sections. In the first section, chapters are included which examine the history of parent education, parent program in the general context of policy for children and families, and portray the policy context with particular reference to the U.S. Congress. Section II contains seven chapters reporting original research or reviews of research on selected aspects of parent education. Parent programs are examined in the chapters in the third section. The final section summarizes all previous sections. References.

Parent Involvement: A Review of Research and Principles of Successful Practice. (1986). Rhoda McShane Becher. In *Current Topics in Childhood Education,* Vol. 6, edited by Lilian Katz. Norwood, NJ: Ablex.

The literature reviewed covers: intelligence, competence, and achievement; cognitive development and school achievement; reading achievement; and parent-teacher relationships and communication. References.

Parent Training: Foundations of Research and Practice. (1984). Edited by Richard F. Dangel, Richard A. Palster. NY: Guilford.

An impressive compilation of the procedures, theories, and research basis of the behavioral approach to teaching parenting. Section I covers goals and objectives including a historical overview of behavioral training programs. Section II outlines programs and applications as well as pioneers of the major parent training projects with detailed accounts of the procedures, theories, research bases, and outcomes of the programs they have developed. The final section of the book looks at important consumer and ethical issues. References.

Parental Participation in Children's Development and Education. (1983). Sheila Wolfendale. London: Gordon and Breach Science Publisher. (Special Aspects of Education).

The ten chapters in this volume explore and look at various projects undertaken to involve parents in the early years of their children's schooling. The author has set about to present an account of developments in parent-professional collaboration in the area of child development and the learning process. She examines the relationship between parents and schools in light of enhancing the developmental and educational needs of children, and she explores the extent to which parents are agents of change in enhancing their children's development and learning. References.

Patterns of Supplementary Parenting. (1982). Edited by Marjorie J. Kostelnik, Albert I. Rabin, Lillian A. Phenice, Anne K. Soderman. NY: Plenum. (Child Nurturance, Vol. 2).

This volume contains ten chapters which discuss and review literature on: day care, foster care, residential homes, Kibbutz child rearing, siblings and peers in the parenting process, parenting by relatives, child rearing in other cultures, and alternatives to parenting. Bibliographies provided.

Research on Parenting: Implications for Primary Health Care Providers. (1982). Robert W. Chamberlin, Barbara B. Keller. In *Advances in Pediatrics, a Research Annual*, Vol. 3, edited by Mark Walraich, Donald K. Routh. Greenwich, CT: JAI.

The chapter reviews the literature of how parents influence the developing child and what factors influence the parent's ability to parent. Suggestions are made on improving the delivery of primary health care by the pediatrician and others. The review covers the infant through preschool. References.

Strengthening Families. (1984). Nicholas Hobbs, Paul R. Dokecki, Kathleen V. Hoover-Dempsey, Robert and May W. Shayne, Karen H. Weeks, M. Moroney. San Francisco, CA: Jossey-Bass. (Jossey-Bass Social and Behavioral Science Series).

Chapter 1 covers the necessity for improved child care and parent education programs. Chapters 2 - 4 examine the knowledge foundation on which various options for strengthening families can be formulated. Chapters 5 - 8 look at policies that could be adopted in relation to child care and parent education along with making recommendations. Chapter 9 sums up the rationale underlying the specific recommendations. References.

Working with Parents and Infants: An Interactional Approach. (1981). Rose Bromwich. Baltimore, MD: Univ. Park Press.

This volume provides information on parent-infant intervention and approaches to parent education in that direction. The book is divided into five parts. Part I introduces the interaction model. Part II describes the Intervention Program used in the UCLA Infant Studies Project. Part III describes 30 case studies. Part IV is a catalog of specific interventions which may apply to specific problems. Appendixes A and B contain the Parent Behavior Progression Forms (RBP) both 1 and 2. References.

Reports of Research

Effects of Dramatic Play as a Basis of a Parent Instructional Model for Home Intervention Programming for Hispanic Parents of Preschool Children. (1986). Thomas D. Yawkey. In *Cultural Dimensions of Play Games and Sport*, edited by Bernard Morgen. Champaign, IL: Human Kinetics. (TAASP, Vol. 10).

This study examines the effects of training Hispanic parents of children in Project PIAGET to develop, use, and practice various dramatic play activities and games with their youngters at home. Project PIAGET is an acronym for Promoting Intellectual Adaptation Given Experiential Transforming and is a Title VII federally funded demonstration project.

Parent Involvement: Perspectives from the Follow Through Experiences. (1983). Patricia P. Olmstead, Robert I. Rubin. In *Parent Education and Public Policy*, edited by Ron Haskins, Diane Adams. Norwood, NJ: Ablex. (Child and Family Policy).

The chapter discusses parent education and involvement in the Follow Through program. Both parents involved in FT and non-follow through (NFT) parents were interviewed. The results of the findings are presented and summarized in this chapter. Parent involvement in the various follow through sponsoring programs are analyzed and discussed. The findings are all positive. References.

Handbooks

Handbook on Parent Education. (1980). Edited by Marvin J. Fine. NY: Academic (Educational Psychology).

Part I of this book provides a historical and contemporary perspective on parent education and the American family. Part II discusses different models of parent education. Part III details the application of parenting programs for specific groups: handicapped children, foster parents, parents of preschoolers, abusive parents, and parenting for teenagers. Anyone involved in parent education will find this book of value.

SIBLINGS

Reviews of Literature

Modeling and Reactive Components of Sibling Interaction. (1969). Brian Sutton-Smith, B. G. Rosenberg. In *Minnesota Symposia on Child Psychology*, Vol. 3, edited by John P. Hill. Minneapolis, MN: Univ. of Minnesota Press.

This paper discusses studies which fall into three distinct groups: (1) those focused on parent-child interactions in which the major dependent variables have been achievement and affiliation; (2) those concerned with child-child interactions in which the major dependent variables have been chiefly those of sex role traits and power; and (3) those in which some attempt has been made to consider patterns of interaction or constellations involving the whole family. References.

Only Children in America. (1982). Toni Falbo, In *Sibling Relationships: Their Nature and Significance across the Lifespan,* by Michael Lamb, Brian Sutton-Smith. Hillsdale, NJ: Lawrence Erlbaum.

The chapter provides a brief description of the social and historical aspects of only childhood during the twentieth century. The major portion of the chapter reviews the psychological literature about only children: intelligence, achievement, interpersonal orientation, self-esteem, and marital success. Sixty-two references.

Sibling Relationships: Their Nature and Significance across the Lifespan. (1982). Michael E. Lamb, Brian Sutton-Smith. Hillsdale, NJ: Lawrence Erlbaum.

This classic compilation of sibling research is comprehensive, informative as to the state-of-the-art, and provides ideas for future research on siblings. The volume takes a life-span approach, including information on siblings from infancy through adulthood. Chapters focus on a variety of topics: the only child; cross-cultural comparisons of sibling relationships; effects of newborn on older siblings; siblings and their mothers; patterns of interaction among preschool-age children; relationship in middle childhood; split parent identification; birth order and sibling status effects; life-span personality in sibling status; sibling loyalties; sibling interdependence; and similarities and differences among siblings. References.

Sibling Studies and the Developmental Impact of Critical Incidents. (1984). Judy Dunn. In *Life-Span Development and Behavior.* Vol. 6, edited by Paul B. Baltes, Orville G. Brim, Jr. NY: Academic.

Studies address two particular aspects of orientation, the impact of critical life events and the question of the significance of early experience in the context of the sibling relationship. The changes accompanying the birth of a sibling demonstrate that the significance of critical incidents in the developmental process should be studied with reference to individual differences in personality and family relationships. Differences in the quality of ther early sibling relationship persist into middle childhood and retrospective material shows that in late adulthood individuals attribute their closeness to their siblings to this early relationship. References.

The Single-Child Family. (1984). Edited by Toni Falbo. NY: Guilford.

Chapter 1 reviews the psychological and sociological literature concerning only children and their parents. The chapter by Boswell and Katz addresses the influence of siblings on sex role development during early and middle childhood. Chapter 4 looks at the development of ego identity and describes the types of family communication patterns that foster healthy development and the role of siblings in these communication patterns. Chapter 5 examines the impact of sibling tutoring on intellectual development. The Polits' chapter deals with the double handicap of growing up without siblings and without a father. Chapter 7 is a longitudinal study which indicates that individuals reared as only children express greater preferences for solitary activities than their peers. The final chapter concludes that only children are not much different from children raised with siblings. References.

Sisters and Brothers. (1985). Judy Dunn. Cambridge, MA: Harvard Univ. Press. (Developing Child Series).

This book looks at recent studies of young siblings in an attempt to answer two questions: first, how do experiences of childhood spent with a sibling influence the way the child develops; and second, why do some siblings get along well while others don't. The author also draws on case histories in an attempt to answer these questions. References.

Reports of Research

The Psychology of Twinship. (1985). Ricardo Ainslie. Lincoln, NE: Univ. of Nebraska Press.

The first two chapters review and critique genetic studies on twinship. The remaining chapters report data gathered by Ainslie when he interviewed twins and their mothers regarding adjustment to being twins, feeling about being a twin, etc. The study is unique in that Ainslie used a life history approach to gathering his data. In the appendix may be found the description of the twins sampled and the questionnaire used. References.

Siblings: Love, Envy and Understanding. (1982). Judy Dunn, Carol Kendrick. Cambridge, MA: Harvard Univ. Press.

This is a study of 40 firstborn children living with their parents in Cambridge, England or vicinity and the effects on these children of the arrival of siblings into the family. The findings indicate that the birth of a baby and the accompanying change in the firstborn's life has a dramatic effect on the behavior of the first child. It was also found that the first born showed a great deal of sensitivity to the emotional expressions of the baby. Most of the children studied were found to show signs of disturbance and unhappiness in addition to affection for the baby. Relationships with parents changed sharply. Data gathered during the study are located in the appendixes.

5

Child Care

 DATABASES TO CONSIDER   Child Abuse and Neglect
Family Resources
Sociological Abstracts   ERIC
PsycINFO

GENERAL

Bibliographies

Child Care Issues for Parents and Society: Guide to the Information Sources.
(1977). Andrew Garoogian, Rhoda Garoogian. Detroit, MI: Gale
Research. (Social Issues and Social Problems Information, Vol. 2).

A bibliography of nontechnical sources of information for parents of children
from birth through adolescence. Books, government documents, periodicals,
and audio-visual aids are included. Coverage is very broad. Included are
sections on: child development; children's rights; day care; death, divorce and
separation; discipline; drugs, alcohol, and their abuse; health topics;
exceptional children including the gifted; sex education; television; and the
working mother. Appendix B lists children's magazines. Appendix C is a
directory of poison control centers.

Reviews of Literature

**Child Care, a Comprehensive Guide: Philosophy, Programs and Practices for the
Creation of Quality Service for Children.** Vol. 1. Rationale for Child Care
Services: Programs vs. Politics. (1975). Edited by Stevanne Auerback, James
A. Rivaldo. NY: Human Sciences Press. (Early Childhood Series).

Chapter 1 reports on a 1971 - 1972 study of day care needs and services in 77
cities. Federal child-care legislation up to 1975 is traced. Chapter 2
examines issues in day care from the perspective of the children, their

parents, and the government. Chapter 3 outlines the history of child rearing from medieval days until the beginning of the twentieth century. Chapter 4 provides a brief history of child care in California, the only state to continue support of day care when federal funding ceased in the 1940s. Chapter 5 looks at the needs of children for various types of programs. Chapter 6 outlines procedures for setting up a comprehensive program with government funding. Chapter 7 discusses private enterprise and child care. Chapter 8 outlines basic requirements of a comprehensive child-care system. Chapter 9 discusses citizens' lobbies. Chapter 10 reports Auerbach's 1971 - 1973 study, "Parents and Child Care: A Report on Child Care Consumers in San Francisco." References.

Do Male Teachers in the Early School Years Make a Difference? A Review of the Literature. (1978). Dolores Gold, Myrna Reis. (ED 171 387).

Examines the influence of teacher gender on child behavior and development from nursery school through the later elementary school grades. Implications of social learning and cognitive theories of gender identification and development are explored. Several studies of the effects of male teachers on students, as well as anecdotal reports, are critically reviewed. A few studies of nursery and kindergarten children indicate that male teachers may positively affect boys' perceptions of spatial relations, attitudes, perception of teachers and school environment, sex role identification, and behavior. Only one of the reviewed studies of elementary school children provides significant positive findings. References.

Juggling Jobs and Babies: American's Child Care Challenge. (February 1987). Martin O'Connell, David E. Bloom. In *Population Trends and Public Policy*. No. 12. Washington, DC: Population Reference Bureau.

This paper summarizes the recent trends in labor force participation and outlines some of the obstacles faced by working mothers attempting to juggle job and family duties. References.

Latchkey Children. (1984). Thomas J. Long, Lynnette Long. In *Current Topics in Early Childhood Education*. Vol. 5, edited by Lilian Katz. Norwood, NJ: Ablex.

The chapter provides a synthesis of research concerning the number of and care of children left alone or unattended by parents or other adults. References.

Public Policy for Day Care of Young Children: Organization, Finance, and Planning. (1973). Dennis R. Young, Richard R. Nelson. Lexington, MA: D. C. Heath.

An analysis of the basic issues regarding day care: rationale for public support, economic aspects, delivery systems, and day care policy. Each contributor based their chapter on research. The volume is footnoted by chapter at the close of the book.

Reports of Research

Child Care, Family Benefits, and Working Parents: A Study in Comparative Policy. (1981). Sheila B. Kamerman, Alfred J. Kahn. NY: Columbia Univ. Press.

This volume reports the results of a six-country study investigating child care issues. After surveying fourteen countries, the authors selected six to study in depth: Federal Republic of Germany, France, German Democratic Republic, Hungary, Sweden, and the United States.   In all countries the teams studied social benefits in governmental support of an at-home option as well as child care services. In the last chapter, policy recommendations are made. Footnoted.

Children and Day Nurseries. (1980).   Caroline Garland, Stephanie White. Ypsilanti, MI: High/Scope Press. (Oxford Preschool Research Project).

In this volume the authors record and discuss their research findings after observing nine day nurseries and checking the interview results of each. The authors spent from five to nine hours observing in each of the nurseries representing one of a type available to parents for child care in Britain. The book not only records the studies' findings, but also may serve as a guide for persons planning to open and operate a day nursery. A review of research findings may be found in Chapter 7 of *Under Five in Britain*. References.

Parental Work Patterns in Alternative Families: Influence on Child Development. (1984). Irla Lee Zimmerman, Maurine Bernstein. In *Annual Progress in Child Psychiatry and Child Development*, 1984, edited by Stella Chess, Alexander Thomas. NY: Brunner/Mazel.

This study collected data from a sampling of 200 working mothers and compared their children's social, emotional, and cognitive development. No evidence of negative effects was traceable to maternal absence due to employment. Twenty-two references are cited.

The Role of the Teacher in the Nursery School. (1975).   Joan E. Cass.   NY: Pergamon.

This study looked at the role of the teacher at the nursery school level. Chapter 4 discusses the qualities good teachers possess.   Chapters 5 and 6 explored the necessity of cooperation between the nursery school and the family.   Factors contributing to good home-school relationships were outlined.   Chapter 7 looked at the handicapped child in the nursery school situation.   Chapter 8 described and commented on the duties and relationship of the nursery assistant to the nursery school environment. References.

Selection and Control: Teachers' Ratings of Children in the Infant School. (1974). Walter Brandis, Basil Bernstein. London: Routledge & Kegan Paul.

This monograph presents a study of teachers' ratings of children from middle and working class areas, taken at the end of the first and second school years. The monograph is organized into two main parts.   The first is a technical description of the logic of statistical description, with a primary focus on common features of the ratings across social class.   The second part represents the authors' interpretations of the major findings in which differences in the patterns of teacher judgments in middle-class and working-class areas are examined.   The monograph also includes an appended presentation of interview segments with mothers of the children prior to their school entry.   Questions concerning the preparation of the child for school were asked.   References.

Other References

Child Care: A Comprehensive Guide.   Vol. 2.   Model Programs and Their Components. (1976). Edited by Stevanne Auerbach, James A. Rivaldo. NY: Human Sciences. (Early Childhood Series).

This volume focuses on the planning of model programs and services. Programs started in Portland, OR; Appalachia; Berkeley, CA; Denver, CO; and College Park, MD are covered in chapters 2 - 6. Two chapters deal with strategies for obtaining financial support and establishing community information and referral services for child care. Four chapters are grouped under the general topic "social-psychological welfare of children in day care." Chapters in the third section deal with health care and nutrition. Indexed.

Child Care and ABC's Too. (1975). Sar A. Levitan, Karen Cleary Alderman. Baltimore, MD: Johns Hopkins Univ. Press.

An exploration of the American child-care system. Emphasis is statistical, providing documentation and relevant discussion on topics ranging from mothers in the labor force and their child-care arrangements to the federal child-care dollar and the role of compensatory education. Data collected on characteristics of working mothers and choices for child care are outlined. Child care programs and the relevant problems of providing quality care for all preschool children are discussed. A comprehensive look at the cost of child care including documentation of who pays at what price and for what kind of care is included. A history of child care and exploration of options is presented. The authors examine the role of the federal government in child care and assess the impact of Head Start. References.

The Child Care Handbook: Needs, Programs, and Possibilities. (1982). Franna Diamond. Washington, DC: Children's Defense Fund.

Part I documents social and economic forces contributing to the need for child-care services. Part II describes 12 day care programs in various sections of the United States. Part III spells out what advocates can do to protect and expand existing child-care programs. The four appendixes give lists of people interviewed, addresses of programs described, a list of federal programs supporting child care, and provide an annotated reading list. Footnoted.

Day Care: A Source Book. (1987). Kathleen Pullen Watkins, Lucius Durant, Jr. NY: Garland.

This handbook covers such topics as the roles of care givers, parent involvement, and infant-toddler programs. Focus is placed on standards in the field, issues, and innovations. Each chapter is essay in form followed by a comprehensive annotated bibliography citing books, journal articles, and dissertations published in English from 1980 to 1986 along with landmark works. Indexed.

Developing and Administering a Child Care Center. (1979). Dorothy June Sciarra, Anne G. Dorsey. Dallas and Palo Alto: Houghton Mifflin.

Provides practical information needed to administer either a newly developed or an ongoing child-care program. The 16 chapters are very practical in orientation. Chapter titles are: (1) Developing Interpersonal Relationships; (2) Assessing Community Need and Establishing a Program; (3) Licensing and Certifying; (4) Establishing and Working with a Board; (5) Handling Financial Matters; (6) Funding the Program and Writing Proposals; (7) Developing a Center Facility; (8) Equipping the Center; (9)

Staffing the Center; (10) Publicizing the Center and Selecting Children; (11) Grouping and Enrolling the Children; (12) Managing the Food and the Health and Safety Programs; (13) Evaluation Center Components; (14) Providing for Personal and Professional Staff Development; (15) Working with Parents, Volunteers, and the Community; and (16) the Working Director. Each chapter includes samples of forms, intake procedures, floor plans, equipment lists, personnel evaluation procedures, budgeting, and exercises. References.

40 Innovative Programs in Early Childhood Education. (1973). Edited by Berlie J. Fallon. Belmont, CA: Lear Siegler/Fearon.

Although dated, the monograph provides detailed descriptions of early childhood education programs in operation in the late 1960s and early 1970s in the United States. Two main sections make up the book. Section I, Innovative Programs in Early Childhood Education, provides the descriptions for the programs selected. Section II, Resources Section, includes an overview of the field of study of early childhood education and includes excerpts from materials provided by the schools with exemplary programs. A glossary and table of descriptor terms are included. References.

The New Encyclopedia of Child Care and Guidance. Revised edition. (1968). Edited by Sidonie Matsner Gruenberg. Garden City, NY: Doubleday.

"Defines terms, lists relevant organizations, contains extensive annotated bibliography, and features 30 chapters by specialists on various aspects of child care and guidance."

Who's Minding the Children? The History and Politics of Day Care in America. (1973). Margaret O'Brien Steinfels. NY: Simon and Schuster.

This book presents a historical overview of child care beginning a century ago and traces its growth to the attitudes and realities. A complete discussion of motivations for day care and the concurrent legislation is included. A typical day care is described in terms of adult-child interaction, physical space and equipment, sponsors and resulting program differences, and curriculum, in family day care as well as group day care. The final chapters explore the elements of political debate concerning child care, the resolution of the debate, and questions of social policy and values which the debate touched upon but did not resolve. References.

PROGRAMS

Reviews of Literature

Advances in Early Education and Day Care: A Research Annual. (1980 -). Edited by Sally Kilmer. Greenwich, CT: JAI.

A series begun in 1980 to provide original research and critical analysis on research in the care of children. Each volume focuses on related issues of a general theme. References.

As the Twig is Bent . . . Lasting Effects of Preschool Programs. (1983). Consortium for Longitudinal Studies. Hillsdale, NJ: Lawrence Erlbaum.

This book is a major report from the Consortium for Longitudinal Studies concerning the long-term effects of early educational intervention. Consortium members presented individual investigations which generally identify the same problem, the below-average performance of economically disadvantaged, mostly black, children in public schools. Some of the studies lack good descriptions but readers are referred to other sources for more information. Taken as a whole, the book represents a good history of the various attempts at early intervention. References.

The At-Risk Infant: Psych/Socio/Medical Aspects. (1984). Edited by Shaul Harel, Nicholas Anastasiow. Baltimore, MD: Paul H. Brookes.

This is probably one of the most comprehensive volumes dealing with the at-risk child currently available. The volume is divided into three major sections. Section 1 concerns ecological factors that foster development of high-risk infants and children. Section 2 focuses on pregnancy and perinatal periods. Section 3 focuses on the infant and early childhood period. Each of these sections contains a combination of reviews, empirical studies, and descriptions of various procedures or programs that have been evaluated. Most of the 46 chapters are quite readable. References.

The Challenge of Employer-Supported Child Care: Meeting Parent Needs. (1984). Dana E. Friedman. In *Current Topics in Early Childhood Education*, Vol. 5, edited by Lilian Katz. Norwood, NY: Ablex. (Current Topics in Early Childhood Education).

The chapter synthesizes the literature about operating an employer-supported child care facility.

The Child and the Day Care Setting: Qualitative Variations and Development. (1984). Edited by Ricardo C. Ainslie. NY: Praeger.

The chapters in this monograph look at the effects day care has on the child. In the first chapter an overview of day care research is given, its accomplishments, and limitations. Subsequent chapters help to differentiate the forms and features of child care as they present opportunities and risks for the developing child. The majority of the chapters focus on the care of infants and toddlers and their care givers. The final three chapters provide summaries of research on children's attachments, response to separation, and maternal separation anxiety. The coverage of the volume is not comprehensive in terms of either the age periods of types of child care settings covered. References.

Child Care: A Comprehensive Guide. Vol. 3.   Creative Centers and Homes. (1978). Edited by Stevanne Auerbach. NY: Human Sciences Press. (Early Education Series).

This volume examines the question, At what age should a child enter a program? The core of the volume focuses on various family day care programs including procedures and problems in certifying and regulating family day care homes. Very briefly, the volume looks at the interior and exterior environments for maximum stimulation, enrichment and efficiency in child care programs. Although outdated, it provides a good description of early home day care systems such as FDCH Systems or a particular program such as the Neighborhood Day Care Program (NDCP). References.

Child Care: A Comprehensive Guide. Vol. 4. Special Needs and Services. (1979). NY: Human Science. (Early Education Series).

Chapter 1 describes the Santa Monica Children's Center in operation since 1943 by the California State Department of Education. Chapter 2 discusses a curriculum whereby high school students can earn credit by working with children in child care settings. Chapter 3 explores the process of preparing child care personnel. Chapter 4 examines the role of play in the physical, mental, and social development of children. Chapter 5 describes the Education for Parenthood Program initiated by HEW in 1972. Chapter 6 reports on the Extended Family Center, established to deal with special problems of abused children. Chapter 7 describes the program at Berkeley's Early Growth Center, a pioneer project in mainstreaming. Chapter 8 looks at the black community's involvement in child care. Chapters 9 - 11 look at programs for Chicano, Filipino, and Chinese children. Chapter 12 discusses the involvement of parents in child care programs. Chapter 13 discusses the services developed by the Child Care Switchboard of San Francisco to help parents in locating dependable child care. Chapter 14 looks into the need of cooperative measures between agencies in child care. Chapter 15 focuses on future needs of child care services. Although now superseded by more recent publications, this volume will be of value to researchers studying early programs and efforts at child care. References.

Contemporary Education for Children Ages Two to Eight: Recent Studies of Educational Intervention. (1973). Edited by Julian C. Stanley. Baltimore, MD: Johns Hopkins Univ. Press. (Blumberg Series).

In this volume five studies reported are experiments or quasi-experiments on preschool intervention with the goal of improving the educability of children ages two through grade three. The emphasis is on starting early, at age four or less, and continuing the facilitation as long as feasible. Chapter 2 is a paper on research on *Sesame Street*. Chapter 4 discusses variations in Head Start and Follow Through. Chapter 6, by Virginia C. Shipman, reports a longitudinal study on first school experiences and disadvantaged children. References.

Current Research in Early Childhood Education: A Compilation and Analysis for Program Planners. (1970). Anne L. Butler. Washington, DC: American Association of Elementary Kindergarten Nursery Educators, NEA Center.

This review of literature covering 1964 to the publication date focuses on the outcomes of early childhood education or on analysis of factors constituting early childhood education. This is one of a series initiated by the Association of Elementary Kindergarten Nursery Educators in 1960. Series titles, cited in the bibliography, are less than 100 pages long. Some are available through ERIC.

Day Care. (1982). Alison Clarke-Stewart. Cambridge, MA: Harvard Univ. Press. (The Developing Child).

This comprehensive volume looks at the effects of day care on young children. The book is factual, research-based, and cogent. Chapter 3 provides a brief history of day care in the United States, including how day care was used as a political football for 50 years. Chapter 4 delves into some of the creative methods families use in arranging care for their children. In the middle chapters, the author examines the effect of day care on the child. She points out that physical development is accelerated for poor families, but not in middle-class children. Health problems of day care children are covered. Her studies show that day care children do as well or better than children at home, even when care standards are only minimal. She also concludes that day care children are as attached to their mothers, just not so intensely physical, as home bound children. Chapter 6 examines why some day care programs accelerate children's development of independence. She examines different types of programs, looking at structured versus unstructured programs. Chapter 7 examines care giver qualities. Chapter 10 looks at alternative care systems in other parts of the world. References.

Day Care and the Public Schools: Profiles of Five Communities. (1978). James A. Levine. Newton, MA: Education Development Center.

This monograph describes public school affiliated day care in five communities throughout the United States. Each program described represents a different type of school involvement with day care: preschool and after-school care; after-school care; infant and toddler care; and family day care. Chapter 4 contains the descriptions of the programs. Chapter 5 is a synthesis of findings and recommendations. The book contains an annotated bibliography of cited resources.

Day Care: Scientific and Social Policy Issues. (1982). Edited by Edward Zigler, Edmund W. Gordon. Boston, MA: Auburn House.

The first section of the book focuses on theoretical and social policy issues related to child care with emphasis on infant care. Chapter 6 deals with environmental differences among day care centers and their effect on the child's development. Chapters are included on the Yale Child Welfare Program and the National Day Care Study. Part II covers the legislator's perspective and the third, and last part, covers social policy issues. In this last section, chapters cover black day care and school-age child care. References.

Development and Policy Concerning Children with Special Needs. (1983). Edited by Marion Perlmutter. Hillsdale, NJ: Lawrence Erlbaum. (Minnesota Symposium on Child Psychology, Vol. 16).

The volume contains six papers concerning children with special needs. The content areas covered include: interactions of high risk infants and parents; maladaptation in preschoolers; self-control in young handicapped children; attention deficit disorder; preschool intervention for the poor; and child abuse. References.

Early Childhood Education: Special Problems, Special Solutions. (1982). K. Eileen Allen, Elizabeth M. Goetz. Rockville, MD: Systems Corp. Publication.

Reviews research related to behavioral analysis of early identification and intervention of developmental problems in young handicapped, normal, and at-risk children. Lengthy bibliographies are provided as well as an index to the volume.

The Effects of Day Care: A Critical Review. (December 1978). J. Belsky,   L. Steinberg. In *Child Development*, 49 (4).

The authors review a substantial amount of the published research on day care after noting that the literature is quite narrow in scope. The research reviewed indicates that day care is neither beneficial nor harmful to the child's intellectual development. Day care does not disrupt the child's bonding with the mother. Day care children compared with home-care children interact more with peers in both positive and negative ways. References.

Experiments in Primary Education: Aspects of Project Follow-Through. (1970). Eleanor E. Maccoby, Miriam Zellner. NY: Harcourt, Brace and Jovanovich.

This book re-examines some of the experimental programs in Project Follow-Through. Some of the psychological assumptions underlying the program are examined. One chapter contrasts the several educational philosophies and pedagogical methods and attempts to discover how the one leads to the other. This is a good overview of Project Follow-Through for those with limited background.

Facilitating Infant and Early Childhood Development. (1982). Edited by Lynne A. Bond, Justin M. Joffe. Hanover, VT: Univ. Press of New England. (Primary Prevention of Psychopathy, Vol. 6).

The twenty papers making up this volume review what is known about the prevention of disturbance and of handicapping conditions. The book ties together broad theories and perennial questions with data from historical and on-going research and service programs. The book is divided into four parts. The first gives a theoretical perspective of the notion of promotion of optimal development as the focus of prevention. Part II delves into identification of risk. Part III reviews intervention programs and how they work. Part IV centers on social policy. References.

Families, Schools, and Delinquency Prevention. (1987). Edited by James Q. Wilson, Glenn C. Loury. NY: Springer-Verlag. (From *Children to Citizens*. Vol. 2).

This volume addresses issues related to opportunities for delinquency prevention through early intervention. Findings suggest that providing quality preschool programs may be an effective way to prevent juvenile delinquency. Part I contains three chapters covering introductory essays on the problem. Part II has two chapters. The first discusses what can be learned from family studies of juvenile conduct problems and delinquency. The second reviews studies of parenting patterns which result in delinquent children. Part III contains Chapters 6 - 8. Schweinhart discusses whether preschool programs can prevent delinquency. Zigler and Hall look at the implications of early intervention efforts. The final chapter in the section looks at prevention through parent training. Part IV, entitled The Family and Public Policy, has four chapters. Each chapter covers a different institutional need for public policy in this area: the courts, the federal government, and the community. Lengthy bibliographies follow each chapter.

Found: **Long-Term Gains from Early Intervention.** (1978). Bernard Brown. Boulder, CO: Westview. (AAAS Selected Symposia Series).

Each chapter is individually authored and presents the research findings of various studies showing positive results of early intervention. Chapters 3 and 4 cover special projects such as the New Haven Project and the Developmental Continuity Consortium Study. Chapter 5 is a review of Head Start research since 1969. Chapter 6 provides an overview of research of long-term gains from early intervention. Cited sources may be found at the end of the text and at the end of some chapters.

The Impact of Head Start on Children, Families and Communities: Final Report of the Head Start Evaluation, Synthesis and Utilization Project. (1985). R. H. McKay, L. Condelli, J. Ganson, B. J. Barnett, C. McConkey, M. C. Plantz, Washington, DC: Government Printing Office.

The project involved the collection of over 1,600 documents related to Head Start and the analysis and synthesis of 210 reports of research on the effects of local Head Start programs. This review is distinguished from others in two ways. First, it includes all Head Start research, both published and unpublished, rather than focusing on a subset of studies related to a specific topic. Second, when possible it uses the statistical techniques known as meta-analysis to produce numerical estimates of Head Start's effects. The report presents findings on: cognitive development, socioemotional development, children's health, families enrollees, and communities where Head Start programs operate. Appendix D is a bibliography of references from Chapters 3 - 7.

Infant Psychiatry: A New Synthesis. (1976). Eveoleen N. Rexford, Louis W. Gander, Theodore Shapiro. New Haven, CT: Yale Univ. Press. (Monographs of the *Journal of American Academy of Child Psychiatry*, No. 2).

This is a collection of papers on infant research and early intervention programs. The papers come from two sources: issues of the journal published during its first decade; and a 1971 symposium on primary prevention and early intervention. Sections I and II deal with studies of the baby and his caretaker. Sections III and IV present reports on clinical efforts to intervene with infants at risk. Substantial bibliography.

Intervention Strategies for High Risk Infants and Young Children. (1976). Edited by Theodore D. Tjossem. Baltimore, MD: Univ. Park Press. (NICHD-Mental Retardation Research Centers Series).

The first section introduces early intervention issues and approaches. The section devoted to case finding, screening, diagnosis, and tracking gives insight into the art of early diagnosis of at-risk infants. The demonstration projects section discusses at length eleven well-known models of early intervention having national recognition (Portage Project, Read Project, National Collaboration Infant Project, Carolina Abecedarian Project). How education, nursing, and medicine discharge their responsibilities is covered in the State-of-the-Art section. International programs of intervention are reviewed in the "international perspective" section. References.

Is Early Intervention Effective? (1975). Urie Bronfenbrenner. In *Handbook of Evaluation Research*, Vol. 2, edited by Marcia Guttentag, Elmer Struening. Beverly Hills, CA: Sage.

This chapter is a reanalysis of many evaluation studies of early intervention. Bronfenbrenner's secondary analysis yields some fresh insights, for example, the suggestion that intervention should be family centered rather than child centered. The chapter concludes with a lengthy bibliography.

Learning from Experience: Evaluating Early Childhood Demonstration Programs. (1982). Edited by Jeffrey R. Travers, Richard J. Light. Washington, DC: National Academy.

This collection characterizes developments in programs and policies for children and families that challenge traditional approaches to evaluations as well as tracing the implications for outcome measurement and for the broader conduct of evaluation studies. Various types of information evaluators of early childhood programs might collect are identified. One paper by Melvin Levine and Judity Palfrey covers a range of issues in health measurement. A taxonomy of measurement approaches to day care is provided. Chapters contain their own references.

Long-Term Effects of Infant Stimulation Programs. (1981). Barry J. Guinagh, R. Emile Jester. In *Advances in Behavioral Pediatrics, a Research Annual*, Vol. 2, edited by Bonnie Camp. Greenwich, CT: JAI.

Reviews research covering programs for infants under the age of three. Indications are that intervention programs that focus on parents show long-term treatment effects but programs ignoring parents do not. References.

The Preschool in Action: Exploring Early Childhood Programs. Second edition. (1977). Edited by Mary Carol Day, Ronald K. Parker. Boston, MA: Allyn & Bacon.

Part I describes programs falling into the category of infant and home-based programs. The second part looks at programs which are center-based preschool programs. The authors of each chapter address the following topics: theoretical and research foundations of the program, curriculum objectives, selection of content, organization of content, methods of implementation, and formative and summative research and evaluation.

Preschool Programs and Later School Competence of Children from Low-Income Families. (1980.) R. B. Darlington, J. M. Royce, A. S. Snipper, H. W. Murray, I. Lazar. In *Science*, 208 (4440), 202 - 204.

A research study looking at the effectiveness of preschool programs for low-income children in light of improved school competence at a later date. The study concluded that children in the preschool program did show achievement gains evidenced by a lower frequency of placement in special education classes and in grade retention. Seventeen references.

Preschool Programs for the Disadvantaged: Five Experimental Approaches to Early Childhood Education. (1972.) Edited by Julian C. Stanley. Baltimore, MD: Johns Hopkins. (Blumberg Series).

The common theme running through the papers in this volume is improving the educational readiness of preschoolers from environments that do not provide the cognitive stimulation most middle-class children receive. References.

Project Head Start: A Legacy of the War on Poverty. (1979). Edward Zigler, Jeannette Valentine. NY: Free Press.

This volume is a very complete account of project Head Start's first thirteen years. Part V is an evaluation of the program at that time. A very valuable and useful bibliography of Head Start during the first ten years follows the text.

Quality in Child Care: What Does Research Tell Us? (1987). Edited by Deborah A. Phillips. Washington, DC: National Association for the Education of Young Children. (Research Monographs of the National Association for the Education of Young Children, Vol. 1).

The first of a new series of annual research monographs summarizes "third wave" research on the issue of quality day care. Individual chapters: report the results from the Bermuda Study which focused on the social development of children; outline the Pennsylvania Day Care Study; discuss the Los Angeles Study; look at dimensions of care giver stability and training, and staff-child ratios in centers that serve infants and toddlers; and describe the Victoria Study Research Project in Canada which focused on children's language development in child care. References.

Sandbox Society: Early Education in Black and White America--A Comparative Ethnography. (1985). Sally Lubeck. Philadelphia, PA: Falmer Press.

This book contains an extensive review of classic research and writings about social systems and cross-cultural studies on child rearing. Lubeck also notes less frequently cited writings and research about the cultural context of functional adaptive strategies observed among African and African-American people. Users should note that a few of the cited resources are missing from the bibliography. Overall the book describes observations made by Lubeck in comparing teachers' child-rearing beliefs and practices on the use of time, space, and activities in two early education settings: one a black Head Start center and the other a white middle-class preschool setting. References.

Social Development in Childhood: Day Care Programs and Research. (1977). Edited by Roger A. Webb. Baltimore, MD: Johns Hopkins Univ. Press. (Hyman Blumberg Symposia on Research in Early Childhood Education).

The papers in this volume all are related to the problems of intervention into social development. Some of the papers are theoretical while others are applied. Chapter 1 discusses home-reared children and mother-child interaction. Chapter 5 looks at peer interaction in preschool children. Chapter 6 by Phyllis T. Elardo discusses the Project Aware, a school program to facilitate the social development of children. References.

Reports of Research

All Things Bright and Beautiful? A Sociological Study of Infants' Classrooms. (1978). Ronald King. NY: John Wiley & Sons.

Study is concerned with describing, analyzing, and explaining the activities occurring in ordinary classrooms. The author observed in three English schools: Social Priority School, Burnley Road; Seaton Park School; and the Langley School; recording the activities of students as well as teachers. Forty references.

Changed Lives, the Effects of the Perry Preschool Program on Youths through Age 19. (1984). John R. Berueta-Clement, Lawrence J. Schweinhart, W. Steven Barnett, Ann S. Epstein, David P. Weikart. Ypsilanti, MI: High/Scope Educational Research Foundation. (Monographs of the High/Scope Educational Research Foundation, No. 8).

This monograph is the eighth in a series reporting the Foundation's longitudinal research on the effects of early childhood education. The Project studied 123 black, low-SES youths who were at risk of failing in school. The purpose of the study was to explore the long-terms effects of participation versus non-participation in a program of high-quality early childhood education. At ages three to four, subjects drawn from a single school attendance area were divided into an experimental group that received a high quality preschool program and a control group that received no preschool program. Information about these youngsters on hundreds of variables has been collected and examined annually from ages three to eleven, and at ages 14, 15, and 19. Results to age 19 indicate lasting beneficial effects of preschool education in improving cognitive performance during early childhood; in proving scholastic placement and achievement during the school year; in decreasing delinquency and crime, the use of welfare assistance, and the incidence of teenage pregnancy; and in increasing high school graduation rates and the frequency of enrollment in postsecondary programs and employment. References.

Children at the Center: Summary Findings and Their Implications. Final Report of the National Day Care Study, Vol. 1. March 1979. (1979). Richard Ruopp, Jeffrey Travers, Frederic Glautz, Craig Coelen. Cambridge, MA: Abt. (ED 131 928).

The central purpose of this first volume of the NDCS final report is to explore the effects of decisions on children and costs as they affect federal policy. Chapters 1 through 5 provide a descriptive content of the study's findings which are presented in chapters 6 and 7. In Chapter 8 the implications of these findings for federal purchasing regulations are examined. References.

Continuity between Home and Day Care: A Model for Defining Relevant Dimensions of Child Care. (1985). Florence Long, Donald L. Peters, Laurie Garduque. In *Advances in Applied Developmental Psychology*, Vol. 1, edited by Irving Sigel. Norwood, NJ: Ablex. (Advances in Applied Developmental Psychology).

The study examined the premise that day care is inferior to home care. For middle-class families the assumption is that there is an ideal standard of child-rearing beliefs practiced, whereas in the low-income families certain discontinuities exist between day care and the home because of less favorable child-rearing beliefs. References.

Day Care and Intervention Programs for Infants. (1972). Marshall M. Haith. Atlanta, GA: Avatar.

This short report was originally written as a review of current infant day care and intervention programs for the guidance of participants in a two-week workshop in 1970. Programs are divided into day care, intervention, and child centers, with some attention given to programs for the handicapped as well as those outside the United States. A similar format is used in describing each program, with interest focused on "purpose, theoretical orientation, characteristics, facilities, and staffing." An insert chart concisely presents fourteen "infant programs at a glance." Anyone tracing the development of infant day care programs or looking for a description of one of the early programs will find this slim volume a fruitful resource. Several pages of references are provided. The appendix is a chart of the specific lesson plans used in the Weikart and Lambie study.

Day Care and Its Effects on Early Development: A Study of Group and Home Care in Multi-Ethnic, Working-Class Families. (1978).   William Fowler. Toronto, Canada: Ontario Institute for Studies in Education.

This monograph presents a five-year study of the effects of group day care and home care on the cognitive (including language and perceptual motor), motivational, and socioemotional development of children six months to five years old in metropolitan Toronto. A group of children reared entirely in the home were studied for comparison. The day care children came primarily from single parent homes. The home-care children came from two-parent homes where the mother was a full-time homemaker. The study's results are complex, although clearly presented in both tabular and graphic form. In essence, the longitudinal analyses present a consistent picture of mean differences across measure favoring the home-reared children, though not significantly. The correlational analyses suggest a differential, changing pattern of associations for the two groups, from infancy to early childhood, between the developmental measures and a complex set of program, child-rearing resource, and parental factors. The clearest patterns of findings seem to indicate: (1) the importance of parent training for early development, particularly language, and (2) the detrimental effects of large staff-child ratios (1:9+) and rapid staff turnover (up to 20% per month) as experienced by the older children. References.

Day Care for Three-Year-Olds: An Interdisciplinary Experimental Study. (1982). Marianne Cederblad. In *The Child in His Family, Children in Turmoil: Tomorrow's Parents,* Vol. 7, edited by James Anthony, Calette Chiland. NY: John Wiley & Sons.

This chapter reports a lengthy study carried out in Stockholm which investigated the effect of care taker to child ratio on behavior. Special emphasis was placed on the reduction of stress level. Findings show that increasing the ratio of caretakers to children does bring about tangible improvements in the children's behavior. Thirteen cited references are given along with a bibliography of all of the reports from the project.

Developmental Intervention with Young Physically Handicapped Children. (1975). Philip L. Safford, Dena C. Arbitman. Springfield, IL: Charles C. Thomas.

This volume provides a comprehensive description of the Human Early Education Development Project (HEED), concerned with developmental intervention for young physically handicapped children. Major contributions to the volume come from physical therapists, teachers, and case workers in collaboration with the authors.

An Economic Analysis of the Ypsilanti Perry Preschool Project. (1978). C. U. Weber, P. W. Foster, D. P. Weikart. Ypsilanti, MI: High/Scope Educational Research Foundation. (Monographs of the High/Scope Educational Foundation, No. 5.)

This paper presents a benefit cost analysis of the Ypsilanti Perry Preschool Project. Results indicate that the costs of this intervention program for disadvantaged children were more than compensated by the benefits to society. The report is well illustrated with charts and tables. References.

Education and Day Care for Young Children in Need: The American Experience. (1973). Tessa Blackstone. London: Bedford Square Press of the National Council of Social Service. (Doughty Street Paper No. 1).

This is the report of 13 British specialists who visited the United States in 1972 through a Ford Foundation grant to study child-care programs. The report sets forth some of the impressions and conclusions reached by the team. Thirty-seven references are provided.

Effectiveness of Early Special Education for Handicapped Children. (1982). Brian A. McNulty, David B. Smith, Elizabeth W. Soper. Report Commissioned by the Colorado General Assembly, Colorado Department of Education.

Study shows that handicapped children who participated in preschool programs: (1) scored significantly higher on language skills testing; (2) significantly fewer needed special education services; and (3) it cost the school district less to serve students who entered the program early. Contains good bibliography on intervention strategies for high-risk infants.

The Evolution of an Intervention Programme for Disadvantaged Children. (1977). Thomas Kellaghan. Atlantic Highlands, NJ: Humanities.

Describes an experimental program which attempted to prevent educational failure of disadvantaged Dublin children. In the first two chapters, the definition of the disadvantaged is discussed and previous educational programs in the United States and Great Britain are reviewed.   The preschool program, which focused on the general cognitive, language, and personality/social development, continued for five years with ninety children starting at three years of age. The curriculum was based on Piagetian principles. The subjects attended classes two and one-half hours each day. Parents participated in parents' meetings and were encouraged to visit classes.   In addition to the Stanford-Binet and Cattrell Culture Fair Intelligence Tests, scales of the perceptual-motor, language, preschool attainment, cognitive style, personality, and home environment were administered to experimental subjects at ages three and eight and to disadvantaged and nondisadvantaged control groups at age eight.   The program was successful in preventing the Binet-IQ decrement with increasing age. The preschool was most effective for low-IQ children but produced little or no effect for above-average children. The experimental subjects did not exceed control groups in other measures. The concluding chapter summarizes the entire book sufficiently for a hurried reader. References.

Family Day Care in the United States: Executive Summary. Final Report of the National Day Care Home Study.   (1981).   Patricia Divine Hawkins. Cambridge, MA: Abt. (ED 211 224).

A synopsis of the findings from all six NDCHS components including data on family day care providers, the children in their care, and the children's parents. The summary additionally presents information on the nature of the day care in each of the NDCHS settings and presents both cost and program data on family day care systems. Lists all the National Day Care Home Studies which may be located in ERIC (ED nos. 221 218 to 211 223).

From 3 to 20:   The Early Training Project.   (1982).   Susan W. Gray, Barbara K. Ramsey, Rupert A. Klaus.   Baltimore, MD: Univ. Park Press.

This book describes the Early Training Project and its longitudinal follow up. The project began in 1962 as an intervention directed at preventing the progressive retardation of a group of 86 black children from low socioeconomic backgrounds in the southern United States.   Unlike most other early intervention projects undertaken during the 1960s, however, the present project followed up on the children who were involved in the study to age 21 (in 1979).   Most previous longitudinal studies of this duration have dealt with middle-class families, making this book a unique contribution to longitudinal studies of early experiences on later achievement.   The follow-up measures included standardized achievement, intelligence, teachers' ratings, and interviews with the participants. The general pattern suggested greater effects from the intervention for females than for males. References.

Home Teaching with Mother & Infants: The Ypsilanti-Carnegie Infant Education Project, an Experiment.   (1974, 1980).   Dolores Lambie, James T. Bond, David P. Weikart.   Ypsilanti, MI: The High/Scope Press.   (Monographs of the High/Scope Educational Research Foundation, No. 2).

The initial account of High/Scope's experiment in home-based parent-infant education.   Chapters cover the project's philosophy of infant education, characteristics of the families selected for the project, implementation of the program, experimental design, and initial results of the research.   The findings show the program's effectiveness in supporting communication between mothers and children. References.

Lasting Effects of Early Education: A Report from the Consortium for Longitudinal Studies.   (1982).   Irving Lazar, Richard Darlington.   In *Monographs of the Society for Research in Child Development*, No. 195, Vol. 47, Nos. 2 - 3.   Chicago, IL: Univ. of Chicago Press.

Monograph assesses the long-term effects of early childhood education experience on children from low-income families.   In 1976, twelve investigators, who had independently designed and implemented infant and preschool programs in the 1960s, pooled their original data and conducted a collaborative follow-up of the original subjects, aged 9 - 19 at the time. Results show that early education programs for children from low-income families had long-lasting effects in four areas; school competence, developed abilities, children's attitudes and values, and impact on the family. Substantial bibliography.

Matchmaking in Neighborhood Day Care. (1971). Arthur C. Emlen, Eunice L. Watson. Corvallis, OR: Oregon State University, Continuing Education.

This monograph describes and evaluates the data obtained through a two-year study of a type of day-care service known as the Day Care Neighbor Service. The Service intervenes at the neighborhood level where families privately and without benefit of a social agency make day care arrangements with neighborhood sitters or care givers. This report concentrates on reporting the findings of the authors and their evaluation of the program. The monograph is footnoted.

Mental Health and Going to School: The Woodlawn Program of Assessment, Early Intervention, and Evaluation. (1975). Sheppard G. Kellam, Jeanette D. Branch, Khazan C. Agrawal, Margaret E. Ensminger. Chicago, IL: Univ. of Chicago Press.

This volume is a report on an urban-based mental health intervention program for first-grade children. Conducted by a team of psychiatrists, social workers, and other mental health specialists, the program addressed the children's psychological well-being and social adaptational status. These two concepts served as the theoretical bases of the specialists' notion of mental health. The core of the program involved weekly small group meetings in the classrooms by a psychiatrist and teacher. The meetings were described as informal sessions during which pupils were allowed to express their feelings, views, and observations about experiences that they had recently encountered. The authors' report that the intervention program had differential results: boys benefitted more than girls; younger children gained more than older children; and mildly maladapted children were helped more. Correlates of academic achievement were also reported. References.

Mental Health Programs for Preschool Children (A Field Study). (1974). Raymond M. Glasscote, Michael E. Fishman. Washington, DC: American Psychiatric Association, Joint Information Service.

This book reports a joint information service field study (American Psychiatric Association and National Mental Health Association) conducted in 1972 - 1973 in eight centers. It focuses on services to children under six years of age, a target group that, according to NIMH studies, receives less than 1% of the direct services provided through mental health. Part I of the book includes a brief review of the literature available on needs and care of young children. Part II presents an overview of seven of eight programs visited and studied: The Dubnoff Center, North Hollywood; a "quartet of programs" in Topeka; Project Enlightenment, Raleigh; Developmental Center for Autistic Children, Philadelphia; M. L. King, Jr. Parent-Child Center, Baltimore; Division of Child Psychiatry, Cedars-Sinai Medical Center, Los Angeles; and the Pre-School Unit, Cambridge-Somerville

Mental Health and Retardation Center, Massachusetts.   The appendix presents a simple and straightforward instrument for data collection. Footnoted.

Research Results of the National Day Care Study: Final Report. (1980). Jeffrey Travers, Barbara Dillon Goodson. Cambridge, MA: Abt Books. (National Day Care Study Series).

Provides sufficient information to judge the soundness of the evidence underlying the study's search for day care center characteristics which can both protect children from harm as well as foster their social, emotional, and cognitive development. Findings indicated that these outcomes are clearly attainable when groups of children are small and when care givers receive training in child-related areas. It also found that relaxing the staff/child ratio would not adversely affect children but could lower costs substantially and this enables more children to receive care. A bibliography of the National Day Care Studies is included.

Take A Giant Step: An Equal Start in Education for All New York City Four-Year-Olds, Final Report. (1986). Early Childhood Education Commission, New York City: Saul B. Cohan, Chairman. New York City: City of New York, Office of the Mayor.

A comprehensive report of the state of four-year-olds in New York City and the programs in which they are enrolled, their educational needs, and recommendations for implementing a universal educational program. In July 1985, Mayor Koch appointed a commission to recommend how best to implement his proposal to phase in universally available preschool education for four-year-olds beginning in September 1986. This is the commission's report. They formulated ten recommendations for implementing the mayor's proposal. Chapter 1 sets forth the ten recommendations and discusses them. Chapter 2 is a review of the literature on effects of early childhood education which the commission looked at in making its recommendations. Chapter 3 gives demographics and enrollment patterns of preschool children in New York City. Chapter 4 reviews already existing publicly funded preschool programs servicing four-year-olds. Chapter 5 looks at elements of quality educational preschool programs. Chapter 6 covers sets in implementation of the New York City program. Chapter 7 goes into the economics of financing the program.   Appendix 1 outlines the preschool programs of the Department of Parks and Recreation. Appendix 2 outlines in chart form the components of the Early Childhood Program. References.

Young Children Grow Up: The Effects of the Perry Preschool Program on Youths through Age 15. (1980). L. J. Schweinhart, D. P. Weikart. Ypsilanti, MI: High/Scope Educational Research Foundation.   (Monographs of the High/Scope Education Research Foundation, No. 7).

A landmark study that found that children who went to preschool had higher scores on achievement tests and were more strongly committed to schooling, and their parents were better satisfied with their school performance. As teenagers, those with preschool were less involved in delinquent activities. This study provides the empirical evidence advocates of early childhood programs need to support their belief in the lasting worth of high quality early childhood education for disadvantaged children. References.

The Ypsilanti-Carnegie Infant Education Project: Longitudinal Follow-Up. (1979). Ann S. Epstein, David P. Weikart.   Ypsilanti, MI: The High/Scope Educational Research Foundation.   (Monographs of the High/Scope Educational Research Foundation, No. 6).

This report on High/Scope's experimental home-visiting program focuses on three major topics: the long-term impact of the parent-infant program on mother-child interactions; children's development as learners; and the relation between interaction and development. Parents and children were studied when the children were two and again when they were seven. The study found that the mother's styles of interaction with their children tended to remain consistent over this five-year period and that certain styles were better than others as predictors of children's academic success and language development. References.

The Ypsilanti Perry Preschool Project: Preschool Years and Longitudinal Results through Fourth Grade. (1978). D. P. Weikart, J. T. Bond, J. T. McNeil. Ypsilanti, MI: High/Scope Educational Research Foundation (Monographs of the High/Scope Educational Research Foundation, No. 3).

This monograph analyzes data obtained on the experimental and control groups as they progressed through fourth grade. Presents solid evidence, grounded in a rigorous methodological framework, that preschool does indeed make a difference for children. This is an early report on results from High/Scope's renowned study of the long-term effects of preschool education. References.

The Ypsilanti Preschool Curriculum Demonstration Project: Preschool Year and Longitudinal Results. (1978). D. P. Weikart, A. S. Epstein, L. Schweinhart, J. T. Bond. Ypsilanti, MI: High/Scope Educational Research Foundation (Monographs of the High/Scope Educational Research Foundation, No. 4).

The Curriculum Demonstration Project was designed to compare the effectiveness, under carefully controlled experimental conditions, of three preschool programs that represented the dominant approaches to early childhood education during the late 1960s: a cognitively oriented "open framework" approach; a programmed approach emphasizing language training; and a "child-centered" approach based on the traditional nursery school. Project children were identified as economically disadvantaged and academically high-risk. Results provide evidence of preschool's impact that is contrary to the well-publicized negative evaluations of other preschool interventions. References.

Other References

The Child Care Catalog: A Handbook of Resources and Information on Child Care. (1985). Randy Lee Comfort, Constance D. Williams. Littleton, CO: Libraries Unlimited.

Like an almanac, the book provides useful information about day-care options, resources and referral centers, starting and operating a day-care facility, information concerning special needs children, and legal aspects of child care. Information on employer sponsored child care, school-age child care, training for day-care providers and staff, and nutrition in day care settings may also be found in the catalog. Guidelines for selecting day care, unique and interesting child care programs and explanations of how to search for, to acquire, and to use library information are given. Pertinent organizations and addresses are provided where applicable. Indexed.

Contemporary Preschool Education: A Program for Young Children. (1973). Shirley G. Moore, Sally Kilmer. NY: John Wiley.

The opening chapters present a brief, but thorough, summary of the preschool program at the University of Minnesota together with a historical overview of preschool education which would be well suited for introductory reading in a course on the history and philosophy of early childhood education. The chapter on discipline presents behavior modification in a positive, realistic manner. A related chapter outlines methods for developing independence and self-confidence such as allowing ample time for assigned tasks and reinforcement upon completion. A fairly detailed discussion is provided of the author's views on curriculum which includes preacademic skills, social studies, geography, science, arts and crafts, and play activities, all of which would be particularly useful and thought-provoking to any preschool teacher. References.

Developing and Administering Early Childhood Programs. (1983). V. Lombardo, E. Lombardo. Springfield, IL: C. C. Thomas.

Intended as a handbook for those involved in developing or administering a child-care program, the books offers regulatory agency requirements, from zoning to parenting, applicable to every state. One chapter deals with the indoor and outdoor and environmental needs including equipment. Information on staff selection and training is given along with a list of books, articles, and audio-visuals to use in training. A section of sample forms and the policy handbook for staff members is given. Practical suggestions on newsletters, parent conferences, open houses, seminars, parent-child workshops, parent libraries, family picnics, and parent handbooks is also given. Common sense budget planning is explored.

Early Childhood Education Study: Washington's Three- and Four-Year-Olds, Dec. 1981. (1983). Olympia, WA: State Printer.

Report of a study made from April 16, 1981 through December 31, 1981 on the condition of early childhood education in the state of Washington.

Early Intervention for Handicapped and At-Risk Children: An Introduction to Early Childhood Special Education. (1987). Nancy L. Peterson. Prospect Hill, NC: Love.

This book covers historical and theoretical issues in early childhood special education, categories of children with special needs, service delivery models of special education, and resources in the field. It is comprehensive in scope, including evaluation models, the impact of an at-risk child upon parents and families, and traditional areas of concern. References.

Employer-Supported Child Care: Investing in Human Resources. (1984). Sandra L. Burud, Pamela R. Aschbacher, Jacquelyn McCroskey. Boston, MA: Auburn House.

The major source of information for this manual was the study of employer-supported child-care programs conducted by the National Employer-Supported Child Care Project in 1982. Written and telephone surveys were used to gather information from 415 active employer-supported child-care programs throughout the country. Information from the study appears throughout the book. Some of it is presented quantitatively, some is used to illustrate program development approaches, and some has been drawn upon in developing the how-to materials. The book is divided into five major topical areas: overview; benefits to companies; determining needs and decision making; implementing program options; and conclusions. The manual will be of help to employers and others investigating employer-sponsored child care. Appendix E lists by state employer-supported child-care programs in existence at the time of publication. References.

The Employer's Guide to Child Care: Developing Programs for Working Parents. (1985). Barbara Adolf, Karol Rose. NY: Praeger.

This is a practical manual for employers who wish to set up a child-care facility for their employees. The book is designed for business professionals who are interested in responding to the specific needs of parents employed in their companies. Each section provides information and relevant worksheets about a specific phase of employer involvement. The worksheets assist employers in assessing needs, identifying options, and outlining program implementation. Information is given about what quality child care is and how to identify it. An excellent bibliography may be found on pages 145 through 151. Six appendixes cover: licensing offices in states; sample operating budgets; tax credit guide; assistance plans for dependent care; and a list of organizations involved in child care.

The Focus Is on Children: The Bank Street Approach to Early Childhood Education as Enacted in Follow Through. (1976). Elizabeth C. Gilkeson, Garda W. Bowman. NY: Bank Street College of Education.

The best description of the Bank Street Approach to Early Childhood Education. The first section describes what happens in a Bank Street classroom. The second section addresses the theoretical foundations of their approach to educating young children. The third section describes the dynamics of the change process which was enacted in Follow Through Project. No bibliography nor index is provided.

The Infant Center: A Complete Guide to Organizing and Managing Infant Day Care. (1977). Emily Herbert-Jackson, Marion O'Brien, Jan Porterfield, Todd R. Risley. Baltimore, MD: Univ. Park Press.

The book is divided into five parts. The first provides an overview to infant day care and discusses arrangement of space. The second part deals with common concerns of the care giver: play, feeding, diapering, sleep, receiving/departures, and handling emergencies and illness. Part III, intended for the supervisor of the day care, covers: parent relations, personnel issues, quality of care, and other duties. Part IV contains two chapters on administration of a center. Part V contains the appendixes which included suggested readings, list of equipment, samples of information materials, and plans for building infant furniture. People planning to open and operate a day care for infants will find the guide helpful.

INTERNATIONAL

Child-Rearing Values: A Cross-National Study. (1979). Wallace E. Lambert, Josiane F. Hamers, Nancy Frasure-Smith. NY: Praeger.

This is a rather technical account based on carefully collected empirical data. In the introduction a review of previous studies on child rearing along with an outline of how this study was conducted is provided. Countries included are: Canada, France, Belgium, Italy, Greece, Portugal, and Japan. The first six chapters concentrate on various aspects of Frenchness in the various countries on child rearing. References.

Childhood in China. (1975). Edited by William Kessen. New Haven and London: Yale Univ. Press.

This book is the result of a three-week trip to China by the American Delegation consisting of eight psychologists, two sociologists, a nursery school teacher, a pediatrician, and a staff member of the committee. The authors visited a variety of settings and observed children ranging in age from two months to eighteen years. They attempted through interviews and observations to gain an understanding of child development and its relationship to the society of new China. The chapters, written by different members of the delegation and edited by Kessen, describe the Chinese family, nurseries, kindergartens, primary schools, middle schools, language development and education, and health and nutritional factors. The book gives an intriguing glimpse into a social system and a child-rearing philosophy divergent from the Western model, and it represents an important first step toward an understanding and appreciation of the new China and the Chinese personality. Indexed.

Children and Families in Australia: Contemporary Issues and Problems. (1979). Ailsa Burns, Jacqueline Goodnow, Richard Chisolm, John Murry. Sydney: George Allen & Unwin. (Studies in Society: 5).

The first and last chapters provide a historical view of children and the status of families in Australia. The middle section of the book looks at nine specific topics: working mothers, unemployed fathers, single parents, television, migrant children, child abuse, custody, adoption, and child welfare. References.

Children and Minders. (1980). Bridget Bryant, Miriam Harris, Dee Newton. Ypsilanti, MI: High/Scope Press. (Oxford Preschool Research Project).

In this volume the researchers report their findings regarding the care givers of preschool-age children in Britain. Different types of care-giving arrangements, quality of care, cost, and effects on child and mothers are investigated and reported. Suggestions for changes needed in public policy are given. A summary of this volume may also be found in another book in the series, *Under Five in Britain*, by Jerome Bruner. References.

The Danish National Child-Care System. (1976). Marsden Wagner, Mary Wagner, Boulder, CO: Westview.

This volume outlines the broad range of publicly and privately supported child and family services operating within the Danish national child care system. Included are discussions of day care, child advocacy, foster care, infant health, and family support. The treatment of each service includes a description of the services provided, administration, funding, personnel support, evaluation, limitations, and implications for the United States. Comparisons are made between services in the United States and Denmark. Some chapters end with references.

Early Child Care in Britain. (1975). Mia K. Pringle, Sandhya Naidoo. London and NY: Garden and Breach. (International Monograph Series on Early Child Care).

A comprehensive account of how British families and the government share the responsibility of caring for infants and young children. All aspects are covered including child-rearing practices, health services, professional care giver training, etc. Chapter 11 reviews research relating to the infant and young child. Lengthy references provided.

Day Care in Canada. (1985). Alan R. Pence. In *The Challenge of Child Welfare*. Edited by Kenneth Levitte, Brian Wharf. Vancouver, BC: Univ. of British Columbia Press.

This chapter provides a historical and contemporary perspective of day care in Canada. Thirty-five references are included.

Early Child Care in Hungary. (1972). Alice Hermann, Sandor Komlosi. London, NY, Paris: Gordon and Breach. (International Monograph Series on Early Child Care).

This small monograph describes and details the Hungarian system of early child care. No index is provided but references for further reading are given.

Early Child Care in India. (1979). Margaret Khalakdina. London and NY: Gordon and Breach. (International Monograph Series).

This book considers the enormous challenge of child care in this vast country. Within its 212 pages are ten chapters; several appendixes, including some useful information tables; about 300 references; a glossary of terms; and photographs of child care.

Early Child Care in Israel. (1976). Chanan Rapaport, Joseph Marcus, Miriam Glikson, Witold Jedlicki, Sheldon Lache. NY: Gordon and Breach. (International Monograph Series on Early Child Care, Vol. 7).

This volume presents a well written and informative account of child-care practices in Israel. The major chapters deal with the division of child-care responsibilities, socialization, and programs available. Others are concerned with historical influences, values, governmental planning, professional training, information and communication and research. Child care in the Kibbutz is also discussed. The mentally and physically handicapped are not discussed.

Early Child Care in Poland. Maria Ziemska. London, NY, Paris: Gordon and Breach. (International Monograph Series on Early Child Care, Vol. 8).

The author gives an authoritative and detailed look at the array of services and provisions which in Poland constitutes the cooperation between state and family for the care and upbringing of the young child. References.

Early Child Care in Sweden. (1973). Ragnar Berfenstam, Inger Williamson-Ollson. N.Y. and London: Gordon and Breach. (International Monograph Series on Early Child Care).

This is a general description of the legal, medical, and social background of Swedish care of preschool children. Chapters cover such topics as abortions, early deaths, adoptions, preschool education, day care centers, family structure, and family income. There are four pages on research relating to the infant and preschool child which cite some references but present no data.

The Evolution of the Nursery-Infant School: A History of Infant and Nursery Education in Britain. (1972). Nanette Whitbread. Boston, MA: Routledge & Kegan Paul. (Students Library of Education).

Whitbread presents in this book the development of the infant school and education in Britain against the historical backdrop of industrialization and social change. The book describes how the development was influenced by the ideas of theorists such as Pestalozzi, Froebel, Montessori, and McMellan. Suggestions for further reading are provided, as well as a lengthy bibliography.

Growing Up in Great Britain: Papers from the National Child Development Study.
(1983). Edited by Ken Fogelman. London: MacMillian Press.

The volume is organized around five headings: social background and development, health and physical development; the school; measuring behavior in the school and home; and written language. Social Background and Development includes papers about: social class and family size; housing; immigrants; single-parent families; and families of low incomes. Health and Physical Development contains papers about the prevalence of speech, vision, and hearing problems, and handedness. The papers included under Schools are about ability grouping, career aspirations, sex education, and patterns of school attendance. Measuring Behavior in School and Home includes papers about the Bristol Social Adjustment Guide and about developmental changes in behavior ratings in the national sample. Lastly, Written Language includes papers about the writing productivity and linguistic maturity of 11-year-olds. References.

Growing Up in New Zealand. (1978). Jane Ritchie, James Ritchie. Sydney and London: George Allen and Unwin.

This volume provides a description of the experience of growing up in contemporary New Zealand. The authors present a wealth of research evidence, including their own extensive studies of child-rearing patterns among both the Pakeha (white) and Maori New Zealanders. The book generally follows the life span from infancy to old age. Special focus is given to the development of sex roles and to the Maoris and Polynesian immigrants from other Pacific islands in contemporary New Zealand society.

Mothering in Greece: From Collectivism to Individualism. (1983). Mariella Doumanis. NY: Academic. (Behavioral Development: A Series of Monographs).

The author compares parenting and family life in rural and urban Greece. The book is devoid of statistics, graphs, and tables, and is based primarily on the subjective impression the author formed from her contacts with urban and rural people. References.

Mothers of Six Cultures: Antecedents of Child Rearing. (1964). Leigh Minturn, William W. Lambert. NY: John Wiley & Sons.

This classical text is a comprehensive cross-national study of child rearing. It is a sequel to *Six Cultures--Studies in Child Rearing* by Beatrice Whiting, and is based on material from the same field work described in that book. The material for the ethnographic summaries in the introduction and chapters 10 - 16 which deals with each of the six communities, was derived largely from data gathered by the field teams of the Six Cultures project. The first few chapters report the differences in the opinions of the mothers in the different societies studied (United States, Mexico, Philippines, Okinawa, India, Africa). The mean differences between the mothers is then discussed and hypotheses formulated. Each of the six cultures is then rated. Chapter 9 is devoted to the presentation of the data and the evaluation of the hypotheses in terms of the degree to which they are confirmed or refuted by the analyses. The second half of the book is devoted to factor patterns within each of the six cultures.

Seven Years Old in the Home Environment. (1976). John Newson, Elizabeth Newson. NY: John Wiley & Sons.

This book is a comprehensive description of the seven-year-old growing up in the culture and context of the British society. The descriptive research reported is intended to contribute to a broader understanding of the dynamics of the parent-child relationship and to stimulate a more critical self awareness in society of the parental role. References.

Sharing the Responsibilities: Minutes of Proceedings and Evidence of the Special Committee. (March 1987). Canada. House of Commons. Special Committee on Child Care. Canada: Queen's Printer for Canada.

This is the final report of the committee on child care needs of the Canadian family. The committee reports on needs of children inside and outside the family as well as parents' views on the kinds of care they would like. The report defines the role of the federal government in child care. Lastly, the report outlines steps the government could take to fulfill this role. Appendix I lists the research studies conducted for the committee.

Soviet Preschool Education. Vol. 1. Program of Instruction. (1969). Edited by Henry Chauncy. NY: Holt, Rinehart and Winston.

The first of two volumes on Russian education contains the operating instruction or curriculum for the public education of children from the age of two months until they enter school. The manual was published by the Ministry of Education and is in effect all over Russia. Divided into the seven age categories, the volume also contains an appendix containing model daily schedules for the different age groups.

Soviet Preschool Education. Vol. 2. Teacher's Commentary. (1969). Edited by Henry Chauncy. NY: Holt, Rinehart and Winston.

This volume is used as the basic text for training all preschool personnel in Russia. In addition it serves as the prototype for dozens of other works on preschool education published in the USSR. The seven areas covered include: the program of instruction; care and upbringing of infants; care and upbringing during the first year, second, and third; education of children from three to seven; and play and organization of children's lives.

Two Worlds of Childhood: U.S. and U.S.S.R. (1970). Urie Bronfenbrenner. NY: Russell Sage Foundation.

This classic compares the child-rearing practices in the United States with those of Russia. The author made a series of seven visits to Russia to observe, interview and analyze Soviet methods of child rearing. Part I reports the author's findings in Russia concerning the Soviet family and child-rearing practices in the collective setting. Part II of the book discusses child-rearing practices in the United States and compares them with those observed in Russian source notes.

Under Five in Britain. (1980). Jerome Bruner. Ypsilanti, MI: High Scope Press. (Oxford Preschool Research Project).

This volume, the only one of the series authored by an American, is a summary of the Oxford Preschool Research Project which provides an in-depth look at each of the major English child-care methods. Chapters 1 and 2 provide an overview of preschooling available in Britain. Chapter 3 discusses the preschool scene in Oxfordshire and relates it to Britain as a whole. Chapter 4 defines the research charge of the Oxford Study. Chapter 5 reviews the principle findings of the group writing the report called *Childwatching at Playgroup and Preschool*. Chapter 6 presents findings from the working group on *Childminding*. Chapter 7 reviews the principal findings set forth in *Children and Day Nurseries*. Chapter 8 discusses implications of the Oxford Study findings as they reflect on future policies regarding child-care methods. References.

A World of Children: Day Care and Preschool Institutions. (1979). Nancy M. Robinson, Halbert B. Robinson, Martha Darling, Gretchen Holm. Monterey, CA: Brooks/Cole.

This book draws together material on day care and early education in selected industrialized countries, mostly eastern and western Europe. Four national models are explicated in some detail; the Latin-European model, the Scandinavian model, the socialist model, and the Anglo-Saxon model. Comparisons across models are highly informative and accomplish their intended purpose. References.

Young Children in China. (1982). Rita Liljestrom, Eva Noren-Bjorn, Gertrud Schyl-Bjurman, Birgit Ohrn, Lars H. Gustafsson, Orvar Lofgren. Clevedon, Avon, England: Multilingual Matters.

This book recounts observations of a group of Swedish professionals including a sociologist, a psychologist, a preschool teacher trainer, a pediatrician, and an ethnologist on a visit to China in early 1982. They studied the Chinese preschool, preschool pedagogy, preschool teacher training, child health care, and family policy. The six chapters individually cover each of the topics. The appendix contains a trial version of a curriculum for preschool.

6

Communication

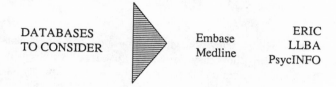

DATABASES
TO CONSIDER

Embase
Medline

ERIC
LLBA
PsycINFO

GENERAL

Reviews of Literature

Children Communicating: Media and Development of Thought, Speech, Understanding. (1979). Edited by Ellen Wartella. Beverly Hills, CA: Sage. (Sage Annual Reviews of Communication Research, vol. 7).

A review of how children communicate. Describes and explains the nature of the communicative differences between children of all ages and adults. The volume examines two aspects of children's communication: (1) how communication activities change as children grow older; and (2) the cognitive aspects of communication. References.

The Communication of Emotion. (1984). Ross Buck. NY: Guilford. (Guilford Social Psychology Series).

A collection and synthesis of information from diverse areas. Chapter 1 outlines a broad framework based upon the concept of two modes of communication. Chapter 2 deals with the evolution of emotion communication as a "read-out" model. Chapter 3 is an explanation of the physiology necessary to support the author's model. Chapter 4 discusses the importance of the developmental processes in the child in relationship to proper emotional functioning and communication. Chapter 5 summarizes research on nonverbal sending accuracy. References.

Human Non-Verbal Behavior: A Means of Communication. (1972). Christopher R. Brannigan, David A. Humphries. In *Ethological Studies of Child Behavior*, edited by Blurton Jones. London: Cambridge Univ. Press.

This chapter deals with the use made of facial expressions and body language in communication. References.

Mind and Media: The Effects of Television, Video Games, and Computers. (1984). P. M. Greenfield. Cambridge, MA: Harvard Univ. Press. (Developing Child Series).

An outstanding summary of what television, video games, and computers can and should do, while describing how they are actually used with children in the real world. Chapter 1 discusses an approach to questions of how media affect development. In Chapter 2 film and television techniques such as zooming in on subjects or cutting from one episode to another are discussed in light of cognitive development. Chapter 3 examines the literature on the effect of television on the young child's information-processing skills and on how style of presentation affects retention of material. Chapter 5 examines attempts to use television to overcome educational disadvantage. Chapter 6 examines skills needed to use print, radio, and television, suggesting that each medium helps teach something slightly different, and drawbacks and advantages. The next two chapters examine video games and computers including a thorough review of the intellectual motor skills required to play such games competently. Chapter 8 examines the changes that computers have made on education and leisure for children. The last chapter is a discussion of future use of media. References.

COMMUNICATION DISORDERS

Bibliographies

Auditory Competence in Early Life: Roots of Communicative Behavior. (1976). Rita B. Eisenberg. Baltimore, MD: Univ. Park Press.

An extensive bibliography of research on infant hearing. This volume provides detailed information on the development of auditory processes during the first three years of life along with information on the procedures and techniques necessary for investigating auditory behavior. The first three chapters describe the physical, physiological, and neurological systems of infants which underlie auditory perception; the general methods used in auditory research with infants; and models of auditory processes. Chapters 4 and 5 present detailed accounts of research in Eisenberg's Bioacoustic Laboratory. Studies investigating the effects of stimulus duration, bandwidth, and frequency on infant state are described, and investigations using heart rate and electrophysiological responses as indexes of auditory processing are discussed. The last two chapters include a review of research which has investigated a wide range of auditory stimulus parameters. An attempt to put the results of research on infant auditory processes into a developmental model is described. Appendix A contains a glossary of terms. Appendix B is a listing of studies relative to the effects of sound on human subjects. Appendix C presents instrumentation and techniques used in the Bioacoustic Laboratory.

Bibliography: The Volta Review, 1899 - 1976; American Annals of the Deaf, 1947 - 1976. (1977). Edited by George W. Fellendorf. Washington, DC: Alexander Graham Bell.

A subject index of *The Volta Review* and the *American Annals of the Deaf*. Entries are chronological according to date of publication with the earliest appearing first. Entries appear only once: There are no cross-references. Articles of less than two pages have been excluded.

DSH Abstracts. (1960 - 1985). Washington, DC: Deafness, Speech and Hearing Publications.

Even though this reference ceased publication in 1985, it still serves as the best index to the literature of speech and hearing sciences. The publication gives brief, noncritical summaries of world-wide literature pertinent to deafness, speech, hearing, and audiology. For publications after 1985, *Index Medicus* should be consulted.

Language and the Brain, in Two Volumes. (1981). William O. Dingwall. NY: Garland.

This set is a compilation of about 5,746 entries investigating language and the brain. There are five separate sections within the two volumes. The first introduces the nervous system (anatomy, physiology, and pathology) along with overviews of neuropsychology and neurolinguistics plus philosophical issues dealing with language and the brain. Part III covers the neurological disorders of language and allied capacities. Part IV addresses the development of language and the brain. Part V discusses the evaluation of the brain and communication. Brief annotations are provided with each entry.

Leopold's Bibliography of Child Language, Revised and Augmented. (1972). Dan Isaac Slobin. Bloomington, IN: Indiana Univ. Press.

All entries deal with child language, speech therapy, mental testing, and the influence of language on behavior and child development. Entries include 746 entries from Leopold's original bibliography plus new items up to June 1967. Entries are not annotated. An update of Werner F. Leopold's *Bibliography of Child Language*, published in 1952. Latter should still be consulted for pre-1952 references.

Reviews of Literature

Bilingualism and Language Disability: Assessment and Remediation.   (1984).
Edited by Nicklas Miller. San Diego, CA: College-Hill.

> Chapter 1 introduces the topic. Chapter 2 delves into language development.
> Chapter 3 addresses myths about the consequences from bilingualism for
> cognition. Chapter 4 is an analysis of which language difficulties of bilingual
> children are more imagined than real. Chapters 5 to 8 review briefly past
> thoughts and controversies on bilingualism. The last three chapters deal with
> the problems for the monolingual remediator with monolingual materials in
> the management of the potentially bilingual child diagnosed as having (first)-
> language acquisition difficulties. Chapter 9 addresses the problems and
> pitfalls in case history compilation in cross-cultural settings. Chapter 10
> outlines the basis for remediation and offers practical advice on problems of
> program implementation and personnel training. Chapter 11 compares the
> difference between children with a second-language learning difficulty and
> those who have problems learning any language at all. References.

Cerebral Palsy. (1983). James Hardy. Englewood Cliffs, NJ: Prentice-Hall.
(Remediation of Communication Disorders Series).

> The first two chapters include an introduction and background to
> communication. Chapter 3 discusses the nervous system and etiologies of
> cerebral palsy. Chapter 4 discusses the characteristics of individuals with
> cerebral palsy. Chapters 5 and 6 address assessment. Chapter 7 discusses
> management of developmental dysarthria.   Chapter 8 discusses other
> disabilities associated with cerebral palsy. Chapter 9 discusses the role of the
> speech pathologist, programs, and prognosis of cerebral palsy. Chapter 10
> outlines some of the alternative methods of communication for those
> individuals unable to communicate verbally. Fifty-two references.

Cleft Palate Speech. (1984). B. J. McWilliams, H. L. Morris, R. L. Shelton.
Philadelphia, PA: B. C. Decker.

> Provides an excellent overview of cleft palate speech. The book is divided
> into sections covering: nature of the problem; medical and dental aspects;
> psychosocial development; velopharyngeal valving; communication disorders;
> and treatments of those disorders. An appendix, tonsils and adenoids,
> clarifies the relevance of this topic. The book is well-illustrated with
> photographs, drawings, charts, tables, and clinical forms. An extensive
> bibliography containing both recent and classic sources follows each chapter.

Disorders of First-Language Development: Trends in Research and Theory.
(1984). Sheldon Rosenberg. In *Malformations of Development: Biological
and Psychological Sources and Consequences*, edited by Eugene Gallin. NY:
Academic. (Developmental Psychology Series).

Chapter reviews applied psycholinguistic literature in the field of
developmental language disorders. A very lengthy bibliography is provided.

A Handbook on Stuttering. Third edition. (1981). Oliver Bloodstein. Chicago, IL:
National Easter Seal Society.

This handbook summarizes the literature and research in the area of
stuttering.

Language Development and Intervention with the Hearing Impaired. (1978).
Richard R. Kretschmer, Laura W. Kretschmer. Baltimore, MD: Univ. Park
Press. (Perspectives in Audiology Series).

Discusses issues and strategies of learning, assessing, and teaching oral
language to the hearing-impaired and deaf child. The book is divided into
seven chapters which present a developmental approach to language
learning. After an overview of language learning, the book details language
acquisition and learning in the hearing-impaired and deaf child. The book
concludes with a chapter devoted to the relations between reading and
language in hearing-impaired and deaf children. References.

Language Disorders in Preschool Children. (1982). Patricia R. Cole. Englewood
Cliffs, NJ: Prentice-Hall. (Remediation of Communication Disorders,
edited by Frederick N. Martin).

This volume delves into the bases and procedures for language intervention
programs for preschool children with language disorders.   Chapter 2
discusses the development of prelinguistic behaviors and concludes with a
brief discussion of language assessment. Chapter 3 discusses strategies for
remediation of language disorders. Intervention procedures are discussed for
deficits at different stages and for different components of language. An
excellent bibliography follows the text.

Language Intervention with Young Children. (1986). Marc E. Fey. San Diego, CA:
College-Hill.

This book, along with discussing theory and clinical matters, provides a
critical analysis of the available literature on intervention. Clinicians will
find the chapters on various intervention methods interesting as well as
enlightening.   A lengthy bibliography at the end of the book is
comprehensive.

Measurement of Audition and Vision in the First Year of Postnatal Life: A Methodological Overview. (1985). Edited by Gilbert Gottlieb, Norman A. Krasnegor. Norwood, NJ: Ablex.

Six chapters deal with various aspects of audiology. Five deal with visual development. Two chapters look at speech perception while one, Chapter 13, addresses techniques of studying cognition in infancy. References.

Nature and Treatment of Stuttering: New Directions. (1984). Richard F. Curlee, William H. Perkins. San Diego, CA: College-Hill.

The volume provides a recent synthesis of research and theory about stuttering. Each chapter is written by a well-known researcher or specialist in the field. Lengthy bibliographies follow the chapters. The book concludes with an author and subject index.

Normal and Disordered Phonology in Children. (1985). Carol Stoel-Gammon. Baltimore, MD: University Park Press.

Reviews and critiques the current body of literature on normal and disordered phonological development in children. The book also relates empirical findings to the clinical issues of assessment and treatment of children with phonological disorders.

Otitis Media and Child Development. (1986). Edited by James F. Kavanagh. Parkton, MD: York. (Communicating by Language Series).

Reviews the literature on the effect of otitis media on the developing child. The 18 chapters are grouped according to five large divisions: role of hearing in child development; identification and diagnosis of otitis media; effect of mild hearing loss on child development during the first three years; prevention, intervention and treatment of otitis media; cognitive development in children with recurrent otitis media. Each chapter provides a bibliography.

Perspectives in Audiology Series: Speech of the Hearing Impaired; Research, Training, and Personal Preparation. (1983). Edited by Irving Hochberg, Harry Levitt, Mary Joe Osberger. Baltimore, MD: Univ. Park Press. (Perspectives in Audiology Series).

This volume contains the papers and discussions falling into the seven areas of: (1) speech production; (2) speech perception; (3) assessment procedures; (4) development of speech; (5) sensory aids and speech training; (6) auditory training; and (7) personnel preparation. References.

The Psychoeducational Assessment of Preschool Children. (1983). Kathleen D. Paget, Bruce A. Bracken. NY: Grune and Stratton.

This volume provides synthesis of the latest research and assessment techniques in all areas that are crucial for assessment of preschool children (language, gross motor, fine motor, speech, creativity, neuropsychology, etc.). References.

Recent Perspectives on American Sign Language. (1980). Edited by Harlan Lane, François Grosjean. Hillsdale, NJ: Lawrence Erlbaum.

Reviews the literature on American Sign Language including topics such as: linguistics, psycholinguistics, developmental aspects, neurolinguistics, and historical. References.

Recent Studies in Early Auditory Development. (1986). John Columbo. In *Annals of Child Development, a Research Annual*, Vol. 3, edited by Grover Whitehurst. Greenwich, CT: JAI.

Chapter reviews recent research into the infant's intermodal capacities. Of special note is the suggestion that binaural fusion is not found in the newborn but is seen in the two-month-old. It is also noted that the six- to seven-month age may mark the onset of the loss of sensitivity to other stimuli. Substantial references.

Remediating Children's Language: Behavioral and Naturalistic Approaches. (1984). Edited by Dave J. Muller. San Diego, CA: College-Hill.

Addresses the application of behavioral techniques and naturalistic approaches in language remediation programs. Section III contains a critical review of parents as therapists and another on remediation programs. References.

Research and Experiment in Stuttering. (1968). H. R. Beech, Fay Fransella. NY: Pergamon.

Highlights research in the area of stuttering up to about 1966. References.

Speech and Language: Advances in Basic Research and Practice. Vol. 1 - . (1979 -). Edited by Norman J. Lass. NY: Academic.

Each annual provides a review of research in the areas of speech and language. Volumes contain individual indexes. No cumulative index is provided. References.

Speech Disorders in Children: Recent Advances. (1984). Edited by Janis Costello. San Diego, CA: College-Hill. (Speech, Language, and Hearing Disorders Series).

Synthesizes current knowledge in speech, language, and hearing. This volume is in three sections. Part I covers assessment and treatment of articulation disorders; motor control perspectives on apraxia of speech and dysarthria; and phonologic systems, problems of second language acquisition. Part II delves into assessment and treatment of voice disorders; speech rehabilitation of the laryngectomized patient; and voice disorders. Part III discusses treatment of fluency and stuttering.

Stuttering and Behavior Therapy: Current Status and Experimental Foundations. (1984). Roger John Igham. San Diego, CA: College-Hill.

The volume reviews and evaluates current practices and principles of behavior therapy used with stutterers. Lengthy references conclude the chapters.

Understanding Language through Sign Language Research. (1978). Particia Siple. NY: Academic.

Initial chapter provides an overview of sign language research. The following fourteen chapters cover research on particular aspects of American Sign Language. References.

Reports of Research

The Causes of Profound Deafness in Childhood. (1976). George R. Fraser. Baltimore, MD: Johns Hopkins Univ. Press.

Presents the combined results of three surveys, personally conducted by the author from 1958 to 1967, of 3,535 deaf individuals born deaf or whose deafness occurred in early childhood. The text is in six parts. The first defines the S group, methods of identification, and arrangement of the material. The second concerns deafness determined by Mendelian inheritance and contains eight chapters detailing deafness with goiter, abnormal EKG, retinitis pigmentosa, recessive syndromes, and clinically undifferentiated deafness. The third part discusses deafness in conjunction with malformation syndromes. The fourth examines acquired causes of deafness and contains three chapters concerning prenatal deafness, perinatal deafness, and deafness in infancy and childhood. The fifth part focuses on the etiology of deafness associated with unknown causes. The sixth part synthesizes information dealing with subgroup comparisons, genetic counseling, and final conclusions. Each chapter presents a very complete review of the literature followed by an extremely detailed presentation of the affected individuals in the survey. The survey results are presented through the use of numerous tables. Each table is self-explanatory, and Fraser highlights the important aspects of each table in the text. Questionnaires used in the survey are reproduced in an appendix. Lengthy bibliography.

Language and Learning Skills of Hearing-Impaired Students. (1986). Edited by Mary Joe Osberger. Rockville, MD: American Speech-Language-Hearing. (ASHA Monographs).

This monograph describes a study carried out on a large group of profoundly hearing-impaired students assessing language, academic, and related learning skills. The subjects consisted of 150, four- to twenty-year-olds, from a residential school for the deaf. The results of the multivariate analyses revealed that language, particularly expressive language, was the major determinant of academic achievement in the sample under study.

Language without Speech. (1977). Ruth F. Deich, Patricia M. Hodges. NY: Brunner/Mazel.

An account of the authors' use of the Premack language system to provide nonverbal retarded children with a nonvocal communication system. Appendix A contains an annotated bibliography for traditional language intervention methods.

Other References

Comprehensive Dictionary of Audiology. Fourth edition. (1983). James H. Delk. Harvard, MA: Laux.

Specialized dictionary for the subject area of audiology.

Developing Systematic Procedures for Training Children's Language. (1974). Edited by Leija V. McReynolds. Rockville, MD: American Speech and Hearing. (ASHA Monograph No. 18).

Chapter 2 presents a descriptive study of the acquisition of the verb *to be* in normal and linguistically delayed children. The third chapter compares the relative effectiveness of imitation and comprehension training for increasing verbal production. The study of noun phrases in Chapter 4 describes procedures for training and testing for generalization that could be directly applied to language intervention programs. Next, two language-training programs using procedures from the experimental analysis of behavior are presented. Both describe methods for evaluation and generalization testing. References.

A Dictionary of American Sign Language on Linguistic Principles. (1976). William C. Stokoe, Dorothy C. Casterline, Carl G. Croneberg. Silver Spring, MD: Linstok.

An illustrated guide to American Sign Language and its variations. Symbol guides that appear at the upper right-hand corner of each page assist in locating particular sign-words. Appendix D discusses the variations of dialects in Virginia and North Carolina. Edition includes a bibliography and index of English words. Not an easy dictionary to use either by novice or experienced individuals because sign language was never intended to be written.

Galludet Encyclopedia of Deaf People and Deafness. 3 vols. (1987). Edited by John V. Van Cleve. NY: McGraw-Hill.

Unique in its coverage, the three volumes contain approximately 273 entries on general, scientific, and biographical topics concerning deafness. All entries are signed and provide references for further study. A detailed index is in Volume 3.

Handbook of Clinical Audiology. (1985). Third edition. Jack Katz. Baltimore, MD: Williams & Wilkins.

Each chapter, written by an expert, synthesizes the current knowledge in the area covered. Depending on the chapter subject, subtopics include methods of measurement, instrumentation, charting, research needs, assessment techniques, and clinical procedure. Section X of this volume deals with hearing aids and Section XI, with communication training. Lengthy bibliographies end each chapter.

Handbook of Speech Pathology and Audiology. (1971). Lee Edward Travis. NY: Appleton Century.

This handbook, considered a classic, covers research, theory and practice in the area of communication disorders. Part I deals with the concepts and factors common to all disorders of communication, such as terminology, phonetics, acoustics, personality, diagnosis, and therapy. Part II deals with hearing: anatomy, physiology, pathology, speech, diagnosis, and treatment. Part III deals with the origin, nature, uses, troubles, and means of voice modification. Part IV deals with speech and speech disorders. Part V deals with the development, nature, and disturbances of language. Aphasia in children is included in this section. Lengthy bibliographies are included at the ends of chapters. A detailed subject index which includes institution names and individual letter sounds is located at the end of the handbook.

Language Assessment Instruments: Infancy through Adulthood. (1981). Arden R. Thorum. Springfield, IL: John C. Thomas.

Describes language assessment instruments for use with infants and children. Normative data is included with each entry.

Language Disorders in School-Age Children. (1982). Mary Lovey Wood. Englewood Cliffs, NJ: Prentice-Hall. (Remediation of Communication Disorders, edited by Frederick N. Martin).

This volume offers a theoretical base for intervention along with specific suggestions for direct work on communication disorders with school-age children. Part I introduces general issues related to identification of and intervention with children in the early primary grades. Part II expands upon identification and assessment processes following the principle that, regardless of how analyzed, the evaluation of a child's communicative competencies must take place within socially interactive contexts. Part III deals with intervention approaches and strategies following the same classification schema presented in Part II. The author supplies specific, and frequently rich, examples of intervention strategies. References are supplied at the end of the volume.

Language Handicaps in Children. (1984). William H. Perkins. NY: Thieme-Stratton.

All the chapters in the volume are devoted to clinical procedures and written by a recognized specialist in the field. The 16 chapters are groups under three general parts: approaches to facilitating development of language and literacy, methods of facilitating language development, and facilitating language development in specific disorders.

Organization of Speech-Language Services in Schools: A Manual. (1985). Rolland J. Van Hattum. San Diego, CA: College-Hill.

Discusses the responsibilities, opportunities, and challenges currently found in the public schools in providing speech and language services. The book is divided into six chapters, the first being an introduction. Chapters 2 and 3 delve into the professional skills, characteristics, and ethics required of the speech-language pathologist as a professional and a member of the educational team. Chapter 4 talks about establishing the therapy program and handling the case load. Chapters 5 and 6 address scheduling and the therapy program itself. The text concludes with an author and subject index. References.

Research Procedures in Speech, Language, and Hearing. (1982). William M. Shearer. Baltimore, MD: Williams & Wilkins.

This handbook is intended to assist graduate students with their research. The book is handy for commonly employed statistical methods.

Terminology of Communication Disorders: Speech, Language, Hearing. Second edition. (1983). Lucille Nicolosi, Elizabeth Harryman, Janet Kresheck. Baltimore, MD: Williams & Wilkins.

This special dictionary defines words peculiar to the field of communication disorders. Appendixes includes: overview of developmental sequences of language behavior; mean length of utterance; general outline of language development from birth to 11 years; developmental sequences of motor behavior; developmental sequences of social behavior; language tests and procedures; articulation tests and procedures; audiometric tests and procedures; psychological measures and tests; and diagnostic differences.

Treatment of Stuttering in Early Childhood: Methods and Issues. (1983). David Prins, Roger J. Ingham. San Diego, CA: College-Hill.

Contains good bibliographies on topics at the end of each chapter. Title conveys subject coverage of volume.

COMPOSITION

Bibliographies

Children's Writings: A Bibliography of Works in English. (1982). Jane B. Wilson. Jefferson, NC: McFarland.

The introduction states, "This is an eclectic bibliography, partially annotated, of books by or about children and youth who wrote and, in most instances, published manuscripts by the age of 21 or younger." There are 737 alphabetically arranged entries, two appendixes, and a combined name and title index. The literature sources are rich and varied; entries at least as early as 1770 and as late as 1980 appear. Citations include books, periodicals, and newspapers. Some of the annotations are extensive. The first appendix is an essay on seven-year-old writers.

Reviews of Literature

Advances in Writing Research. Vol. 1. Children's Early Writing Development. (1985). Edited by Marcia Farr. Norwood, NJ: Ablex. (Advances in Writing Research).

In this first volume of the series, the focus is on children beginning the task of writing. The first three studies explore emergent literacy. The last two studies, conducted in early elementary school settings, explore emerging literacy capacities within the formal school setting. References.

Children's Writing and Reading: Analyzing Classroom Language. (1984). Katharine Perera. Oxford, England: Basil Blackwell. (Language Library).

The major focus of this book is on the grammatical structures of written language of the children themselves and the materials used with the children. Chapter 3 outlines children's grammatical development from 18 months to 14 years. Chapter 4 illustrates some differences between speech and writing. Practical recommendations useful to teachers in their classrooms are the subject of chapters 5 and 6. The book provides a scholarly integration of empirical data, theory, and practical recommendation. References.

Development and Disorders of Written Language: Studies of Normal and Exceptional Children. Vol. 2. (1973). Helmer R. Myklebust. NY: Grune and Stratton.

Part I, Learning to Use the Written Word, provides a very brief introduction which emphasizes the importance of studying written language and its relationship to spoken and read language. Part II, Disorders of Written Language, describes a series of studies of exceptional children: a group of urban children (9 - 15 years old) with reading disabilities; 66 dyslexics (7 - 18 years old) referred by schools to a nonmedical clinic; mentally retarded children (9 - 15 years of age) in EMH classes of an urban school system; 127 children (7- 13 years old) with articulation disorders and in speech therapy; 68 socially and emotionally disturbed children (9 - 16 years of age) in special education programs; and 228 third and fourth graders with learning disabilities. Part III, Diagnosis-Remediation-Classification, provides comparisons of the various disability groups with each other on the battery of tests used and offers suggestions for remediation and classification. References.

Learning to Write. (1982). Gunther Kress. London: Routledge & Kegan Paul.

Detailed analyses of essays produced by children ages 6 - 14 serve to illustrate various aspects of the child's developing mastery of written language. Particularly interesting is a chapter on the development of the child's concept of the sentence. The author argues that children's early written sentences correspond to textual rather than syntactic units. The book reflects current perspectives in text linguistics and sociolinguistics, but is weak in failing to acknowledge cognitive aspects. References.

The Relations between Reading and Writing in Young Children. (1984). Lee Galda. In *New Directions in Composition Research*, edited by Richard Beach, Lillian Bridwell. NY: Guilford. (Perspectives in Writing Research).

This chapter examines selected research in reading and writing to determine possible relations between these two aspects of literacy. The chapter offers a good bibliography.

Reports of Research

Social Cognitive Ability as a Prediction of Quality of Fourth-Graders' Written Narratives. (1984). Donald L. Rubin, Gene L. Piche, Michael L. Michlin, Fern L. Johnson. In *New Directions in Composition Research*, edited by Richard Beach, Lillian Bridwell. NY: Guilford. (Perspectives in Writing Research).

This study reports an investigation to determine the influence of social cognitive ability in predicting fluency and error incidence in narrative writing of fourth graders. Subjects of the study were 19 fourth graders from middle-class public schools in suburban Minneapolis. The study results indicate a link between social cognition and writing quality. Furthermore, there is an indication that programs designed to enhance social sensitivity in general may do more to promote composing skill than does didactic training in writing conventions.

The Writing Report Card: Writing Achievement in American Schools. (1986). Arthur N. Applebee, Judith A. Langer, V. S. Mullis. Princeton, NJ: Educational Testing Service.

This report is based on NAEP's 1984 national assessment of writing achievement of American children. Chapter one provides a summary and implications of the study. Part I of the monograph addresses the question of how well do students write according to the national survey. Part II looks at the writing students do and the help they receive. Charts and graphs showing the results of the assessment are located throughout the text and help in visualizing the results.

COMPUTERS

Reviews of Literature

Children and Microcomputers: Research on the Newest Medium. (1985). Edited by Milton Chen, William Paisley. Beverly Hills, CA: Sage. (Sage Focus Editions).

A compilation of empirical studies of children and microcomputers. The book is divided into four sections. Part I looks at research on microcomputers within the context of media technology and social research.

Part II presents studies of microcomputer utilization which emphasizes investigations of software applications as well as hardware acquisition. Part III examines individual cognitive, attitudinal, and behavioral effects of microcomputers on children. Part IV looks at future developments of educational uses of microcomputers. References.

Computers and Young Children, a Review of Research: Research in Review. (November 1987). Douglas H. Clements. In *Young Children* 43 (1).

This journal article reviews recent literature on the use of computers with young children, including preschoolers. Subjects reviewed include: the appropriate age to introduce computers; sex differences; social/emotional development; attitudes; and development of various aspects of communication via the computer. Sixty-six citations make up the bibliography.

Microcomputers in Early Childhood Education. (1984). Mima Spencer, Linda Baskin. In *Current Topics in Early Childhood Education*, Vol. 5, edited by Lilian Katz, Chapter 4, pp. 105 - 120. Norwood, NJ: Ablex.

A review of research on the use of microcomputers in early and elementary education settings. CAI, programming, and word processing all are covered in this brief chapter. References.

Reports of Research

Computers, Children and Classrooms: A Multisite Evaluation of the Creative Use of Microcomputers by Elementary School Children. (1985). Hilda W. Carmichael, J. Dale Burnett, William C. Higginson. Toronto: Ontario Ministry of Education.

Study examines the creative uses of computers in elementary schools and their impact on students' confidence and self-esteem, student-peer interaction, student-teacher interaction, male and female students, classroom management, the role of the teacher, special education, teacher training, and curricular areas. Classrooms had constant use of one to five computers over a year. LOGO and word processing were studied extensively with graphics and Musicland explored for a short period. Report discusses in detail various software used and offers extensive illustrations of what children from kindergarten to eighth grade are able to accomplish with them. Substantial references.

HANDWRITING

Reviews of Literature

Handwriting: Theory, Research, and Practice. (1987). Jean Alston, Jane Taylor. NY: Nichols.

Reviews theory and research on handwriting problems. Seventeen chapters cover all aspects of the topic: motor skills; pencil grasp; left- and right-handed writers; assessment; scope and sequence of teaching; and writing and the handicapped. References.

LANGUAGE

Bibliographies

Body Movement and Nonverbal Communication: An Annotated Bibliography, 1971 - 1981. (1982). Edited by Martha Davis, Janet Skupien. Bloomington, IN: Indiana Univ. Press.

A sequel to *Understanding Body Movement: An Annotated Bibliography*, the references, mostly published in the 1970s, are in alphabetical order. A subject index is provided. Reviews of research may be located by using the term "overview, literature review."

Reviews of Literature

Acquiring Conversational Competence. (1983). Elinor Ochs, Bambi B. Schieffelin. Boston, MA: Routledge & Kegan Paul.

A collection of collaborative studies encompassing over ten years of research by the authors. The first and largest section of the book looks at how young children in adult-child and child-peer conversations sustain coherent, relevant discourse. In the second section of the book, the authors challenge the widely-held belief that in the process of developing communicative competence children discard early discourse strategies and replace them with adult strategies. In the third section the authors stress that children develop communicative competence simultaneous with their socialization into a particular culture. References.

Age in Second Language Acquisition. (1986). Birgit Harley. Clevedon, Avon: Multilingual Matters.

This book examines the empirical studies investigating the question of at what age should second language learning take place. Part II concentrates on some specific aspects of oral language proficiency at different ages. References.

Bases of Language Intervention. (1978).   Edited by Richard L. Schiefelbusch. Baltimore, MD: Univ. Park Press. (Language Intervention Series, Vol. 1).

Subject variables addressed by chapter are neurophysiological (Chapter 1); auditory/perceptive (Chapter 2); and cognitive (Chapter 3). The content variables identified are psycholinguistic-syntactic and semantic (Chapter 4) and pragmatic (Chapter 5).   Environmental variables are addressed in Chapters 5 and 8. The reviews of neurological processes, semantics, syntax, pragmatics, audition, etc., are detailed and impressively current. References.

Child Language: An Interdisciplinary Guide to Theory and Research.   (1977). Adele A. Abrahamsen. Baltimore, MD: Univ. Park Press.

This guide to literature of child language contains approximately 1,500 entries, one-third published from 1971 - 1974, one-third published earlier, and one-third published after 1974. The guide is organized topically into five parts: general resources, syntactic development, semantic development, beyond grammar, and phonology and orthography. Each of these five parts is further divided into 13 sections with 53 subsections with further subdivisions where appropriate. Entries are listed chronologically within the lowest level of classification.   Of great importance is a section providing basic bibliographies on linguistics, cognitive psychology, adult psycholinguistics, Piagetian theory, philosophy of language, and artificial intelligence. Each section is prefaced with introductory remarks which define important terms and print out issues and research directions in the subject area. An author and publication index is provided. References.

Child Language and Cognition, Contemporary Issues. (1984).   Mabel L. Rice, Susan Kemper. Austin, TX: Pro Ed. (Child Language Acquisition Series).

This particular volume looks at theoretical as well as applied research on the relationship of language and cognition. Chapter 1 provides an orientation to the central issues. Chapter 4 discusses the major theoretical positions about children's mastery of object terms. Chapters 5 and 6 focus on the early stages of the child's learning formal grammar and the use of language as a cognitive tool. References.

Child Language and Education. (1972). C. B. Cazden. NY: Holt, Reinhart, & Winston.

The book title is misleading because the book is really about child language and child speech. A detailed analysis of curriculum is not covered. The first four chapters deal with language development, syntax, sounds and meanings, developmental processes, and environmental assistance.   The middle grouping of chapters deals with language differences and language use: dialect and bilingualism, communication styles, and the roles of language in cognition. The last chapter discusses oral language education. The appendix looks at methods of analyzing child language. Substantial bibliography.

The Child's Conception of Language. (1978). A. Sinclair, R. J. Jarvella, W. J. M. Levelt. NY: Springer-Verlag. (Springer Series in Language and Communication).

This book explores the growth of children's linguistic awareness in a series of papers written by psychologists and linguists from both the United States and Europe. The book is divided into two major sections plus an introduction and appendix. In the introduction some of the major theoretical and empirical issues involved in the study of linguistic awareness are discussed. The section Empirical Studies includes papers utilizing a number of approaches, experimental studies, literature reviews, case studies, and field studies. The section on Theoretical Aspects is limited to three papers. Presented in this section are a discussion of awareness in Piaget's theory, a proposed resolution of the incompatibility between linguistics and psychology with respect to grammar, and a model of linguistic awareness discussed in terms of "EMMA functioning." References.

Children Communicating: Media and Development of Thought, Speech, Understanding. (1979). Ellen Wartella. Beverly Hills, CA: Sage. (Sage Annual Reviews of Communication Research, Vol. 7).

Research studies describing how children communicate are presented in this volume. Each chapter concludes with references of varying lengths. The volume is not indexed.

Children's Conversation. (1985). Michael McTear. Oxford: Basil Blackwell.

McTear examines the development of conversational skills in children from early interaction with care givers through preschool and beyond. The focus is primarily on normal children's conversational skill development but he also discusses the implications of the research for the study of conversational disability and for clinical and educational applications. The book opens with a very careful, detailed analysis of the structure and components of conversation, including a discussion of turn-taking, appropriateness of utterances, initiations, responses, and repairs of conversational breakdown. This is followed by a review of the literature on conversational skills in very young children below the age of three. In the final chapters, the author argues that the school environment demands that some new conversational skills be learned by the child; that there is cultural variation in the rules governing conversational exchanges; and that in the diagnosis and treatment of language disorders, it is essential to distinguish deficiencies in the linguistic system from deficiencies in conversational skills, and that one does not necessarily imply the other. One asset of the book is that the data come from child-child, rather than child-adult, interaction. References.

Children's Language. Vol. 1. (1978). Edited by Keith E. Nelson. NY: Gardner.

This volume covers the normal child's spoken words, sentences, and conversations. Chapters 1 through 4 look at the child's production and comprehension of figurative expressions, semantic development and semantic memory development, semantics of adjectives, and language development during the school years. Chapters 5 through 10 cover various aspects of the child's language in relation to the language and expectations of peers and adults. Chapter 11 looks at early language development between the ages of two and four and one-half years. References.

Children's Language. Vol. 2. (1980). Edited by Keith E. Nelson. NY: Gardner.

This volume describes the theoretical and empirical work on the process of rule learning in child speech. Chapter 2 tries to answer the questions of how to conceptualize the task of the child learning his native language and what part environment plays in facilitating the learning. Chapter 3 synthesizes various theories and empirical studies of how the child forms descriptions of grammatical structure. Chapter 4 reviews the major issues involved in bilingualism. Chapters 5 - 9 address the symbols, phrases, and sentences used by nonhuman primates to communicate. Chapter 10 reviews the study of Greenfield and Dent, which found that the number of elements verbally encoded increased as uncertainty increased across the tasks. References.

Children's Language. Vol. 3. (1982). Edited by Keith E. Nelson. Hillsdale, NJ: Lawrence Erlbaum. (Children's Language).

This volume looks at various situations in which the child learns through social interaction with language "masters" or "models" both the rules for sentences and the rules of conversation. The first two chapters discuss what is known about early communication between mother and child and its effect. Chapter 3 discusses how the preschooler and the school-age child acquire a broader and more flexible set of language skills. Chapter 4 is a case study of a four-year-old's conversation with two different adults, his natural mother and his foster mother. Chapter 5 reports a study on how children acquire complex syntactic forms over time using a sentence repetition test. In Chapter 6, Baker and Cantwell review the literature on language difficulties. Chapters 7 and 8 address the topic of sign language. Chapter 9 investigates other types of language difficulties such as aphasics, reading difficulties, dyslexia, etc. References.

Children's Language. Vol. 4. (1983). Edited by Keith E. Nelson. Hillsdale, NJ: Lawrence Erlbaum.

Chapter 1 presents a study on the development of discourse about objects not in the child's nor the parent's view. Chapter 2 looks at imitations in children's language. Chapters 3 and 4 discuss transfer of rules and information from one context to another. Chapter 5 examines the development of indirect and direct requests as it affects various perspective-taking skills. Chapters 7 and 8 cover phonology. Chapter 9 discusses language acquisition in a deaf child of deaf parents. Chapter 10 investigates the development of summarization skills in children. Chapter 11 discusses developmental differences in schemata for story comprehension. Chapter 12 summarizes studies in language development in the neuropsychiatric disordered child. References.

Children's Language. Vol. 5. (1985). Edited by Keith E. Nelson. Hillsdale, NJ: Lawrence Erlbaum.

Chapter 1 reviews several studies dealing with how infants discriminate speech sound categories. Chapter 2 looks at the intonational communication of 12-month-old children with their care givers. Chapter 3 examines pretend play during the second year in relation to language. Chapter 4 summarizes some studies investigating noun and verb concepts by preschool children. Chapter 5 critiques research comparing good and poor readers. Chapters 6 - 11 review the various aspects of language acquisition in language-handicapped children including the deaf. Chapter 12 discusses language errors occurring between two and five years and the child's continuing reorganization of language skills. Chapter 13 looks at various issues of the language learning process. References.

Children's Language and Communication. (1979). Edited by W. Andrew Collins. Hillsdale, NJ: Lawrence Erlbaum. (*Minnesota Symposia on Child Psychology*, Vol. 12).

The six papers in the book cover such divergent topics as reviewing empirical studies in the acquisition of passives, negatives, and tense; development of semantic systems; children's processing of phonology; emergence of symbols; role of social interaction in language acquisition; and peer teaching in a primary classroom and the act of listening. Each paper ends with references. Indexed.

Children's Oral Communication Skills. (1981). Edited by W. Patrick Dickson. NY: Academic. (Developmental Psychology Series).

The volume provides a synthesis of theory and research on children's communication skills. Areas covered include speaking, listening, and communication competency. References.

Children's Talk. (1984). Catherine Garvey. Cambridge, MA: Harvard Univ. Press. (Developing Child Series).

The volume summarizes information on the child's attempts to use language in a social context from several research groups. The children whose language is reported come from white, upper-middle-class homes with very well-educated parents. Garvey gives examples of young children learning different strategies for opening and closing a conversation and examples of situations where the strategies used are inappropriate or ineffective. Finally, Garvey discusses the ways in which children learn about turn-taking and temporal sequencing of conversations. References.

Children's Talking to Themselves: Its Developmental Significance, Function, and Therapeutic Promise. (1983). Anne P. Copeland. In *Advances in Cognitive-Behavioral Research and Therapy*, Vol. 2, edited by Philip Kendall. NY: Academic.

Chapter reviews studies focusing on the effects that overt and covert private speech have on various cognitive, behavioral, and emotional performance. Some theoretical interpretations of the function of private speech are discussed along with issues of developmental significance. References.

Communication and Children.   (1987).   Ellen Wartella, Byron Reeves.   In *Handbook of Communication Science*, edited by Charles Berger, Steven Chaffee. Beverly Hills, CA: Sage.

The chapter reviews three broad areas: (1) learning to communicate; (2) communication with others; and (3) mediated communication. A lengthy bibliography is included.

Communication in Development.   (1981).   Edited by W. P. Robinson.   NY: Academic. (European Monographs in Social Psychology, 24).

The papers report international research studies focusing on the impact of social and environmental factors on language or cognitive development in the child, infancy to age eight.   David Messer discusses the role of nonlinguistic information as an aid to interpretation of referents of maternal speech in one- and two-year-olds. Freeman, Sinha, and Condliffe discuss problems involved in interpreting two- and three-year-olds' understanding of the prepositions *in* and *on*. W. P. Robinson's chapter surveys his research on the differences in maternal question-answering and their relationship to child speech and social class "codes."   Perret-Clermont and Schubauer-Leoni describe the role of differential types of social interaction within a Piagetian framework.   E. J. Robinson discusses the development of communication failures in children and the role of maternal feedback. References.

Concept Development and the Development of Word Meaning. (1983). Edited by Thomas B. Seiler, Wolfgang Wannenmacher.   NY: Springer-Verlag. (Springer Series in Language and Communication).

This volume of the series consists of 18 chapters reflecting international viewpoints on theoretical and empirical studies. The introductory chapter provides an excellent historical overview and synthesis of work on concept and word meaning. Several chapters focus primarily on theoretical issues including reviews, criticisms, and reinterpretations of the Piagetian position.

A number of the chapters address the acquisition process and consider the principles governing word formation, the relevant constraints on acquisition, and the impact of adult word usage on children's word usage. Several chapters are empirical reports on the acquisition of specific locative prepositions, action verbs, and emotional concepts. The volume concludes with a focus on directions for research in this area and synthesis of major theoretical and methodological problems. References.

The Development of Communication. (1978). Edited by Natalie Waterson, Catherine Snow. NY: John Wiley & Sons.

A selection of papers representative of child language research between 1970 and 1975. The different areas of interest included are: semantic and pragmatic components; social-communicative nature of language; language and cognitive development; perceptual processing; and innate structures for language acquisition. Several of the papers included provide new data on different languages: Dutch, English, French, German, Persian, Polish, Serbo-Croatian, and Thai. References.

The Development of Metalinguistic Abilities in Children. (1980). David T. Hakes. NY: Springer-Verlag. (Springer Series in Language and Communication).

The book examines metalinguistic abilities of children between the ages of four and eight years, and on only three tasks: the recognition of sentence synonymy; acceptability; and phonemic segmentation on the word level. The author also examined children's response strategies, comparing them with previously reported data. The major contribution of this work is methodological in illustrating difficulties of tapping children's linguistic intuitions. References.

The Development of Oral and Written Language in Social Contexts. (1984). Edited by Anthony Pellegrini, Thomas D. Yawkey. Norwood, NJ: Ablex. (Advances in Discourse Processes, Vol. 13).

This volume contains papers documenting the interaction among context, language functions and structure. The reports in Section 2, The Context of Social Play, describe ways children use oral language while they interact with peers and adults in play contexts. In Section 4, Language Development in a Social Context, the papers suggest that a child's language develops in the context of dialogue with a more mature language user. In the final section of the volume there are papers which examine the relations between social contexts and written language. References.

The Development of Word Meaning: Progress in Cognitive Development Research. (1986). Edited by S. A. Kuczaj II, M. D. Barrett. NY: Springer-Verlag.

This book provides a survey of children's lexical acquisition to cognitive development. Chapter 1 reviews the traditional feature theories of acquisition. Chapter 2 describes how word meanings are mapped into underlying representations that are gradually decontextualized. Chapters 4, 5, 8, and 10 consider different aspects of the developments of the lexicon that occurs during all phases of word-meaning acquisition. Chapters 6, 11, and 12 consider various aspects of word meaning acquisition that occur during the third year of life when vocabulary growth continues at the rate of 50 or more new words per month. Chapters 4 and 5 discuss the similarities and differences that characterize the acquisition of object names, action names, nouns, verbs, logical connections, etc. The final chapter deals with the need to consider context when examining children's acquisition of relational terms. References.

Discourse Analysis in Second Language Research. (1980). Diane Larsen-Freeman. Rowley, MA: Newbury House.

This volume introduces the user to the research relevant to learning to converse smoothly and adequately in a second language. The book is divided into ten topical areas, each written by a separate specialist in the field of second language learning. References.

Discourse Development: Progress in Cognitive Development Research. (1984). Edited by Stan A. Kuczaj II. NY: Springer-Verlag. (Springer Series in Cognitive Development).

The focus of this volume is on the development of communication skills in children. Three chapters are possibly outstanding because they present relevant theoretical and ethodological concerns while still presenting concrete examples or original data supporting their positions: Chapter 2 by Shatz and McClosky on developmental perspectives of conversational knowledge; Chapter 3 by McTear on structure and process in children's conversational development; and Chapter 4 on skill in peer learning discourse by Cooper and Cooper. Chapter 5 by Susan Kemper provides a comprehensive review of the literature on the development of narrative skills. Chapter 6 by Stan A. Kuczaj and Leslie McClain presents a case study on fantasy narratives. Chapter 7 by Rodger Wales discusses children's didactic reference, suggesting that children use terms such as *this* and *that* selectively, according to both the spatial location of referents and intimacy. Finally, Chapter 8 by Sandy Friel-Patti and Gina Conti-Ramsden provides a unique perspective, examining discourse development in language-impaired children. References.

Early Childhood Bilingualism: With Special Reference to the Mexican-American Child. (1983). Eugene E. Garcia. Albuquerque, NM: Univ. of New Mexico.

In eight chapters the author looks at the theory and research dealing with the study of young children simultaneously acquiring more than one language during the early years. Chapter 2 provides the reader with a short review of bilingual acquisition. Chapter 3 discusses the incidence of bilingualism and records a study of bilingual mother-child discourse. Language transfer is explored in Chapter 4. Two studies are recorded in Chapter 5 regarding language switching. Chapter 6 looks at intellectual functioning and cognitive development. Chapter 7 covers the area of bilingual education. The last chapter discusses methodological and empirical considerations in carrying out research in this area. References.

Early Language. (1979). Peter A. De Villiers, Jill G. De Villiers. Cambridge, MA: Harvard Univ. Press. (Developing Child Series).

After an introductory chapter, Chapter 2 discusses the first sounds of language development with a careful distinction made between babbling and word production. The third chapter discusses early use of words and some of the problems children encounter in understanding that words are both arbitrary and specific. Chapter 4 presents the learning of rules and some of the mistakes commonly made on the way to the understanding of rules. Chapter 5 details difficulty in learning to convey relationships and gives many examples of the various strategies adopted by children to make themselves understood. Chapter 6 discusses how language is freed from concrete references to become a tool that allows the child to use language in a non-egocentric fashion. In chapters 7 and 8, children with atypical learning experiences are examined, and how their lack of early language exposure affects language development. Chapter 8 examines constraints on language in the chimpanzee and in the very young child. References.

A First Language: The Early Stages. (1973). Roger Brown. Cambridge, MA: Harvard Univ. Press.

A resource useful to those interested in retrospective research on the topic up to 1972. Most of the research reported was done by the author or his students. Stage I of the volume deals with semantic roles and grammatical relations discussing topics such as telegraphic speech and the role of word order. Stage II deals with grammatical morphemes and the modulation of meanings. References.

How Twins Learn to Talk: A Study of the Speech Development of Twins From 1 to 3. (1980). Svenka Savic. NY: Academic.

Chapter 1 reviews older studies on speech development in twins. Subsequent chapters contain a discussion of problems in twins' language acquisition and Savic's study which looked at 28,620 utterances collected from three sets of Yugoslav twins and three single children. From this data, Savic computed the rate of directed, nondirected, and semidirected speech for the twin children. It was concluded that adult input plays a significant role in the language development of twins as well as that of single children. Savic also examines repetition, correction, completion, and explication in twins' conversations. Savic concludes with a discussion of autonomous speech between twins; she argues that this type of speech is a form of baby talk. References.

Infant Crying: Theoretical and Research Perspectives. (1985). Edited by Barry Lester, C. F. Zachariah Boukydis. NY: Plenum.

The 17 chapters making up this monograph include studies of characteristics of infants' and children's normal and abnormal cries. References or bibliographies are provided at the ends of chapters.

Information and Meaning in Child Communication. (1981). Peter Loyd, Michael Beveridge. NY: Academic. (Applied Language Studies).

Volume summarizes empirical research on the ability of normal preschool children and older retarded children of similar mental age to engage in communication tasks. The book presents a series of studies with normally developing preschool children engaged in structured contexts with peers, adults, and a talking doll. The results of the studies indicated a considerable range of performance within the normal preschool population. The results with the retarded children showed that these children were not merely functioning at a lower developmental level with respect to referential communication skills but interacted differently than normal preschool children in referential communication tasks. References.

Interaction, Conversation, and the Development of Language. (1977). Edited by Michael Lewis, Leonard A. Rosenblum. NY: John Wiley & Sons. (Origins of Behavior).

The chapter presents a comprehensive overview of the early development of language from the viewpoint of its social genesis. The chapters reflect a broad range of interests, linked together by their underlying theme, the social genesis of language and its relationship to social acts. References.

Language Acquisition in the Early Years: An Introduction to Paedolinguistics. Translated by Katherine Turfler. (1983). Els Oksaar. London: Batsford Academic and Educational.

A review of research and theory of the interdisciplinary study of language acquisition from birth to age seven. The book is divided into four sections. The first is concerned with the definition of paedolinguistics and the history of the field. The second section discusses the theoretical and methodological foundations of paedolinguistics. The study of child language by Oksaar's method is delineated. The third section considers the biological and social conditions for language acquisition. The fourth section contains a description of language development from birth to age seven, including phonology, semantics, morphology, syntax, and pragmatics. The book provides excellent coverage of non-English data, including the author's extensive Estonian, Swedish, and German data concerning her multilingual son. Study questions are included at the end of each section. The book is translated from the 1977 German publication. Some references to post-1977 research have been added. Many of the foreign materials cited are available in English translation. References.

Language Development. Vol. 1. Syntax and Semantics. (1982). Edited by Stan A. Kuczaj. Hillsdale, NJ: Lawrence Erlbaum. (Child Psychology).

Chapter 1 by Ruth Clark synthesizes 10 - 15 years of research into the acquisition of syntax. In Chapter 2 the editor attempts to answer the question, How do young and relatively cognitively immature children acquire the complex, abstract, productive rule-governed conceptual system that underlies their use of the mother tongue? Chapter 3 looks at Brian MacWhinney's theory of the acquisition of word-order patterns. Chapter 4 compares child syntax and adult syntax and what evidence moves the child from incorrect grammar to correct grammar. Chapter 5 examines research on various aspects of children's language learning. Chapter 6 deals with the development of sentence coordination. Chapter 7 examines the child's development of relative clauses. Chapter 8 concerns word meaning acquisition. Chapter 9 explores acquisition of the meaning of object names. Chapter 10 focuses on the holistic or synthetic nature of acquiring meaning of words by the child. Chapter 11 traces experience as a variable to acquiring word meaning. Chapter 12 synthesizes 25 years of literature, both theoretical and empirical, as it relates to learning the meaning of language. Chapter 13 explores the growth of connotations of noun-like words. The last chapter outlines two developments: acquisition of distinctive meanings of mental verbs, and development of distinctive reference to the world of mind. References.

The Language of Children and Adolescents: The Acquisition of Communicative Competence. (1984). Suzanne Romaine. NY: Basil Blackwell. (Language in Society).

This volume includes nine chapters which show the interrelatedness of a growing body of literature of sociolinguistics and psycholinguistics along with the author's own data collected from interviews with school children in Edinburg, Scotland. Chapters 1 - 4 present new and intriguing data along with literature reviews. In Chapter 4 Romaine compares sociolinguistic patterns in the language of children in Britain, the United States, and Sweden relating the findings to major urban sociolinguistic studies of adult populations. References.

The Language of Children Reared in Poverty: Implications for Evaluation and Intervention. (1982). Lynne Feagans, Dale C. Farran. NY: Academic. (Educational Psychology).

The book is divided into five general sections: environmental effects on language learning; language use and school; language evaluation; language intervention; and theory-into-practice, some implications. References.

New Dimensions in Second Language Acquisition Research. (1981). Edited by Roger Andersen. Rowley, MA: Newbury House.

The twenty-three papers in this book focus on some of the different circumstances under which second languages are acquired and used. Three of the papers present new research (chapters 11, 12, and 17). The other papers explore new dimensions of previously researched areas. References.

The Ontogenesis of Grammar: A Theoretical Symposium. (1971). Edited by Dan I. Slobin. NY: Academic. (Child Psychology Series).

This volume covers the process of grammatical development in the young child. Four facts emerge from the theoretical discussions set forth in the four chapters making up the book: (1) early two-word sentences are structured; (2) with the advent of three-word sentences, the structure of many sentences is hierarchical; (3) regular forms are over generalized, even to highly practical forms; and (4) there is a succession of short-lived devices for performing grammatical transformations such as negation and interrogation. Susan Ervin-Tripp's paper, "An Overview of Theories of Grammatical Development" is included in the volume. References.

Phonological Development in Children 18 to 72 Months. (1983). Edited by John V. Irwin, S. P. Wong. Carbondale and Edwardsville, IL: Southern Illinois Univ. Press.

A collection of studies relative to distinctive feature theory bearing on speech development. Part I is a review of the literature by Leslie Paschall and John V. Irwin. The volume includes a bibliography.

Play, Language, and Story: The Development of Children's Literate Behavior. (1985). Edited by Lee Galda, Anthony D. Pellegrini. Norwood, NJ: Ablex.

The nine chapters of this volume explore aspects of the relationship between play and literate language of children. The first chapters look at the influence of scripts on the use of language in play. Several chapters document the change in language to fit play roles and thereby develop communication competence. Several chapters delve into play routines which help children master new language skills. The studies reviewed present a view of the multifaceted nature of the language of play. References.

Precursors of Early Speech. Proceedings of an International Symposium Held at the Wenner-Gren Center, Stockholm, September 19 - 22, 1984. (1986). Edited by Bjorn Lindblom, Rolf Zetterstrom. NY: Stockton.

This book covers investigations related to infant vocalizations and babbling. The 19 chapters are organized into seven parts: introduction; stages of infant vocalization; prognostic use of early vocalization; transition from babbling to spoken language; motor aspects; perceptual and intermodal aspects; and interaction. Only one chapter (Kuhl) is devoted to infant speech perception. Infant cry research is covered in the chapter by Michelsson, who gives a concise review of Finnish cry research from 1960 - 1984. Mother-infant interaction as motivation for speech is covered in the Trevarthen and Marwick chapter. References.

Prelinguistic Communication in Infancy. (1981). Alan Ziajka. NY: Praeger.

The majority of this volume, chapters 3 through 8, reviews the literature in various disciplines, including anthropology, psychology, and child development, regarding the communication choices available to infants during their first year of life. The remainder of the book describes the longitudinal study carried out by the author of communicative interaction in the home environment between six infants, ages six to twelve months, and their primary caretakers. Extensive bibliography.

Pronominal Reference: Child Language and the Theory of Grammar. (1983). Lawrence Solan.   Boston, MA: D. Reidel.   (Studies in Theoretical Psycholinguistics).

This book looks closely at a particular set of linguistic structures with respect to both linguistic theory and language development, exploring the relationship between the theoretical claims and the results of a series of language experiments. Chapters 2 through 4 are concerned with theoretical analysis of structural principles limiting pronominal reference and relationships between focus and pronominal reference. Chapters 3 through 5 discuss experimentation designed to test the claims made in the theoretical chapters about language acquisition.   Chapter 6 summarizes the major findings. References.

Research in Second Language Acquisition: Selected Papers of the Los Angeles Second Language Acquisition Research Forum. (1980). Robin C. Scarcella, Stephen D. Krashen. Rowley, MA: Newbury House.

This volume contains a select group of papers presenting data gathered on almost every aspect in the second-language learning field. References.

Research on Language Acquisition: Do We Know Where Are We Going? (1970). David S. Palermo. In *Life-Span Development Psychology: Research and Theory*, edited by Goulet, Baltes. NY: Academic.

A brief historical review and critical evaluation of research approaches to the problem of language acquisition.   Major attention is focused upon psycholinguistic research and the linguistic as well as psychological environment from which it has grown. Research results, which seem to be incompatible with current learning theories, are summarized.

Second-Language Acquisition in Childhood. (1978). Barry McLaughlin. Hillsdale, NJ: Lawrence Erlbaum.

A synthesis of literature on second language acquisition in childhood viewed from the perspective of the psycholinguist. Chapter 1 is an introduction, historical overview of second language learning, and review of approaches to learning a second language. European and U.S. philosophies are contrasted. Chapter 2 looks at the acquisition process and skills the child must use for the task. An overview is given of the developmental stages characteristic of first language acquisition. Chapter 3 compares second language acquisition in children and adults. Chapters 4 and 5 look at the simultaneous and successive acquisition of second language. Chapter 6 deals with U.S. and Canadian second language programs. Chapter 7 focuses on effects of bilingualism and on research dealing with cognitive processes in bilingualism. References.

Second-Language Acquisition in Childhood. Vol. 1. Preschool Children. Second edition. (1984). Barry McLaughlin. Hillsdale, NJ: Lawrence Erlbaum. (Child Psychology).

This second edition is a thorough review of the literature on second language acquisition during childhood. Chapter 2 discusses the models of language acquisition. Chapter 3 compares second language acquisition in children and adults. Chapters 4 and 5 look at simultaneous and successive acquisition of second languages. Chapter 6 covers the topic of individual differences in language learning. Chapter 7 discusses the effects of early bilingualism on language development and intellectual and cognitive functioning. Chapter 8 discusses the limits of knowledge in the area. References.

The Social Foundations of Language and Thought, Essays in Honor of Jerome S. Bruner. (1980). Edited by David R. Olson. NY: W. W. Norton.

The book is divided into three parts: cognition and language in their social contexts; child language in its social context; cognitive process and cultural products. Parts II and III will be of particular use to the linguistic student. Chapter 6 reviews the literature of acquiring linguistic skills and reports a study investigating sentence construction in preschool children. Chapter 7 looks at the development of the negative in language. Chapter 8 discusses conversational or discourse aspects. Chapter 9 reports a study concerning dialogue between mothers with two-year-olds. Chapter 10 discusses the cross-cultural aspects of perception and communication in infancy. Chapter 11 looks at the sequential aspect of interaction behavior in early child language. Chapter 12 covers the area of teaching the young child. Chapter 13 reviews communication between mothers and infants. Chapter 14 looks at the development of interpersonal and cooperative understanding in infants. References.

Studies in the Cognitive Basis of Language Development. (1975). Harry Beilin. NY: Academic. (Child Psychology Series).

The book reports studies designed to evaluate the general Piagetian hypothesis that linguistic development is dependent on cognitive development. This hypothesis was tested with reference to four cognitive-linguistic domains: knowledge of the passive construction, temporal reference, number lexicon and number agreement, and connectives (*and/or/not*). For each domain a review of the linguistic and psychological literature precedes formulation of more or less specific hypotheses regarding the dependence of certain linguistic acquisitions on certain cognitive abilities. Research is then reported in which the relevant linguistic and cognitive skills are assessed using a cross-sectional sample and inferences made about sequential dependencies between the various abilities. References.

Symbolic Functioning in Childhood. (1979). Edited by Nancy R. Smith, Margery B. Franklin. Hillsdale, NJ: Lawrence Erlbaum. (Child Psychology).

The volume is divided into four parts. The papers in the first part are concerned with basic questions of conceptualizing symbolic functioning and in part with specific symbolizing activities considered developmental. In the second part, Play, Gesture and Graphic Representation, ways in which tangible materials are structured and transformed in non-verbal symbolizing activities are discussed. The papers in the third section focus on aspects of symbolic functioning in the verbal domain. The concluding section, Symbolism and the Mythic World, is concerned with how different domains are spanned in the process of symbolizing in adults as well as children. References.

Topics in Cognitive Development. Vol. 2. Language and Operational Thought. (1978). Edited by Barbara Z. Presseisen, David Goldstein, Marilyn Appel. NY: Plenum. (Topics in Cognitive Development).

Like the first volume, this work includes theoretical, empirical, and applied aspects of Jean Piaget's seminal epistemology. The focus of this publication is the intricate interplay of language development and the development of operational thought. Four chapters make up Part I on language development. Part II, on formal reasoning, has three chapters. Part III deals with social cognition. Part IV contains a report on Rawson's research considering relationships between cognitive operations in concrete and reading situations as well as the relationship between cognitive operations and learning to read. The last chapter in the part examines science activities at various levels and in various scientific fields in order to identify the type of reasoning that may occur. References.

The Transition from Prelinguistic to Linguistic Communication. (1983). Edited by Roberta Michnick Golinkoff. Hillsdale, NJ: Lawrence Erlbaum.

This book provides interesting and important discussions of current issues by leading researchers from a variety of theoretical perspectives. The major importance of the book is that many of the contributors take the time to reflect on the successes and failures of the social/cognitive approaches that have dominated the study of language acquisition in the post-Chomsky era. Only a few papers present data. Harding presents longitudinal data on prelinguistic communication. Golinkoff presents a few examples of mother and child engaged in the "negotiation of failed messages." Messer presents quantitative evidence that redundancy between the adult's nonlinguistic and linguistic behaviors provides the child with important clues in learning referential words. Sugarman, in a general theoretical discussion, argues that much recent research has acted as if issues of continuity-discontinuity and nature-nurture are empirical issues. The final section of the book involves clinical issues of assessment and intervention. It contains papers by Levenstein on an ongoing intervention project; Braunwald on the language of abused and neglected toddlers; Chapman and Miller on the relations between normal and delayed language; and Johnson on explanations of abnormal language development. References.

The Use of Definite and Indefinite References in Young Children: An Experimental Study in Semantic Acquisition. (1976). Michael P. Maratsos. Cambridge, MA: Cambridge Univ. Press.

This monograph addresses children's command of the linguistic rules governing the use of the articles *a* and *the* and also of the semantic rules for their interpretation. It studies whether three- and four-year-olds realize that *a* is used to indicate class membership and *the* to indicate an individual within the class. The book begins with a judicious review of the rules for adult usage. It goes on to summarize the findings of naturalistic observations of children's speech. The rest of the book reports a series of attractive and sensibly interpreted experiments. The general finding is that young children grasp well the difference between definite and indefinite reference. They are slower to take account of whether or not the listener knows to which particular objects they are referring. References.

Reports of Research

Acquiring Language in a Conversational Context. (1981). Christine Howe. NY: Academic.

Chapter 1 introduces the reader to Howe's focus in conversational exchanges and the literature on mother-child conversations. Chapter 2 describes the methodology. Chapter 3 examines mother-child conversational patterns. Chapter 4 records the results of the study. References.

The Acquisition of Syntax in Children from 5 to 10. (1969). Carol Chomsky. Cambridge, MA: MIT Press. (MIT Research Monograph Series).

This book looks at several aspects of children's acquisition of syntactic structures. The question of to what extent children from five to ten have achieved mastery of their native language is explored including the area of disparity between adult grammar and child grammar. The study indicates that mastery of grammar in native languages takes up to nine years or longer. References.

Amy, Wendy, and Beth: Learning Language in South Baltimore. (1982). Peggy J. Miller. Dallas, TX: Univ. of Texas Press.

The book reports a study of three young children's language socializations into an urban, working-class community. Miller examines early language development of two-year-olds from poor families. Chapter 1 reviews the research literature on the relationship between language development and social class. Chapter 2 describes subject selection data collection methods, and the qualitative and quantitative techniques used in discussing the findings. Chapter 3 portraits the study's children and their families. Chapter 4 describes the study's findings. It examines the contexts and content of the mothers' instructions as they teach daughters how to care for babies, to talk back, assert, challenge, and to comply. In Chapter 5 Miller presents a question adopted from Bloom's research, asking whether children of the urban poor express the same kinds of meanings, in the same developmental sequence, as do middle class children in their two- and three-word utterances. Miller gives in this book ethnographic research at its finest. References.

Bilingual Education of Children: The St. Lambert Experiment. (1972). Wallace E. Lambert, Richard G. Tucker. Rowley, MA: Newbury House. (Studies in Bilingual Education).

This volume describes the classic longitudinal study known as the St. Lambert Experiment which studied the effects of the French immersion program on young elementary school children. The study mainly looked at the effects on the linguistic, intellectual, and attitudinal development of children.

Change and Continuity in Infancy. (1971). Jerome Kagan. NY: John Wiley & Sons.

The volume summarizes the findings of a longitudinal study looking at the different degrees of articulation of schemata used by infants encountering human faces, forms, and speech. The researchers gained some insight into the pattern of psychological continuities during the first two years, encountering provocative sex and social class differences in attention dynamics, and sufficient evidence to sustain hope that the preschool child's conceptual tempo might be previewed from his reaction patterns during the first year of life. They found that fixation, vocalization, deceleration, and smiling each mirror different aspects of the attention process with varying degrees of fidelity. References.

The Child's Grammar from I to III. (1969). Roger Brown, Courtney Cazden, Ursula Bellugi-Klima. In *Minnesota Symposia on Child Psychology*, Vol. 2, edited by John Hill. Minneapolis, MN: Univ. of Minnesota.

Paper presents a study made of three preschool-age children's knowledge of language structure at given points of time. The I to III in the title refer to periods of development and are offered by the authors as tools in comparative linguistics studies. Nineteen references cited.

Cognitive Basis of Language Learning in Infants. (1972). J. MacNamara. In *Psychological Review*, 79, 1 - 13.

This paper asserts that infants learn language by first determining, independent of language, the meaning which the speaker intends to convey by working out the relationship between meaning and the expression they hear. Evidence to support the thesis is drawn from three levels: lexicon, syntax, and phonology. References.

Crib Speech and Language Play. (1983). Stan A. Kuczaj. NY: Springer-Verlag.

This book is a report of a study of language practice divided into five types: exact repetitions and imitations; build-ups (that is, an utterance sequence of two or more parts; each successive part including words of the previous utterance and additional linguistic units); breakdowns (the opposite of build-ups); completions (two or more utterances . . . separated by a pause but which form a more complex utterance); and substitutions (a substitution in the second or third utterance of a different word . . . in a sentence grammatically parallel to the original). Each of the five types of language practice is studied in two speech settings (for example, self-model situations and other-model situations). Data are reported on fourteen children (15 - 24 months of age at the start of the study), who were followed until they stopped producing crib speech (6 - 27 weeks). The detailed description of the findings occupies two-thirds of the book's pages. The last section provides discussion, conclusions, and speculation. The use of figures to present data in detail should prove useful to other researchers for the comparison of data sets and the generation of hypotheses relevant to language practice. References.

Developmental Psycholinguistics: Three Ways to Look at a Child's Narrative. (1983). C. Peterson, A. McCabe. NY: Plenum.

The book describes a cross-sectional study of the development of narrative skills that was conducted with 96 children ranging from three to nine years of age. The children engaged in conversation with an experimenter who prompted for narratives describing specific experiences in the child's life. Each child provided several different narratives, and one of the excellent features of the book is the inclusion of 73 complete narratives that could be used by readers for their own purposes. The major portion of the text is a detailed description of three scoring analyses: High Point, Episode, and Syntactic Dependency. The results are described and evaluated thoughtfully and critically by the authors. References.

Language Development: Form and Function in Emerging Grammars. (1970). Lois Bloom. Cambridge, MA: MIT Press. (MIT Research Monograph Series, No. 59).

The volume reports part of an extended study on language development of three children. Section II reviews the psycholinguistic investigations carried out over the past decade which studied the emergence of grammar in children's spontaneous speech. Chapter 1, along with describing the children studied, discusses the theory, notations, and terminology of generative transformational grammar for the grammatical description of the children's language. Chapters 3 - 5 discuss each child of the study separately. Chapter 6 outlines the linguistic rules proposed in the grammars to account for the results of the constraints that appear to operate on length and complexity of the children's utterances. Chapter 7 describes the development of the syntax and semantics of negation. Chapter 8 presents the different strategies that children appear to use in their approaches to learning the model language and the relationship between the children's linguistic expression and development of cognition. The study is a classic in this field. References.

Language Development in the Pre-School Years. (1985). Gordon Wells. NY: Cambridge Univ. Press. (Language at Home and at School, Vol. 2).

The volume reports on the longitudinal study called *The Bristal Language Development Study* which set out to analyze the speech of children learning English as their first language from 15 months up to the age of five. The appendixes provide data from the various transcripts for the reader. References.

Language Development: Kindergarten through Grade Twelve. (1976). Walter Loban. Champaign, IL: National Council of Teachers of English.

This monograph is a continuation of the earlier study, *The Language of Elementary School Children* (1963). Of the original 338 subjects from kindergarten through the twelfth grade 211 were studied regarding: (1) differences between those who use language effectively and those who do not, and (2) predictable sequences in children's language. This study attempts to identify stages and velocity of language development. References.

Learning Lessons: Social Organization in the Classroom. (1979). Hugh Mehan. Cambridge, MA: Harvard Univ. Press.

This work reports a study involving child language in a cross-aged, ethnically mixed, elementary class in the San Diego Unified School District which was videotaped regularly. The research group reviewed these tapes, generated ideas, and drew conclusions. The book reports the year-long study. References.

Observing Composing Behaviors of Primary-Age Children: The Interaction of Oral and Written Language. (1984). Grant Cioffi. In *New Directions in Composition Research*, edited by Richard Beach, Lillian Bridwell. Chapter 8. NY: Guilford. (Perspectives in Writing Research).

Chapter reports a study investigating the role played by oral language in the development of composition skills by first grade students during the first two years of elementary school. The study also sought to document and categorize the kinds of reading that composing required. References.

One Word at a Time: The Use of Single Word Utterances before Syntax. (1973). Lois Bloom. The Hague: Mouton.

This classical study attempts to explain the emergence of grammar by looking at changes in children's use of single-word utterances in the period of time before they use syntax in their speech. Bloom looked at the linguistic behavior in relation to the nonlinguistic behavior and context which go along with what children hear and what they say. The study concludes that, first, children say only one word at a time because of both linguistic and psychological limitations. Second, what children know at different points in time, in terms of cognitive development, appears to influence the linguistic inductions they make about the grammar of their language. The report is divided into four sections. Chapter 2 delves into literature explaining the transition from using only one word at a time to the use of two-word utterances. Chapter 3 presents the argument that single-word utterances before children use syntax in their speech are not sentences. Chapter 4 describes one child's use of single-word utterances in terms of developmental change in form and function of words over the 12-month period they are used before emergence of grammar. Chapter 5 discusses the conceptual notions underlying single-word utterances. Over half of the volume is the appendix where transcripts of video-taped sessions appear. References.

Predication: A Study of Its Development. (1974). Carol Wall. The Hague: Mouton.

The book reports an investigation of the development of predication in the speech behavior of fourteen children ages 15 - 54 months. The first three chapters deal essentially with theoretical considerations, experimental procedures, and methods of observation. Considerable attention is given to the development of noun phrases in chapters 4 - 7. References.

Prelude to Literacy: A Preschool Child's Encounter with Picture and Story. (1983). Maureen Crago, Hugh Crago. Carbondale and Edwardsville, IL: Southern Illinois Univ. Press.

This book is on a diary of the authors' daughter's spontaneous responses to more than 400 books read or discussed during the first four years of her life. The book is organized into three parts. Part I (chapters 1 - 7) presents the protocols for one book selected to be characteristic of each six-month period during the time the child was studied. Part II (chapters 8 - 9) records the child's use of story in her games and monologues outside the time spent in actual reading. Finally, Part III (chapters 10 - 15) presents the child's response to picture, plot, humor, and fantasy.

Social Class, the Nominal Group, and References. (1969). P. R. Hawkins. In *Language and Speech*, 12, 125 (1969).

One of the most quoted research reports from the Bernstein project dealing with language of children and different social backgrounds. References.

Social Class, the Nominal Group, and Verbal Strategies. (1977). P. R. Hawkins. London: Routledge & Kegan Paul. (Primary Socialization, Language, and Education).

This book expands and qualifies an early journal article by Hawkins, "Social Class, the Nominal Group and Reference." *Language and Speech* (1969), which is probably the single most quoted research report from the Bernstein project. The author notes major areas of social class differences which he calls "verbal strategies": (1) noun usage; (2) adjective versus verb usage; and (3) use of verbs of tentativeness versus tag questions. References.

The Structure of Communication in Early Language Development. (1976). Patricia Marks Greenfield, Joshua H. Smith. NY: Academic. (Child Psychology Series).

A report of investigations into one-word utterances the young child uses in the nonlinguistic situation to make his meanings clear. The authors look at the one-word utterances made by two boys between the second half of their first year of life and the end of their second year. Data came from two sources: diaries kept by the boys' mothers (one of whom was Greenfield herself) and formal observation sessions during which the mother and another observer were present. The earliest utterances were "performatives" in which word and action were barely separable (*bye-bye* accompanied by a wave). The most advanced are labeled "modification of an event" (*again* to have something repeated). Experiments involving infants are reviewed to make the point that in their early language children reveal categories that they have long been revealing in other ways, such as through hand or eye movements. Book includes reviews of earlier work on language development in which one-word utterances were virtually ignored, and of studies of one-word utterances which were carried out at the same time as his research. References.

Syntax of Kindergarten and Elementary School Children: A Transformational Analysis. NCTE Research Report No. 8. (1967). R. C. O'Donnell, W. J. Griffin, R. C. Norris. Champaign, IL: National Council of Teachers of English.

This study analyzes language samples of 180 boys and girls, kindergarten through grade seven, from white middle-class families in Tennessee. Some conclusions of the study are: (1) there's a positive correlation between advances in grade and increasing word-length of total responses to a situation; (2) largest overall increases and most frequent statistically significant increments from grade level to grade level were found in the use of coordinate constructions within clauses, of subclausal adverbial constructions, and of nominal constructions containing adjectives, participles, and prepositional phrases; (3) deletion transformations may be better indicators of development than subordinate clauses; and (4) development of oral expression appears to occur fastest in the time span between kindergarten and the end of the first grade and between the end of the fifth grade and the end of the seventh. References.

LISTENING

Reviews of Literature

Talking, Listening, and Learning in Elementary Classrooms. (1985). Greta Morine-Dershimer. NY: Longman.

In this volume the author explores the social meaning of language in naturalistic classroom settings. The study began in 1977 and ended seven years later. This book presents the first complete synthesis of the findings from the entire study. The observational aspects of the study focus on how students develop an understanding of who and what to listen to in a discussion and how this understanding shifts as the social situation or the instructional task varies. References.

READING

Bibliographies

Children, Parents and Reading: An Annotated Bibliography. (1985). Compiled by Mary Maher Boehnlein, Beth Haines Hager. Newark, DE: International Reading Association.

This is a briefly annotated bibliography of materials useful to both parents and educators concerning parent involvement in reading. The monograph has four sections. The first is entitled Parents and Reading. In this section the largest group of citations falls into the preschool readiness category. The books and articles included will assist parents in developing general cognitive skills from birth through preschool years. Section II contains materials for professionals and home/school involvement. Section III lists booklets and pamphlets for parents. Section IV lists periodicals for children and parents, audio-visual materials, and other miscellaneous materials useful in parent education.

Early Reading: An Annotated Bibliography. (1980). Compiled by William H. Teale. Newark, DE: International Reading Association.

Entries are divided into six categories: comprehensive studies of early reading; theoretical issues in early reading; pedagogical issues; empirical issues; reviews; and bibliographies of early reading.

An Introduction to the Cloze Procedure: An Annotated Bibliography. Revised. (1980). Michael C. McKenna, Richard D. Robinson. Newark, DE: International Reading Association.

Sources cited are arranged in nine categories: background reference; reviews; comprehension and readability; statistical and constructional issues;

psychology of cloze; contextual phenomena; cloze as a teaching device; foreign language applications; and cloze and maze.

Reading in American Schools: A Guide to Information Sources. (1980). Maria E. Schantz, Joseph F. Brunner. Detroit, MI: Gale Research. (Vol. 5, Education Information Guide Series).

Guide to the literature in reading philosophy, research, theory, practice, and programs. References.

Reviews of Literature

The Acquisition of Literacy: Ethnographic Perspectives. (1986). Bambi B. Schieffelin, Perry Gilmore. Norwood, NJ: Ablex. (Advances in Discourse Processes, Vol. 21).

This volume examines the acquisition of literacy from an ethnographic view. The chapters have been organized into four sections. Part I examines the organization and meaning of literacy events that involve adults reading to and using written texts with young children. Part II examines how young children acquire an orientation towards literacy as well as skills required to achieve it. Part III examines issues related to school success and failure. The final section focuses on the impact literacy has on different aspects of the social order and looks at Western Samoa, Morocco, and the United States. References.

Advances in Reading/Language Research: A Research Annual. Vol. 1 - . (1982 -). Greenwich, CT: JAI.

The chapters included in each annual describe pertinent research carried out since publication of the previous annual. Volumes do not focus on any single topic. No cumulated index is provided but each annual contains an index. References.

Aspects of Reading Acquisition: Proceedings of the Fifth Annual Hyman Blumberg Symposium on Research in Early Childhood Education. (1976). Edited by John T. Guthrie. Baltimore, MD: Johns Hopkins Univ. Press. (Blumberg Series).

Much of this book consists of highly technical reports of data from ongoing research in reading acquisition. Topics discussed include: (1) a typology of the neurological aspects of some forms of alexia, (2) a description of research concerned with the relationship between a child's expectations for reading success and his success at reading in terms of marks in first grade, (3) a detailed discussion of evidence regarding the relationship between the acquisition of oral and written language, (4) a description of two different research efforts at providing predictors of reading success, (5) an in-depth treatment of the debate between advocates of the *part* and *whole* methods of reading instruction, and (6) a description of several possible models for teaching by the *part* approach. Now outdated but still quite informative. References.

Children's Knowledge of Events: A Causal Analysis of Story Structure. (1981). Tom Trabasso, Nancy L. Stein. In *The Psychology of Learning and Motivation: Advances in Research and Theory*, Vol. 15, edited by Gordon Bower. NY: Academic.

This chapter contains a good review of research on children's causal understanding of narrative events. References.

Clairmont Reading Conference Yearbook. Vol. 1 - . (1936 -). Clairmont, CA: Clairmont Graduate School. (Clairmont Reading Conference).

The Clairmont Yearbooks focus on a general theme with each volume. Some of the papers included in the yearbooks are research and include lengthy bibliographies. The yearbooks are indexed.

Cloze Instruction Research: A Second Look. (1980). Eugene A. Jongsma. Newark, DE: International Reading Association. (Reading Information Series).

This monograph critically reviews and synthesizes twenty-six studies dealing with the use of cloze as a teaching technique. Basically the literature is limited to 1970 - 1980. This is a companion to the earlier publication entitled *The Cloze Procedure as a Teaching Technique* by Eugene Jongsma, published in 1971.

Competent Reader, Disabled Reader: Research and Application. (1982). Edited by Martin H. Singer. Hillsdale, NY: Lawrence Erlbaum.

This book abstracts experimental results relevant to developing effective reading programs. Concentration is on the more mechanical aspects of reading skill such as visual discrimination ability, visual and auditory memory, visual-to-phonetic translation skills, and attention strategies. Stress is placed on the heterogeneity of the reading-disabled population. The book is divided into three sections: Section I reviews experimental evidence on competent reading; Section II reviews research on poor reading; and Section III is an "applications" section. References.

The Complete Handbook of Children's Reading Disorders: A Critical Evaluation of Their Clinical, Educational, and Social Dimension. 2 Vols. (1982). Hilde L. Mosse. NY: Human Sciences.

This two volume handbook provides an overview of how careful clinical examination of children can assess factors involved in the causation of reading and related disorders. Practical and useful diagnostic categories of reading disorders are discussed along with guidelines suggesting treatment and prevention. Disorders included in Volume 1 include reading, writing, and arithmetic. Volume 2 covers speech disorders, musical ability disorders, rhythmic disorders, attention disorders, convulsive disorders, and others. Bibliographic references are listed at the end of each volume. Both volumes contain indexes.

Comprehension and Teaching: Research Reviews. (1981). Edited by John T. Guthrie. Newark, DE: International Reading Association.

This volume presents a new topography in research on the processes and teaching of reading. The twelve papers are divided into two sections. The first section covers generally the processes of reading including schemata, comprehension, inferences and reading, vocabulary knowledge, social context of learning to read, and social-psychological perceptions and reading comprehension. The second section deals with practices in education and includes: instructional variables; academic learning time; reading in bilingual contexts; exemplary reading programs; overcoming educational disadvantages; and recognizing a reading comprehension program. References.

Contexts of Reading. (1985). Edited by Carolyn N. Hedley, Anthony N. Baratta. Norwood, NJ: Ablex. (Advances in Discourse Processes, Vol. 18).

The book focuses on the social, cognitive, and personal contexts in which reading occurs. Some of the papers are more empirically based than others. The twelve chapters are divided among four parts: context of learning; context of reading instruction; variations in language and reading development; and assessment. References.

Effects of Pictures on Learning to Read, Comprehension and Attitudes. (1970). S. Jay Samuels. In *Review of Educational Research*, 40 (3).

This review article summarizes the research findings indicating that pictures interfere with learning to read.

Findings of Research in Miscue Analysis: Classroom Implications. (1976). Edited by P. David Alen. Urbana, IL: National Council of Teachers of English.

This volume brings together the concepts and assumptions underlying children's miscues in oral reading as studied from 1965 to 1974 by researchers at Wayne State University. Individual studies are not presented in depth. A summary is given to clarify for the reader what oral reading miscue research is about. References.

Handbook of Reading Research. (1984). Edited by P. David Pearson. NY: Longman.

This handbook gives an overview of the research-based knowledge about reading and related topics. The 25 chapters are divided among three parts. Part I contains chapters dealing with methodological issues such as history of reading research; traditions of reading research; design and analysis of experiments; ethnographic approaches to research; and assessment. Part II looks at basic process: models of the reading process; word recognition; listening; metacognitive skills; social and motivational influences; and cognitive processes. Part III deals with instructional practices; early reading; beginning reading; word identification; comprehension; studying; readability; classroom instruction; and oral reading. References.

Issues Concerning the Acquisition of Knowledge: Effects of Vocabulary Training on Reading Comprehension. (1983). Karen Mezynski. In *Review of Educational Research* 53 (4).

The eight studies reviewed show increases in students' word knowledge but little improvement was shown in reading comprehension. References.

Metalinguistic Awareness and Reading Acquisition. (1984). William E. Tunmer, Judith A. Bowey. In *Metalinguistic Awareness in Children, Theory, Research, and Implications*, edited by Tunner, Pratt, Herriman. NY: Springer-Verlag. (Springer Series in Language and Communication).

This chapter reviews research dealing with the role metalinguistic awareness plays in the acquisition of reading skills.

New Methods in Reading Comprehension Research. (1984). Edited by David E. Kieras, Marcel A. Just. Hillsdale, NJ: Lawrence Erlbaum.

Provides an overview to the research and methodologies being carried out in the area. Examples of topics covered in the fifteen chapters include: single-word paradigms; eye-movement data; reading entire sentences; think-out-loud protocols; and word-by-word reading. References.

Parental Involvement in Children's Reading. (1985). Edited by Keith Topping, Sheila Wolfendale. London: Croom Helm.

This volume provides insight into the various programs, research efforts, and practices being carried out in England in the area of parental involvement in reading. Many of the contributions to the volume bridge the gap between practice and research. Part I is a general introduction describing modern international trends and an analysis of why parental involvement works. Part II is divided into four subsections; parent listening, paired reading, behavioral methods, and variations. Part III comprises three chapters concerned with the implementation of projects to promote parental involvement. Each chapter ends with a short bibliography.

Reading: A Research Retrospective, 1881 - 1941. (1984). William S. Gray. Newark, DE: International Reading Association.

This reprint, initially published in the *Encyclopedia of Educational Research*, edited by Walter Monre in 1941, is now considered a classic.

Reading Ability. (1985). Charles A. Perfetti. NY: Oxford Univ. Press.

Comprehensively reviews pertinent literature on the topic. Chapter 7 is a review of investigations designed to explore the role of local processes in comprehension. The final two chapters deal with beginning reading and reading instruction. Chapter 10 provides a balanced treatment of beginning reading. The author also gives a very complete account of the verbal efficiency theory. Substantial references.

Reading and Deafness. (1985). Cynthia M. King, Stephen P. Quigley. San Diego, CA: College-Hill.

Although this research review deals mainly with the acquisition of reading by the deaf, many of the chapters provide concise reviews on the topic of reading generally. Chapter 1 covers cognition, language, and reading. Chapter 2 reviews the literature on reading in hearing children. Chapters 5 and 6 cover reading materials. Chapter 7 looks at the research of reading assessment. Chapter 8 covers reading and other language variant populations like the ESL population. Appendix A is an outline of procedures for preparing reading materials. Appendix C is a bibliography of reading material developed for hearing children. Appendix D is a selected bibliography of reading skills taxonomies and comprehension question hierarchies. Appendix E is a bibliography of how to prepare informal reading tests. Lengthy bibliography.

Reading Disability Research: An Interactionist Perspective. (Spring 1986). Marjorie Youmans Lipson, Karen K. Wixson. In *Review of Educational Research*. 56 (1), 111 - 136.

The first part of the article provides a brief historical perspective of the events leading to current views of reading disability and research practices. The second part reviews the literature from an interactionist perspective on reading disability. The last part discusses the implications of the research on future research in the area of reading disabilities. References.

Reading Research: Advances in Theory and Practice. Vol. 1 - . (1979 -). D. T. Besner, Gary Waller, G. E. Mackinnon. NY: Academic.

Each annual focuses on a particular reading topic. The chapters included in each volume review recent research or present reports on the topic. Chapters conclude with bibliographies. No cumulative index but each volume is indexed.

A Short Survey of the Research on Text and Story Comprehension and Retention. (1980). Lynne Reder. In *Twenty-ninth Yearbook of the National Reading Conference: Perspectives in Reading Research and Instruction.* Washington, DC: National Reading Conference.

This literature review focuses on aspects of comprehension of text and story. References.

Stress and Reading Difficulties; Research, Assessment, Intervention. (1987). Lance M. Gentile. Newark, DE: International Reading Association.

Summarizes the research suggesting that stress is a major factor in emotional maladjustment to reading. The four chapters of the monograph cover research, assessment, intervention, and differentiated intervention. A bibliography is provided at the end of the monograph along with suggested readings.

Theoretical Models and Processes of Reading. Third Edition. (1985). Edited by Harry Singer, Robert B. Ruddell. Newark, DE: International Reading Association.

This volume begins with a review of landmark research on reading starting in 1879. Seventy percent of the material in this edition is new. The chapters in the volume appear under one of four sections: historical changes in reading, processes of reading, models of reading, and teaching and research issues. New theories, models, and processes of reading can be found in the second and third sections. Most chapters conclude with lengthy bibliographies. Users will find the context index very useful for retrieving particular subject information.

Theory and Practice of Early Reading. 3 Vols. (1979). Lauren B. Resnick, Phyllis A. Weaver. Hillsdale, NJ: Lawrence Erlbaum.

These volumes explore the range and depth of the theoretical and practical knowledge about early reading instruction. The chapters are based on papers presented at a series of three conferences held at the Learning Research and Development Center, University of Pittsburgh, 1976. References.

The Word Identification Process in Reading. (1977). John Theios, J. Gerard Muise. In *Cognitive Theory*, Vol. 2, edited by N. John Castellan, Jr., David Pisoni, George Potts, Chapter 11. Hillsdale, NJ: Lawrence Erlbaum.

This chapter reports a study made of the word identification process in reading as well as providing a review of literature on the topic. The researchers' experiments with paired homophonic words and nonwords showed that good phonology or letter-to-sound correspondence is not sufficient to completely mediate the transformation from visual representation of a word to its articulation. Their experiments also showed that frequency of the word in the English language has a very small but consistent effect on the speed of articulating individually presented words. Fifty-seven references.

Yearbook of the National Reading Conference. (1964 -). Washington, DC: National Reading Conference.

This yearbook publishes research and reviews of research presented at the annual National Reading Conference. No general theme or focus may be found in any one yearbook. It is necessary to consult each volume's table of contents to determine if something relevant to a topic is included. Papers are arranged under broad categories such as reading instruction, comprehension, vocabulary, beginning reading, research and measurement concerns, teacher effectiveness, review of research, story structure, writing, study skills, and early reading. Papers conclude with bibliographies.

Reports of Research

How Reading Difficulties Develop: Perspectives from a Longitudinal Study. (1982). Alan M. Lesgold, Lauren B. Resnick. In *Theory and Research in Learning Disabilities*, edited by J. P. Das, R. F. Mulcahy, A. E. Wall. NY: Plenum.

This chapter reports a longitudinal study of the relationship between word recognition efficiency or automaticity and reading comprehension. Conclusions reached suggest that the lack of word processing efficiency may lie at the heart of reading disability. A lengthy bibliography is provided.

Inquiry Into Meaning: An Investigation of Learning to Read. (1985). A. M. Bussis, E. A. Chittenden, M. Amarel, E. Klausner. Hillsdale, NJ: Lawrence Erlbaum.

The researchers, primarily classroom teachers, examined children's use of background knowledge, their understanding of grammatical structure, sense of rhythm in reading, lexical skills, spelling, and other aspects of the reading process. They looked at the children's use of readers, literature, drawings, three-dimensional construction, and other parts of classroom life that applied. References.

Literacy Before Schooling. (1982). Emilia Ferriero, Ana Teberosky. Exeter, NH: Heinemann Educational Books.

Chapter 2 explores how children respond to graphic information such as letters, numbers, and punctuation marks. Chapter 3 explores the relationship between drawing and writing. Chapter 4 investigates oral response to the text and graphic aspects of the text and how printed words become apparent to children. Chapter 5 discusses how children determine differences in texts based on newspaper, story, and conversational modes. Chapter 6 looks at production of written language. Chapter 7 delves into dialect differences and concerns about correct pronunciation. The basic population used in this research is Argentinean children four to six years old. References.

One Second of Reading Again. (1977). Philip Gough, J. Michael Cosky. In *Cognitive Theory*, Vol. 2, edited by N. John Castellan, David B. Pisoni, George Potts. Hillsdale, NJ: Lawrence Erlbaum.

This chapter, part of Section IV in the book, is a sequel to Gough's well-known attempt to propose a model describing the processes taking place during one second of reading. In this chapter the authors review the progress made in the last five years since the original model was proposed. The data they collected indicate that if features are involved in word recognition, their organization into letters is important. Thirty-four references.

Dictionaries

A Dictionary of Reading and Related Terms. (1981). Edited by Theodore L. Harris, Richard E. Hodges. Newark, DE: International Reading Association.

This specialized dictionary for the subject area of reading contains approximately 5,400 terms drawn from some 10,000 terms identified from the reading literature. Entries are concise and where necessary a pronunciation key is given.

SPELLING

Reviews of Literature

Children's Creative Spelling. (1986). C. Read. London: Routledge & Kegan Paul.

Provides an extensive review of current research on spelling in the primary grades. Individual chapters describe research on dialects and spelling as well as spelling in other languages. The author gives a comprehensive discussion of beginning spelling including his own research carried on over the past fifteen years.

Cognitive Processes in Spelling. (1980). Edited by Uta Frith. NY: Academic.

A wide variety of issues regarding spelling is included from experimental psychology and education. Lengthy list of references.

Sources of Difficulty in Learning to Spell and Read. (1986). Linnea Ehri. In *Advances in Developmental and Behavioral Pediatrics*, Vol. 7, edited by Mark Walraich, Donald Routh. Greenwich, CT: JAI.

The chapter identifies various sources of difficulty involved in learning to spell and learning to read. The author first outlines the developmental steps good spellers go through. Then the author points out where poor spellers run into problems. Reading difficulties are only eluded to in context to spelling problems in the chapter. References.

TELEVISION

Bibliographies

Children and Families Watching Television: A Bibliography of Research on Viewing Processes. (1985). Compiled by Werner Muller, Manfred Meyer. NY and London: K. G. Saur.

The bibliography contains studies that investigate the mental processes and interpersonal communication that occur when children alone, with their siblings, peers, mothers, or within the family view television. The thirteen chapters of the bibliography are divided into four general parts.   Part I contains basic bibliographical material for study, literature reviews, general papers, and other publications.   Part II deals with individual aspects of the reception process which includes all the mental processes which a child uses to transform reality as presented on TV into his own ideas: excitement, emotional reaction, process of attention, comprehension and cognition, discrimination between fiction and reality, social perception, and media literacy.   Part III deals with the social aspect of reception.   Part IV includes studies and material on aspects of application of the research covered previously in the book.

CTW Research Bibliography; Research Papers Relating to the Children's Television Workshop and Its Experimental Education Series: "Sesame Street" and "The Electric Company", 1968 - 1976. (1977). NY: Children's Television Workshop.

An annotated bibliography of research related papers and reports in connection with the development of *Sesame Street* and *The Electric Company*. Entries are divided into sections under the appropriate television show title as well as CTW research on *Sesame Street* and other reports on media and children.

Effects and Functions of Television: Children and Adolescents. A Bibliography of Selected Research Literature, 1970 - 1978. (1981). Manfred Meyer, Ursula Nissen. Hamden, CT: Linnet Books (K. G. Saur).

The 914 references primarily cover empirical studies published from 1970 to March 1978. Entries are grouped into categories such as cognitive and emotional effects, and aspects of socialization. The bibliography appears to be very well done and has both an extensive author index and subject index. Many of the citations are from the literature normally not cited in the child and development literature, including marketing research, communication journals, and the U.S. government publications. Additionally, unpublished convention papers are cited. There are extensive references to ERIC documents. Many European, mostly German, entries also are included.

Mass Communication Effects and Processes, Comprehensive Bibliography, 1950 - 1975. (1978). Thomas F. Gordon, Mary Ellen Verna. Beverly Hills, CA: Sage.

In the literature overview section (pp. 27 - 28) the author covers adolescents as well as children, further dividing the topic of children into five subcategories: violence, advertising, learning, modeling, and language. *The Electric Company* and *Sesame Street* are noted under the category of language but not in the subject index provided. Most users will find the subject index helpful in locating studies published from 1950 - 1975. Unfortunately, document numbers are not provided for these entries.

Television: A Guide to the Literature. (1985). Mary Cassata, Thomas Skill. Phoenix, AZ: Oryx.

This guide to the literature is divided into three parts: test patterns, the environment, and directions. Within Part I is a section on reference sources. Part II contains a section about television processes and their effects on children.

Television and Social Behavior: An Annotated Bibliography of Research Focusing on Television's Impact on Children. (1971). Edited by Charles K. Atkin, John P. Murray, Oguz B. Nayman. Rockville, MD: National Institute of Mental Health.

Annotated bibliography of research on television and social behavior initiated in 1969. The bibliography contains about 300 annotated and 250 unannotated citations.

Television's Impact on Children and Adolescents. (1981). Sara Lake. Phoenix, AZ: Oryx.

Chapter 1 cites studies of viewing habits: how much TV is watched; why TV is watched; and programs preferred. Chapter 3 deals with TV as a shaper of children's attitudes, behavior, and thought. Entries for this bibliography were selected from: ERIC, Comprehensive Dissertation Index, NTIS, Psychological Abstracts, Sociological Abstracts, and SSCI. Magazine Index.

Reviews of Literature

Activity in the Effects of Television on Children.   (1986).   Robert P. Hawkins, Suzanne Pingree.   In *Perspectives on Media Effects*, edited by Jennings Bryant, Dolf Zillmann.   Chapter 12.   Hillsdale, NJ: Lawrence Erlbaum. (Communication).

The authors review studies on children as active participants in their use of television. The chapter differentiates between the cognitive activities applied in processing television and the cognitive efforts applied to these activities. A model of the various elements which play a part in the effects of television on children is presented.   Several suggestions are put forth on how researchers may keep the different types of cognitive activities in processing television separate in order to study the effects on children. References.

Children and Television.   (1976).   Edited by Ray Brown. Beverly Hills, CA: Sage.

Reviews twenty years of research dealing with children and television. Part I covers the aspect of how much time children watch television. Part II covers the influence of family on the child's functional orientation on viewing patterns. Part III deals with the general effects of television on the child. References.

Children and Commercials: Issues, Evidence, Interventions.   (1983).   Donald F. Roberts.   In R_x *Television, Enhancing the Preventive Impact of TV*, edited by Joyce Sprafkin, Carolyn Swift, Robert Hess.   NY: Haworth.   (Prevention in Human Services, Vol. 2, No. ½).

Reviews studies dealing with general impact of commercials on children. The author examines closely the developmental changes in children's processing of and responses to commercials. Roberts suggests that teaching children to evaluate commercials might moderate the impact of the selling messages. References.

Children, Television, and Sex-Role Stereotyping.   (1981).   Frederick Williams, Robert LaRose, Frederica Frost.   NY: Praeger.

This volume describes research dealing with sex-role stereotyping and television. Lengthy bibliography included.

Children's Processing of Television Content: Implications for Prevention of Negative Effects. (1983). W. Andres Collins. In *R$_x$ Television, Enhancing the Preventive Impact of TV*, edited by Joyce Sprafkin, Carolyn Swift, Robert Hess. NY: Haworth.

This chapter reviews the research on cognitive processing in children watching television. It is revealed that pronounced age differences in children's retention of essential information exists with preschool and young school-age viewers retaining or comprehending less than preadolescents and adolescents.

Children's Understanding of Television: Research on Attention and Comprehension. (1983). Edited by Jennings Bryant, Daniel R. Anderson. NY: Academic.

This book reviews the literature on the fundamental nature of children's television viewing. The first four chapters focus on the topic of attention. Chapters 5 - 9 address comprehension. Chapters 10 - 13 deal with research application or intervention. The last chapter is a synthesis of the research reported throughout the book and gives direction for possible future research. References.

The Early Window: Effects of Television on Children and Youth. Second edition. (1982). Robert M. Liebert, Joyce N. Sprafkin, Emily S. Davidson. NY: Pergamon. (Pergamon General Psychology Series).

This book provides an account of the theory and research on television and children's attitudes, development, and behavior, and explores the social, political, and economic factors that surround these issues. Chapter 1 provides an overview of the topic. Chapter 2 covers the topic of commercial television as a business rather than a social force. Chapter 3 reviews the theories and research on TV violence. Chapters 4 and 5 look at the Surgeon General's Report and aftermath of the report. Chapter 6 is devoted to the topic of television advertising and children. Chapter 7 focuses on stereotyping and sex roles on TV. Finally, Chapter 8 looks at the potential for good in television. Appendix B is a list of U.S. government documents available on the topic. Each entry is briefly annotated. References.

The Effects of Television Advertising on Children: Review and Recommendations. (1980). Richard P. Adler et al. Lexington, MA: Lexington Books.

Reviews existing research on the effects of television advertising on children. References.

Effects of Television on the Developing Child. (1980). Ronald G. Slaby, Gary R. Quarfoth. In *Advances in Behavioral Pediatrics*, Vol. 1, edited by Bonnie Camp. Greenwich, CT: JAI.

This chapter reviews the research and discusses the impact of television on the developing child. A lengthy bibliography is provided at the end of the chapter.

The Future of Children's Television: Results of the Markle Foundation/Boys Town Conference. (1984). John P. Murray, Gavriel Salomon. Boys Town, NE: Boys Town Center.

This is a collection of papers growing out of a conference held in March 1982 at the Boys Town Center in Nebraska. The focus of the conference was an assessment of the accumulated research evidence on the impact of television on children. Part I of this volume contains ten papers, written by participants, which are not really reviews of literature but rather the authors' reflections on their own experiences and personal statements of what they think are the important issues, conclusions, and implications of research in their particular domain. The papers in Part I are organized in a structured sequence beginning with overviews of research on the long standing issue of television violence. Next are more recent studies such as children's understanding of the content of television. Two essays look at the roles of parents and teachers in assisting children in getting the most out of television. In Part II there is a summary of the main research issues that emerged during the three-day conference. One paper looks at cable and the future of children's television. Another, by Judah Schwartz, discusses issues surrounding video, computers, and new technologies. The book is intended for professionals interested in the topic.

Interaction of Media, Cognition, and Learning. (1979). Gavriel Salomon. San Francisco, CA: Jossey-Bass.

The book provides a very readable integration of theory, experimental evidence, and implications for pedagogy. Four chapters are theoretical treatments: Chapter 1 on media; Chapter 2 on symbol systems; Chapter 3 on symbol systems and cognition; and Chapter 5 on the role of media's symbol systems in skill cultivation. Another four chapters describe empirical studies; Chapter 4 examines the role of symbolic elements in knowledge acquisition, and chapters 6 through 8 look at their role in skill cultivation. Chapter 9 summarizes all eight chapters. References.

Learning from Television: Psychological and Educational Research. (1983). Edited by Michael J. A. Howe. NY: Academic. (Educational Psychology).

The ten chapters in this book cover most, but not all, of the major categories of research studies investigating the effects of television upon children and adults. The first three chapters consider the influences of those forms of television that are deliberately designed to achieve educational goals. Chapters 4 - 8 examine some of the ways in which people are affected by their everyday television viewing. The final two chapters address the issue of ways people learn from television. References.

Out-of-School Television and Schooling, Hypothesis and Methods. (Summer 1981). Robert Hornik. In *Review of Educational Research*, 51 (2).

This review of the literature indicates that television viewing does affect school achievement in the area of reading.

Quality in Instructional Television. (1972). Edited by Wilbur Schramm. Honolulu, HI: Univ. of Hawaii Press.

The first two papers in the volume, by Lundgren and Egly, are excellent representations of the viewpoints of experienced and successful producers toward the problems of building quality into instructional television. The third and fourth papers, by Schramm and Lunsdaine, give the scholars' viewpoint. The Schramm paper is a brief review of the literature on content elements as related to effectiveness. Part III of the book contains two papers by Lesser and Palmer. The two papers are of major importance in the study of instructional television because they outline how writers of television programs can use the guidelines from previous scholarship and experience and produce highly effective productions like *Sesame Street* and *The Electric Company*. Few references.

Research on the Effects of Television Advertising on Children: A Review of the Literature and Recommendations for Future Research. (1977). Washington, DC: U.S. Government Printing Office.

This report is composed of an "Executive Summary," a series of chapters on various issues, a bibliography, recommendations for future research, and current voluntary regulatory codes for advertising to children. The report contains many unpublished studies as well as virtually all the published research on the topic. This volume is quite useful as an annotated bibliography.

Studies in Violence and Television. (1976). M. S. Heller, S. Polsky. NY: American Broadcasting.

This book consists of a collection of eleven original and partially integrated projects commissioned over a five-year period by the American Broadcasting Corporation. The approach taken is based on the assumption that if TV violence affects the young, it is likely to be most pronounced in children with emotional impairments. Consequently, the effects of TV violence are investigated with respect to institutionalized children, emotionally troubled children, and youthful offenders in a series of intensive small-sample experiments and clinical interviews. The appendix contains questionnaires and the details of numerous measures which could be used when assessing the effects of TV violence on children. In the face of the rather convergent set of findings that TV violence has a negative impact on children, the conclusion of these studies, that TV violence has little negative effect and potentially a prosocial one, may be related to the way in which the data are analyzed and interpreted and directly or indirectly to the nature of the sponsor of the research. Footnotes.

Summative Research of "Sesame Street": Implications for the Study of Preschool Children. (1972). Samuel Ball, Gerry Ann Bogatz. In *Minnesota Symposia on Child Psychology*, Vol. 6, edited by Anne Pick. Minneapolis, MN: Univ. of Minnesota Press.

The authors of this chapter focus on providing some generalizations about research related to the effect of *Sesame Street* on preschool children's development. Seven references cited.

Television and Its Educational Impact: A Reconsideration. (1986). Samuel Ball, Patricia Palmer, Emilia Millward. In *Perspectives on Media Effects*, edited by Jennings Bryant, Dolf Zillman. Hillsdale, NJ: Lawrence Erlbaum. (Communication).

Chapter examines the direct influence of television viewing on IQ, school achievement, and reading; the indirect influence of television viewing in the development of social relationships; and the mediating factors of family context on learning from television. References.

Television and Social Stereotypes. (1983). Bradley S. Greenberg, Carrie Heeter. In R_x *Television, Enhancing the Preventive Impact of TV*, edited by Joyce Sprafkin, Carolyn Swift, Robert Hess. NY: Haworth.

Noting that the very young and the elderly watch TV more than any other age group, Greenberg and Heeter discuss the contents of television programs in light of sex roles, ethnic roles, occupational roles, and age roles portrayed. Research on the impact of these portrayals is reviewed as well as research on programming, critical viewing skills, and parental mediation strategies presented.

Television and the Socialization of the Minority Child. (1982). Edited by Gordon L. Berry, Claudia Mitchell-Kerman. NY: Academic.

The volume pulls together diverse theories and research on the topic of television and the socialization process. Part I gives an overview of television and its role in the socialization of the minority child. Part II focuses on minority children and personal identity issues as well as mental health. Part III reviews research findings in available literature. References.

Reports of Research

Children's Television: An Analysis of Programming and Advertising. (1977). R. Earle Barcus, Rachel Wolkin. NY: Praeger. (Praeger Special Studies in U.S. Economic, Social, and Political Issues).

A study of three related context analyses of children's television programming and advertising in 1975. The first analysis was performed on weekend morning programming and on the advertising appearing on weekend mornings. The second was directed to after-school programming and advertising on ten independent stations across the country. The final analysis was a comparison of weekend morning advertising in April and November. Programming was analyzed for violent content, sex and racial stereotypes, subject matter, format, and other variables. Advertising was examined in light of products advertised; the age and sex of characters; the use of personalities, endorsements, previews, contests, disclaimers, and qualifiers; product information; and basic themes of types of appeals. References.

The Impact of Television: A Natural Experiment in Three Communities. (1986). Edited by Tannis Macbeth Williams. NY: Academic.

A classic in the field of research describing three Canadian communities before and after obtaining television. The first chapter provides an overview of research. Descriptions of the three communities and their comparability are also included. Chapters 2 - 8 describe the individual studies. Chapters 2, 3, and 4 deal with television's potential displacement effects on children's reading competence, thinking, and participation in other leisure activities. Chapters 6 and 7 look at the issue of sex-role attitudes and aggression as affected by television viewing. Chapter 9 is a summary of the data. References.

Television and the Aggressive Child: A Cross-National Comparison. (1986). Edited by L. Rowell Huesman, Leonard D. Eron. Hillsdale, NJ: Lawrence Erlbaum.

This book reports a three-year, longitudinal, cross-national research program in five different countries (Australia, Finland, Israel, Poland, and the United States) looking at television viewing habits and aggressive behaviors in children and their parents. Chapter 1 outlines the theoretical rationale, social importance, and historical background of the study. Chapter 2 discusses the methodology of the study. Chapter 3 outlines the findings in the United States. Chapters 4 through 7 report the findings in each of the other countries. Chapters 8 and 9 discuss the findings in a cross-cultural perspective. References.

The Television Experience: What Children See. (1979). Mariann Pezzeila Winick, Charles Winick. Beverly Hills, CA: Sage. (People and Communication).

Reports on a large cross-sectional study of children's experiences with television using an interview/observational technique in the child's home. Congruence was measured on six dimensions derived rationally from the developmental and television literature.   Dimensions included fantasy, believability, identification, humor, morality, and violence. Findings indicate that little congruence exists between adults' and children's experiences. A short chapter at the end of the book discusses the study's implications for understanding how children use television. Footnotes.

Television, Imagination, and Aggression: A Study of Preschoolers. (1981). Jerome L. Singer, Dorothy G. Singer. Hillsdale, NJ: Lawrence Erlbaum.

The volume describes two studies carried out at Yale University Family Television and Consultation Center in the psychology department. The studies looked at the viewing patterns of preschool children as they affected their spontaneous behavior, play, aggression, and language used in nursery school settings. References.

Video Violence and Children. (1985). Geoffrey Barlow, Alison Hill. NY: St. Martin's.

This study looked at the effects of children viewing films primarily intended for an adult market. Data gathered suggest that young viewers are adversely affected by exposure to scenes of violence on video film. Children with a strong propensity toward aggression show obsessive characteristics that may result in addiction to ever more increasing stimulation. Study indicated a strong link between viewing of violence and violent behavior.   Parents' attitudes are a major determinant affecting the view patterns of children. Lists of "violent" videos make up the appendixes. References.

Violence on the Screen: A Report on Research into the Effects on Young People of Scenes of Violence in Films and Television. (1971). Andre Glucksmann. London: British Film Institute Educational Department.

Good analysis of topic at the time. References.

Other References

The Media, Social Science, and Social Policy for Children. (1985). Eli A. Rubinstein, Jane D. Brown. Norwood, NJ: Ablex. (Child and Family Policy).

The volume begins with case histories of major national social policy efforts like the Coleman Report, the obscenity and pornography report, and the President's Commission on Mental Illness. In Section II there is a look at the evaluation of knowledge into action; in others words, how the slow accumulation of scientific information affects social policy. Examples used are the effects of television on children, studies of the effectiveness of health education, and research concerned with child mental health. Finally the book suggests how the social scientists and media could communicate. References.

7

Cognition

DATABASES
TO CONSIDER

Embase
Medline
Mental Health Abstracts

ERIC
PsycINFO

GENERAL

Reviews of Literature

Applications of Cognitive-Developmental Theory. (1984). Edited by Barry Gholson, Ted L. Rosenthal. NY: Academic. (Developmental Psychology Series).

Discusses major theoretical components and research findings to solve children's problems whether social, emotional, educational, or cognitive. The majority of the volume is divided into three sections of three chapters each. The chapters in Part II concern promotion of the acquisition and generalization of basic cognitive competencies, that is, the role these competencies play in reading, mathematical cognition, and instructional factors in the child's transsituational application of basic cognitive strategies. The chapters in Part III discuss intervention strategies. Part IV describes and evaluates intervention strategies used to readily identify populations of children. In Part V the three major theoretical components constituting a comprehensive applied theory of development (competence, acquisition, and intervention) are discussed. Chapters conclude with references.

Bloom's Taxonomy of Educational Objectives for the Cognitive Domain: Philosophical and Educational Issues. (Winter, 1981). Edward J. Furst. In *Review of Educational Research*, 51 (4).

A comprehensive review of research over a twenty-five year period. Focus is on the claimed properties of neutrality, comprehensiveness, cumulative hierarchical structure, and usefulness. Supplements a previous review by Seddon in 1978 published in the *Review of Educational Research*, 48. References.

Cognitive and Affective Growth: Developmental Interaction. (1981). Edited by Edna K. Shapiro, Evelyn Weber. Hillsdale, NJ: Lawrence Erlbaum. (Child Psychology).

The book is divided into six parts with part three addressing the issue of reciprocal relations in the first years of life. In Chapter 10, Dorothy Z. Ullian reviews the literature on gender and children, offering a "constructivist" hypothesis that links many of the differences observed between males and females to early cognitive structures that shape and distort concepts in inevitable and predictable ways. References.

Cognitive Assessment. (c. 1981). Edited by Thomas V. Marluzzi, Carol R. Glass, Myles Genest. NY: Guilford. (Guilford Clinical Psychology and Psychotherapy Series).

Part I of the book provides an introduction to the field. Part II covers methods, issues, and approaches to cognitive assessment. Part III summarizes and evaluates the current status of cognitive assessment. References.

Cognitive Development. (1985). T. F. Gross. Monterey, CA: Brooks/Cole.

Reviews the major dimensions of cognitive research. Chapter 1 presents a historical examination of the roots of cognitive psychology in both America and Europe. Chapters 2 and 3 introduce the basics of information processing and Piagetian theory. Chapters 4 and 5 focus on major research in the area of perceptual development during infancy. Chapters 6 - 8 look at memory development. Chapter 6 concentrates on the multistory model and Chapter 7 on the levels of processing model. Chapter 8 concentrates on Piaget's model of memory function. Chapters 9 and 10 look at Piagetian approaches to problem solving. Chapter 10 examines Piaget's belief that there are stage related changes in children's knowledge. Chapter 11 reviews research in the area of metacognition. Chapter 12 looks at the relationship of language and cognition. Chapter 13 addresses the question of how knowledge of cognitive development might be applied to practical problems confronting mankind. References.

Cognitive Development. Vol. 3. *Handbook of Child Psychology*. Fourth edition. (1983). Edited by John J. Flavell, M. Markman Ellen. NY: John Wiley & Sons.

Provides a review of all aspects of cognition. The volume is divided into 13 chapters covering the following areas: perception; learning, remembering, and understanding; Piagetian concepts; theory and research of the Genevan School; logical reasoning; intelligence; representation; social cognition; morality; creativity; acquisition of grammar; meanings and concepts; and communication. Chapters are by well known specialists and are comprehensive. Lengthy bibliographies follow each chapter.

Cognitive Development. (1978). Rochel Gelman. In *Annual Review of Psychology*, Vol. 29. California: Annual Review. (Annual Review of Psychology).

Reviews the literature on early cognitive development in children up to the date of publication. About 57 citations are provided. Subcategories covered in the review include: early cognitive capacity, quantitative invariance concepts, classification abilities, sensitivity to order and causal relationships, and perspective taking abilities. Near the end of the chapter is a section addressing problems encountered by researchers in the area. References.

Cognitive Strategy Research: Educational Applications. (1983). Michael Pressley, Joel R. Levin. NY: Springer-Verlag.

This book is one of a two-volume set concerning cognitive strategy research. The 10 chapters cover an array of topics representing both Piagetian and information processing approaches. One chapter is an exhaustive review of research on moral education strategies. Brainerd reviews 30 years of studies exploring the trainability of Piagetian concrete operations in one chapter. Willows, Borwick, and Butkowsky synthesize reading research during its 100 year history. The last section looks at practical applications of studies to encourage the use of specific cognitive strategies in the decoding process. Levin's chapter considers limitations of using pictorial stimuli in language learning. The chapters in this book compliment each other nicely and provide an innovative look into the interface of research and application.

Cognitive Styles in Infancy and Early Childhood. (1976). Nathan Kogan. NY: Lawrence Erlbaum.

Reviews and critiques research in four areas of cognitive styles: field independence-dependence, reflection-impulsivity, breadth of categorization, and styles of conceptualization. Separate chapters are devoted to research on each style and include discussion of theoretical background and analyses of assessment, construct validation with respect to cognitive and personality correlates, sex differences, and patterns of continuity and discontinuity from early to later years.   In the final chapter Kogan suggests: pervasive sex differences exist in cognitive styles in preschool years; lack of stability of cognitive style is common during the early years; a relationship exists between cognitive style and personality emotional factors, but these do not appear to be stable; a limited relationship can be found between cognitive style and IQ; development of categorization and conceptualization styles is multilinear; and demand characteristics of tasks used to assess cognitive styles influence their measurement. References.

Cognitive Theory. Vol. 2. (1977).   Edited by H. John Castellan, Jr., David B. Pisoni, George R. Potts. Hillsdale, NJ: Lawrence Erlbaum.

The 11 chapters are subdivided into four sections. The chapters in Section 1, Problem Solving, discuss computer stimulation approaches used to describe the internal representation of problems. In Section 2, Decision Processes, are found chapters presenting formal models of decision making in tasks having probabilistic cues. The two chapters in Section 4, Reading, present supporting evidence for quite different models of the reading process. Section 3, Cognitive Development, consists of three chapters on different topics: Motherese; young children's reasoning about small numbers; and verbal learning in children compared to adults. References.

The Growth of Reflection in Children. (1985). Edited by Steven R. Yussen. NY: Academic. (Developmental Psychology Series).

Volume is concerned with two types of insight that develop in children. The book is organized so that chapters on metacognition and attribution processes are intermingled with one another from section to section. Part I, Approaches to Development, starts with a paper on metacognitive assessment and discusses the advantages and pitfalls of interviews, concurrent think-aloud assessments, task and performance analyses, and training studies.   The next major paper deals with three methods for measuring children's personality attributions. Part III, Descriptive Trends, consists of two major papers: H. M. Wellman's classes of knowledge that develop as young children's understanding about the mind evolves; S. R. Yussen and P. T. Kane's study in which first, third, and sixth graders were asked 20 specific questions about intelligence.   Part IV, Contextual Considerations, starts with a paper by E. Fennema, who considers the value of attribution theory for understanding gender differences in children's mathematics achievement. A final major paper deals with the concept of mindlessness. The papers and commentaries included in this volume are of uniformly high quality. References.

Home Environment and Early Cognitive Development: Longitudinal Research.
(1984). Edited by Allen W. Gottfried. NY: Academic. (Developmental
Psychology Series).

Presents investigations carried out to determine the home environment
variables that correlate with and possibly regulate cognitive development
during infancy and the preschool years. The book contains ten chapters. The
first is a brief introduction to the issues investigated. Each of the following
seven chapters is devoted to a longitudinal investigation. The ninth chapter
focuses on the issue of comparability and generalizability of findings across
the longitudinal studies. Chapter 10 deals with the implications for
intervention. It is in this last chapter that applications of the theoretical and
empirical findings are discussed. References.

Humor: Its Origins and Development. (1979). Paul E. McGhee. San Francisco,
CA: W. H. Freeman.

Summarizes all aspects of children's humor. Chapter 1 gives a foundation for
understanding the studies reviewed. Chapter 2 deals with the origin of
incongruity of humor in infancy and describes four stages of development in
early childhood. Chapter 3 addresses whether animals other than human
beings express humor. Chapter 4 draws attention to the transition period
between ages six and eight. Chapter 5 deals with other cognitive processes
and factors related to the initiation or appreciation of humor. Chapter 6
examines the social nature of most humor situations. Chapter 7 looks at the
origin of individual differences in laughter and humor. Chapter 8 looks at
sex differences. Footnoted.

Metacognition, Cognition, and Human Performance. Vol. 2 - Instructional
Practices. (1985). Edited by D. L. Forrest-Pressley, G. E. MacKinnon, T.
Gary Waller. Orlando: Academic.

This second volume focuses on the current status of work in the field of
education. Chapter 1 describes an instructional program in reading that
incorporates training in metacognition. Chapter 2 discusses the importance
of metacognition in the early stages of reading acquisition. Chapter 3 focuses
on the central role in instruction of asking questions with specific reference
to the relationship of both student- and teacher-generated questions to the
development of reading comprehension. Chapter 4 reviews current theory
and research on the nature of the disability in learning disabilities. Chapter 5
reviews the research on meta-attention. Chapter 6 reviews research related
to the effectiveness of metacognitive intervention programs. The final
chapter explores the relationship between metacognition and learned
helplessness. This chapter reviews studies that suggest that learned
helplessness is determined in part by the availability of metacognitive
strategies for coping with failure. References.

Motivation, Reinforcement, and Problem Solving in Children. (1972). E. Kuno Beller, Peter Adler, Alan Newcomer, Arnold Young, In *Minnesota Symposia on Child Psychology*, Vol. 6, edited by Anne Pick. Minneapolis, MN: Univ. of Minnesota Press.

Chapter reports studies investigating the interrelated effects of motivation and reinforcement on the learning of cognitive tasks. Twenty-five references.

Neonate Cognition: Beyond the Blooming Buzzing Confusion. (1985). Edited by J. Mehler, R. Fox. Hillsdale, NJ: Lawrence Erlbaum.

This book is concerned with the infant's mind and the means, methods, and procedures used to study it. Only studies of very young infants are included. In the first chapter of the volume, Mehler raises issues related to natural language acquisition. Chapter 3 discusses the behavioral and neuronal development of binocular vision. Chapter 4 discusses the development of visual space perception in young infants. Chapter 5 summarizes the literature on visual development, particularly binocular deprivation. Chapter 6 is concerned with the perception of unit, persistence, and identity in three- to five-month-old infants. Chapter 7 gives a good summary on the development of visual categorization. Chapter 8 refutes the position that infant facial imitation is a sophisticated cognitive achievement. In Chapter 9, data on visual neurophysiology, genetic constraints, fusion, binocularity, stereopsis, strabismus, and astigmatism is presented. Chapter 10 deals with perception and auditory/cognitive functioning in infants over one month of age. Chapter 12 reviews experiments on the perception of similarity among speech sound by infants. Chapters 13 and 14 discuss the infantile nervous system. Chapter 15 discusses neuroanatomical substrates of language. Chapter 17 provides a brief treatise on the effects of early sensory and language experiences on the human brain. Chapter 18 surveys the behavioral prowess of the newborn. Chapter 19 discusses constraints on semantic development. References.

Origins of Cognitive Skills. The Eighteenth Annual Carnegie Symposium on Cognition. (1984). Edited by Catherine Sophian. Hillsdale, NJ: Lawrence Erlbaum.

Integrates research on both infant cognition and cognitive development in childhood. The volume is divided into three parts: origins on spatial skills; origins of number skills; and origins of categories. A commentary at the end of each section brings together the different lines of research discussed in the preceding chapters. The section of spatial development looks at the abilities ranging from the young infant's perception of how far away an object is to the elementary school child's ability to infer how an array of objects would look from a different perspective. Some discussion focuses on the recurrent problems of how children cope with movements and how they make use of landmarks. The section on number development looks at abilities ranging from the infant's discrimination between two small numerical quantities to the elementary child's selection of appropriate addition and subtraction strategies for problems of varying difficulty. The section on the development of categorization reviews developments from infants' early perception of color categories to the acquisition of hierarchical relationships among taxonomic categories. References.

Piagetian Research: A Handbook of Recent Studies. (1974). Sohan Modgil. Windsor, Berks: NFER.

Catalogs, up to December 1972, a number of Piaget-oriented research studies and offers a variety of research approaches to investigating cognitive development. Subjects included in the research studies range from birth to 94 years old. Chapters consist of an integrated review of the studies followed by abstracts of the reports of research arranged in chronological order.

Predicting Cognitive Development from Assessments in Infancy. (1980). Michael Lewis, Nathan Fox. In *Advances in Behavioral Pediatrics*, Vol. 1, edited by Bonnie Camp. Greenwich, CT: JAI. (Advances in Behavioral Pediatrics).

Reviews research related to problems of predicting later cognitive development from assessments in infancy. Problems inherent in infant tests are covered as well as demographic factors predictive of later cognitive functioning. Research relating characteristics of mother and child interaction on later cognitive development is also reviewed. Lengthy bibliography included.

Recent Advances in Cognitive-Development Theory: Progress in Cognitive Development Research. (1983). Edited by Charles J. Brainerd. NY: Springer-Verlag. (Springer Series in Cognitive Development).

Summarizes current investigations in the area of cognitive development theory. The specific theories that are covered in the text and for which the chapters are entitled include: social learning theory; rule-oriented; sociobiology; working-memory and cognitive development; and the ethological approach. References.

The Relationship between Social and Cognitive Development. (1983). Edited by Willis F. Overton. Hillsdale, NJ: Lawrence Erlbaum. (Jean Piaget Symposium Series).

The volume is comprised of a set of papers originally presented at the Tenth Annual Symposium of the Jean Piaget Society. In Chapter 2 Turiel emphasizes the need to carefully consider the specific nature of social domains in approaching an understanding of social-cognitive development. Turiel critiques earlier research in this area and presents a model of social cognition that integrates both structural and contextual components. Chapter 3 concerns the question of the distinction between the cognition of social and physical events. Chapter 8 is a discussion of the history and implications of a traditional model in which social existence and social functioning have been explained on the basis of the organism's individual character. Chapter 9, by Sutton-Smith, considers several theoretical and research issues concerning both social and cognitive features of play. References.

Schooling and Cognitive Development: Is There a Season for Learning? (October 1987). Barbara Heyns. In *Child Development*, 58 (5). Chicago, IL: Univ. of Chicago Press.

This article reviews the literature on the effects of summer programs and analyzes the role summer learning has on cognitive development. Thirty-six references.

Sex Related Differences in Cognitive Function: Developmental Issues. (1979). Edited by Michele Andrisin Wittig, Anne C. Petersen. NY: Academic. (Academic Press Series in Cognition and Perception).

The volume focuses on aspects of cognitive functioning that are sex linked. Each chapter provides a scholarly integration of theoretical formulations, empirical data, and methodological concerns. The editors admit in the preface that the book's organization is biased in the direction of biological factors with only twenty-five percent of the book discussing sociocultural factors. The volume is divided into seven parts: introduction, genes, brain organization, hormones, socialization, measurement, and conclusion. Included in Part II are chapters dealing with intellectual performance, spatial ability, and handedness. Part III includes chapters dealing with cerebral organization and maturation of cerebral cortical functions. Part IV, Chapter 9 is of particular interest because the authors focus on prenatal influence on cognitive abilities. In Part V, Chapter 12, achievement in mathematics is reviewed. Chapter 13 outlines the implications of test content and context for sex-related research. References.

Social Cognition: Studies of the Development of Understanding. (1982). Edited by George Butterworth, Paul Light. Chicago, IL: Univ. of Chicago Press.

An overview of current thinking on the topic of social cognition. Child development specialists will be most interested in Section II, Origins of Social Cognition in Infancy, containing three chapters that discuss the origins of social cognition in universal processes of perception and action observable in infancy and early childhood. In Section III, Chapter 9 by Harris and

Olthof is on children's cognitive appraisal of their own emotions; the metacognition of emotional development. References.

Time, Mind, and Behavior. (1985). Edited by John A. Michon, Janet L. Jackson. NY and Berlin: Springer-Verlag.

Two chapters deal exclusively with children. Chapter 6 by Pouthas discusses time behavior in young children, including at what age temporal discriminations reach a stable level in the course of development. Chapter 19 by Jacques Montangero deals with the development of temporal reasoning and with the constituent components of the concept of duration as they develop with age. References.

Topics in Cognitive Development. Vol. 1. Equilibration: Theory, Research, and Application. (1977). Edited by Marilyn H. Appel, Lois S. Goldberg. NY: Plenum. (Topics in Cognitive Development).

Reviews various aspects of Piagetian theory, research, and application. The first few chapters cover the process of equilibration. One chapter in the theory section covers strategies for understanding order of development, particularly as applied to the sensory motor period. The section entitled Research begins with a chapter describing Genevan procedures for training children's concepts of conversation and class inclusion with the goal of learning about transitions from one stage to the next. The chapter by Langer describes research investigating the development of transductive preoperations and its manifestation in physical, social, and personal preconcepts. The next chapter describes the child's growing awareness of syntactic and semantic properties or language. In the "application" section one chapter reviews some basic concepts of Piagetian theory, and their implications for education are discussed. References.

Reports of Research

Closely Observed Children: The Diary of a Primary Classroom. (1980). Michael Armstrong. Oxford: Oxford Univ. Press.

The chapters making up this small observation study describe the thoughts and actions of children in Stephen Roland's class as displayed in their work and play within the intellectual, social, and physical environment of the classroom. Concentrated attention is given to the moments of intellectual absorption, occasions when the children were engrossed in the subject matter of their activity and evidently concerned with the significance of what they were saying, writing, painting, making, experimenting with, calculating, designing, or inventing.

Cognitive Development of Children and Youth: A Longitudinal Study. (1978). Herbert J. Klausmeier, Patricia S. Allen. NY: Academic. (Educational Psychology).

Reports an extensive study of children's concept development from kindergarten to grade 12 interlaced with a theoretical discussion. The research represents a comprehensive and well designed combined cross-sectional and longitudinal study using 50 children at each of grades K, 3, 6 and 9. A battery of test was administered measuring the mastery of four hierarchically conceived levels (concrete, identity, classificatory, and formal) and in terms of three types of usages (principle, taxonomic, and problem solving). Included is a brief reference to a small scale intervention study aimed at facilitating the cognitive growth of slow developing children through fostering parent-teacher intervention over a brief period. References.

How Infants Form Categories. (1985). Barbara A. Younger, Leslie B. Cohen. In *The Psychology of Learning and Motivation, Advances in Research and Theory,* Vol. 19, edited by Gordon Bower. New York: Academic.

Chapter explains human ability to categorize and demonstrates that infants possess it. The authors examine how infants acquire and represent category information and separate items into different categories. Lastly the chapter looks at the infant's ability to acquire categories as it develops during the first year and what percursors of these abilities may exist in infants who are not able to form actual categories. Charts, tables, and graphs illustrate data collected during the authors' investigations. Thirty-six references.

Infants as Problem-Solvers: A Psychobiological Perspective. (1983). Carolyn K. Rovee-Collier. In *Advances in Analysis of Behavior*, Vol. 3, *Biological Factors in Learning*, edited by Zeiler and Harzem. NY: John Wiley & Sons.

Chapter supplies evidence that the young infant is a rapid and efficient learner. The author suggests that what the infant learns is subject not only to biological constraints which influence the timing as well as the type of behavior. The author provides a substantial bibliography.

Teaching Strategies and Cognitive Functioning in Elementary School Children: Cooperative Research Project No. 2404. (1966). Hilda Taba. San Francisco, CA: San Francisco State College Press.

A classical study of developing cognitive potentials of young elementary school children. Despite recognized limitations, the chief hypothesis of the study was confirmed: if students are given a curriculum designed to develop their cognitive potential and theoretical insights, and if they are taught by strategies specifically addressed to helping them master crucial cognitive skills, then they master the more sophisticated forms of symbolic thought earlier and more systematically than expected if left to the accidents of experience or if their school experience is guided by less appropriate teaching strategies.

INTELLIGENCE

Reviews of Literature

Achievement-Related Motives in Children. (1969). Edited by Charles P. Smith. NY: Russell Sage Foundation.

This volume presents reports of four extensive research projects that deal with achievement related motivation in children. Chapter 2 looks at motivation for academic and intellectual achievement. The chapter summarizes a number of studies looking at the relationship of expectancies to performance, and sex differences in expectancies. Chapter 3 discusses the importance of social comparisons with respect to skills. Chapter 4 investigates how achievement motivation develops and how test anxiety develops. Chapter 5 focuses on anxieties aroused in achievement situations. References.

Advances in Motivation and Achievement, a Research Annual: The Effects of School Desegregation on Motivation and Achievement. (1984). Edited by David E. Bartz, Martin L. Maehr. Greenwich, CT: JAI.

This is the first volume in a series on motivation. The focus is primarily on black children. The contributors have done a good job in reviewing the history of school desegregation in the United States and integrating these historical antecedents with the theoretical and empirical social science literature. A paper by Krol notes that the literature on bussing and academic achievement is replete with poorly conceived and designed studies. The volume concludes with a discussion of some solutions to the problems of desegregation. References.

Intellectual Development: Birth to Adulthood. (1985). Robbie Case. NY: Academic. (Developmental Psychology Series).

Gives a general theory about the topic developed by the author over a six- or seven-year period. Summarizes appropriate research of other groups on the subject. Presents new data gathered by the author's research group. Places theory of the topic in a historical perspective. References.

Organization of Data on Life-Span Development of Human Abilities. (1970). John L. Horn. In *Life-Span Development Psychology: Research and Theory*, edited by Goulet and Baltes. NY: Academic.

Reviews data pertaining to the development of intellectual abilities in childhood and adulthood within the framework of a general theory in which the cohesion producing influences associated with acculturation and neurophysiology are emphasized and contrasted. Attention is given to the fact that when abilities are measured at quite different points in development, excluding the first two years of life, they are not predictive of intellectual abilities measured in later childhood and thereafter. References.

Perspectives on Intellectual Development. (1986). Edited by Marion Perlmutter. Hillsdale, NJ: Lawrence Erlbaum. (Minnesota Symposium on Child Psychology, Vol. 19).

Twelve papers presented in this volume focus on intellectual development. References are included with each paper.

Reports of Research

Cognitive Development: The Child's Acquisition of Diagonality. (1970). David R. Olson. NY: Academic. (Child Psychology Series).

The focus of the book is on the theoretical and empirical study of the child's development of a conceptual system to the concept of the diagonal during the age range three to six years. The purpose of the study was to refine the conception of the nature of intelligence of the child and its transformation over the ages of four to seven years. The author recommends that the reader begin with the last chapter, the conclusions and conjectures, and then sample chapters according to need. References.

The Growth of Logical Thinking from Childhood to Adolescence: An Essay on the Construction of Formal Operational Structures. (1958). Barbel Inhelder, Jean Piaget. NY: Basic Books.

This classic describes the formal structures that mark the completion of the operational development of intelligence. Each of the first 15 chapters includes an experimental part by the first author and a brief final analysis by the second author. References.

Preschool IQ: Prenatal and Early Development Correlates. (1975). Sarah H. Broman, Paul L. Nichols. Hillsdale, NJ: Lawrence Erlbaum.

Study identifies factors in the first years of life which relate to intellectual performance by age four. From 1959 to 1965, 44,000 pregnant women participated in the investigation called the Collaborative Perinatal Project. Data gathered included: family characteristics, maternal characteristics, prenatal period, labor and delivery data, neonatal period, black versus whites, and infancy/childhood variables such as weight, head circumference, height, and Bayley scores. References.

Relations between Piagetian and Psychometric Assessment of Intelligence. (1977). Rheta De Vries, Lawrence Kohlberg. In *Current Topics in Early Childhood Education.* Vol. 1, edited by Lilian Katz. Norwood, NJ: Albex.

Study looks at the empirical relationship between Piagetian and psychometric conceptions of intelligence. Sixty-seven middle class white kindergarten children enrolled at the University of Chicago Laboratory School and first grade children enrolled in a suburban public school were administered psychometric tests and subtests. Each child's performance on the psychometric tests was assessed by means of mental age using published norms for each test. Performance on Piaget-type tasks was assessed by means of Guttman scales constructed for each task. The study's findings call into question the expectation that early stimulation and education will necessarily increase a child's psychometric intelligence. References.

Other References

Intelligence Testing with the WISC-R. (1979). Alan S. Kaufman. NY: John Wiley & Sons. (Wiley Series on Personality Process).

This volume is essentially a guide to the clinical interpretation of the WISC-R, incorporating the latest research and considering recent attacks on intelligence testing. After detailing the deficiencies and misuses of intelligence tests, including the obvious failure to encompass all significant mental operations, Kaufman presents a compelling defense of the utility of these instruments which have been refined, restandardized, and researched for over a generation. He covers the application of these tests to children from various ethnic backgrounds, to children who have suffered educational and cultural deprivation, and to children afflicted by various learning disorders and emotional difficulties. An indispensable volume for the professional who works with the WISC-R. Bibliography included.

LEARNING

Reviews of Literature

Advances in Child Development and Behavior. Vol. 8. (1974). Edited by Hayne W. Reese. NY: Academic.

Reviews research in the area of learning including experimental work on transfer of learning as conceptualized from the Hill-Spence view. Some of the articles look at birth order and the effect on development of behavior. One article critically discusses fear of strangers during the latter third of an infant's first year. References.

At What Age Should Children Enter First Grade: A Comprehensive Review of Research. (1977). William D. Hedges. Ann Arbor, MI: University Microfilms.

This slim volume reviews the literature regarding the relationship of chronological age of school entrance to success in school. References.

Basic Processes in Memory Development: Progress in Cognitive Development Research. (1985). Edited by Charles J. Brainerd, Michael Pressley. NY: Springer-Verlag. (Springer Series in Cognitive Development).

Chapter 1 examines theory and research concerned with the presumed retrieval deficits that children show on traditional long-term memory tasks. Chapter 2 considers current work on children's encoding that is usually called cognitive mapping. However, Bjorklund argues in Chapter 3 that organization is largely an automatic process and, consequently, that the development of organization is the result of age changes in automatic rather than strategic processes. Chapter 4 discusses the problem of how to factor the relative contributions to memory development of variables that are responsible for getting traces into memory (storage) and variables that are responsible for getting them out again (retrieval). Chapter 5 surveys the literature on the development of short term memory. References.

Brain and Learning, Directions in Early Childhood Education. (1980). Marlin Languis, Tobie Sanders, Steven Tipps. Washington, DC: National Association for the Education of Young Children.

The volume provides a synthesis of the research and theories regarding brain functioning of young children in the context of learning. Organized into three parts, the book in Part I examines theory and evidence for three mutually reinforcing models: an evolutionary model; the hemispheric brain model; and a program of the brain model. There is a suggestion that learning experiences may result in changes in brain organization and in expectancy. Part II relates brain functioning theories to the learning process in three areas of children's language development, in human development, and in a generative learning model. Part III covers recommendations for further research in the area. Each section lists some suggested readings on the topic. Cited references within each chapter are listed among the references at the end of the book. A concise glossary of terms is provided at the end of the book.

Children's Metamemory and the Teaching of Memory Strategies. (1985). Michael Pressley, John G. Borkowski, Julie O'Sullivan. In *Metacognition, Cognition, and Human Performance*, Vol. 1, Theoretical Perspectives, edited by Forrest-Pressley, MacKinnon, and Waller. NY: Academic.

Reviews literature on metamemory and the teaching of memory strategies with children. Also discusses metamemory-memory behavior relationships. A comprehensive bibliography is provided by the authors.

Cognitive Learning and Memory in Children: Progress in Cognitive Development Research. (1985). Edited by Michael Pressley, Charles Brainerd. NY: Springer-Verlag.

A chapter by Daehle and Greco reviews work on memory development during the transitional period from infancy to preschool. Two chapters look at the role of social interactions as the key to memory development. The chapter by Rogoff and Mistry looks at the role of culture in memory development. A chapter by Reyna examines the development of understanding metaphors and fantasy-based language. The chapter by Marx, Winne, and Walsh focuses on instructional psychology, discussing classrooms as settings for cognitive research. The final chapter of the book details errors in methodology and statistical analyses commonly found in studies of children's learning, and offers solutions. References.

Cognitive Learning in Children: Theories and Strategies. (1976). Edited by Joel R. Levin, Vernon L. Allen. NY: Academic. (Educational Psychology).

The book is divided into three major sections. Part III, Learning, Development, and Cognitive Abilities, focuses on the presumed cognitive operations used by children in a variety of learning situations. Part II, Strategies for Improving Cognitive Learning, focuses on experimental manipulations and instructional training techniques that purportedly facilitate the learning process. Part III, Strategies for Improving Classroom Instruction, provides examples of how educational researchers can move into the "real world" phase of the research into practice. References.

Developing Young Children's Curiosity: A Review of Research with Implications for Teachers. (September 1978). Marilyn R. Bradbard, Richard C. Endsley. Urbana, IL: ERIC Clearinghouse on Early Childhood Education.

This review of the literature on the development of young children's curiosity is directed specifically toward teachers and other practitioners and emphasizes what socialization agents can do to influence children's curiosity. Gaps in current knowledge about children's curiosity, including trait, perceptual, mastery motivational, learning, cognitive and ethological theories, are briefly delineated.   Developmental and situational factors related to curiosity are pointed out and individual differences among children's expressions of curiosity are probed.   Correlates of curiosity, including intelligence, play, creativity, authoritarianism, anxiety and self-concept, are examined. The influence of situation and setting variations on curiosity, such as maternal absence, environmental deprivation, the presence of strangers, educational programs, group size, the opportunity to manipulate objects, and object novelty, are reported. Findings show that adults can be instrumental in fostering and maintaining children's curiosity by being attentive, sensitive, and supportive of children's needs to explore, by answering children's questions informatively, and by displaying the positive characteristics of curious people. Areas for further research are indicated. References.

Developmental and Motivational Perspectives on Cooperative Learning: A Reconciliation. (October 1987). Robert E. Slavin. In *Child Development*, 58 (5). Chicago, IL: Univ. of Chicago Press.

This article reviews research on the two major theoretical perspectives dealing with cooperative learning strategies, developmental and motivational. A theory for reconciling these perspectives that emphasizes the role of group rewards for individual learning in motivating students is set forth. Twenty-seven references.

The Development of Memory in Children. (1979). Robert Kail. San Francisco, CA: W. H. Freeman. (Series of Books in Psychology).

After an introduction, six chapters deal with the development of mnemonic strategies, metamemory, recognition memory, knowledge and memory development, individual differences in children's memory, and memory and cognition. The body of the text is a series of clearly written discussions of a number of representative experiments in the field. The book successfully brings out the major themes of the literature in the field of memory development. Subject and author index included.

Emergent Literacy: Writing and Reading. (1986). Edited by William Teale, Elizabeth Sulzby. Norwood, NJ: Ablex. (Writing Research; Multidisciplinary Inquiries into the Nature of Writing).

Examines the concept of legitimate, conceptual, and developmental literacy learning occurring during the first years of a child's life leading up to and preparing for what by adult standards is called reading and writing. The chapters in this volume are authored by many leading researchers of written language development in very young children. Most of the eight chapters report one or more research investigations. Chapter 5 by Snow and Ninio looks at what book reading contributes to a child's literacy development. Also very interesting is Chapter 8 by Teale, which addresses the relationship between home background and preschool children's literacy development. References.

Exceptional Infant. Vol. 1. The Normal Infant. (1967). Edited by Jerome Hellmuth. NY: Brunner/Mozel. (Exceptional Infant).

This first volume of a three-volume series contains studies by leading experts from various disciplines. The focus is on normal infant development, mainly learning. References.

The Experiential Origins of Human Behavior. (1970). Lewis Lipsitt. In *Life-Span Development Psychology: Research and Theory*, edited by Goulet and Baltes. NY: Academic.

The chapter reviews studies of the learning processes in infants and young children. The author concludes that human infants, including newborns, are capable of learning under either classical or instrumental procedures, as well as some procedures combining features of both of these. Learning capacity seems most enhanced with experiential circumstances capitalizing upon the congenital and sometimes idiosyncratic response repertoire of the infant. Individual differences, reflected through measures at chronological age and physiological dispositions, set limiting conditions upon capacity for learning, but those limiting conditions must always be determined empirically rather than merely presumed. References.

Hemispheric Function and Collaboration in the Child. (1985). Edited by Catherine T. Best. NY: Academic. (Educational Psychology).

A collection of literature on hemispheric function in children. The book is organized into three parts. The three chapters in the first part, Theoretical Perspectives, discuss various issues crucial to building a comprehensive and developmental model of hemispheric function and collaboration in the normal as well as the learning disabled child. The three chapters in the second part of the book, Developmental Views, are devoted to research on the contributions of both hemispheres to the development of complex skills: language, recognition of faces, and the ability to manually copy a visually presented pattern. The four chapters in the third part, Educational Considerations, evaluate the "right-brain" educational movement and the notion that LD students fail to establish left-hemisphere dominance. References.

Learning in Children and in Older Adults. (1970). Jack Botwinick. In *Life-Span Development Psychology: Research and Theory*, edited by Goulet and Baltes. NY: Academic.

Chapter reviews studies based on children integrated with comparable studies based on older adults. Classical conditioning studies were represented primarily by the eyeblink response with the processes of habituation and extinction receiving special attention. Learning based upon prior experience, including pretraining studies, was discussed giving emphasis to the distinction between learning and performance. The problem of speed of response is examined in the context of paired-associate and serial learning, and finally, studies on incidental learning are reviewed indicating that typical growth and decline curves do not always apply to abilities across the life span. References.

Learning in Children: Progress in Cognitive Development Research. (1983). Edited by Jeffrey Bisanz, Bay L. Bisanz, Robert Kail. NY: Springer-Verlag. (Springer Series in Cognitive Development).

Volume sets forth new themes of research on learning in children. The first new theme is the goal of integrating social, motivational, and cognitive aspects of learning. The second theme deals with identifying the competencies of very young children. The third theme involves the generality and application of research on children's learning. The final theme involves a heightened concern for sophisticated methodological tools to allow more perceptive insights into children's behavior. Particular chapters of interest are the Bransford and Heldmeyer chapter outlining motivational and cognitive factors that may enhance learning in preschool children; the Perry and Perry chapter which reviews research on the development of moral behavior; and the chapter by Heth and Cornell identifying concepts acquired in the first two years of life. References.

Learning in Infants and Young Children. (1975). Michael Howe. Stanford, CA: Stanford Univ. Press.

Chapter 1 describes how learning in infants is influenced by characteristics of the child at birth. Chapter 2 surveys the evidence produced by experimental investigations of learning in infants. Chapter 3 considers theoretical issues important to psychology such as reinforcement and the effects of early learning on the infant. Chapter 4 looks at the mother's importance in early social learning. Chapter 5 looks at the role of language in learning. Chapter 6 extends the discussion started in Chapter 4 on social learning. Chapter 7 is concerned with the differences between individuals and learning. References.

Learning, Speech, and the Complex Effects of Punishment: Essays Honoring George J. Wischner. (1982). Edited by Donald K. Routh. NY: Plenum.

The editor of this book in the introduction terms this book a "Festschriff" honoring a multifaceted man, George J. Wischner. The scholar researcher is fortunate that the editor decided to combine a potpourri of topics because in doing so a number of excellent references are cited. Chapter 2 covers the young child's discrimination learning. Chapter 3, on learning sets, focuses on the work on sets called the Pittsburgh Studies by Wischner. In the chapter on punishment, a small section deals with the treatment of bed-wetting, citing important studies from 1904 to the present.

Memory Development and Motor Skill Acquisition. (1986). Jerry R. Thomas. In *Physical Activity and Well-Being*, edited by Vern Seefeldt, Chapter 4. Reston, VA: American Alliance for Health, Physical Education, Recreation, and Dance.

Reviews theory and research concerning the function of cognition in motor skill acquisition and performance. Selected studies identify the major mechanisms of memory and how they operate to influence skilled performance and learning. The chapter first delves into why cognitive processes are important to skill acquisition. This leads to the concept of the development of motor programs in memory followed by a specific model, Schema Theory, followed by developmental questions. Two important types of information are discussed within this framework, knowledge of results and motor development as well as psychomotor skills modeling. This is followed by an account of how memory and knowledge development influence children's skill acquisition. The chapter concludes by presenting factors that may be influenced during practice and motor performance. References.

Memory Development in Children. (1978). Peter A. Ornstein. Hillsdale, NJ: Lawrence Erlbaum.

Chapters 2 - 7 are syntheses and assessments of current research being carried on in the area of memory. Chapter 7 focuses on memory in young children ages two to five. Position papers make up the remaining chapters. References.

Metacognition, Cognition, and Human Performance. Vol. 1. Theoretical Perspectives. (1985). D. L. Forrest-Pressley, G. E. MacKinnon, T. Gary Waller. NY: Academic.

A comprehensive discussion and review of theories and research on metacognition. Chapter 1 gives general background to metacognition, its origins and development. Chapter 2 reviews studies regarding interaction between adults and young children. Chapter 3 analyzes the literature on the relationship between metamemory and memory behavior. Chapter 4 looks at the relationship between metamemory and memory strategy use. Chapter 5 deals with monitoring of skill execution and specifically with the monitoring of comprehension during reading. Chapter 6 develops a framework to account for the development of first and second language skills. Chapters end with references.

Psychological Perspectives and Early Childhood Education: Some Relations between Theory and Practice. (1977). Margery B. Franklin, Barbara Biber. In *Current Topics in Early Childhood Education*, Vol. 1, edited by Lilian Katz, Chapter 1, pages 1 - 32. Norwood, NJ: Ablex.

The chapter delineates some of the central issues regarding the application of psychological theory and research to early childhood education. Three approaches are discussed: behavioristic learning theory, cognitive-developmental theory, and developmental-interaction or "whole" child approach. Of the three approaches the authors believe that the behavioristic learning theory is the most limiting when applied to education. The cognitive-developmental theory appears to contribute to learning and growth in terms of constructing knowledge of the world through interaction. The authors note that the whole child approach has goals comprised of affective social, as well as cognitive, aspects of development. References.

Questions and Children's Cognitive Processing. (1985). Michael Pressley, Donna Forrest-Pressley. In *The Psychology of Questions*, edited by Arthur Graesser and John Black, Chapter 10. Hillsdale, NJ: Lawrence Erlbaum.

Reviews the effects of self-questions, teacher questions, and text questions on children's learning. Reading the review will also be helpful to researchers in the area of memory. Authors describe the new area of research involving "interrogative MAPs" (metacognition acquisition procedures). References.

Stimulus Control in Children's Learning. (1972). Thomas J. Tighe, Louise S. Tighe. In *Minnesota Symposia on Child Psychology*, Vol. 6, edited by Anne Pick. Minneapolis, MN: Univ. of Minnesota Press.

Paper presents a new analysis of discrimination shift performance and the implications of this on the concept of learning in general. References.

Thinking and Learning Skills. Vol. 1: Relating Instruction to Research. (1985). Edited by Judith W. Segal, Susan F. Chipman. Hillsdale, NJ: Lawrence Erlbaum.

The first of two volumes, which is organized by a classification of cognitive skills into three groups: intelligence and reasoning, knowledge acquisition, and problem solving. This, the first volume, attempts to bring theory and practice into close perspective. Programs already implemented by schools are described. Leading cognitive psychologists then analyze these programs. In the final section of the volume there are chapters by other educators who have implemented instructional programs in cognitive skills. Not all programs described in the volume deal with children, but there is sufficient material covered to be of interest to educators of children in elementary grades. References.

Thinking and Learning Skills. Vol. 2: Research and Open Questions. (1985). Edited by Susan F. Chipman, Judith W. Segal. Hillsdale, NJ: Lawrence Erlbaum.

This second volume of the set contains a representative sample of contemporary research on cognitive skills and considers research issues and open questions that indicate further research directions. Each of the papers included provides insight into theory and methodology currently being studied by cognitive scientists in the area of thinking and learning. Each of the topics (knowledge acquisition, problem solving, and intelligence and reasoning) includes perspectives from developmental psychology and from study of cultural influences on human learning. References.

Trends in Memory Development Research. (1983). Edited by Michelene T. H. Chi. NY, London: Karger. (Contributions to Human Development, Vol. 9).

The major theme of this volume is the relationship between existing knowledge and remembering. The first four chapters of the volume are on current research topics with the final two chapters providing a general overview of the past decade and a look at the future of memory development. References.

Reports of Research

Computer Experience and Cognitive Development: A Child's Learning in a Computer Culture. (1985). Robert W. Lawler. NY: John Wiley & Sons. (Ellis Harwood Series in Cognitive Science).

Reports the interaction between Mr. Lawler and his six-year-old daughter over an extended period of time, primarily working on computer problems utilizing the computer language LOGO. The emphasis is on the problem-solving processes revealed by the child in carrying out simple arithmetic sums, constructing simple geometric patterns, and division game-playing strategies. For those tolerant of this unsystematic, intuitive reporting of a single case, there is much to intrigue the student of cognitive development.

Conceptual Change in Childhood. (1985). Susan Carey. Cambridge, MA: MIT Press. (MIT Press Series in Learning, Development, and Conceptual Change).

A case study of the acquisition of biological knowledge during the years four to ten. Within the first six chapters, the author shows that the child's knowledge of animals and living things shifts much like the theorists of the novice-expert suggest. Using several different phenomena and the results from four different research methods: inductive projection, Piagetian clinical interview, appearance versus reality, and judgments of category errors, the author supports this view. The appendixes provide data from some of the experiments presented in the chapters. References.

Dimensions of Preschool: The Effects of Individual Experience. (1985). Louise B. Miller, Mary B. Bugbee, Duane W. Hybertson. In *Advances in Applied Developmental Psychology*, Vol. 1, edited by Irving Sigel. Norwood, NJ: Ablex.

The study reported in this chapter looks at the relationship between program dimensions and program outcomes. The data collected suggest that drill, didactic instruction, and higher ratios of negative to positive reinforcement appear to have adverse effects on the receptive skills of boys. The data also suggest that the examination of process product relationships indicates that the child behavior variables are more frequently and more influentially related to outcome measures than the teacher contact variables. The study clearly indicates that teachers interact differently with the two sexes. References.

The Early Growth of Logic in the Child: Classification and Seriation. Barbel Inhelder, Jean Piaget. Translated from the French by E. A. Lunzer and D. Papert. (1964). London: Routledge and Kegan Paul.

This is a classic study of the way children come to a gradual awareness of the criteria of their own actions. A sampling of 2,159 children was studied. The greater part of the volume deals with the classification. In summary Inhelder and Piaget concluded that there is a very close relation between the development of logical operations; little children have difficulty in coordinating intension and extension; the starting point for understanding is the actions and operations of the subject; and transition from one stage to another is governed by the beginnings of hindsight and anticipation.

How Children Learn to Buy: The Development of Consumer Information-Processing Skills. (1977). Scott Ward, Daniel B. Wackman, Ellen Wartella. Beverly Hills, CA: Sage. (People and Communication).

Study examines children's development of consumer buying skills. The authors interviewed 615 kindergarten, third-grade, and sixth-grade children and their mothers, from blue-collar and middle class neighborhoods. The researchers checked on recall of information from television advertising, awareness of brand names, comprehension of the purpose of commercials, judgment of truth in advertising, purchase requests, and use of money for savings or spending. The study includes a bibliography.

Intellectual and Personality Characteristics of Children: Social-Class and Ethnic-Group Differences. (1979). Regina Yando, Victoria Seitz, Edward Zigler. Hillsdale, NJ: Lawrence Erlbaum.

Looks at how children from different social classes and ethnic groups behave in problem-solving situations. The first study compared economically advantaged second- and third-grade children with economically disadvantaged children equivalent in IQ, chronological age, and mental age. The second study compared economically advantaged and economically disadvantaged children. Comparisons were made of two-parent and one-parent families. References.

The School Lives of Seven Children: A Five Year Study. (1982). Patricia F. Carini. Grand Forks, ND: Univ. of North Dakota. (North Dakota Study Group on Evaluation).

The monograph is based on data from a five-year evaluation of the New York State Experimental Prekindergarten Study, also known as the Indepth Study, that focused on the way children learn. In this study seven of the 30 children involved in the five-year study are described in detail regarding their educational experience and modes of thinking and learning. The study shows the children's pervasive need for context, wholeness, and continuity in the learning environment. It is suggested that schools need to look closely at practices such as yearly promotion, pull-out programs, school schedule interruptions, and classroom organization that compartmentalize the learning experience.

Young Children Learning. (1984). Barbara Tizard, Martin Hughes. Cambridge, MA: Harvard Univ. Press.

A supplemental report of a research project that examined mother-child conversations in the home and adult-child conversations in a nursery school. Fifteen children were from middle-class families and 15 were from working-class families. Tizard and Hughes demonstrate that the children from both social classes learned whenever they interacted with the mother, whether at play, during mealtimes, when the child was helping the mother, or "when mother and child were doing nothing in particular." The authors found the nursery school setting to be quite sterile in contrast to the home. There was less conversation and less informal learning. Footnotes.

MATHEMATICS

Reviews of Literature

The Child's Understanding of Number. (1978). Rochel Gelman, C. R. Gallistel. Cambridge, MA: Harvard Univ. Press.

The authors begin by looking at the preschool child's conception of number and how that conception develops. Previous work on the young child's use and understanding of number is reviewed. The authors note that there is need for investigating the counting abilities in children and they present a model for studying the topic. Other chapters look at the preschoolers how-to-count principles, abstraction, and order irrelevance principles. Chapter 10 looks at the way young children reason with numbers. Users will find the lengthy references provided on pages 246 - 254 highly useful.

Children and Number: Difficulties in Learning Mathematics. (1986). Martin Hughes. NY: Oxford, UK: B. Blackwell.

This book proposes a new perspective on children's early attempts to understand mathematics. Citing his own research and others', the author argues that children need to build links between their informal and their formal understanding of number. The book also describes how LOGO can have a positive effect on children's learning to understand numbers. The book concludes with an excellent bibliography which researchers will find helpful.

Children's Counting Types: Philosophy, Theory, and Application. (1983). Leslie P. Steffe, Ernst von Glasersfeld, John Richards, Paul Cobb. NY: Praeger. (Praeger Special Studies).

This monograph reports results of investigations carried out within the framework of the project Interdisciplinary Research on Number (IRON). Chapter 1 attempts to elucidate the structure of the concept of unit by relating insights found in the literature of philosophy and mathematics. Chapter 2 develops the theory of counting types at the various developmental stages of children. Research in mathematics education is represented in chapters 3 and 4 which report experiments with first graders. Chapter 5 is a summary and perspective of the entire volume. In the appendix von Glaserfeld gives a model for the conceptual construction of units and numbers.

Children's Mathematical Concepts: Six Piagetian Studies in Mathematics Education. (1975). Edited by Myron F. Rosskopf. NY: Teachers College Press.

Each study presented in this volume is concerned with aspect of the child's growing mathematical concepts, and with the development and evaluation of related instruction. In the first study, The Concept of Bilateral Symmetry in Young Children, Elaine Genkins compares the concept of bilateral symmetry in kindergarten and second-grade children. The second, by Helen Bass, Topological Understandings of Young Children, specifically concerns concepts of order, enclosure, and equivalence. In the third chapter, Harriett Wagman discusses The Child's Conception of Area Measure, particularly the concept of the area of a polygonal region in children's understanding of four concepts relevant to the limiting process, including functional rule of correspondence, convergence, neighborhood of a point, and limit point. H. Laverne Thomas examines The Concept of Function in seventh- and eighth-grade children of high ability who were given instruction in function. In the final study included in the book, Low Achievers' Understanding of Logical Inference Forms, Constance Anne Carroll reports investigation of low achievers' understanding of "if . . . then" reasoning using various types of arguments, and discusses their ability to profit from small group instruction on conditional reasoning. References.

The Development of Mathematical Thinking. (1983). Edited by Herbert P. Ginsburg. NY: Academic. (Developmental Psychology Series).

The chapters in this volume review, criticize, and analyze relevant literature on mathematical cognition. Chapter 2 is an analysis of early use and understanding of number words. Chapter 3 discusses a new theory on the manner in which young children's concepts of numbers become elaborate during early school years. Chapter 4 provides a model of the child's solution of arithmetic word problems. Chapter 5 looks at the concept of subtraction. Chapter 6 looks at more complex mathematical cognition. Chapter 7 discusses the development of numbers as embedded in social life. Chapter 8 examines learning difficulties in children's mathematics. Chapter 9 examines the relevance of Piaget's theory for understanding children's knowledge of academic mathematics.

How Young Children Reason about Small Numbers. (1977). Rochel Gelman. In *Cognitive Theory*, Vol. 2, edited by John Castellan Jr., David Pisoni, George Potts. Hillsdale, NJ: Lawrence Erlbaum.

This chapter discusses the arithmetic reasoning principles of young children regarding abstract numerical representation of a set of objects. The author presents data indicating that the young child does have some ability to reason about numbers up to five. Nineteen references are provided.

Mathematical Talent: Discovery, Description, and Development. Proceedings of the Third Annual Hyman Blumberg Symposium on Research in Early Childhood Education. (1974). Julian C. Stanley, Daniel P. Keating, Lynn H. Fox. Baltimore, MD: John Hopkins Univ. Press. (Blumberg Series).

This volume is a result of the Third Annual Hyman Blumberg Symposium. The research and discussion in the nine separate papers stem directly from the Study of Mathematically and Scientifically Precocious Youth (SMSPY), a five-year project at John Hopkins University. The first three papers provide background for the study. The fourth paper reports on the study done by Helen S. Astin regarding sex differences in math and scientific precocity. Chapter 6 discusses rapid teaching of math and science. Chapters 7 and 8 examine the social and emotional development of the gifted.

Reports of Research

Linear Structural Models for Response and Latency Performance in Arithmetic on Computer-Controlled Terminals. (1967). Patrick Suppes, Lester Hyman, Max Jerman. In *Minnesota Symposia on Child Psychology*, Vol. 1, edited by John Hill, Minneapolis, MN: Univ. of Minnesota Press.

This paper reports research done in the area using computers to present carefully programmed sets of problems to children in school. The authors did not test the merits of the computer based instruction but rather the determinants of problem solving abilities of the children. Fourteen references are given.

The Psychology of Mathematical Abilities in Schoolchildren. (1976). V. A. Krutetskii. Chicago, IL: Univ. of Chicago Press.

This book reports on the author's extensive research program exploring the nature and structure of mathematical abilities in children ranging from six to seventeen years. In the initial chapters Krutetskii presents an extensive review of the literature on mathematical abilities. The review, although very useful, is biased and has a strong political component. Beginning in Chapter 5, Krutetskii describes the various methods he used in his investigation and presents his hypotheses about the nature of mathematical abilities. The main body of the book is concerned with Krutetskii's major experimental study. The data for this study came from extensive interviews with almost 200 schoolchildren who were given 26 series of problems to solve. Because Krutetskii was especially interested in the processes involved in solving problems, his data consist largely of "thinking aloud" protocols as well as solution time and solution accuracy measures. Based on this data, Krutetskii concludes that there are three stages of mental activity in solving a mathematical problem: gathering the information needed to solve the problem, processing the information to obtain a solution, and retaining information about the solution. Although the work presented in this book differs considerably from experimental research by Western psychologists, it presents a tremendous wealth of descriptive data about children's mathematical thinking which should make a contribution to our work in cognitive development.

PERCEPTION

Bibliographies

Annotated Bibliography on Perceptual-Motor Development. (1973). American Association for Health, Physical Education, and Recreation. Washington, DC: American Association for Health, Physical Education, and Recreation.

This annotated bibliography came about through the efforts of the Perceptual-Motor Task Force of the Physical Education Division of AAHPER, which operated from 1967 - 1972. The bibliography is divided into three broad sections. The first lists the works of six individuals: A. Jean Ayres, Ray Barsch, Robert Doman and Carol Delacato, Marianne Frostig, Newell Kephart. The second section, the subject bibliographies, includes: auditory perception and movement; body image and movement; depth and distance perception and movement; feedback and regulation of movement behavior; figure-ground perception/field dependence/field independence; reduced and supplementary perceptual cues and movement; and visual and size perception and movement. The last section is a bibliography on perceptual-motor programs: tests, programs, and materials sources; and assessment instruments.

Reviews of Literature

Children's Searching: The Development of Search Skills and Spatial Representation. (1985). Edited by Henry M. Wellman. Hillsdale, NJ: Lawrence Erlbaum.

This volume brings into sharp focus the last two decades of studies on search behavior in children. New studies as well as classic findings are included. The first chapter, by Presson and Somerville, argues that existing data on infant search do not support the idea that early spatial representation is egocentric, or purely body-referenced. The Bremner and Bryant chapter reviews evidence linking physical maturation and motor development to changes in spatial awareness in infancy. Somerville and Haake, in their chapter, outline evidence that some logical search skills are present as early as 15 - 18 months of age. Harris suggests that search skills may be related. The Wellman, Fabricius, and Sophian chapter tries to connect search skills with problem-solving skills in children. DeLoache presents data indicating that children 18 months to three years of age make active efforts to remember the location of hidden objects. Heth and Cornell review ethological and anthropological data on search. Finally, Corrigan and Fischer analyze search tasks using concepts taken from Fischer's skill theory. This book is intended for the researcher. References.

The Development of Sensory-Motor Function in Young Children. (1986). Harriet G. Williams. In *Physical Activity and Well-being*, edited by Vern Seefeldt. Reston, VA: American Alliance for Health, Physical Education, Recreation, and Dance.

The chapter presents a brief overview of the development of selected sensory-motor functions in young children. It describes and explains what the role of sensory-motor experiences may be in the development of motor and cognitive functions in young children. The chapter tries to show how neural development may be related to the sensory and motor experiences which the child undergoes early in life.

Emergence and Characterization of Sex Differences in Spatial Ability: A Meta-Analysis. (December 1985). Marcia C. Linn, Anne C. Petersen. In *Child Development.* 56 (6), pp. 1479 - 1493.

This article synthesizes empirical studies investigating various aspects of sex differences in spatial ability. A lengthy bibliography concludes the journal meta-analysis.

Life-Span Changes in Visual Perception. (1970). Peter E. Comalli, Jr. In *Life-Span Development Psychology: Research and Theory*, edited by Goulet and Baltes. NY: Academic.

The chapter discusses the empirical evidence demonstrating life-span changes in perceptual achievement. The studies cited show perceptual performance between children and the aged to be more similar than between young adults over the course of the life span. Complete citations to studies mentioned in the chapter must be located in the bibliography at the end of the book.

Many Facets of Touch - The Foundation of Experience: Its Importance Through Life, with Initial Emphasis for Infants and Young Children. (1984). Edited by Catherine Caldwell Brown. Skillman, NJ: Johnson & Johnson Baby Products. (Johnson & Johnson Baby Products Company Pediatric Round Table Series).

The monograph summarizes the Round Table #10 symposia that brought together a multidisciplinary faculty of distinguished scholars to discuss the importance of touch to growth and development. The topic was covered from birth to death. Special emphasis was given, however, to infants and young children during the symposium. Part I gives a general overview of the different philosopher's views on touch. Part II contains three papers covering touch and brain plasticity. Part III, made up of four papers, looks at touch and attachment in animals and humans. Part IV discusses touch and the preterm infant. The topic is covered with six papers. Part V, entitled Touch in Childhood and Adolescence, covers in three papers such varied topics as reading achievement and the child's body image. Part VI contains three papers on the topic of therapeutic touch. Part VII is made up of two papers discussing touch near the end of life. References and suggested readings conclude the text.

Measurement of Audition and Vision in the First Year of Postnatal Life: A Methodological Overview. (1985). Edited by Gilbert Gottlieb, Norman Krasnegor. Norwood, NJ: Ablex.

Volume is a collection of 16 chapters providing an overview of measurement of audition and vision in the first year of postnatal life. The volume is divided into four general sections. The four chapters in Section I cover significant dimensions of auditory stimulation for infants, the characterization of visual stimuli, and auditory development and environmental constraints on infant perception. Section II covers psychophysics of infant audition and vision. Section III, containing six chapters pertaining only to human infants, is devoted to higher cognitive processes. Emphasis is on the infant-head-turning response, high amplitude techniques of studying speech perception, and preferential looking and reaching methods for studying higher psychological processing. The final section which consists of three chapters concentrates on psychological measures of auditory and visual function. Chapter 14 discusses brainstem auditory-evoked response. Chapter 15 discusses event-related brain potentials in relation to visual development. This is a highly recommended source.

Perception and Understanding in Young Children: An Experimental Approach. (1974). Peter Bryant. NY: Basic Books.

This book contributes to the study of child thought, both for providing a plausible theory which integrates a number of isolated research areas and as an example of the creative use of experimentation. Generally the book covers the question of how young children of three to eight years perceive and interpret their surroundings. Chapter 3 presents evidence that, contrary to the findings of Piagetian research, children as young as four are capable of making transitive inferences. The final chapter discusses the value of experimentation for understanding children's behavior and focuses on (1) the relationship between the controlled circumstances of the experiment and real life and (2) the role of the experiment in studying the causes of developmental change.

The Perceptual World of the Child. (1977). T. G. R. Bower. Cambridge, MA: Harvard Univ. Press. (Developing Child).

Part of The Developing Child Series, this volume presents research findings regarding perception in the infant. The third chapter discusses experimental studies of the infant's perceptual capacity in detail. The fourth chapter covers studies which show the limitations of the infant's capacity to process information. Three chapters cover studies which show how the infant adjusts to the growth of his own system. Chapter 8 provides a case history of a blind child fitted with an echo sounding device. The book is clearly written and should be of interest to readers on all levels. One major flaw with the book is the lack of adequate references.

Perspectives on Non-Sexist Early Childhood Education. (1978). Edited by Barbara Sprung. NY: Teachers College Press.

This volume looks at sex differences in light of the way girls and boys are socialized from birth. The twelve individually authored chapters were first presented at the 1976 Conference on Non-Sexist Early Childhood Education at Airlie House, Airlie, Virginia. Chapters 5 - 8 fall under the general category of research overviews and look at overall sex stereotype that children learn through media; how teaching reinforces sex-role stereotypes; effect of social class on sex-role stereotyping with children; and levels of use of sex-role stereotyping. After each of the research chapters, other reports of research are cited. In the appendixes there are guidelines for developing and evaluating unbiased educational materials as well as sources of non-sexist materials.

Rules That Babies Look By: The Organization of Newborn Visual Activity. (1980). Marshall Haith. Hillsdale, NJ: Lawrence Erlbaum.

This book reports five studies carried out by the author on infant perception and attention. Chapter 1 provides a review of the literature with the remaining chapters describing the studies. The author has provided a summary statement at the beginning of each results section. A lengthy bibliography is provided (pp. 131 - 138).

Sensorimotor and Postual Behaviors: Their Relation to Cognitive Development. (1982). Pierre Mounoud, Claude-Alain Hauert. In *Review of Child Development Research*, Vol. 6, edited by Willard Hartup. Chicago, IL: Univ. of Chicago Press.

The authors review research contradicting Piaget and Wallon's theory that an infant's behavior during the first weeks of life is not characterized by a lack of intersensory or sensorimotor coordination. The research reviewed indicates that the child's interchanges with his physical as well as social environment are well-organized. Furthermore, it appears that the infant reorganizes his interchanges with the outside world several times by the sixteenth to eighteenth month after birth. In fact, during certain stages of development the interchanges between child and environment are organized, automatic or automated, preprogrammed, and based on well-defined representations. The reviewers suggest that "there exist at birth preformed, constituted representations that can be termed sensory representations." The authors suggest that the new capacities of representation that appear at birth should be called perceptive, those that appear around 18 months, conceptual, and those that appear around ten years of age, formal or semiotic.

Some Aspects of the Development of Space Perception. (1971). Seymour Wapner, Leonard Cirillo, A. Harvey Baker. In *Minnesota Symposia on Child Psychology*, Vol. 5, edited by John Hill. Minneapolis, MN: Univ. of Minnesota Press.

This paper summarizes some of the empirical findings and theoretical concepts pertaining to perception in which the authors have been engaged for several years. Although the majority of the research deals with adults, references to age changes from childhood to adulthood are made. A lengthy bibliography is provided. Researchers in the area of perception will find the paper helpful.

Spatial Abilities: Development and Psychological Foundations. (1982). Edited by Michael Potegal. NY: Academic.

This collection contains 15 chapters dealing with the ability of organisms to organize the space around them and the nature of the brain mechanisms underlying this organization. Seven of the fifteen chapters are primarily about children or developmental issues. The topics covered include: perceptual cues related to spatial orientation; impaired and nonimpaired children's coding of spatial information in different modalities; spatial orientation and mobility in blind pedestrians; object localization in infancy; children's cognitive mapping; children's perception of obliques; mental rotation; heredity and spatial ability, sex-related differences in spatial ability; history of brain-related disorders in spatial thinking; cerebral lesions and spatial orientation disorders; single-cell mechanisms and spatial skill in the monkey; spatially organized behaviors in animals; and vestibular and neostriatal contributions to spatial orientation. Of real note are the chapters by Gremner on object constancy in infants, by Pick and Rieser on cognitive mapping by Hart and Berzok on cognitive mapping in natural environments, and by Newcombe on sex-related differences in spatial ability.

The Visual World of the Child. (1976). Elaine Vurpillot. NY: International Universities Press.

This book is primarily concerned with research on perception in children from three to seven years of age. The first section of the book comprises a review of developmental research and theories in some of the classical areas of perception - the perceptual constancies, embedded figures, reversible and ambiguous figures, closure, and form orientation. The second major section summarizes the extensive literature on verbal mediation and selective attention models of discrimination learning. Vurpillot concludes that this literature largely confirms the results of classical perceptual identification tasks in showing significant developmental changes in the child's ability to analyze and extract perceptual structures or properties of stimuli. The final section of the book summarizes Russian, American, and Western European observations of visual activity in children. The book is not written for beginners; however, the researcher who is theorizing and conducting developmental experiments on perception and attention will find this book to have some merit.

X-Linkage of Spatial Ability: A Critical Review. (September 1980). David B. Boles. Child Development, 51 (3), 625 - 635.

Critical review of literature on sex differences and spatial ability.

Reports of Research

Children's Experience of Place. (1979). Roger Hart. NY: John Wiley & Sons.

The focus of this book is on children's knowledge and feelings about different places. Hart's book is both a research monograph and a series of appendixes containing reviews of theory and research about children's spatial activity, place knowledge, place feelings, and place use. Data was gathered from all the children in a small New England town plus integrative data from individual children in eight families. The focus of the book is not upon children's knowledge of the spatial structure of the environment but upon their knowledge and feelings about different places. A lengthy and meaty bibliography is provided.

An Experimental Approach to the Effects of Experience on Early Human Behavior. (1967). Burton L. White. In *Minnesota Symposia on Child Psychology*, Vol. 1, edited by John Hill. Minneapolis, MN: Univ. of Minnesota Press.

White's paper looks at the development of visual accommodation and visual motor coordination during infancy. His research suggests that extra handling of the infant, making increased motility possible, and providing a visually compelling environment can have decelerating as well as accelerative effects on the age at which onset of certain accommodative and visually directed reaching responses occur. The paper is an excellent example of the combination of longitudinal and experimental approaches to the study of development in children. Thirty-four references are included.

Light Detection and Pattern Recognition: Some Comments on the Growth of Visual Sensation and Perception. (1970). Harry Munsinger. In *Life-Span Development Psychology: Research and Theory*, edited by Goulet and Baltes. NY: Academic.

The chapter is a description of a study looking at the differentiation between energy detection and pattern recognition. Evidence from neonatal and infant studies shows the human newborn is not sensitive to changes in brightness and his visual acuity is comparable to adults' rod vision.

The Role of Modalities in Perceptual and Cognitive Development. (1971). Jacqueline Goodnow. In *Minnesota Symposia on Child Psychology*, Vol. 5, edited by John Hill. Minneapolis, MN: Univ. of Minnesota Press.

In this paper Goodnow reports "on the empirical studies that were inspired by a general non-modality-specific framework and that have contributed to the development of her stimulus sampling view." Two and one-half pages of references are provided.

The Scanning Patterns of Human Infants: Implications for Visual Learning. (1982). Gordon W. Bronson. Norwood, NJ: Ablex. (Monographs on Infancy).

Study of the scanning patterns of two-month- to five-month-old babies (ten) by recording their visual fixation during one and one-half minutes of experimental exposure. Good bibliography on the topic is included.

THINKING

Reviews of Literature

Children's Thinking. (1986). Robert S. Siegler. Englewood Cliffs, NJ: Prentice-Hall.

This book presents major theories and research findings on the development of problem solving, reasoning, memory, language, perception, and the 3 R's. Individual chapters end with suggested readings. The volume ends with a lengthy bibliography of cited sources. Separate author and subject indexes are provided.

Children's Thinking: What Develops?   (1978).   Edited by Robert S. Siegler. Hillsdale, NJ: Lawrence Erlbaum.

This volume covers three broad areas of children's thinking: (1) memory development;   (2) development of problem solving skills;   and (3) the development of representational processes.   Chapter 1 is an overview of current research in memory development.   Chapter 2 presents a new general theory of memory development.   Chapter 3 looks at causes of developmental differences in memory.   Chapter 5 explores the origins of scientific reasoning. Chapter 6 reviews children's understanding of class inclusion.   Chapter 7 examines three- to five-year-olds' ability to plan ahead.   The final chapter in the problem-solving section analyzes the development of counting skills, with two- to four-year-olds.   Chapter 10 covers the development of language skills. Chapter 11 examines children's ability to take perspectives other than their own.   Chapter 12 examines the development of visual imagery.   References.

Cognitive Development.   Second edition.   (1985).   John H. Flavell.   Englewood Cliffs, NJ: Prentice-Hall.

A very readable book for anyone interested in human cognitive development. Many references are cited, especially secondary sources which will provide ready access to the primary research literature.   This edition differs from the first in that it contains two more chapters plus thoroughly revised and updated chapters on developmental changes during early childhood, during middle childhood and adolescence, and in social cognition, perception, memory, and language.   This is less emphasis on Piaget in this edition and more emphasis on Gibsonian information processing and growth of knowledge approaches.   Emphasis is also given to the cognitive competencies of infants and young children that recent research has documented.

Individual Differences in Cognition.   Vol. 1.   (1983).   Edited by Ronna F. Dillon, Ronald R. Schmeck. NY: Academic.

The volume tries to establish connections between psychometrics, theories of individual differences, and modern cognitive psychology.   The chapters review research and theories concerning individual differences in short-term memory; verbal processes that influence differences in reading ability; process models of spatial and verbal aptitudes as measured by psychological tests; relationship between developmental and individual differences; differences in mathematical competence; and individual differences in problem solving in learning styles including play.

Piaget and the Foundation of Knowledge. (1983). Edited by Lynn S. Liben. Hillsdale, NJ: Lawrence Erlbaum. (Jean Piaget Symposium Series).

This volume is drawn from the 10th annual symposium of the Jean Piaget Society whose theme was "Piaget and the Foundations of Knowledge." A number of common themes emerged from the symposium; one was that context is of critical importance to the study of the foundation of knowledge. Chapter 1 focuses on "regularities in the environment" and the development of child thought. Chapters 2, 3, and 4 address ways in which "preadapted coordinations," "unlearned sensitivity to relationships," and "natural biological characteristics of the organism" play a role in shaping the categorization and interpretation of what is encountered in the environment. Chapter 5 looks at the role of logical structures on categorization. Chapter 6 discusses the variation in subjects' performance on logical reasoning tasks. Chapter 7 deals with the effect of operational schemes on memory. Chapter 8 looks at the effects of self-awareness or consciousness on the construction of knowledge. Chapter 9 looks at infant social cognition. Chapter 10 relates research on delay of gratification. Chapter 11 examines the ways in which different metatheoretical assumptions influence the kinds of questions asked. I can think of no other book that better represents the diversity of contemporary thought on cognitive development and how deeply it reflects the influence of Jean Piaget.

Young Children's Knowledge of Relational Terms: Some Ifs, Ors, and Buts. (1985). Lucia A. French, Katherine Nelson. NY: Springer-Verlag. (Springer Series in Language and Communication, Vol. 19).

The four chapters in this book discuss research data gathered on ways in which children convey their understanding of the temporal and logical structure of the events they describe through both sequential reporting and the provision of relational terms such as *before, after, because, so, if, or, but, first,* and *when.* Data were also gathered on the ways in which these productions contrast with previous literature on young children's understanding of temporal relationships and related terms. The last chapter addresses the question of why there is such a disparity between the present studies and previous investigators' data.

Reports of Research

Children's Early Thought: Developments in Classification. (1983). Susan Sugarman. NY: Cambridge Univ. Press.

This book describes changes in the way children think during the period in which they learn to talk. The study charts cognitive organizational change during the second and third years. Chapter 2 presents the overall research design and procedure. Chapters 3 - 10 present the main results on spontaneous and elicited organization of subjects into two groups. Chapter 11 extends the inquiry to coordination of convergent criteria in spontaneous and provoked organization. Chapter 12 indicates that the main trends occur in seriation as well, and Chapter 13 shows that children's verbal references to classes and between class relations also follow the main sequence of development. Chapter 14 provides some concluding remarks on cognitive development in the light of the results of the investigation. An appendix presents some classification data from six deaf preschoolers also showing the increasing ability to coordinate conceptual comparisons of objects. The volume is rich in interesting data, including many detailed descriptions of children's behavior sequences with the various tasks.

Logical Thinking in Second Grade. (1970). Edited by Millie Almy. NY: Teachers College Press, Columbia Univ.

The major question in this study has to do with the effects of early instruction on the logical thinking abilities of young children. This three-year study involved 914 children, 26 kindergarten teachers, and 58 first-grade teachers. The primary objective of the study was to find out whether children who receive instruction in kindergarten and first grade in one or more of the "new" programs dealing with basic concepts in math and science show a more advanced level of thinking when they reach the second grade than children of similar background not receiving such instruction. New programs used in the study were the AAAS, Science--A Process Approach; SCIS, Science Curriculum Improvement Study; and GCMP, Greater Cleveland Mathematics Program. The results of the study appear to pose a paradox. The children who participated in the new programs initiated at the kindergarten level performed somewhat better in the logical thinking tasks in the second grade than did the children whose participation in the new programs did not begin until grade one. On the other hand children participating in the new programs beginning in kindergarten did no better than those who did not participate at all in the new program by grade two.

Directories

Cognitive Development among Sioux Children. (1983). Gilbert Voyat. NY: Plenum. (Cognition and Language: A Series in Psycholinguistics).

Reports a study comparing the cognitive development of non-Indian and American Indian children ages four to eleven. The researchers used a small cross-sectional sample of 71 Sioux children and a group of European children. This work is presented as a descriptive work without benefit of full statistics or comparative analysis. The presentation and conclusion from experiments of spatial relationships and spatial perspective provide some of the most interesting reading of the book. The ethnographic material in this study presented at the beginning is largely political history rather than a psychocultural background. The crosscultural material is not related to the outcome of the Piagetian tasks. The second part of the book explores the application of Piagetian theory to education. References.

An International Directory of Spatial Tests. (1983). John Eliot, Ian Macfarlane Smith. Oxford: NFER-Nelson.

A very unusual reference in that the scope of the volume is limited to visual-spatial tests which appear to require the perception and retention of visual forms and/or the mental manipulation of visual shapes. It is also unique in that the volume contains a broad sampling of commercially available, out-of-print, and experimental tests in the English language. The volume is unique in its organization. The tests are organized and presented in a classification based on the perceived similarity of test stimuli and requirements. The volume is unusual because the test instructions and practice items are reproduced directly from test specimens wherever possible. Cross references to Buros are given as well as others where available. Examples of tests which might be of interest to scholars and researchers in child development include: Thurstone's Primary Mental Ability Tests, Primary Mental Abilities Test, and Lanzo's Pictorial Test of Positional Concepts.

8
Behavior Development

DATABASES
TO CONSIDER

Embase   CJPI
Medline   ERIC
Social Work Abstracts   NCJRS
Sociological Abstracts   PsycINFO

GENERAL

Bibliographies

The Consumer Behavior of Children and Teenagers: An Annotated Bibliography.
(1969). Robert O. Herrmann. Chicago, IL: American Marketing.
(Bibliography Series, No. 16).

Entries in this annotated bibliography are those published since 1955. Some
important sections in this work include: social influences on youth, the young
consumer, learning the consumer role; and problems, needs, and interests of
the youth market.

Research in Infant Behavior: A Cross-Indexed Bibliography. (1964). Edited by
Yvonne Brackbill. Baltimore, MD: Williams & Wilkins.

This list of references to infant behavior is over two decades old. However, it
lists older journal articles and books on the topic which will be helpful to
researchers doing retrospective literature searching. The book is divided into
seven broad categories: perception; motor behavior; learning and
conditioning; language, vocalization, and communication; cognitive
development; social behavior and variables; and emotion and personality
development. At the end of the text is an author and subject index.

Reviews of Literature

Can Television Teach Prosocial Behavior? (1983). Valeria O. Lovelace, Aletha C. Huston. In R_x *Television: Enhancing the Preventive Impact of TV*, edited by Joyce Sprafkin, Carolyn Swift, Robert Hess. NY: Haworth.

> Prosocial television and its effect on children's learning and behavior is reviewed. Three different methods of presenting favorable prosocial behavior are discussed and evaluated. The chapter concludes with references.

Child Neuropsychology: An Introduction to Theory, Research, and Clinical Practice. (1983). Byron P. Rourke, Dirk J. Bakker, John L. Fisk, John D. Strang. NY: Guilford.

> Chapters 2, 3, and 4 deal with aspects of developmental neurology, brain asymmetry, and lateralization of function within a developmental context, and the notion of plasticity and its relationship to brain and behavior development. Chapter 5 looks at neuropsychological assessment of children. Chapter 7 gives 21 case illustrations relating aspects of developmental neuropsychological theory, assessment findings, and treatment approaches. Descriptions of tests administered to children ages 5 - 15 may be found in the appendix. References.

The Development of Prosocial Behavior. (1982). Edited by N. Eisenberg. NY: Academic.

> The 15 chapters are grouped into five broad categories: conceptual issues, early development of prosocial behavior and socialization mechanisms, the role of cognition, the role of affect, and personality and prosocial development. In Section I (conceptual issues) two chapters cover altruism in children and one is devoted to social learning theory and the development of prosocial behavior. Three chapters make up the early development section, covering altruism in some aspect. In Section III (role of cognition) one chapter covers helping behavior development while two address the development of reasoning in regard to prosocial behavior. In Section IV, Chapter 11 looks at prosocial motivation, empathy, and guilt. Chapter 12 lists six differences in empathy. Chapter 13 looks at the effect of mood on prosocial behavior. In Section V, Chapter 14 covers personality development while Chapter 15 looks at the development of prosocial motivation. References.

Effects of Stimulus Familiarization on Child Behavior. (1969). Gordon N. Cantor. In *Minnesota Symposia on Child Psychology*, Vol. 3, edited by John Hill. Minneapolis, MN: Univ. of Minnesota Press.

This paper looks at Stimulus Familiarization Effect (SFE). The author summarizes and analyzes eight studies on the subject. On pages 8 and 9 these studies are shown in chart form for the reader. References.

Ethological Studies of Child Behavior. (1972). Edited by N. Blurton Jones. London: Cambridge Univ. Press.

The book brings together work where methods used in studying behavior of animals, especially social behavior, have been directly applied to studies of human behavior. Most of the chapters included in the two sections involve methods of studying causation, particularly in interaction between individuals, to the study of child behavior. The five chapters in Part I deal with child and peer interactions. The seven chapters in Part II cover interactions between mother and child. References to works or studies cited in the text are located at the ends of chapters. This volume is considered a classic.

Imitation: A Developmental Perspective. (1978). Regina Yando, Victoria Seitz, Edward Zigler. Hillsdale, NJ: John Wiley & Sons.

This book provides a synthesis of theories and research on the phenomenon of imitation in young children. The first half of the book is a review of theory and literature on imitation through 1976 with special attention given to studies investigating developmental differences. Most of the second half of the book is devoted to reporting an empirical study conducted with children from 4 to 13 years of age. The final chapter is a theoretical integration which corresponds to the reviews of theory and literature in the first half of the book. References.

Out of School. (1980). Edited by Lionel Hersov, Ian Berg. NY: John Wiley & Sons.

This volume investigates the causes, problems, and ramifications of physically healthy children who do not attend school. The first nine chapters look at the problem of truancy. The remaining eight chapters of the book deal with school phobics. Most of the truancy data comes from England with only one study from the United States, and it concerns adults. The problems surrounding school phobia are thoroughly discussed and clinical treatment plans from several different orientations are suggested. References.

Research in Infant Behavior: A Cross-Indexed Bibliography. (1964). Edited by Yvonne Brackbill. Baltimore, MD: Williams & Wilkins.

Most of the more than 1,700 entries are articles, but over 400 monographs and serial publications also are analyzed. An innovative technique in subject indexing, providing multi-faceted access to entries, is employed. Eight separate subject indexes (Sensation and Perception; Motor Behavior; Learning and Conditioning; Language; Vocalization and Communication; Cognitive Development; Social Behavior and Social Variables; and Emotion and Personality Development), each prepared by a specialist, attempt to direct researchers to those references specifically concerned with certain topics. Underscored numbers refer to those studies considered important. Entries in indexes are arranged first by broad subject, then appropriately under successively narrower headings.

Storage Mechanisms in Early Experience. (1972). William R. Thompson. In *Minnesota Symposia on Child Psychology*, Vol. 6, edited by Anne Pick. Minneapolis, MN: Univ. of Minnesota Press.

Paper reviews the author's research, along with others in the field, on the effect of early experience on later behavior. Forty-two references.

Type A Behavior: Emergence, Development, and Implications for Children. (1986). Patrice G. Sabb, Karen A. Matthews. In *Advances in Developmental and Behavioral Pediatrics*, Vol. 7, edited by Mark Walraich, Donald Routh. Greenwich, CT: JAI.

Chapter is an overview, since 1984, of the origins of the type A behavior pattern. Type A in children is examined and its implications on the mental and physical health of children. A substantial bibliography is included.

U-Shaped Behavioral Growth. (1982). Edited by Sidney Strauss, Ruth Stavy. NY: Academic.

This book discusses the theories and research of U-shaped behavior growth curves. The eleven chapters are based on a workshop held at the University of Tel Aviv under the joint auspices of that university and the Massachusetts Institute of Technology. The first four chapters consider the question in the context of information processing. Chapter 5 looks at certain types of errors in children's spontaneous speech. Chapter 6 addresses the child's early artistic flair. Chapter 8 discusses a study in which the authors revisited a class and retested the drawing of a "rhythm" to which subjects listened. References.

Reports of Research

Behavioral Individuality in Early Childhood. (1963). Alexander Thomas, Stella Chess, Herbert G. Birch, Margaret E. Hertzig, Sam Korn. NY: New York Univ. Press.

A classical study of the behavioral characteristics of eighty children during the first two years of life. The findings of the longitudinal study suggest that all infants will not respond in the same fashion to a given environmental influence. The reaction will vary with the personality characteristics of the child upon whom the constant stimulus is brought. Specifically, the tactics utilized by parents and others in child rearing will have different behavioral results depending on the nature of the child. References.

The Child from Five to Ten. Revised edition. (1977). Arnold Gesell, Frances L. Ilg, Louise Bates Ames. NY: Harper & Row.

The author sees this volume as a developmental sequel to the earlier volume, *Infant and Child in the Culture of Today*, first published in 1943 and revised in 1974. The two volumes supplement each other and are further supplemented by a third, *Youth: The Years from Ten to Sixteen.* All three may be considered companion volumes, but each is written to stand alone. The author considers this volume a biographic developmental study of the patterning of behavior throughout the first ten years of life. The findings of the longitudinal study are presented in the form of "growth gradients" embracing some eighteen age levels and ten major fields of behavior. Part I is intended to give the reader preliminary orientation to the central theme of development and is rather theoretical. Part II describes the progressive stages in the growth of the child's mind. Part III deals with the total growth complex and outlines the process of development. This is a classic in the area of behavior. References.

A Comparison of the Social Behavior of Some Normal and Problem Children. (1972). Gill M. Leach. In *Ethological Studies of Child Behavior*, edited by Blurton Jones. London: Cambridge Univ. Press.

This study observed social interactions of 24 preschool children. Results showed that problem children have unsatisfactory and fewer interactions with both peers and mothers. Problem children appear less responsive to their mothers than normal children. Mothers of problem children tend to avoid interactions with their children. References.

Development of Hierarchical Configurational Models for Parent Behavior and Child Behavior. (1971). Earl S. Schaefer. In *Minnesota Symposia on Child Psychology*, Vol. 5, edited by John Hill. Minneapolis, MN: Univ. of Minnesota Press.

This paper presents a hierarchical, configurational approach to the study of conceptual domains as applied to the study of parent and child behavior. The change from circular to spherical conceptual models for parent and child behavior suggests that major replicable dimensions and configurations can be isolated for these and other domains. A lengthy bibliography is included.

Perspectives on School at Seven Years Old. (1977). John Newson, Elizabeth Newson, Peter Barnes. London: George Allen and Unwin.

This book is a study of a child's educational experience as seen by parents. The authors report the results of 700 interviews with mothers based upon a 200-item questionnaire. When answers to several questions about such topics as discipline or school relationships are considered together, the authors find that a pattern, or an index, emerges. The book, then, is a discussion of such patterns as the children's initial reluctance to attend school, the tribulations of their "settling-in," the different kinds of parental support provided the children at home, the parents' concerns about their children learning to read, their ambitions for their children, and so forth. References.

Preschool to School: A Behavioral Study. (1982). N. J. Richman, Stevenson Graham, P. Graham. London: Academic. (Behavioral Development).

A longitudinal study focusing on the behavior problems and developmental delays of three-year-old children. The study not only looks at the percentage of behavior problems within the population but also identifies the other related factors such as material deprivation, disturbance of family relationship, parental health, and rate of development of the child in language and other abilities. The researchers studied the link between disturbance in the preschool child and the presence of similar difficulties later in life. References.

Social Competence, Symptoms, and Underachievement in Childhood: A Longitudinal Perspective. (1977). Martin Kohn. NY: John Wiley & Sons.

This volume reports the results of a large scale longitudinal study of children's social and academic performance.   Two dimensions of the preschool children's functioning were included in the study.   One was the extent to which children exhibit interest-participation versus apathy-withdrawal, and the other is the extent to which children exhibit cooperation-compliance versus anger-defiance.   Sampling continued through the fourth grade. Boys were found to score much higher than girls on anger-defiance and to do worse than girls in verbal achievement. Social class contributed minimally to scores on the apathy-withdrawal or anger-defiance scales. A third focus of the study was on the relationship between social-emotional functioning and academic performance. It appeared that apathy-withdrawal in preschool and elementary school predicted academic achievement, even when demographic factors were excluded. References.

Guides

The Gesell Institute's Child from One to Six: Evaluating the Behavior of the Preschool Child. (1979). Louise Bates Ames, Clyde Gillespie, Jacqueline Haines. NY: Harper & Row.

Tests described in this book represent an updated version of those found in the earlier book, *The First Five Years of Life*. The volume tells educators and psychologists how to examine preschoolers and describes general behavioral characteristics and age changes which may be expected in the first six years. Four fields of behavior are covered: motor, adaptive, language, and personal/social. The appendixes contain the materials, examiner's record sheets, and the personal/social interview forms used by the authors.

Listening to Children. (1985). Carol R. Lewis. NY: Jason Aronson.

The guide encompasses cases where children are struggling to cope with bereavement, adoption, divorce, school problems, chronic illness, and many other normal developmental problems. The author has tried to illustrate a number of therapeutic approaches throughout the book. References.

ANTISOCIAL

Bibliographies

Research on Suicide, a Bibliography. (1985). Compiled by John L. McIntosh. Westport, CT: Greenwood. (Bibliographies and Indexes in Psychology, No. 2).

A comprehensive guide to the literature. Noteworthy entries are annotated. Materials included are general reference sources to literature directed at a specific professional group. A number of the entries concern children and youth. Includes a subject index.

Suicide: A Guide to Information Sources. (1980). David Lester, Betty H. Sell, Kenneth D. Sell. Detroit, MI: Gale Research. (Social Issues and Social Problems Information Guide, Series 3).

Guide to general reference sources for information concerning suicide.

Reviews of Literature

Advances in the Study of Aggression. Vols. 1 - . (1984 -). Edited by Robert J. Blanchard, D. Caroline Blanchard. Orlando, FL: Academic. (Advances in the Study of Aggression).

This new series reviews investigations on the topic of aggression. The first volume contains a paper on the role of child rearing practices on control of aggression as well as a paper on siblings and aggression. References.

Aggression: Social Learning Analysis. (1973). Albert Bandura. Englewood Cliffs, NJ: Prentice-Hall. (Prentice-Hall Series in Social Learning Theory).

Reviews aggression research and social learning theory. Represented are child and adult, animal and human, lab and field, and experimental and nonexperimental research. Five chapters consider theories, origins, instigators, maintaining conditions, and modification and control of aggression. Reviews include: frustration-aggression; catharsis; displacement; pain-elicited and extinction-induced aggression; and psychoanalytics, instinct, ethological, and drive theories. Television influences and gang behavior are also covered. Book was considered a landmark at publication. References.

Attributional Bias in Aggressive Children. (1985). Kenneth A. Dodge. In *Advances in Cognitive-Behavioral Research and Therapy,* Vol. 4, edited by Philip Kendall. NY: Academic.

This chapter looks at the literature dealing with the cognitive processes involved in the evolution of aggressive interchanges among children. References included.

Childhood Antecedents of Alcoholism. (1986). Mark A. Stewart, James Allen Wilcox. In *Advances in Developmental and Behavioral Pediatrics*, a Research Annual, Vol. 6, edited by Mark Walraich, Donald Routh. Greenwich, CT: JAI.

Chapter reviews literature about patterns of behavior and family background that predict a child's abuse of alcohol as an adult. The discussion includes literature concerning young children who drink to excess. A number of tables are provided within the chapter. Forty-seven references are cited.

Development of Antisocial and Prosocial Behavior: Research, Theories, and Issues. (1986). Edited by Dan Olweus, Jack Block, Marion Radke-Yarrow. NY: Academic.

Book is divided into five broad themes, two of particular interest to the child development specialist: Part II, early developmental patterns; and Part IV, socialization in the family, childhood groups, and society. Part II begins with a chapter on early development. Chapter 5 by Rheingold and Emery describes nurturing acts of young children. Chapter 6 by Waters, Hay, and Richters examines prosocial and antisocial behavior within the context of the parent-child attachment relationship. Chapter 7 describes a large project predicting preschool social behavior from home behavior. Chapter 12 written by Maccoby outlines differences between girls' and boys' social interaction and implications for prosocial/aggressive behavior. Chapter 13 examines the variables that mediate the social learning effect of television on both aggression and prosocial behavior. References.

Sex Differences in Aggression: A Rejoinder and Reprise. (December 1980). Eleanor Maccoby, Carol Nagy Jacklin. In *Child Development*, 51 (4), 964 - 980.

A meta-analysis of observational studies of peer directed aggression by children age six or younger. References.

The Stability of Antisocial and Delinquent Child Behavior: A Review. (December 1982). Rolf Loeber. In *Child Development*, 53 (6), 1431 - 1446.

Review of research on the stability of antisocial and delinquent behavior showing that children who initially display high rates of antisocial behavior are more likely to persist in this behavior than children who initially show lower rates of antisocial behavior. Studies suggest that more children drift into higher levels of antisocial behavior than revert to a lower level. The number of children engaged in overt acts such as fighting and disobedience declines between ages six to sixteen. Early identification of chronic offenders is discussed. References.

The Suicidal Child. (1986). Cynthia R. Pfeffer. NY: Guilford.

A comprehensive overview of current knowledge about suicidal behavior in preadolescents. Chapter 1 reviews the early scientific literature about childhood suicidal behavior. In Chapter 2 a definition of suicidal behavior offers a classification of the behavior. Chapter 3 looks at the incidence of completed suicides in children. Chapter 4 is a detailed clinical description of and hypothesis about the development of suicidal episodes in children. The second section, containing six chapters, discusses key factors that enhance risk of childhood suicidal behavior. Two chapters focus on the effects associated with suicidal behavior and discuss characteristics of childhood depression.   Chapter 7 discusses the development of normal children's concepts of death and compares these to the unique death concepts found in suicidal children.   Family characteristics and psychodynamics of suicidal children and suicidal parents are discussed in chapters 8 and 9.   The last chapter in the section talks about the process of change in ego functioning leading to suicidal behavior.   Section III of the book is devoted to evaluative techniques useful with at-risk suicidal children. Excellent bibliography.

Why People Kill Themselves: A 1980s Summary of Research Findings on Suicidal Behavior. Second edition. (1983). David Lester. Springfield, IL: Charles C. Thomas.

Reviews research conducted in the 1970s. Various parts of the book cover predisposition to suicide, behavioral and sociological aspects of suicide, and personality types.   Childhood suicide is mentioned where appropriate throughout the book. Chapter 4 specifically addresses suicidal behavior in children. References.

Reports of Research

Children of War. (1983). Roger Rosenblatt. Garden City, NY: Anchor/Doubleday.

This book, one of only a few published on the topic, is an account of the impressions gained in interviewing children in Northern Ireland and Israel, and refugees from Palestine, Cambodia, and Viet Nam. Rosenblatt collected his data without attempting to select representative samples, did not investigate the cultures with which he was dealing, and in many cases spoke with the children only through interpreters.

A Generation Divided: German Children and the Berlin Wall. (1987). Thomas A. Davey. Durham, NC: Duke Univ. Press.

Reports a study which interviewed children, teachers, and families on both sides of the Berlin Wall. The author examined the moral and political subtleties of their lives. Presents a portrait of how political tensions shape the developing personality of children.

Growing Up to be Violent: A Longitudinal Study of the Development of Aggression. (1977).   Monroe M. Lefkowitz, Leonard D. Eron, Leopold O. Walder, Rowell L. Hues-Mann. NY: Pergamon. (Pergamon General Psychology Series).

This book is written not only for specialists interested in aggression but also for readers who are less familiar with psychological terminology and methodology. It represents the final report on a longitudinal study of the development of aggression from ages eight to eighteen. Findings suggest that: (a) individual differences in aggression exhibit considerable temporal stability from ages eight to eighteen; (b) males and females differ not only in level of aggression but also in the variables that predict aggression at both ages; (c) exposure to and preference for television violence among third-grade boys is more strongly related to aggression at eighteen than at eight; and (d) among males, aggression is related to other signs of psychopathology, and in both sexes social success and attainment are negatively correlated with aggression. References.

Kids Who Run Away. (1984). Joseph Palenski. Saratoga, CA: R & E.

Palenski uses a combination of interviewing, observation, and analysis to study the subject. Chapter 2 provides a survey of the literature. Chapter 3 is an overview and discussion of the key theoretical concepts. Chapter 4 discusses methodological issues which are important to understanding the problem. Chapters 5 and 6 present the findings of the study. References.

War and Children. (1943). Anna Freud, Dorothy Burlingham. NY: International Univ. Press.

A lucid account of the psychological effect of war on British children during World War II. The authors note, through observations of the children, reactions, both physical and mental, to the actual experiences of bombings, separation from families, and evacuations. Book is considered a classic.

EMOTIONS

Bibliographies

The Bereaved Child: Analysis, Education, and Treatment. An Abstracted Bibliography. (1981). Gillian S. Mace, Faren R. Akins, Dianna L. Akins. NY: IFI/Plenum Data.

Abstracts 550 citations focusing on the reactions and coping mechanisms of children and adolescents to the death of parents, siblings, friends, teachers, pets, or well-known personages. Publications dealing with both normative and pathological stages of bereavement are reviewed. Materials covering childhood concepts and attitudes toward death are included. Citations appear which explore child death education and counseling issues. The arrangement is alphabetical by author. The subject index is rather limited and users may have to use some ingenuity to locate particular citations. Most of the material is post-1960.

Reviews of Literature

Anxiety in Children. (1984). Edited by Ved P. Varma. NY: Methuen.

Each chapter in this volume is authored by a well-known expert in the field and covers research and theory on issues of anxiety in children, focusing particularly on what these involve in mental health, educational, and clinical psychology. The chapter, authored by David Jones, reviews various assessment methods. Chapter 3, by Philip Barker, discusses the psychiatric interview as a clinical method of assessment. Chapter 4 discusses projective techniques of measurement. Chapter 5, by Vaman G. Lokare, looks at the cross-cultural aspects of anxiety. Chapter 6, by Philip Barker, covers family problems as they contribute to children's anxiety. Chapter 7 discusses theory and therapy for anxieties about death. Chapter 9, by Elsie L. Osborne, discusses the various aspects of anxiety and schooling, such as starting school, separation from mother, termination in bonding, and other transitions such as relationships with teachers and peers. Chapter 10, by Lindy Burton, presents case studies of anxiety resulting from illness and being treated for illness. Chapters 11 and 12 discuss the psychological and psychiatric treatment of childhood anxiety. References.

Behavioral Treatment of Children's Fears and Phobias: A Review. (1985). Richard J. Morris, Thomas R. Kratochwill. In *School Psychology Review* 14 (1).

This article reviews current behaviorally oriented fear reduction methods used with children. The article is well referenced.

A Child's Parent Dies: Studies in Childhood Bereavement. (1974). Erna Furman. New Haven, CT: Yale Univ. Press.

Provides both theoretical and practical approaches used with young children experiencing the death of a parent. The ten clinical reports written illustrate the many different ways children experience and react to the death of a parent. The bibliography as well as the text is an extensive literature review up to the time of publication.

Children's Concepts of Death. (1986). Cynthia R. Pfeffer. In *Suicidal Child*. NY: Guilford.

The first part of this chapter focuses on normal children's concepts about death, showing that children's fantasies, feelings and concepts about death evolve through a developmental process that begins at an early age. The second part of the chapter highlights death concepts in suicidal children. Normal and suicidal children's verbatim statements about death are provided to clearly illustrate their thoughts about death. References.

Children's Understanding of Death: A Review of Three Components of a Death Concept. (October 1984). Mark W. Speece, Sandra B. Brent. In *Child Development*, 55 (5), 1671 - 1686.

A review of the empirical literature on the development of the concept of death focuses on three components of the concept: irreversibility, nonfunctionality, and universality. Review suggests that children achieve an understanding of all three components between five and seventeen years of age. References.

The Communication of Emotion. (1984). Ross Buck. NY: Guilford. (Guilford Social Psychology Series).

An overview of studies of emotion and emotion communication carried out for the most part over the past fifteen years. After a definition of communication in Chapter 1, chapters 2 and 3 discuss the basic nature of motivation and emotion. Chapter 4 looks at how this process occurs in animals and considers the similarities and differences between animals and humans. The chapter also discusses cognitive development of children, language and emotional education. Chapter 5 summarizes studies of nonverbal sending accuracy, including evaluation of different techniques of study and methods of analysis. Chapter 6 discusses processes in which the spontaneous emotional display is altered. Chapter 7 summarizes studies of nonverbal receiving ability with evaluations of different methods of measurement and analysis. Chapter 8 looks at the implications of emotion communication to the analysis of interaction. References.

Distress and Comfort. (1977). Judy Dunn. Cambridge, MA: Harvard Univ. Press. (Developing Child).

This volume discusses the capabilities and limitations of the newborn and the course of development over the first few months. The causes for crying and distress are covered, followed by an examination of the relationship between attachment and distress in Western cultures as well as in other cultures. The problem of long term separation is discussed. The last two chapters cover the long term effect and practical applications of caretaker reactions to early distress. Appropriate research studies are cited through the book's chapters. Other references and suggested readings are provided at the end of the text.

Emotion and Early Interaction. (1982). Edited by Tiffany M. Field, Alan Fogel. Hillsdale, NJ: Lawrence Erlbaum.

This book is a collection of papers on the development in infancy of emotional expression and social interaction. The twelve papers are grouped in three parts: five papers about face-to-face interactions in early infancy, three papers on play interactions in later infancy, and four papers on methodology of observational data collection and analysis. The studies making up Part II report on older infants and use more varied procedures. Demos describes facial expressions as they occur spontaneously in the home using Ekman's method of microanalysis of facial movements. Brooks-Gunn and Lewis report on social interactions between handicapped children and their mothers observed in a standard playroom and find them to differ from those of normal children. Part III focuses on observational methodology. References.

Emotional Disorders in Children and Adolescents: Medical and Psychological Approaches to Treatment. (1980). G. Pirooz Scholevar. NY: SP Medical and Scientific Books. (Child Behavior and Development).

This handbook summarizes what is known about various syndromes classified as emotional disorders. Each chapter, authored by a specialist, provides background to the disorder, developmental considerations, clinical methods, follow-up steps where necessary, and references.

Emotions, Cognition, and Behavior. (1984). Edited by Carrol Izard, Jerome Kagan, Robert Zajonc. London: Cambridge Univ. Press.

This volume approaches the topic from several areas: cognitive psychology, developmental psychology, social psychology, psychophysiology, and personality-clinical psychology. The problem of definition is dealt with in Chapter 1. In Chapter 2 Kagan urges that constructs must be used for emotions that follow from detected or undetected physiological changes. Chapter 3 discusses the role of the motor system in emotion and cognition. In Chapter 4, Hoffman discusses his theory of empathy. Chapter 5 suggests other mechanisms which may provide a key for understanding emotion-cognitive relationships. In Chapter 6 Weiner and Graham describe their approach to the study of emotional development. Chapter 7 provides empirical findings and insights on cognition-emotion-action relationships. Chapter 8 contains a review on the infant's use of "social referencing." Chapter 10 presents empirical studies on the effects of social interaction. References.

Epidemiology of Anxiety Disorders in Children: A Review. (1986). Helen Orvaschel, Myrna M. Weissman. In *Anxiety Disorders of Childhood*, edited by Rachel Gittleman. NY: Guilford.

This chapter on the correlates, origins, and outcomes of childhood anxiety disorders gives a glimpse of where the field stands. The summaries of the epidemiologic studies give insight into the prevalence of fears in children, and their stability. Thirty-two references.

Helping Children Cope with Stress. (1984). Avis Brenner. Lexington, MA: D. C. Heath.

Volume describes a wide spectrum of stresses affecting children from infancy to age twelve and identifies typical coping patterns. Chapter 1 provides a general overview of the topic. Chapters 2 - 4 look at stress in one-parent, two-parent, and multiparent families. Chapters 5 - 7 look at stress during different types of separation; death, adoption, temporary separation from caretaker, and divorce. Chapters 8 - 11 discuss different types of abuse or neglect, including parental alcoholism causing stress. Chapter 12 talks about helping the child under stress. References.

Helping Young Children Cope with Death. (1977). Joanne E. Bernstein. In *Current Topics in Early Childhood Education*, Vol. 1, edited by Lilian Katz. Norwood, NJ: Ablex.

This chapter concisely reviews the literature and discusses various aspects of assisting children to cope with death. How children view death, how to explain death to children, and other aspects of children's mourning are covered. References.

Infant Stress under Intensive Care. (1985). Edited by Allen W. Gottfried, Juarlyn Gaiter. Baltimore, MD: Univ. Park Press.

Looks at all aspects of the environment of newborn special care facilities and their impact on the medical and developmental status of sick infants: neonatology, pediatrics, nursing, psychology, engineering, and social work. Chapter 1 is a brief historical overview of issues in the early development of newborn intensive care. Chapter 2 delves into the structure and organization of newborn intensive care facilities. Chapters 3 - 8 contain observational studies documenting the physical and social environment of newborn special care units. Chapter 9 focuses on thermal characteristics and engineering in newborn intensive care. Chapter 10 is an extensive review of the potentially adverse consequences of intensive care on the newborn. Chapter 11 looks at the impact of newborn intensive care on staff. Chapter 12 delves into some implications for intervention based on environmental data. The last chapter addresses ethical issues. References.

The Origins of Fear. (1974). Edited by Michael Lewis, Leonard Rosenblum. NY: Wiley-Interscience. (Origins of Behavior).

Volume two of the Origins of Behavior series, the chapters discuss such topics as the cognitive basis of fear, the situational determinants of fear, and the role of organismic factors (for example, temperament) in infants and young children. References.

Parental Death and Psychological Development. (1982). Ellen B. Berlinsky, Henry B. Biller. Lexington, MA: D. C. Heath.

Provides an exhaustive review of studies examining the impact of parental death during childhood. Includes almost 100 empirical studies on the topic augmented with an equal number of theoretical and review papers. Findings are organized under three broad headings: (1) behaviors that have been identified as consequences of parental death; (2) studies identifying family and situational variables that may affect the impact of parental death, such as the sex of the parent and the reason for the parent's absence; and (3) review of findings concerned with the characteristics of the child at the time of the parent's death. References.

Parental Death during Childhood, and Adult Depression: A Critical Review of Literature. (1980). Thomas Crook, John Eliot. In *Psychological Bulletin*, 87 (2), 252 - 259.

A synthesis of research on the relationship between parental death and depression indicates that there is no sound basis to support the theory that there is a relationship between parental loss during childhood and adult depression or any subtype of adult depression. References.

Psychological Deprivation in Childhood. (1975). J. Langmeier, Z. Matejcek. NY: John Wiley & Sons.

Reviews and discusses varied dimensions of deprivation in childhood, from extreme loss of orphans, to school phobias. A lengthy analysis of institutionalized children in Czechoslovakia is included. The authors present their own research on "types of deprived personality." One chapter explores individual differences in response to loss as a function of age, sex, temperament, and various sorts of psychological and physical disorders. The final chapters deal with diagnosis, treatment, and prevention of deprivation. The breadth of coverage attempted by the authors makes this book somewhat chaotic, but research reviewed may be new to English readers. About one-third of the 1,200 references are not available in English.

School Stress and Anxiety: Theory, Research, and Intervention. (1978). Beeman Phillips. NY: Human Sciences.

This book investigates the impact of school environment on children. The major part of the book reports on studies done with the Children's School Questionnaire (CSQ) developed by the author. After describing the procedures used for developing the CSQ, studies are reported which deal with (a) race, sex, and social class differences in school anxiety; (b) cross cultural differences based on a study done in India and Malaysia; (c) effects of different school environments on anxiety, that is, nongraded classrooms, racial integration, grade level; and (d) the relationships of anxiety to IQ and reading achievement. All of the United States data was obtained in Texas, and racial comparisons involved Anglos, blacks, and Mexican-Americans. The final chapter in the book describes a model for the role of the school psychologist as an interventionist in reducing the stress and anxiety in school settings. References.

"So the Witch Won't Eat Me": Fantasy and the Child's Fear of Infanticide. (1978). Dorothy Bloch. Boston, MA: Houghton Mifflin.

The book is a mingling of the author's own experiences with children she has treated and a discussion of the author's theories and research on the topic of childhood fantasies. The book is broken into two parts, one covering childhood and the other follow-up studies. The volume is quite readable and cites many of the older studies and theories. References.

Stress, Coping, and Development in Children. (1983). Edited by N. Garmezy, M. Rutter. NY: McGraw-Hill.

A cogent survey of stress and coping as interwoven variables in children's experiences. The book contains twelve chapters organized in five sections. In the first section Garmezy reviews the literature about the effects of war or loss of caretaker upon children's stress and coping behavior. The second section contains a chapter by Ciaranello about the nature of neurochemical systems, and a chapter by Levine about the study of stress and coping from a psychobiological approach. The third section of the book contains four chapters, each of which focuses upon a different age period. The fourth section concerns the family as a stress agent. Finally, in the last section of the book, Segal asks questions involving the general public in creating less stressful lives for children. References.

Unspoken Grief: Coping with Childhood Sibling Loss. (1986). Helen Rosen. Lexington, MA: D. C. Heath.

The book addresses the little-explored issue of sibling death. The author's overview of basic issues includes an examination of the recent but sparse literature on sibling relationships and bereavement. Explores questions of the child's comprehension of death, mourning behaviors, and reactions to specific losses. Children's experiences of parent loss are compared with sibling loss, showing a major difference in the degree of adult awareness or understanding of the child's deep feelings upon the sibling death. The chapter on society and bereaved family contributes insights into the unfortunate social isolation endured by bereaved children. Coping behaviors found useful by surviving siblings are reported. Chapter 6, Living with a Dying Sibling, presents findings from a clinical study of a support group of healthy children experiencing a sibling's terminal illness. Chapter 7 reports changes over a period of time in the lives of surviving siblings in such aspects as their interpersonal characteristics and behaviors of intimacy, domination, self-control, and death anxiety. The final chapter makes recommendations of ways to help bereaved children and families cope with the death of a child. References.

Reports of Research

Children's Dreams, Longitudinal Studies. (1982). David Foulkes. NY: John Wiley & Sons.

This volume details the finding of two concurrent longitudinal dream studies done with children over a five-year period in a laboratory setting. Part I of the text describes how the studies were set up. Part II describes what, when, and why the children dreamed, according to age categories. Part III provides two summary essays on dream development in children. A list of references is provided along with a subject index. Charts of data gathered may be found in the appendixes.

Developmental Course of Emotion Expression in the Human Infant. (1985). Carol Zander Malatesta. In *The Development of Expressive Behavior: Biology-Environment Interaction*, edited by Gail Zivin. NY: Academic. (Communication and Behavior, an Interdisciplinary Series).

This chapter delves into the development of emotional expression in the human infant. The chapter originated as a paper presented at a symposium jointly sponsored by the Ninth International Congress of Primatology and the Meeting of the International Society for Human Ethology. References.

Emotional Behavior and Development in the First Year of Life: An Analysis of Arousal, Approach-Withdrawal and Affective Responses. (1972). Henry N. Ricciuti, Robert H. Poresky. In *Minnesota Symposia on Child Psychology*, Vol. 6, edited by Anne Pick. Minneapolis, MN: Univ. of Minnesota Press.

This paper describes research clarifying the nature and development of emotional behavior and associated approach withdrawal responses in infants during the first year of life. It also refines the procedures for assessing such behaviors. Thirteen references are provided.

Emotional Expression in Infancy: A Biobehavioral Study. (1976). Robert N. Emde, Theodore J. Gaensbauer, Robert J. Harmon. NY: International Universities. (Psychological Issues, Monograph 37).

This study is based on two groups of infants--an initial sample of twelve, who were seen weekly for the first three and one-half months, and a second sample of fourteen, who were seen approximately bi-weekly throughout the first year. Home visits alternated with laboratory visits. The data are organized around the development of two prominent, affective changes; namely, social smiling and distress at the approach of a stranger. These two affective behaviors are seen as benchmarks of major biobehavioral shifts of not only affective development but of cognitive development and brain maturation as well. The authors stress the notion that development is discontinuous, and the biobehavioral shifts are regulated by maturational factors. Their presentation of data is selective, and sometimes only brief summary statements are given. This volume makes an important contribution to the literature on affective development. References.

The Fears of Childhood: A Guide to Recognizing and Reducing Fearful States in Children. (1986). Edward P. Sarafino. NY: Human Sciences.

This volume shows how the development of fears takes several sources: inborn temperaments, conditioning, seeing fear in other people, thinking and imagination, and unconscious memories. The book uses extensive research to describe what fears are, why they develop, and which fears are the most common at different stages of a child's development. Finally the book stresses the uniqueness of each child and each fear. The author uses case studies to illustrate his approach to minimizing and alleviating common childhood fears. References.

Reactions of Pre-School Children to a Strange Observer. (1972). Kevin Connolly, Peter K. Routh In *Ethological Studies of Child Behavior*, edited by Blurton Jones Smith. London: Cambridge Univ. Press.

Reports the findings of a study made of reactions of children in day nurseries to an unfamiliar observer. The conditions under which the observers were allowed to respond to the children were carefully defined. From time-sampling observations over a one-hour period each day, the kinds of approaches made to the observer were classified into seven main types. Almost all kinds of approach occurred with increased frequency at those nurseries where the observer responded to the children. In all three nurseries studied, there was a tendency for younger children in the group to show more responses than older children. No consistent sex difference was found, nor was any difference found between children with or without their father in the home. The findings suggest that the nursery environment, rather than the home background, may be more important in accounting for the differences found between children. References.

Resourceful and Vulnerable Children: Family Influence in Hard Times. (1986). G. H. Elder, Jr., A. Caspi, T. van Nguyen. In *Development as Action in Context: Problem Behavior and Normal Youth Development*, edited by Rainer Silbereisen, Klaus Eyferth, Georg Rudinger. NY: Springer-Verlag.

Chapter examines selected personal and social resources that had important implications for resilient or vulnerable status of children in two Depression periods in Berkeley and Oakland, California.   Thirty-nine references provided.

Vulnerability, Coping, and Growth: From Infancy to Adolescence. (1976). Lois B. Murphy, Alice M. Moriarty. New Haven, CT: Yale Univ. Press.

This book is an overview of twenty years of a longitudinal study carried on in Topeka, Kansas, concentrating on a group of thirty-two children who were studied intensively from infancy into young adulthood. The study sought to understand how the individual learns to deal with stress, with particular emphasis on how early response styles related to later coping behaviors. The study focused on the development of positive traits; in other words how these children coped with life's stresses, rather than how they failed. The second section of the book summarizes the longitudinal data from contacts made in infancy, preschool, latency, puberty, and late adolescence. The third section is more theoretical, and the authors attempt to pull together many of the contradictions and somewhat unrelated findings of the longitudinal study. In particular, they discuss in some detail the relationship between early individual styles and the type of coping mechanisms developed, and try to determine why in some cases stress appears to strengthen the individual, whereas in others, the child cannot seem to learn adequate coping mechanisms. The fourth section includes a case history of one child and a summary of findings. Included is a bibliography of coping studies and related discussions.

The Widening World of Childhood, Paths toward Mastery. (1962). Lois Murphy. NY: Basic Books.

Now considered a classic, this is one of a group of publications based upon longitudinal studies of normal children observed in infancy and periodically to adolescence, supported by the Menninger Foundation and the U.S. Public Health Services. In Appendix C other research with this group is listed. The book first describes a number of children confronting new experiences. Descriptions of the children's responses to difficulties in taking the intelligence test are outlined. The discussion then describes how a child copes with an accident or physically distressing situation. Part III examines the major coping devices and patterns observed. Part IV deals with the contributions of coping efforts to development. References.

Other References

Childhood and Death. (1984). Edited by Hannelore Wass, Charles A. Corr. NY: Hemisphere Publishing Corporation. (Death Education, Aging and Health Care Series).

A handbook covering all aspects of working with children affected by death. The volume combines theoretical issues with practical information. Research based, chapters cover children's concept of death; children facing death; patterns of coping; staff stress in caring for dying children; children's mourning patterns; and suicidal behavior in children. References at the end of chapters.

Measuring Emotions in Infants and Children. Based on seminars by the Committee on Social and Affective Development During Childhood of the Social Science Research Council. (1982). Edited by Carrol E. Izard. London: Cambridge Univ. Press. (Cambridge Studies in Social and Emotional Development).

This volume contains contributions on methodology, research strategies, measurement procedures, and techniques for each of the three components of emotion: biological; behavioral expressive; and subjective experimental. Chapters on psychoendocrinology, psychophysiology, facial, vocal and gaze behavior, as well as self report scales are included. The final section of the book consists of commentaries by three experts, each of whom focus on a major issue in one or more of the other three sections of the volume. References.

MANAGEMENT TECHNIQUES

Bibliographies

Behavior Modification and the Child, an Annotated Bibliography. (1979). Hazel B. Benson. Westport, CT: Greenwood. (Contemporary Problems of Childhood).

Covers the subject of behavior modification with children between 1956 and 1977. Entries are grouped by general topics: general introductory material, behavioral techniques for specific behaviors and handicapping conditions, the use of behavior modification techniques in specific settings, and training in behavioral techniques. Within each section, arrangement is alphabetical by author.

Reviews of Literature

A Bio-Developmental Approach to Clinical Child Psychology: Cognitive Controls and Cognitive Control Therapy. (1978). Sebastiano Santostefano. NY: John Wiley & Sons. (Wiley Series on Personality Process).

This volume integrates theory and research in developmental psychology with the professional practice of clinical child psychology. The book is divided into parts that cover a historical review, the biodevelopmental concepts and their implications for diagnosis and practice, the heart of the theory and practice advocated, the implications of cognitive control theory for clinical techniques, programs of cognitive control therapy, and research in cognitive control therapy. One appendix contains a useful summary of the studies conducted by the author and another appendix describes the tests he and his colleagues used. References.

Biofeedback in Pediatrics: Current Status and Appraisal. (1985). Frank Andrasik, Virginia Attanasio. In *Advances in Developmental and Behavioral Pediatrics*, Vol. 6, edited by Mark Wolraich, Donald Routh. Greenwich, CT: JAI.

Chapter reviews the literature dealing with biofeedback studies of children ranging from four years old to the late teens. Topics covered include: headaches; asthma and airway biofeedback; movement disorders including cerebral palsy, torticollis, and epilepsy; learning disabilities; writing disabilities; academic performance; emotional disabilities; and hyperkinesis. Various types of biofeedback are discussed. A lengthy bibliography of references is included.

Children in Adult Prisons, an International Picture. (1986). Katarina Tomasevski. NY: St. Martin's.

This book contains the basic documents resulting from the Exploratory Study on Children in Adult Prisons. Also included are national surveys undertaken by researchers in the twenty-seven countries encompassed by the first phase of the study; *A Study on Alternatives to Imprisonment*, written by Daniel O'Donnell; and the *Final Report on the Exploratory Study on Children in Adult Prisons*, prepared by Sanford Fox. One section discusses infants in prisons. Users will find some footnotes at the ends of chapters.

Cognitive-Behavioral Interventions: Theory, Research, and Procedures. (1979). Edited by Philip C. Rendall, Steven D. Hollon. NY: Academic. (Personality and Psychopathology: A Series of Monographs, Texts, and Treatises.)

The volume synthesizes the theory, research, and procedures in which cognitive behavioral strategies have been applied. The opening chapter traces the history of the movement and describes the professional environment of it. The chapters that follow represent major contributions by leading investigators across a number of areas of intervention. Each chapter gives a review of research in the perspective area, a description of the actual intervention procedures with supporting empirical data, and a consideration of the theoretical foundations and potential implications associated with the intervention. Chapter 2 deals with behavior modification with children. Chapter 3 looks at developing nonimpulsive behavior in children. Chapter 4 covers problem-solving, role-taking, and self-control with delinquents. References.

Cognitive-Behavioral Therapy for Impulsive Children. (1985). Philip C. Kendall, Lauren Braswell. NY: Guilford. (Guilford Clinical Psychology and Psychotherapy Series).

This volume summarizes the research of Kendall and his colleagues in the area of cognitive-behavioral therapy and developmental principles with attention deficit disordered children. Following an interview of the author's basic premises in Chapter 1, the second chapter reviews the literature. Subdivided into the categories of self-instructional and problem-solving training, the studies are summarized and evaluated in terms of two themes: (1) their use or nonuse of explicit contingencies, and (2) the degree of child and therapist/experiment involvement within the reported research settings. Symptomology, prevalence, etiology, and prognosis are foci of the third chapter. Assessment procedures are thoroughly presented in a chapter, while the three final chapters deal with treatment issues-interventions, techniques for maximizing parent and teacher involvement in treatment, posttherapy generalization, and termination. The appendix contains the therapy manual and a twelve-session step-by-step guide to implementing the proposed therapy. References.

The Development of Sleep Patterns and Sleep Disturbances from Infancy through Adolescence. (1981). Thomas F. Anders. In *Advances in Behavioral Pediatrics, a Research Annual*, Vol. 2, edited by Bonnie Camp. Greenwich, CT: JAI.

This chapter reviews studies devoted to sleep disorders and disturbances of infants, children, and adolescents. The author has used a developmental framework constituting "tasks" of sleep state organization to note stages of development. In infancy the developmental task involves both structural and temporal organization of sleep. Abnormalities of structural organization are correlated with serious central nervous system impairments and gross signs of brain damage. Disturbances of temporal organization may be linked to difficulties in environmental synchronization and produce common clinical conditions of irregular settling and night walking. In preschool and school-age children the developmental task seems related to the change in temporal organization during the first hours of sleep. References.

Increasing Children's Self-Control through Cognitive Interventions. (Spring 1979). Michael Pressley. In *Review of Educational Research* 49 (2), 319 - 370.

Reviews the experimental literature of cognitive interventions which affect children's self control. References.

Managing Children's Behavior Problems in Pediatric Practice. (1983). Carolyn S. Schroeder, Betty N. Gordon, Kornel Kanoy, Donald K. Routh. In *Advances in Developmental and Behavioral Pediatrics, a Research Annual*, Vol. 4, edited by Mark Walraich, Donald Routh. Greenwich, CT: JAI.

A summary of the pediatrician's and mental health worker's role in managing children's behavior. One section addresses the types and frequency of behavioral problems in children. Research directions are discussed as well as pertinent studies cited. The chapter is illustrated with several tables. A lengthy bibliography of cited references is provided.

The Neonatal Behavioral Assessment Scale: Assessing the Behavior Repertoire of the Newborn Infant. (1982). Frances Degen Horowitz, Patricia L. Linn. In *Advances in Behavioral Pediatrics, a Research Annual*, Vol. 3, edited by Mark Walraich, Donald Routh. Greenwich, CT: JAI.

The chapter provides a brief history and description of the Neonatal Behavioral Assessment Scale (NBAS). A review of the research is given along with clinical and educational uses of the NBAS. References.

Psychological Processes in Early Education. (1977). Edited by Harry L. Hom, Jr., Paul A. Robinson. NY: Academic.

Volume reviews research and theory about the development and modification of behavior from both laboratory and field studies and to suggest the applicability and relevance to early education. References.

Punishment. (1977). Gary C. Walters, Joan E. Grusec. San Francisco, CA: W. H. Freeman.

This book is a good overview of the two types of punishment research and will familiarize readers with the two different viewpoints. References.

Recent Progress in Understanding and Treating Sleep Disorders. (1986). Naomi Richman. In *Advances in Development and Behavioral Pediatrics, A Research Annual*, Vol. 7. Greenwich, CT: JAI.

Reviews the literature on sleep disorders in children and the implications for treatment. Focus is on difficulties with falling asleep and with night waking.

No sex differences are found in either the development of sleep patterns or in the rates of sleep patterns. Pediatricians appear to favor bedtime routines, consistent bedtimes, and minimal attention at night. It is apparent that parents are the key to promoting good sleep habits according to this writer. References.

Review of Behavior Therapy, Theory and Practice. Vol. 11. (1987). G. Terence Wilson, Cyril M. Franks, Philip C. Kendall, John P. Foreyt. NY: Guilford.

Chapter 7, by Cyril M. Franks, reviews recent literature on behavior therapy. Subsections in the chapter include topics such as: home and family therapy, compliance and noncompliance in children, behavior parent training, parent training of children with special needs, child abuse and neglect, autism and therapy, superactivity, behavior modification, and the school system. References.

The Utilization of Classroom Peers as Behavior Change Agents. (1981). Edited by Phillip S. Strain. NY: Plenum. (Applied Clinical Psychology).

Chapters focus on specific approaches to intervention: peer tutoring, role of peer imitation in development, use of peer social initiations with withdrawn children, vicarious reinforcement and punishment in the classroom, group-oriented contingency procedures, and a package program for the remediation of social aggression (RECESS program developed by the Center at Oregon for the Behavioral Education of the Handicapped). Each chapter includes a substantive review of pertinent research.

PERSONALITY

Bibliographies

Longitudinal Studies of Child Personality: Abstracts with Index. (1959). Alan A. Stone, Gloria Cochrane Onque. Cambridge, MA: Harvard Univ. Press.

An abstracted bibliography of pertinent longitudinal research studies in *Child Development Abstracts, Psychological Abstracts*, and other sources up to 1955. A subject index is provided. Although almost thirty years old, the bibliography is a valuable source of early studies in this area.

Sex Roles: A Research Bibliography. (1975). Helen S. Astin, Allison Parelman, Anne Fisher. Rockville, MD: National Institute of Mental Health.

This annotated bibliography covers the years 1960 - 1972. Besides research, some theoretical papers have been included. Entries have generally been divided into four broad categories: sex differences, development of sex differences and sex roles, specialized sex roles in institutional settings, and cross-cultural overviews of the status of the sexes. The volume is made up of 346 journal articles, 54 books, and 49 chapters of book.

Sex Studies Index, 1980. (1982). Alfred C. Kinsey, Institute of Sex Research. Boston, MA: G. K. Hall.

The Institute searched many sources including *Psychological Abstracts, Sociological Abstracts, Index Medicus,* and *Index to Legal Periodicals* in locating the entries included in this index. In the beginning of the monograph are listed the journals indexed. The index itself consists of two parts; an author index where entries are alphabetical by author's last name; and the subject index where entries are categorized by appropriate terms. Although the monograph indexes mostly articles concerning adults, a few entries may be found concerning children under such subjects as: child behavior, child-rearing advice, child victims, and child-parent relationships.

Reviews of Literature

The Assessment of Child and Adolescent Personality. (1986). Edited by Howard M. Knoff. NY: Guilford.

A comprehensive review of the literature and techniques of assessment. Concepts discussed include: reciprocal determinism; multitrait, multisetting, multimethod assessment; ecological assessment and evaluation; and multimodal therapy and intervention. Also included are some of the newest assessments in the behavior rating scale, projective technique, objective inventory, and family and ecological approach areas. References.

Birth Order: Its Influence on Personality. (1983). Cecile Ernst, Jules Angst. NY: Springer-Verlag.

The first part of this monograph is a world survey of studies, occurring between 1946 and 1980, on the relationship between birth order and socialization, intellectual functioning, and various aspects of personality. The eight chapters in the section generally cover: fallacies in birth order research, birth order and biological differences, twins and only children, birth order and IQ, school achievement, birth order and occupational status, birth order differences in socialization and personality, and birth order and mental illness. Part II of the book is an analysis of empirical data. A comprehensive bibliography is included.

The Concept, Measurement, and Interpretation of Temperament in Young Children: A Survey of Research Issues. (1986). Ronald Seifer, Arnold J. Sameroff. In *Advances in Developmental and Behavioral Pediatrics, a Research Annual*, Vol. 7, edited by Mark Wolraich, Donald Routh, pp. 1 - 43. Greenwich, CT: JAI.

Discusses research issues pertinent to the concept of temperament in young children as they relate to (1) theoretical conceptualization, (2) measurement, (3) clinical applications, and (4) the importance of the parent-child context in interpretation. Future directions of temperament research are explored. The emphasis throughout is on temperament during infancy and early childhood since that is the age range where most of the empirical work has been done and to which most theories apply. References.

The Development and Sustaining of Self-Esteem in Childhood. (1983). John E. Mack, Steven L. Ablon. From the Study Group of the Division of Child Psychiatry of the Cambridge Hospital, Department of Psychiatry, Harvard Medical School and the Cambridge-Somerville Mental Health and Retarded Center. NY: International Universities.

A collection of fifteen articles that address the development, regulation, and sustenance of self-esteem in childhood and the later years. In the introductory chapter, Mack provides an overview of relevant constructs and issues. Articles in the first section address clinical and theoretical considerations, mostly case studies with some research data to support the author's respective positions. Chapters by Demos and Ablon explore the role of affect in self-esteem development and maintenance, as well as its therapeutic implications. The relationship between self-esteem and body image is discussed in chapters by Harrison and Belfer. Cotton presents a life-cycle developmental perspective. The relationship between self-esteem and narcissism, parent-child relationships, and depression are explored by Huizenga, Givelber, Van Buskirk, and Malquist, respectively. The second section deals with the clinical and therapeutic considerations relative to the understanding of and interventions for special populations. The effects of neurological defect, learning disorder, and ego deficiency on self-esteem are examined by Jacobs. Three chapters are devoted to the roles of the educational system, the community, and the family on children's self-esteem. References.

The Development of Self. (1985). Edited by Robert L. Leahy. NY: Academic. (Developmental Psychology Series).

Chapter 1 reviews the cognitive-developmental approach to self-concept development. Chapter 2 provides insight into the history of the study of self and competence. Chapter 3 looks at social cognitive abilities affecting self-image. Chapter 4 looks at how the self has a variety of domains (physical, active, social, and psychological selves) which develop in a manner similar to understanding others. Chapter 5 by Robert Kegan looks at the development of self from ages five to seven. Chapters 6 and 7 cover the adolescent. Chapter 8 covers the cost of the lack of normal development of self and its clinical implications. References are provided with chapters.

Developmental Approaches to the Self. (1983). Edited by Benjamin Lee, Gil B. Noam. NY: Plenum. (Path in Psychology).

A collection of eight papers describing developments in three areas of developmental psychology: psychoanalytics, cognitive-developmental, and Vygotskian. Readers will find the papers more theoretical than research based. The general theme running through most of the papers is that interactions between the child and the social environment play a critical role in the development of the self. In the first six papers, the focus is on integrating cognitive-developmental and psychoanalytic views. The final two chapters present views of the development of self, based on Vygotsky's general theory of psychology. Although concrete suggestions for research are relatively scarce, this book provides provocative thought for those interested in the development of the self across the life span. References.

The Effects of Familial Variables on Sex Typing, on Parent-Child Similarity, and on Imitation in Children. (1967). E. Mavis Hetherington. In *Minnesota Symposia on Child Psychology*, Vol. 1, by John Hill. Minneapolis, MN: Univ. of Minnesota Press.

This paper on the child's development of sex role behavior focuses on the distribution of power within the family. The importance of the father for sex typing in children of both sexes is discussed and demonstrated. Hetherington's studies encompass both parents and children of both sexes. Thirty-six references.

From the Cradle to the Grave: Comparison and Self-Evaluation Across the Life-Span. (1982). Jerry Suls, Brian Mullen. In *Psychological Perspectives on the Self,* Vol. 1, edited by Jerry Suls. Hillsdale, NJ: Lawrence Erlbaum.

Outlines a model of how modes of self-evaluation change in importance with age. There are specific sections addressing a mix of theoretical and empirical studies on infants (up to four years), early childhood, middle childhood (four to eight years), and later childhood. Social comparisons are made with each group. A lengthy bibliography concludes the chapter.

Gender Influences in Classroom Interaction. (1985). Louise Cherry Wilkinson, Cora B. Marrett. NY: Academic. (Educational Psychology).

The chapters in this book link the research about the kinds of differences that occur and the consistency, prevalence, and influences on male-female differences in the elementary school years. The majority of the research deals with teacher-student interaction. A small proportion deals with student-peer interaction. Chapter 1 highlights recurrent themes in the research on teacher-student interaction and on peer interaction. Chapter 2 looks at the research findings regarding the differences of high-level cognitive skills between males and females. Chapters 3, 4 and 5 discuss teacher expectations and students. Chapter 6 by Brophy presents a review of research on teacher student interaction and the changing concerns about gender and the classroom. Chapter 7 discusses indications that generalized gender differences may be in place before the child enters school. Chapters 8 and 9 look at the effects of the existence or nonexistence of cross-sex interaction in the classroom. Chapter 11 examines gender and grade level differences in students' perceptions of salient interactional characteristics that determine friendship choices. References.

Interactions of Temperament and Clinical Conditions. (1985). William B. Carey. In *Advances in Developmental and Behavioral Pediatrics, a Research Annual*, Vol. 6, edited by Mark Walraich, Donald Routh. Greenwich, CT: JAI.

The chapter summarizes current theory, empirical data, and recommendations dealing with the relationship between temperament and the many aspects of physical health, development, and behavior. A formidable body of research is reviewed.

Personality Development in Childhood. (1976). Lee C. Lee. Monterey, CA: Brooks/Cole. (Core Books in Psychology Series).

Provides a brief overview of select topics in the area of personality development. The author concentrates on the early years. Topics covered include attachment, autonomy, identification, and moral development. Each topic is discussed from psychoanalytic, behavioral, and cognitive perspectives. References.

Presentations of Gender. (1985). Robert J. Stoller. New Haven, CT: Yale Univ. Press.

This volume examines the development of gender identity from the perspective of a psychoanalyst and researcher who has devoted 25 years to the study of the topic. The author reviews the concept of gender identity from biological, psychological, and sociological viewpoints, and on this basis presents a classification of gender disorders. He illustrates the development of marked femininity of boys with a number of cases he has treated, discussing the relative influence of mothers and fathers. Scholars, students, and researchers of gender development will find the volume a good reference. The emphasis in the volume is on the development of masculinity. References.

The Psychology of Sex Differences. (1974). Eleanor Emmons Maccoby, Carol Nagy Jacklin. Stanford, CA: Stanford Univ. Press.

This exhaustive review questions many beliefs about sex-related differences. Recognized as a definitive and an indispensable review of the field at the time of publication, the book is a sequel to the volume, *The Development of Sex Differences* by Maccoley in 1966. The book focuses on the development of sex differences through childhood and adolescence with some work with adults included. The volume includes an annotated bibliography of studies published since 1966. Users of the volume will find it helpful to turn to Chapter 10 first to scan the summary of findings before reading through the individual chapters. Chapters 2 - 7 review the unfounded beliefs about sex differences. Chapters 8 and 9 explain the patterns of similarities and differences found in studies. References.

The Rorschach: A Comprehensive System. (1982). John E. Exner, Jr., Irving B. Weiner. NY: Wiley-Interscience. (Assessment of Children and Adolescents, Vol. 3).

This volume deals with the assessment of children's personalities. The norms for the various scores included in the book cover the age range of 5 - 16 years and are used extensively in the sample cases presented. After a preliminary discussion of basic principles of interpretation, application of normative data, and research bearing on interpretation, nineteen cases are presented, including case history, protocols and scoring, interpretation, and follow-up clinical notes. Structural interpretation, scoring sequence, and content are thoroughly discussed and integrated in a summary interpretation. The types of cases covered include normal children, depression, schizophrenia, school learning problems, problems in behavior, and forensic issues. The volume concludes with recommendations for report writing. The major drawback of the volume is that it assumes knowledge of the Comprehensive System of scoring as presented in Volumes I and II. References.

The Self-Concept of the Young Child. (1980). Edited by Thomas D. Yawkey. Provo, UT: Brigham Young Univ. Press.

This volume describes growth, development, and learning of self concept by young children ages two through eight. Four parts make up the book: developmental changes and self concept learning; components of the self concept; play exploration and creative expression in self concept development; and self concepts of young children in special settings. The lack of an index curtails use. Individuals chapters are referenced.

Sex Differences in Children's Behavior. (1983). Harriet Shaklee. In *Advances in Developmental and Behavioral Pediatrics*, Vol. 4, edited by Mark Walraich, Donald Routh. Greenwich, CT: JAI.

The chapter reviews the literature dealing with sex differences and children's behavior. Studies cited are categorized generally under social, academic, and behavioral. The social interaction is further subdivided under playmates, play activities, aggression, social influence, and comfort giving and taking. The body of research within the academic area is subdivided under verbal, math and spatial skills, trial theories of achievement, expectancy and attributions, and hemispheric specialization. A formidable body of research is reviewed and cited in the chapter.

Temperament: Early Developing Personality Traits. (1984). Arnold H. Buss, Robert Plomin. NY: Lawrence Erlbaum. (Wiley Series in Behavior).

Reviews theory and research pertinent to all perspectives of temperament while emphasizing recent conceptual, measurement, and empirical advances associated with author's own position--the behavioral genetics. Chapter 1 describes the recent history of temperament theory and research. Chapter 2 considers the relations between evolution and the early appearance and development of traits. Chapter 3 presents an informative review of the pediatric approach and describes and evaluates the measures of temperament associated with, and critiques of, the conceptual issues. The nature and kinds of arousal are discussed in Chapter 4, and the topic of emotionality is treated in Chapter 5. Chapter 6 includes a presentation of interaction social rewards and a very useful analysis of the role of temperament as a moderator of mother-infant attachment. Chapter 7 presents the theory and measurement associated with the three temperaments within the authors' current theory, that is, Emotionality, Activity, and Sociability (EAS). The chapter includes an excellent discussion of the influence of EAS on the environment. In Chapter 8 the components of behavioral genetics methods are analyzed and discussed, and Chapter 9 considers the issue of heredity and the EAS temperaments. In Chapter 10 the topics of continuity, environment, and the EAS are considered. References.

Theories of Personality: Primary Sources and Research. Third Edition. (1973). Edited by Gardner Lindzey, Calvin S. Monosevitz, Martin Hall. NY: Wiley.

Comprises an excellent collection of original papers and research studies. More than half of the material included was not cited in the first edition. The papers are grouped according to the appropriate personality theory.

Each section contains an original paper written by the innovator of a particular personality theory. The anthology includes many excellent and provocative papers, such as those by Neal Miller, Allport, and Rogers, to name a few. References.

Too Tall, Too Small. (1982). John S. Gillis. Champaign, IL: Institute for Personality and Ability Testing.

This book discusses the effect height has on people's lives: personality development, mate choice, self esteem, achievements, and overall life successes. Although most of the book deals with adult topics, the child development specialist will find Chapter 4 on height and personality relevant. Chapter 6, although written for parents, will be of interest to professionals. Appendix 3 provides a list of organizations for the very tall and the very small. The notes at the end of the text will be helpful in following up on cited sources. This is a very readable book, full of interesting data on height.

Reports of Research

Gender Segregation in Childhood. (1987). Eleanor E. Maccoby, Carol Nagy Jacklin. In *Advances in Child Development and Behavior*, Vol. 20, edited by Hayne Reese. NY: Academic.

This paper reports the findings from the Stanford Longitudinal Study on the degree of gender segregation during the preschool years. Most of the children were observed during free play periods at nursery school when they were four and one-half years old and then again two years later during first grade recess periods. Section II of the paper is a review of literature. Section III summarizes relevant data. Section IV discusses the hypothesis about the origins of gender segregation in childhood. References.

Nicknames: Their Origins and Social Consequences. (1979). Jane Morgan, Christopher O'Neill. London and Boston: Routledge & Kegan Paul. (Social Worlds of Childhood Series).

This volume examines the psychological impact of nicknames on the development of the individual. Drawing on survey and common sense the authors examine the origins, purposes, roles, influences, and values which nicknames assume between parent and child as well as peers. The prime source of data and theory is the children themselves. Nicknaming varies culturally: it is more elaborate in the United Kingdom than in the United States; in other societies, for example, Japan, it is largely prohibited. Nicknames function in the autonomous world of children in multiple ways: to represent personality, to affect control, to enforce norms, or to insult. Further, good evidence exists that nicknames directly influence behavior and that the namegiver possesses considerable social influence and power. The use of nicknames raises interesting cognitive- and social-developmental questions. For example: together, two parents may use up to twelve names in addressing a child of six months; yet, the child appears to grasp that it is the single referent. The authors append a few "nickname autobiographies" to give those of us who traversed childhood without such a nickname insight into what actually being nicknamed means. References.

The Psychological Birth of the Human Infant: Symbiosis and Individualization. (1975). Margaret S. Mahler, Fred Pine, Anni Bergman. NY: Basic Books.

This classic work of Margaret Mahler and her co-authors delineates their observations on the normal individualization separation process which culminates at the psychological birth of the human infant. Her account of the accumulation and analysis of clinical data, recording observations, and direct work with mothers and children is presented in four parts. Part I is an overview of the infant's emergence from symbiotic fusion with the mother until he assumes his own individual characteristics through adaptation to his environment. Part II presents a sequential description of the individualization process and its forerunners, the normal autistic and normal symbiotic phases. Part III profiles the individual process with five children. Part IV summarizes a study which spans more than a decade and a half with special references to differentiation, epigenesis of separation anxiety, basic mood, identity, and approachment. Appendix A presents available data on the children and their mothers, methods of data collection, observations, interviews, film records, home visits, testing, conferences. Appendix B traces events and circumstances leading to the Research Rationale, and Appendix C shows the strategies finally used. References.

Social Cognition and the Acquisition of Self. (1979). Michael Lewis, Jeanne Brooks-Gunn. NY: Plenum.

Explores the knowledge of self and social cognition during the period of infancy. Chapter 1 presents various theories regarding the origin of self and briefly reviews previous research concerning the development of self-recognition. The research in Chapter 5 focuses on infants' and young toddlers' production and comprehension of labels of pictures of the self, familiar others, and nonfamiliar others. The empirical portion of the book closes with a chapter exploring the relationship between self-recognition and emotional response to approach by a stranger. The final three chapters summarize the author's findings. References.

Stable Patterns of Behavior: The Significance of Enduring Orientations for Personality Development. (1969). Wanda C. Bronson. In *Minnesota Symposia on Child Psychology*, Vol. 2, edited by John Hill. Minneapolis, MN: Univ. of Minnesota Press.

This paper uses data from the Berkeley Guidance Study to identify two dimensions of personality--emotional expressiveness reserve and placidity explosiveness--which are central and stable from childhood through adulthood. Bronson suggests these orientations play an important role in determining the nature of the individual's experience, his effectiveness in coping with developmental tasks, and the kind of beliefs about himself and others that he maintains. Eleven references.

Temperament and Development. (1977). Alexander Thomas, Stella Chess. NY: Brunner/Mazel.

This is the third book by the authors and their associates reporting results from the twenty-year New York Longitudinal Study (NYLS) of individual differences in temperament and their significance for normal and deviant psychological development. The NYLS identified dimensions of temperament (including activity level, rhythmicity, approach to new situations, adaptability, quality of mood, and persistence) and temperamental types (the easy child, the difficult child, and the slow-to-warm-up child). The research from the NYLS and other sources, summarized in several chapters by the authors clearly indicates the importance of an awareness of temperamental patterns for understanding and coping with the child's response to environmental demands (including parental practices, schooling, and health care). Other topics covered in the book are: the historical background of the NYLS; the theoretical and operational framework of the temperament concept; the genetic and environmental origins of temperament; and the consistency or inconsistency of temperament over time. In addition, the authors provide, in a series of appendixes, several short questionnaires and a list of interview questions for the identification of temperamental characteristics in infants and young children. References.

Youth: The Years from Ten to Sixteen. (1956). Arnold Lucius Gesell, Francis L. Ilg, Louise Bates Ames. NY: Harper and Brothers.

This classic covers the topic of the growth of mind and personality of children between the ages of ten and sixteen. It is a companion volume to Gesell's *The Child from Five to Ten*. Part I is an outline of the study. Part II contains seven chapters, each of which covers one of the ages from ten to sixteen and profiles maturity levels and traits. Part III, composed of nine chapters, falls under the general heading of Maturity Trends and Growth Gradients. Covered in this section are self-care, emotions, self, interpersonal relationships, activities, school life, ethical sense, and philosophic outlook. References.

9

Social/Cultural Development

DATASES
TO CONSIDER
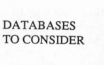
Social Work Abstracts   ERIC
Sociological Abstracts   PsycINFO

GENERAL

Bibliographies

Child Labor and National Development: An Annotated Bibliography. (1983)
Elizabeth B. Moore. In *New Directions for Child Development*, No. 20. San
Francisco, CA: Jossey-Bass.

Provides an introduction to, and a bibliography on, the issue of child labor
and its relationship to economic development in the Third World.

Reviews of Literature

Children of the Troubles: Children In Northern Ireland. (1983). Edited by Joan
Harbison. Belfast: Stranmillis College.

The first chapter of this volume reviews a number of research studies which
examined the responses of children in Northern Ireland today and discusses
some of the effects of the past fifteen years on young people. Each of the
remaining eleven chapters looks at a different aspect of how the turmoil in
Northern Ireland is affecting the development of children. References.

The Development of Social Cognition. (1985). Edited by John B. Pryor, Jeanne D.
Day. NY: Springer-Verlag.

This is a collection of original essays covering areas of recent social cognition
research. The volume is divided into three general sections: (1) Attribution
and Social Judgment; (2) Moral Development and a Sense of Self; and (3)
Social Influences on Cognitive Development. Not all chapters relate to

children's social cognition. Chapter 2 by Dodge and Richard bridges the gap between cognition and behavior by examining how attributional biases mediate the social behaviors of aggressive children. Chapter 3 reviews recent research from the information integration perspective. Chapter 5 by Widaman and Little describes a contextual model of sociomoral development in children. The final chapter in the last part of the volume focuses on how children's social interactions with peers foster individual cognitive growth. References.

The Development of Social Knowledge: Morality and Convention. (1983). Elliot Turiel. Cambridge, MA: Cambridge Univ. Press.

This volume reviews the last decade of literature by Turiel and colleagues which challenges important aspects of the traditional structuralist perspective on the development of social knowledge in children. Turiel shows that even quite young children distinguish between moral and social conventional rules and issues. Turiel maintains that children consistently view social-conventional rules as arbitrary, changeable, and dependent on social context, whereas moral rules are understood as nonarbitrary, universal, and intrinsically related to actions and their consequences. References.

Issues in Childhood Social Development. (1978). H. McGurk. London: Methuen. (Psychology in Progress).

Chapter 1 discusses the interaction between genotype and environment. Chapter 2 looks at the significance of the mother-infant relationship and social development. Chapter 3 discusses acquisition of knowledge of self and others through interaction with society. Chapter 4 looks at social perception and social cognition in middle childhood. Chapter 5 is an overview of the influence of peers on the development of social behavior and social knowledge. Chapter 6 addresses the topic of sex differences in social development. Chapter 7 argues that social development involves the acquisition of social knowledge as conceptions of interpersonal relations. Chapter 8 looks at Piaget's development of formal operational thinking and presents Furth's research findings. References.

Prosocial Behavior: Theory and Research. (1976). Daniel Bar-Tal. NY: John Wiley & Sons.

This book identifies various indicators of prosocial behavior and reviews the theory and research of each indicator. In all eight chapters, the author describes the interaction between donor and the recipient, and between the harm-doer and the victim. All the chapters end with summaries. References.

The Psychology of Infancy and Childhood: Evolutionary and Cross-Cultural Perspectives. (1984). Harold D. Fishbein. Hillsdale, NJ: Lawrence Erlbaum. (Child Psychology).

This volume is a continuation of the author's first book, *Evolution, Development, and Children's Learning* (1976). The two books, according to the author, have only a 5% overlap. The emphasis in this volume is cultural. The eight major sections of the book cover theories and methods of developmental psychology; evaluation, culture, and socialization; personality development; social development; cognitive development and social cognition; language, intelligence, and symbol use; socialization; and schools, television, and the family. References.

Putting the Child into Socialization: The Development of Social Categories in Preschool Children. (1984). Kurt W. Fischer, Helen H. Hand, Malcolm W. Watson, Martha M. Van Parys, James L. Tucker. In *Current Topics in Early Childhood Education*, Vol. 5, edited by Lilian Katz. Norwood, NJ: Ablex. (Current Topics in Early Childhood Education).

This chapter synthesizes the literature on social role acquisition and social cognition during the preschool period. A number of studies cited show that cognitive capacities of children are much greater than Piaget thought. An excellent table may be found in the chapter giving the sequence of social role development from ages two to ten. A second table shows the developmental sequence for understanding nice and mean social interaction. Substantial references.

Roots of Caring, Sharing, and Helping: The Development of Prosocial Behavior in Children. (1977). Paul Mussen, Nancy Eisenberg-Berg. San Francisco, CA: W. H. Freeman.

The major contribution of this volume is the carefully written and exceptionally well-organized review of literature on sources of variation in children's prosocial behavior, both interindividual (individual differences) and intraindividual (situational determinants). Situational determinants are treated in one chapter, subheadings of which include moods, reinforcements, preaching and characteristics of the beneficiary. Yarrow, Waxler, and Scott's study on modeling and nurturance effects, Friedrich and Stein's study on prosocial television, and Hoffman's work on disciplinary techniques in relation to prosocial behavior are given special attention. Also noteworthy is the chapter on cognitive factors related to prosocial behavior. The authors provide a detailed treatment of theoretical issues and empirical research in those areas of cognition (moral reasoning, role playing, and empathy) which have been considered in relation to prosocial development. Footnoted.

Social and Personality Development. (1983). William Damon. NY: W. W. Norton.

The book presents contemporary research, using sophisticated filming and videotaping, that demonstrates that the infant becomes an active partner in social relations shortly after birth. Bonding, attachment to the care giver, play behavior with other children, the place of role-taking in learning and social behaviors, empathy, prosocial behaviors, and the child's developing sense of fairness are all investigated. Individuality is the second major theme of Damon's study. Personality development is studied as it progresses through childhood, and the role of such dimensions as ego-resilience, field dependence and independence, sex differences, and the child's cognitions about these, and self-esteem and self-understanding are examined. Case histories are also used to exemplify the development of personal identity in adolescence. References.

The Social Life of Children in a Changing Society. (1982). Edited by Kathryn M. Norman. Hillsdale, NJ: Lawrence Erlbaum/Ablex.

The papers presented in this volume provide an integrative, multidisciplinary discussion of the social development of preschool and young elementary school-aged children. The volume is organized around four major sections: (1) parents and others; (2) language as a primary socializer with normally developing children; (3) language as a primary socializer with developmentally delayed children; and (4) the cross-cultural perspective. References.

Social Perception in Infants. (1985). Edited by Tiffany M. Field, Nathan A. Fox. Norwood, NJ: Ablex.

This volume provides an overview of current research on early social perception by researchers actively studying infants' perceptions of social stimuli. The volume is divided into three sections. In the first section infants' innate responses to social stimuli are discussed. In the second section are chapters discussing perception and discrimination of faces. The third and fourth sections contain a chapter with a model of infant contingent behavior during social interaction. This is followed by chapters describing the infant's competence at social interaction. A final chapter presents data on social perception in toddlers. Lengthy bibliographies conclude each chapter.

The Social World of the Child. (1977). William Damon. San Francisco, CA: Jossey-Bass. (Jossey-Bass Behavioral Science Series).

This integrative account of the development of social cognition in early and middle childhood focuses on four aspects of social knowledge: positive justice; friendship; authority; and social regulation. Children's ideas about social relations and principles are viewed as more important than specific social behaviors; the distinction between cognition and action is dismissed as artificial. The studies reported aimed to elucidate the underlying structure of children's social concepts and their developmental progressions. References.

Socialization and Social Class. (1972). Alan C. Kerckhoff. Englewood Cliffs, NJ: Prentice-Hall.

Although there are occasional references to studies in other countries, the exclusive concern of this book is with the socialization process as it operates within the stratification system of the United States. The association between social origins and socialization is examined in two ways: first, by examining the relationship between socioeconomic origins and the content and form of socialization experiences; and second, by examining the association between socialization experiences and social class destinations. Focus is on the early years and, of course, emphasizes the crucial role of the family in the socialization process. Particular attention is paid to class-related child training practices and to the way parental values influence parent-child relationships. Evidence is presented to show that middle-class parents are more likely to use affection-oriented and explanatory child rearing practices, whereas lower-class parents are more likely to depend on the assertion of power and the exercise of authority, with the consequence that middle-class children tend to show greater moral development, a higher level of achievement motivation, a clearer and more favorable self-concept, and greater role-playing and role-taking abilities. References.

Young Children in Context: Impact of Self, Family, and Society on Development. (1985). Edited by Caven S. McLoughlin, Dominic F. Gullo. Springfield, IL: Charles C. Thomas.

This volume is divided into three sections: child's individual or personal ecology; individual skill development of the child in family and social situations; and evaluation of the young child and optimizing the facilitation of children's development. The four chapters in the first section cover: developmental changes in children's thinking; acquisition of social communication skills; sex and gender similarities and differences in the young child; and the young handicapped child. Section two is made up of five chapters that cover such topics as: development of social relationships; family influences on development; multicultural influences on development; effect of technology (television and computers) on young children; and social and personal ecology factors influencing public policy for young children. The two chapters in the last section look at evaluating the ecology of the young child, both internally and externally; and the natural unfolding process required to facilitate development. References.

Reports of Research

Children and Work: A Study of Socialization. (1979).   B. Goldstein, J. Oldham. New Brunswick, NJ: Transaction Books.

Book reports the authors' survey of 905 children in grades one, three, five, and seven of north central New Jersey. The younger children (grades one and three) were generally interviewed individually, while the fifth and seventh grade students responded in writing to questionnaires or other verbal tasks. The authors discovered that: (1) there is a general trend of steady cognitive growth throughout the elementary years regarding occupational knowledge; (2) work does not occupy a central position in the world of the child as it does in mainstream American culture; (3) children tend to adhere to a double standard regarding work in that they seem to perceive that work is generally disliked, but they themselves demonstrate relatively positive feelings about it, and the children demonstrated clear signs of occupational/sex stereotyping in their work orientations; and (4) children are aware of social class and use this awareness in their classifications of occupations and their estimations of occupational income differentials. The volume is recommended for anyone planning research related to children and their socialization to work. References.

The Serious Business of Growing Up: A Study of Children's Lives Outside School. (1982). Elliott A. Roizen, Judith A. Medrich, Victor Rubin, Stuart Buckley. Berkeley, CA: Univ. of California Press.

Reports the findings of an interview study of 764 preadolescents and their parents in five Oakland, CA neighborhoods.   Children's after-school activities were divided into five domains: time spent alone; time spent with parents; time spent in jobs and chores; time spent in organized activities; and time spent watching television. The results reveal a blend of life satisfaction and dissatisfactions. The authors discuss some constraints on children's use of their time, including limited geographic mobility. A noteworthy area of this study involves children's participation in the world of work, which, in this age group, was largely confined to household chores. Most of the children studied saw work simply as a means to money. References.

The Smallest Pawns in the Game. (1980). Peter Townsend. Boston, MA: Little, Brown.

Part I describes atrocities against children in the past through war and persecution. Data presented in this section come from documents and written testimonies. Crimes against children during World War II are included here. Part II, based on oral testimony, tells of recent wrongs committed against children. Experiences in Asia, the continent of Africa, Northern Ireland, and South America are included. A list of child advocates along with addresses ends the text. Sixty-five references.

Other References

Child Welfare: A Source Book of Knowledge and Practice. (1984).   Edited by Frank Maidman.   NY: Child Welfare League of America.

Provides an overview of the current professional literature of child welfare. Chapters cover a variety of topics: child protection; day care; child neglect and abuse; foster care; residential child care; and adoption.   References.

CROSS CULTURAL

Bibliographies

The Education of Poor and Minority Children, a World Bibliography.   2 vols. (1981).   Compiled by Meyer Weinberg.   Westport, CT: Greenwood.

This is an unannotated bibliography of over 40,000 entries dealing with the education of the poor and minority child.   Volume 1 is divided into sixteen different subsections including different ethnic groups, plus general sections covering history, children, and the American scene.   Volume 2 contains six sections covering topics such as law and government; church; community; general; world scene; and higher education.   An author index is located at the end of Volume 2.

Research in Black Child Development: Doctoral Dissertation Abstracts, 1927 - 1979. (1982).   Hector F. Meyers, Phyllis Gabriel-Rana, Ronee Harris-Epps, Rhonda J. Jones.   Westport, CT: Greenwood.

The scope of the work included in this document covers a span of 52 years, from 1927 - 1979.   Arrangement is into five major areas of emphasis: language development, physical development, cognitive development, personality development, and social development.

Reviews of Literature

Beginnings: The Social and Affective Development of Black Children. (1985). Edited by Margaret Beale Spencer, Geraldine K. Brookins, Walter R. Allen. Hillsdale, NJ: Lawrence Erlbaum.   (Child Psychology).

Each chapter addresses black children's social and emotional development by providing empirical assessments of the ecological contexts, interpersonal relationships, and psychological states which influence their growth and development.   The seventeen chapters are divided into three sections.   Part I offers four contrasting perspectives for scientifically studying minority-child development.   Part II has three sections: social competence, identity, and family.   In this part individual authorities discuss such topics as pretend play, student-teacher interactions, aspects of black identity formation, and aspects of black-child development in relation to family patterns.   Part III is a summation of all the various themes presented in the book regarding the growth and development of black children. References.

Bilingualism: Psychological, Social, and Educational Implications. (1977). Peter A. Hornby. NY: Academic.

The volume provides the reader with the historical developments, theoretical controversies, and major research findings, as well as applications from the disciplines of psychology, sociology, linguistics, and education on the topic. Much of the material deals either directly or indirectly with the young child. References.

Black Children: Their Roots, Culture, and Learning Styles. (1982). Janice E. Hale. Provo, UT: Brigham Young Univ. Press.

Volume reviews research investigating the effect Afro-American culture has on child-rearing practices in the home. Suggestion is that black children may have distinctive learning and expressive styles observable in their play behavior. The seven chapters of this text are organized around a central theme of encouraging the reader to become more sensitive to the unique features of the Afro-American child's culture and how these cultural patterns influence the way these children think and learn. The chapters discuss, in order, the African background, the way culture shapes cognition, culture and child-rearing, play behavior and cognition style, the humanities and black culture, Afro-American roots, a curriculum relevant to Afro-Americans, and implications for early childhood education. References.

Children and Race, Ten Years On. Second edition. (1983). David Milner. NY: Penguin.

This second edition is a completely revised and updated version of the 1975 edition. Only the historical material remains intact from the earlier edition. The eight chapters review and assess major research related to racial attitudinal development in children. This edition, like the first, is an important addition to the literature of racial attitudes. A lengthy bibliography is provided.

Culture and Early Interactions. (1981). Tiffany M. Field, Vietze Anita M. Sostek, P. Herbert Leiderman. Hillsdale, NJ: Lawrence Erlbaum. (Child Psychology).

The volume provides research findings, reference sources, and a methodology for considering the variable effects of cultural values and contexts on early social interaction patterns. The studies reported were conducted by psychologists, anthropologists, pediatricians, and psychiatrists among Hispanic, Hopi and Navajo cultures in the United States, and in cultures of Europe, Africa, and South America as well as islands of the South Pacific. The volume is organized in sections according to major variable studies: cultural contexts, cultural and socioeconomic status, cultural values, and growth, and developmental status of infants. References.

Eskimos, Chicanos, Indians. (1977). Robert Coles. Boston, MA: Little, Brown. (Children of Crisis, Vol. 4).

After fifty pages of preamble, chapters are devoted to individual types of minority child. The book is impressive in the details conveyed. Coles offers some conclusions but the work is primarily raw data. The index is adequate and references are provided.

Privileged Ones: The Well-Off and the Rich in America. (1977). Robert Coles. Boston, MA: Little, Brown. (Children of Crisis, Vol. 5).

The book begins with a fifty-page introduction before going into individual chapters on each of the children. An impressive amount of raw data is provided in the book rather than conclusions drawn from that data. Indexes and references included.

Race, Education, and Identity. (1979). Gajendra K. Verma, Christopher Bagley. NY: St. Martin's.

This volume of original papers provides a wealth of scholarly and empirical research looking at racism and its effects upon minority children. The material highlights four major areas: scholastic and cognitive attainment; race-relations teaching; identity and self-esteem; and adoption policy and practice.

The School Achievement of Minority Children: New Perspectives. (1986). Edited by Ulric Neisser. Hillsdale, NJ: Lawrence Erlbaum.

Each of the seven papers addresses the question, Why is school achievement of American minority children, especially black, so often below their white counterparts? Chapter 2 talks about the effects of caste. Chapter 3 describes aspects of Afro-American culture that are more or less in conflict with the social and cognitive structure of the school. Chapter 4 talks about ineffective schools. Chapter 5 discusses instructional methods used with poor readers. Chapter 6 looks at the effects of prejudice and stress. Chapter 7 analyzes the findings of the Consortium for Longitudinal Studies on the effectiveness of preschool programs (Head Start). Chapter 8 reviews recent cross-cultural and subcultural research regarding cultural deprivation. References.

Reports of Research

Navajo Infancy: An Ethological Study of Child Development. (1983). James S. Chisholm. NY: Aldine. (Biological Foundations of Human Behavior).

This book describes field research carried out during the years 1974 - 1976 in the Navajo community of Cottonwood Springs. Chapter 1 describes the process of adaptation and outlines the evolutionary biological reasons that the process of development constitutes an important adaptive mechanism. Chapter 2 describes the Navajo and his environments, noting what is most likely to affect child development. Chapter 3 focuses on the cradleboard and its long-term effects on child development. Chapter 4 describes the author's research with not only Navajo but Anglo-American infants. Chapter 5 compares the behavior of newborn Navajo infants to Anglo infants. Chapter 6 covers the topic of fear of strangers. Chapters 7 and 8 analyze the interaction between Navajo infants and mothers versus Anglo infants and mothers. The summary and conclusions to the study are given in Chapter 9. References.

ENVIRONMENT

Reviews of Literature

The Child in the City. (1979). William Michelson, Saul V. Levine, Ellen Michelson. Toronto: Univ. of Toronto Press.

This two-volume set is based on a lecture series organized by the Child in the City research program at the University of Toronto. Volume 1 is a compendium of expert opinion on issues related to the influence of a contemporary urban environment on the development of the child. Leading researchers in the field comment on such dimensions of the issue as: the influences of man-built environment, the spatial world of the child, the child and the law, as well as day care, problems of delinquency, health, and the role of community social services. Volume 2 integrates the opinion expressed in the initial volume and as such represents a state-of-the-art summary. Broad considerations include children, families, and community services, child-rearing systems, ethnic diversity and children, and issues for adolescents.

Children within Environments: Toward a Psychology of Accident Prevention. (1985). Tommy Garling, Joan Valsiner. NY: Plenum.

This book looks at the environmental contexts in which children interact with care givers, other children, and objects. Several of the chapters of this volume are based on invited presentations in a symposium, organized by the editors, at the Inaugural European Conference on Developmental Psychology, "Individual Development and Human Welfare," held in Groningen, the Netherlands, in 1984. These chapters and the remaining ones that were written for the volume, cover a wide range from theoretical analyses of children's relationships with their environment (chapters 1, 2, 3, and 9) to the presentation of data from empirical studies of children within concrete environmental settings, in Sweden (chapters 6 and 7), in Italy (Chapter 8), in West Germany (Chapter 10), in the United States (chapters 11 and 12), and in Russia (Chapter 13). Some of the chapters address exclusively the issue of childhood accidents, either directly through empirical studies (chapters 4 and 5) or indirectly through a discussion of legislation (Chapter 14). References.

Children's Behavior in Preschool Settings: A Review of Research Concerning the Influence of the Physical Environment. (1980). Elizabeth Phyfe-Perkins. In *Current Topics in Early Childhood Education*, Vol. 3, edited by Lilian Katz. Norwood, NJ: Ablex. (Current Topics in Early Childhood Education).

This chapter discusses and examines the literature on the effect of environment on behavioral development of the child. The paper looks at crowding, physical space, and use of space in the preschool setting. References.

Early Experience: Myth and Evidence. (1976). Ann M. Clarke, A. D. B. Clarke. London: Open Books.

The authors believe that early environmental learning influences are reversible. In the volume they review literature and studies supporting this theory. The book is divided into five sections. The first reviews the origins of the view that the first few years of life are of vital long-term importance. Made up of four chapters, Part II looks at studies concerning formerly isolated children, such as Itard's "wild boy," and more modern accounts, such as those of Kingsley Davis. A case study of isolated twins is recorded in Chapter 4. Part III and Part IV make up the bulk of the volume and discuss studies supporting the authors' hypothesis that the course of human development can be reversed. Chapter 14 in the last section will be of interest to people studying early intervention. Part V gives an overview and implications of the research and data provided in the book. References.

Ecological Factors in Human Development. (1977). Edited by Harry McGurk. NY and Amsterdam: North-Holland.

The first five papers in this book address a number of conceptual and methodological issues (that is, how do ecological factors differ from environmental factors of traditional research, and how do we document the range, intensity, and frequency of behavior-environment interrelations?). The next two papers report findings from research in the Kansas tradition (Barker and his colleagues). Four papers examine problems in large scale spatial representation, crowding, the environmental correlates of selective attention, and the development of hypothetic-deductive thinking in school environments. Four more papers deal with the effects of poverty, psychiatric disorder, social class, and similarly adverse conditions upon development. A final section of four papers presents such cross-cultural comparisons as the study of perceptual organization, nomadic style, and infant-care giver attachment. The book concludes with a succinct overview and summary of ecological issues by Urie Bronfenbrenner. References.

Habitats for Children: The Impacts of Density. (1985). Joachim F. Wohlwill, Willem van Vliet. Hillsdale, NJ: Lawrence Erlbaum. (Child Psychology, edited by David S. Palermo).

Nine chapters examine and review research on various aspects of the ways and extent different density levels in residential environments affect the development of children. Chapter 2 reviews the literature on the topic, citing the best known works. Chapter 3 looks at the effects crowding and noise in the home have on perceptual-cognitive development. Chapter 4 reviews the theoretical and empirical literature on the effects density has on play and exploration. Chapter 5 addresses the effects environment has on social behavior. Chapter 6 discusses how habitats shape behavior and development of individuals. Chapter 7 reviews what is known about housing type and household crowding and its effect on children. Chapter 8 reviews literature concerning household type, household density, and neighborhood density and their effect on socialization. References.

Reports of Research

Flats, Families and the Under-Fives. (1976). Elizabeth Gittus. London: Routledge & Kegan Paul. (International Library of Social Policy).

This volume reports the results of the Tyneside Survey which was designed to explore the implications of various forms of public urban housing on young children and their families in Great Britain. The data were obtained by interviewing mothers. The impetus for the research appeared to be a commonly-held belief in Britain that young children who lived in apartments near the top of tall buildings would suffer, assumedly due to confinement and a diminished opportunity to play. Findings suggest that "living off the ground, whether in high- or low-rise, can be problematic for young children and those responsible for their care." The report of the study is divided into nine chapters with three appendixes interspersed throughout the book. References.

The Urban Education Task Force Report. Final Report of the Task Force on Urban Education to the Department of Health, Education and Welfare. (1970). Wilson C. Riles. NY: Praeger.

More commonly known as the Riles Report, this work concentrates on the effect of environment on a child's development and how that effect must be taken into consideration in urban education. As expected this work is loaded with tables, figures, and statistics but they are important to understanding the problem and formulating solutions. References.

MORAL DEVELOPMENT

Reviews of Literature

Development of Internal Moral Standards in Children. (1971). Martin L. Hoffman. In *Research on Religious Development, a Comprehensive Handbook*, edited by Merton Strommer. NY: Hawthorn Books.

This review of research is limited to one major factor in moral development, that of the external behavior of parents. The chapter is organized according to the basic areas of moral development concepts, child-rearing concepts, dynamics of the discipline encounter, and guilt. Following the lengthy bibliography is an appendix giving descriptions of discipline techniques classified within the text as love withdrawal or induction.

The Development of Religious Understanding in Children and Adolescents. (1971). David Elkind. In *Research on Religious Development, a Comprehensive Handbook*. A project of the Religious Education Association. NY: Hawthorn Books.

This chapter reviews research pertinent to children's religious development. Chapter focuses on cognitive changes in understanding, how children perceive God, view prayer, and understand their religious identity. The findings of this chapter are reported under three major headings: descriptive, developmental, and pedagogical research. The descriptive studies explore some aspect of religious conversion or assess the variety of religious experiences; the developmental studies delineate the content and/or form of the religious understanding which seems to characterize successive age levels; and the pedagogical studies deal with the child's understanding of both verbal and pictorial biblical material. Special attention is given to the studies of Goldman and DeValensart. References.

Lawrence Kohlberg: Consensus and Controversy. (1985). Edited by Sohan Modgil, Celia Modgil. Philadelphia, PA: Falmer. (Falmer International Master-Minds Challenged).

This volume provides a concise analysis, supported by research, of the elements of Kohlberg's theory of moral development. In a number of the chapters, references to the moral development of the child as theorized by Kohlberg may be found. John Rick's chapter, elaborating on the role of emotions in morality, discusses children's emotions and morality. David Gordon challenges Kohlberg's idea of the "hidden curriculum" as not being effective nor pervasive. Brian Gates' chapter critically analyzes Kohlberg's ideas regarding religious education as one of the exponents of an evolutionary sequence of child development, that is, moral development. References.

Moral Development. (1986). Maureen Weiss. In *Physical Activity and Well-Being*, edited by Vern Seefeldt, Chapter 13. Reston, VA: American Alliance for Health, Physical Education, Recreation, and Dance.

The chapter summarizes studies relating moral development to physical education or sport experiences. The chapter begins with a brief overview of the major theoretical approaches to moral development. This provides a framework for the subsequent critical review of empirical studies of moral growth among physical education and sports' participants. References.

Moral Development: Current Theory and Research. (1975). Edited by David J. DePalma, Jeanne M. Foley. NY: John Wiley & Sons. (Child Psychology).

Provides a selective coverage of the area of moral judgment and moral behavior. Chapters 2 and 3 focus on cognitive variables associated with the development of moral judgment or thought. In Chapter 4 James Rest reviews research on his objective test of moral judgment, the Defining Issues Test (DIT). Bryan's chapter reviews much of the research on the effects of models on children's donation behavior. In Staub's report, the interest is on what one, as a teacher or parent, can teach a child to facilitate prosocial behavior. The final chapters focus on both affective and cognitive components in the development of altruistic motives in children. References.

Moral Development: Theory, Research, and Social Issues. (1976). Edited by Thomas Lickona. NY: Holt, Rinehart, & Winston.

This book brings together a distinguished group of scholars whose contributions to the book synthesize the theory, research, and issues involved in moral development at the time of publication. The book is divided into four parts. Part I is an introduction and will assist the reader in organizing the wealth of theory and research in the field around eight basic questions confronting the science of morality. Part II, Theoretical Perspectives, sets forth eight distinctively different theoretical views of how moral development occurs. Part III deals in Research. It examines, critically, findings in selected areas of moral functioning. Part IV on Morality and Special Issues, looks at the moral dimensions of social issues and attempts to derive intervention strategies from the accumulated theory and research about moral behavior. References.

Moral Stages: A Current Formulation and a Response to Critics. (1983). Lawrence Kohlberg, Charles Levine, Alexandra Hewer. NY and London: Karger. (Contributions to Human Development, Vol. 10).

This monograph provides a synopsis of some of the critiques of Kohlberg's theory of moral stage development. Most of the critiques to which replies are included are mainly responses to statements of the theory made in articles such as "Stage and Sequence" (1969) and "From Is to Ought" (1971). Anyone interested in cognitive development will find this monograph invaluable. It is well written and concise. It contains a helpful bibliography and presents the current status of one of the most important programs of ongoing research in psychology today.

Parental and Peer Influences on Moral Development. (1981). David R. Shaffer, Gene H. Brody. In *Parent-Child Interaction, Theory, Research, and Prospects*, edited by Ronald Henderson. NY: Academic. (Educational Psychology).

The chapter provides a synthesis of research on the development of moral maturity. Both the psychoanalytic approach and the social-learning approach are reviewed. A separate section covering parental influences on the child's moral development briefly discusses problems involved in comparing studies and drawing inferences from laboratory studies of child-rearing. One section of the chapter reviews research of parental discipline, providing two very informative tables. The last major section of the chapter covers peers as agents of moral socialization. References.

The Religion of Youth. (1971). Robert J. Havighurst, Barry Keating. In *Research on Religious Development, a Comprehensive Handbook*, edited by Merton Strommer. NY: Hawthorn Books.

Synthesizes studies dealing with children's religious attitudes and experiences. The review indicates a remarkable consistency among children. References.

Reports of Research

The Children's God. (1986). David Heller. Chicago, IL: Univ. of Chicago Press.

This is a study that illustrates rather than defines a "major, unifying image" of a children's God, whatever the titles or names they use. Heller interviewed forty children, ages four to twelve selected from a Roman Catholic parish, a Baptist congregation, a Jewish day school, and an American Hindu ashram. The method included direct questions and discussion, play, drawing, storytelling with lifelike dolls, and an exercise in which each child wrote a letter to the deity. Heller organizes his general analysis and conclusions by age range (4 - 6, 7 - 9, 10 - 12), religious tradition, and gender themes. He notes that certain human personality traits--"God" as inconsistent, loving, distrustful, therapeutic--seem to arise in the children's view. Strong familial and social images also recur in what Heller sees as "strikingly universal" ways. The writing is lucid and the analysis and reporting are clearly organized and presented. References.

The Child's Reality: Three Developmental Themes. (1978). David Elkind. Hillsdale, NJ: Lawrence Erlbaum. (John M. MacEachran Memorial Lecture Series).

Book reconstructs the author's earlier research studies of children's conceptions of religious denominations and of prayer; children's gradual development of perceptual regulations and their relationship to reading; and the evolution of egocentrism from infancy through the formal operational period. Throughout the book, the author contends that children construct their reality from experience with their surroundings and further, that their reality differs from adult reality. In particular, the author argues that only when we regard children as having similar feelings but different constructions of reality can we break the chains of misunderstanding which too frequently characterize child-adult relationships.

The Moral Life of Children. (1986). Robert Coles. Boston & NY: Atlantic Monthly.

Robert Coles used his same method of researching and studying this topic as he did in his *Children of Crisis* series--interviews to glean what he could about the moral life of children. The study is broken down into seven chapters covering various aspects of morals. Chapter 1 covers psychoanalysis and moral development. Chapter 2 looks at movies and moral energy. Chapter 3 covers moral purpose and vulnerability. Chapters 4 and 5 are on character and young idealism. Chapter 6 discusses social class and moral order. The last chapter discusses children and the nuclear bomb. References.

The Original Vision: A Study of the Religious Experience of Childhood. (1977). Edward Robinson. Oxford: Religious Experience Research Unit, Manchester College. (Studies in Religious Experience).

A report analyzing the responses from a questionnaire sent out to adults inviting them to detail the experience they had which they felt had affected their lives by some power beyond their control. The majority responded indicating a religious type experience. Fifteen percent of the 4,000 responding wrote about experiences occurring in childhood. The author then followed up on those who responded to the original questionnaire. In this monograph the results of these answers are discussed and analyzed according to content area; for example, of vision and reality, death, morality, etc. In the appendix may be found the questionnaire and the analysis of the replies received. References.

Other References

The World Sunday School Movement. (1979). Gerald Knoff. NY: Seabury.

A history of the Sunday School Movement begun over 200 years ago by Robert Raikes of Gloucester, England. The Sunday School Movement

spread quickly through. England and the United States.   It became an
institution in all Protestant congregations on both sides of the Atlantic.
Toward the end of the nineteenth century the movement became a
worldwide institution and was embraced by non-protestant churches.   The
book recounts the spread and development of the movement.

PLAY

Bibliographies

Play.   (1982).   K. H. Fein, G. Rubin, B. Vandenberg.   In *Handbook of Child
Psychology: Social Developments*, Fourth edition, edited by Hetherington.
NY: John Wiley & Sons.

The chapter cites approximately 450 different journal articles, books, and
convention presentations concerning the psychological aspects of children's
play of which twenty percent are dated between 1970 and 1974, thirty-eight
percent between 1975 and 1979, and fourteen percent after 1980.

Reviews of Literature

Biology of Play.   (1977).   Edited by Barbara Tizard, David Harvey.   Philadelphia,
PA: Lippencott.   (Clinics in Developmental Medicine No. 62).

This volume, a group of fourteen papers, delves into the problems of the
effect of play on the child's behavior, present and future.   Rosenblatt's
observations of twenty infants led her to the conclusion that maturity of play
correlated with the speed of language development and general intellectual
functioning by age two.   Dunn and Wooding saw the mother's initiation of
representational or pretend play with their 18- to 24-month-old children in
39% of the play sequences as an indication that social learning is both taught
and sought in play and that the adult has a major function in interpreting and
responding to the child's play activities.   Self-initiation, with the goal
direction of play, in three-, four-, and five-year-olds was noted to contribute
to subsequent problem solving in Sylva's study of the relationship between
play and learning.   Chapter 11 is oriented toward the clinical applications of
play, dealing with the measurement of play in clinical application, the need
for adult-directed play of children in a hospital setting, the special problems
of handicapped children in play activities, and the therapeutic relearning that
is achieved through play.   References.

Child Studies through Fantasy: Cognitive-Affective Patterns in Development.
(1972).   Rosalind Gould.   NY: Quadrangle Books.

In this volume the author records her findings from a study of fantasy
expression of children three, four, and five years old who are being observed
in the natural setting of a nursery school where the opportunity was provided
for the expression of spontaneous fantasy.   Chapter 1, an overview, defines

fantasy and looks at aggression in fantasy, sex differences, and individual differences.   Chapter 2 generally covers self-representations in fantasy. Chapter 3 looks at affective factors in regressive and variable cognitive function.   Chapter 4 looks at pattern relationships of defense and individualization in fantasy. Chapter 5 delves into morality and superego development reflected in fantasy and reality behavior. Chapter 6 covers the basic concepts in understanding morality development. References.

Children's Play. (1985). Peter K. Smith. In *Early Child Development and Care*, 19 (1, 2).

The entire issue is devoted to play. The eight articles cover symbolic play, language of play, play with computers, play and the handicapped, play therapy, and outdoor play and play equipment. References.

Child's Play. (1982). R. E. Herron, Brian Sutton-Smith. Malabar, FL: Robert E. Krieger.

This collection of scholarly literature on children's play provides a comprehensive overview of the viewpoints and styles of numerous thinkers on play. Research covering seventy years in the field is provided along with a lengthy bibliography at the end of the text.

Child's Play: Developmental and Applied. (1984). Thomas D. Yawkey, Anthony D. Pellegrini. Hillsdale, NJ: Lawrence Erlbaum. (Child Psychology).

The volume brings together in nineteen chapters a scholarly integration of theoretical and empirical research on play. Several chapters address pretend play and symbolic play. Play therapy and creative dramatic play each have separate chapters. Play in various settings such as school, preschool, and hospitals is also reviewed. Chapter 12 focuses on humor, suggesting that play and humor are closely related. The volume represents one of the most comprehensive reviews of play published to date. References.

The Child's World of Make-Believe: Experimental Studies of Imaginative Play. (1973). Jerome L. Singer. NY and London: Academic. (Child Psychology Series).

This volume examines the nature of imaginative or symbolic play focusing specifically on make-believe play and children's games. An attempt is made to relate make-believe play to the general issue of daydreaming. Whenever possible the author ties the work of the child psychology specialists Piaget, Erikson, and Werner to the broader theoretical positions of Freud, White, Sullivan, Bandura, and Tomkins. The book includes chapters on theory, relevant historical literature, and formal research. References.

Cultural Dimensions of Play, Games, and Sport. (1986). Edited by Bernard Mergen. Champaign, IL: Human Kinetics. (The Association for the Anthropological Study of Play [TAASP], Vol. 10).

The book is divided into four parts. Part I examines play and the reliability of using children as informants in play research. Part II deals with theories of play. Part III covers games, with chapters on video games, writing as a game, dramatic play as a basis of home intervention for preschool Hispanic children, and cultural analysis. Part IV covers sport. This is a scholarly treatment of the sociological aspects of play. References.

Curiosity, Imagination, and Play: On the Development of Spontaneous Cognitive and Motivational Process. (1987). Dietmar Gorlitz, Joachim F. Wohlwill. Hillsdale, NJ: Lawrence Erlbaum.

Volume presents a cross-section of current research on the topics of children's curiosity, imagination, and play. The volume also summarizes current work done in child and developmental psychology in Germany, Great Britain, and the United States. References.

The Development of Play. (1987). David Cohen. NY: New York Univ. Press.

In Chapter 1 the author critiques other books and research on the topic of play. Chapter 2 reviews the historical attitudes toward play and how they have influenced play research. Chapter 3 addresses the issue of the way children play with objects and toys. Chapter 4 looks at the social games and pretend play of young children, focusing on games with peers. Chapters 5 through 7 focus on the many aspects of children's play with their parents. Chapter 8 covers kinds of adult games. References.

The Ecology of Preschool Behavior. (1980). Peter K. Smith, Kevin J. Connolly. London: Cambridge Univ. Press.

The volume reviews several play-group studies conducted in England. A history of research in this area may be found in Chapter 8. References.

Gender Differences in Play and Sport: A Cultural Interpretation. (1982). Susan L. Greendorfer. In *The Paradoxes of Play. Proceedings of the Annual Meeting of the Association for the Anthropological Study of Play*, edited by John Lay, pp. 198 - 204. West Point, NY: Leisure.

The chapter reviews past literature dealing with gender differences in play and sport suggesting that it centers on the socialization process. The author suggests that variations in play and sport could be viewed as aspects of the enculturation process, so that differences between sexes would not be viewed as cultural products but would be viewed as evidence that socialization into the culture of gender role is taking place. This perspective allows the researcher to analyze the underlying cultural ideology inherent in the socialization practices and processes that lead to two distinctive behavioral manifestations, one for males and one for females. The author then presents research to support this proposition. Twenty-two references.

Imaginary Playmates and Other Useful Fantasies. (1984). John T. Partington, Katherine Grant. In *Play in Animals and Humans*, edited by Peter Smith. NY: Basil Blackwell.

This chapter reviews the aspect of children's fantasy play, the imaginary companion phenomenon. Most of the information in the chapter is based on interviews with children and their parents. The analysis of the subjects' replies is usually correlational or employing multivariate statistics. References.

Imaginative Play and Pretending in Early Childhood: Some Experimental Approaches. (1976). Jerome L. Singer, Dorothy G. Singer. In *Child Personality and Psychopathology: Current Topics*, Vol. 3, edited by Anthony Davids. NY: John Wiley & Sons. (Child Personality and Psychopathology: Current Topics, pp. 69 - 112).

This chapter explores empirical research on imaginative play as well as methodologies of studying play. The ties between television watching, spontaneous fantasy, play, and various prosocial behaviors are briefly discussed. Substantial references.

Journal of Research and Development. 14 (3). (Spring 1981).

Entire issue is devoted to the role of play in early childhood education. The reviews and research articles in the issue outline the importance of play to the multidisciplinary area of early childhood education. Glickman's article is a historical review tracing the role of play in early childhood and elementary school curricula. Donmayer's article discusses the political assumptions of incorporating play into school curricula. Tipps' article reviews research examining the relationship between young children's play and neurological growth. Yawkey's research suggests that play positively affects children's mathematical achievement. References.

Object Play, Problem-Solving, and Creativity in Children. (1984). Peter K. Smith, Tony Simon. In *Play in Animals and Humans*, edited by Peter Smith, Chapter 9, pp. 199 - 216. NY: Basil Blackwell.

Chapter looks at research on object play in young children focusing on the aspects of studies linking play to problem-solving and divergent thinking. The chapter contains a detailed table on eleven experimental studies which relate play experience to problem-solving skills and creativity. Details of another four unpublished studies are given in the chapters' appendix. References.

Play. (1977). Catherine Garvey. Cambridge, MA: Harvard Univ. Press. (Developing Child Series).

This volume defines play and briefly summarizes the literature. Environmental components of play which are reviewed include: motion and interaction, objects, language, social materials, rules, and rituals. The book ends with a short section on learning to play. Unless the reader has some background in current theories of play and some knowledge of the experimental paradigms used to study play, the book may prove difficult reading. References to sources cited and suggested readings follow the text.

Play. (1983). K. H. Rubin, G. G. Fein, B. Vandenberg. In *Handbook of Child Psychology*, Fourth edition, Vol. 4, edited by Mussen and Hetherington. NY: John Wiley & Sons.

Excellent review of play with infants and preschool children. References.

Play and Social Cognition. (1984). E. P. Johnsen, James F. Christie. In *The Masks of Play*, by Brian Sutton-Smith, Diane Kelly-Byrie. NY: Leisure.

This chapter is a review and critique of correlational and experimental studies which have investigated the relationship between play and social cognition during childhood. It suggests problems which arise when play is considered in relation to social and cognitive skills within experimental paradigms and points to the serious limitations of these studies. Its thrust is primarily methodological. References.

Play and the Preschool Child. (1984). Edited by Charles H. Wolfgang. In *Early Child Development and Care*, 17 (1).

Play curriculum, creative playgrounds, symbolic development, language of play, and writing with a computer as play are all covered in the special issue.

Play in Animals and Humans. (1984). Peter K. Smith. NY: Basil Blackwell.

This book is perhaps the most comprehensive and up-to-date collection of reviews and essays on the developmental and evolutionary functions of play. The book is divided into five sections. The first two address the evolutionary origins of play and review the existing literature for four nonhuman species. The third section is a bridge between the later sections on human play and the earlier ones on animal play. In this section, three theorists explore adaptive features of play that might be common to all species. The fourth section addresses several aspects of children's play, including object play, rough-and-tumble play, and imaginary playmates. Literature on fantasy play has not been included for review. The last section includes developmental and anthropological perspectives on play and games in humans. References.

The Play of Children: Current Theory and Research. (1982). Edited by D. J. Pepler, K. H. Rubin. NY: S. Karger. (Contributions to Human Development, Vol. 6).

This volume provides an overview of the major theoretical and research-based issues in the field of play. One chapter examines the connection between symbolic play and language development. The chapter by Pepler examines empirical evidence connecting play and divergent thinking or creativity. Cheyne critically evaluates studies in which investigators demonstrated a causal link between play and convergent problem-solving. The chapters by Saltz and Brodie and Brainerd critically examine the causal link between pretense play training and social, cognitive, and social-cognitive development. A final issue addressed in this volume concerns ecological influences on children's play. References.

Playfulness: Its Relationship to Imagination and Creativity. (1977). J. Nina Lieberman. NY: Academic.

Sex differences, levels of intelligence, and social class are some of the variables considered in relation to playfulness. One section is a presentation of the author's own studies of playfulness in kindergarten-age children, adolescents, and adults. Through the use of observational techniques and playfulness rating scales, these studies isolate sense of humor, manifest joy, and spontaneity as the major components of playfulness. This section is followed by an examination of current research literature for further clarification and modification of the author's original conceptualizations. The volume then proceeds to a theoretical framework in which the role of playfulness is presented as a catalyst between play and imagination, play and creativity, and imagination and creativity. A final section of the book presents conclusions and recommendations for future research and application. References.

Recent Research on Play: The Teacher's Perspective. (1984). Millie Almy, Patricia Monighan, Barbara Scales, Judith Van Hoorn. In *Current Topics in Early Childhood Education*, Vol. 5, edited by Lilian Katz. Norwood, NJ: Ablex. (Current Topics in Early Childhood Education).

The chapter provides a synthesis of research concerning the educational functions of play and guides readers in ways of understanding those functions. Emphasis is on teachers of two- to six-year-olds. References.

The Relations between Symbolic Play and Literate Behavior: A Review and Critique of the Empirical Literature. (Spring 1985). A. D. Pellegrini. In *Review of Educational Research*, 55 (1), pp. 107 - 121.

Reviews recent theoretical and empirical evidence for relations between children's symbolic play and literate behavior. Studies are classified and discussed accordingly. References.

The Role of Play in Social-Intellectual Development. (Spring 1983). James F. Christiek, E. P. Johnsen. *The Review of Educational Research*, 53 (1), pp. 93 - 115.

Discusses the role of play in major developmental theories and then reviews a number of experimental and correlational studies which are classified in terms of their major correlates or dependent variable: creativity, problem-solving, language development, logical skills, and social knowledge. References.

Rough-and-Tumble in Preschool and Playground. (1984). Anne P. Humphreys, Peter K. Smith. In *Play in Animals and Humans*, edited by Peter K. Smith, Chapter 11. NY: Basil Blackwell.

This chapter looks at the studies done on children's rough-and-tumble play mainly using naturalistic and observational techniques. The authors look at definitions of the term, significance of the play, and how the type of form of play changes with age. Play-fighting studies are discussed and a number of gender-related studies included. References.

School Play: A Source Book. (1987). Edited by James H. Block, Nancy R. King. NY: Garland.

This volume reviews research and practice on the importance of play as a developmental activity. Part I contains chapters on the historical, anthropological, and sociological perspectives of the importance of play activities in school settings. Part II deals with educational perspectives of play at preschool and elementary levels. Part III provides an excellent review and commentary on the importance of play in the development and education of children. References.

Social and Cognitive Skills: Sex Roles and Children's Play. (1983). Edited by Marsha B. Liss. NY: Academic. (Developmental Psychology Series).

This book reviews the various theories and research regarding sex role acquisition by children via certain types of play activities or toys used during play. Chapter 1 looks at early sex differences in play activities and preferences. Chapter 3 looks at sex-typed toy choices. Chapter 4 looks at social fantasy play in preschoolers. Chapter 5 discusses activity structure and play as it affects socialization. Chapter 7 explores learning gender-related skills through play. Chapter 8 looks at the cognitive consequences and early interventions and sex differentiated play. Chapter 9 looks at the preschool classroom and sex differences in play. Chapter 10 explores patterns of sex typing in an open school. References.

The Social Psychology and Anthropology of Play and Games. (1981). Brian Sutton-Smith. In *Handbook of Social Science of Sport*, edited by Luschen and Sage. Champaign, IL: Stripes.

The author selectively reviews the literature dealing with the social psychology and anthropology of play and games. The focus is on children. References.

The Study of Games. (1971). Elliott M. Avedon, Brian Sutton-Smith. NY: John Wiley & Sons.

Considered a classic, this volume outlines historical studies of game origins, the practical uses of games, and the scientific study of game functions and structures. Each chapter includes an introductory account of a particular field of inquiry, representative readings from relevant literature, and related bibliographic reference. Several unique indexes are included in the volume: authors and researchers index, historic personages index, cultural index, subject index, and references to games in English literature (Tudor-Stuart Period) cited in Chapter 2. References.

When Children Play: Proceedings of the International Conference on Play and Play Environments. (1985). Edited by J. L Frost, S. Sunderlin. Wheaton, MD: Association for Childhood Education International.

The book presents a number of papers covering various aspects of play. Included are reports of research as well as statements of opinion and theory. The book is divided into seven parts, each dealing with one of the following: understanding play; play, learning, and development; how children use playgrounds; trends in designing and developing playgrounds; indoor play and materials; role of adults in promoting play; play as an assessment tool. References.

Reports of Research

Are Toys (Just) Toys? Exploring Their Effects on Pretend Play of Low-Income Preschoolers. (1985). Vonnie C. McLoyd. In *Beginnings: The Social and Affective Development of Black Children*, edited by Margaret Beale Spencer, Geraldine Kearse Broakins, Walter Recharde Allen, Chapter 5. Hillsdale, NJ: Lawrence Erlbaum. (Child Psychology).

McLoyd set up a study of pretend play among low-income black children with "high" and "low" structure play materials. Although the study gleans critical differences in pretend play according to structural contexts, the role of the developmental-cognitive-racial connection is left unanswered.

Boys and Girls at Play: The Development of Sex Roles. (1983). Evelyn Goodenough Pitcher, Lynn Hickey Schultz. NY: Praeger.

The authors and students in the Department of Child Study at Tufts University observed and recorded play sessions at several nursery schools or kindergartens in the Boston area. The five chapters making up this book record their findings and observations. The four appendixes describe the coding categories, discuss reliability and data analysis, and provide statistical tables.

Categories of Child-Child Interaction. (1972). N. Blurton Jones. In *Ethological Studies of Child Behavior*, edited by Blurton Jones. London: Cambridge Univ. Press.

This chapter reports an investigation of a sampling of twenty-five children from two to four years old and their observable behavior during free play time on a playground. Behaviors such as hit, smile, run, cry, point were recorded for each of the children. Factor analysis of these correlations was done. Three main factors, or axes, emerged in each of the four classes of child interaction which were named "rough-and-tumble play versus work," "aggression," "social behavior." Comparisons of behavior between age and sex groups and across individuals were made. Results indicate that taking toys did not change in the same way as fighting over toys changed. Individuals who did more rough and tumble did less aggression, but the evidence suggests that this was because they were less-often using toys and therefore less-often in aggression-provoking situations. References.

Cognitive Aspects of Young Children's Symbolic Play, Final Report. (1976). Virginia Stern, Nancy Bragdon, Anne Gordon. NY: Bank Street College of Education.

This study carried out at Bank Street College of Education assessed aspects of the cognitive functioning of young children from their symbolic play. Primarily a methodological study, the authors noticed developmental changes during group play with their sampling of three- to six-year-olds. The increased complexity of symbolic representation in play manifested itself through the children's behavior and speech. The ability to organize play is indicative of advanced cognitive skills. The study also indicates that white, middle-class three- and four-year-olds are similar in the quality of their symbolic play as three- and four-year-old black children. References.

Patterns of Play and Social Interaction in Preschool Children. (1972). Peter K. Smith, Kevin Connolly. In *Ethological Studies of Child Behavior*, edited by Blurton Jones. London: Cambridge Univ. Press.

This chapter records the results of a time-sampling study of free play in three day nurseries. Twelve five-minute samples of behavior were taken for each of the forty children observed. The mean frequency of occurrence of the various behaviors, inter-observer agreements, and split-half reliabilities were computed. Determinants of behavior examined in this way included particular day nursery, age, sex, presence or absence of a father in the home, length of nursery experience, whether activity indoors or outdoors, and time of day. References.

Play Patterns of Primary School Children. (1985). Julie F. Crum, Helen M. Eckert. In *Motor Development, Current Selected Research*, Vol. 1. Princeton, NJ: Princeton.

The authors videotaped primary children during recess and noon hour play periods. They found that the only sex difference play occurred at the age of six years in activity orientation. By eight years of age they found significant sex differences in activity organization, activity orientation, and size of play group with boys having the higher mean values in all instances. There were no significant sex differences in motor skill competency at either age level. At both ages, same sex children were the preferred playmates.

Social Relations and Innovation: Changing the State of Play in Hospitals. (1977). David J. Hall. London: Routledge & Kegan Paul.

This book outlines a hospital-based research project involving play leaders in children's wards in an attempt to change behavior of groups of children. Part I reviews the traditional psychological literature on hospital and maternal separation and the later work on children's efforts to cope with the trauma and change in the hospital situation. Parts II and III report the author's study of play leaders in hospitals. References.

Symbolic Functioning and Children's Early Writing: The Relations between Kindergartners' Play and Isolated Word Writing Fluency. (1984). Anthony D. Pellegrini. In *New Directions in Composition Research*, edited by Richard Beach, Lillian Bridwell, Chapter 13. NY: Guilford. (Perspectives in Writing Research).

This chapter reports a study investigating the effect play has on children's early writing. Sixty-five kindergarten children from mixed socioeconomic backgrounds were observed. The findings suggest that a child's level of play is a powerful predictor of writing achievement in kindergarten. References.

Understanding Children's Play. (1952). Ruth Edith Hartley, Lawrence K. Frank, Robert M. Goldenson. NY: Columbia Univ. Press.

This book grew out of research conducted by Ruth Edith Hartley to study play in fostering healthy personality development of young children. The book is now considered a classic. The volume discusses all types of play and their value and effects on the growing child. Anyone doing research on children's play should at least read Chapter 1 on the function of play in child development. The remaining chapters go into specific types of play: blocks, water, clay, drawing, music, and movement.

Vicissitudes of Play in Child Analysis: A Seven-Year-Old Tells His Unique Intrapsychic Story. (1984). Maurice Apprey. In *The Masks of Play*, by Brian Sutton-Smith, Diane Kelly-Byrie. El Cerrito, CA: Leisure.

An account of the language of play behavior of a seven-year-old boy in a psychoanalytic relationship with a male analyst. It is a diagnostic and therapeutic study, therefore different from many other published studies on play. The study claims that the child uses play and language to recreate and construe significant parts of his world. References.

Other References

Design for Play. (1969). Richard Dattner. NY: Van Nostrand Reinhold.

This book presents many different playgrounds, all of which have as their goal the creation of an environment where play, learning, and human spirit are nurtured. Interspersed with the descriptions is a general philosophy of children's need for play facilities. The book is well-illustrated with photographs and graphic designs of playgrounds. References.

One Potato, Two Potato: The Secret Education of American Children. (1976). Mary Knapp, Herbert Knapp. NY: W. W. Norton.

The authors state that this is not a comprehensive collection but representative and illustrative of how traditional lore functions in the lives of contemporary children from kindergarten through sixth grade. They give more space to sociological and sexual material than is usual in surveys of child lore; although taboos are relaxing, children are still reluctant to reveal such knowledge to adults, as the authors quickly discovered. Their attention to ethnic humor is only an introduction, and their attention to the lore of girlhood neglects somewhat the extensive lore of boyhood. The Knapps used questionnaires and some interviews with children in a number of U.S. locations, scattered informants from late adolescence from a much wider range of communities, and are familiar with most of the available literature.

A Pediatric Play Program: Developing a Therapeutic Play Program for Children in Medical Settings. (1975). Pat Azarnoff, Sharon Flegal. Springfield, IL: Charles C. Thomas.

Written for doctors, nurses, and administrators of pediatric units who wish to introduce play programs, this book will also be useful to play directors, pediatric nurses, parents, or volunteers who already have play programs but need advice about suitable activities. Organization, staffing, supplies and materials, volunteer assistance, and budgeting of therapeutic pediatric play programs are among the topics discussed in the book. References.

Planning Environments for Young Children's Physical Space. (1969). Sybil Kritchevsky, Elizabeth Prescott. Washington, DC: National Association for the Education of Young Children.

This monograph presents ideas and solutions to analysis of play space and organizing it for optimal use by children. Goals of different play programs are examined. Methods of play space analysis are given. Common problems in space development and suggested solutions are discussed. Examples of excellent play space are given. References.

Play Activities and Elementary School Peer Groups. (1984). Andrew W. Miracle. In *The Masks of Play*, by Brian Sutton-Smith, Diane Kelly-Byrie. NY: Leisure.

This paper deals with the organization of play in an elementary school by school personnel and by groups of fourth graders.

Play Dreams and Imitation in Childhood. (1962). Jean Piaget. NY: W. W. Norton.

Translated by C. Gattegno and F. M. Hodgson, this classic written by Piaget outlines his theories and study regarding the first years of the child's development. Part I covers the six stages of imitation in children. Part II deals with play. Part III looks at cognitive representation.

A Playground for All Children: User Groups and Site Selection. 3 vols. (1976). United States Department of Housing and Urban Development. Washington, DC: Government Printing Office.

These three booklets describe in considerable detail a project that HUD encouraged: the development, by the city of New York, of the nation's first outdoor public playground to be especially designed for integrated play between handicapped and able-bodied children. The first booklet describes the special play needs of children ages three to eleven who are expected to use the playground, considering their abilities and disabilities. Also describes the comprehensive research studies that underlay the project, including site analysis and criteria. The second booklet deals with the design competition, devised by the city of New York to encourage the widest variety of approaches and solutions to the assignment. The third booklet, the resource volume, documents the playground's development and deals with both process and product. Included is the survey of existing playgrounds made in preparation for the competition, the four winning entries, and a description of other innovative concepts, designs, and play components.

Your Child at Play: Birth to One Year. (1983, 1985). Marilyn Segal. NY: Newmarket. (Your Child at Play).

This book gives information on play/learning activities for infants. The suggested activities, fully illustrated, follow the development stages of normal infant development. Others in the series include: *Your Child at Play: One to Two Years*; and *Your Child at Play: Two to Three Years*.

SOCIAL INTERACTION

Bibliographies

Friendship: A Selected, Annotated Bibliography. (1985). Janet L. Barkas. NY: Garland. (Garland Bibliographies in Sociology).

Entries are categorized under four topical areas: books, booklets, dissertations, and reports; articles and chapters in journals, books, encyclopedias, magazines and newspapers; unpublished materials; and organizational resources. A subject index is provided.

The Human-Animal Bond: An Annotated Bibliography. (1985). Karen Miller Allen. Metuchen, NJ: Scarecrow.

Sources of the entries in this volume were located by searching appropriate terms through: Dissertation Abstracts, Hospital Literature Index, Humanities Index, Index Medicus, Index to Nursing and Allied Health, Index Veterinarius, International Nursing Index, Masters Abstracts, Psychological Abstracts, Readers' Guide to Periodical Index, and Social Work Abstracts. Arrangement is under seven broad categories. Under the fifth section, therapeutic values of animals, there is a subtopic of "companion animals and children." About fifty-three entries are listed of studies dealing with pets and children, or pets in families. Several entries refer to abused children and their pets. Another interesting and fruitful subsection in this fifth section is "Companion Animals in Schools . . . "

Reviews of Literature

Altruism and Helping Behavior: Social, Personality, and Developmental Perspectives. (1980). Edited by J. Philippe Rushton, Richard M. Sorrentino. Englewood Cliffs, NJ: Prentice-Hall. (Prentice-Hall Series in Social Learning Theory).

This book provides a conceptual analysis of the literature about how social learning occurs. Chapter 1 discusses altruism. Chapter 2 reviews altruism in animals and discusses the capacity for altruism in humans. Chapter 3 considers motivation of altruistic behavior. Chapter 4 looks at individual differences of altruism. Chapter 5 looks at the principles of social learning in individuals. Chapters 6, 7 and 8 look at the roles the family, mass media, and education play in socializing altruism. References.

Attitudes toward Handicapped Students: Professional, Peer, and Parent Reactions. (1985). Marcia D. Horne. Hillsdale, NJ: Lawrence Erlbaum. (School Psychology).

This volume summarizes and interprets research and theory on attitudes toward exceptional children. Bibliographies may be found at the end of chapters. A separate author and subject index concludes the book.

Children as Teachers: Theory and Research on Tutoring. (1976). Vernon L. Allen. NY: Academic. (Educational Psychology).

The book is divided into four major sections. The first presents a historical perspective and some theoretical foundations for the use of children as tutors. A review of socialization literature in both human and nonhuman social groups suggests that same age peer interactions are more useful and more satisfying than cross-age interactions. At times the younger child will have a better command of the content, be socially more mature, and be able to help socialize an older child. A number of specific programs are reviewed. The second section deals with helping relationships with children. The third looks at tutoring programs in schools. In the final section entitled Problems and Possibilities, Chapter 15 gives a review of research on children tutoring children. The last chapter deals with implementation of a tutoring program. References.

Children's Friendship. (1980). Zick Rubin. Cambridge, MA: Harvard Univ. Press. (Developing Child Series).

Nine short chapters discuss and give further references to such topics as: worth of friendship, early friendships, definition of a friend, skills of friendship, being friends, loss of friends; boys, girls and groups; and cross-age friendship. References.

The Development of Interaction in the First Seven Years of Life. (1982). M. I. Lisina. In *Review of Child Development*, Vol. 6, edited by Willard Hartup. Chicago, IL: Univ. of Chicago Press.

A synthesis of research on the genesis of interaction in children from birth through seven years of age. Focus is mainly on interaction with adults and only briefly on interaction with other children. The research indicates that there is a possibility of improving the development of institutionalized infants through interaction between children and adults. Interaction between infant and adult also contributes to speech development, emotional development, verbal development, and cognitive activity. The research reviewed also indicates that social interaction plays a dominant role in the concepts children form of other individuals. References.

Friendship and Peer Culture in the Early Years. (1984). William A. Corsaro. Norwood, NJ: Ablex. (Language and Learning for Human Service Professionals).

Each of the six chapters reviews research on peer culture, children's play, friendships, and interactions with other children in the nursery school setting.

Friendship and Social Relations in Children. (1980). Edited by Hugh C. Foot, Anthony J. Chapman, Jean R. Smith. NY: John Wiley & Sons.

Chapters are grouped under four headings reflecting recent research interests: value of friendship; processes of acquaintance; dynamics of friendship; and cliques. Reviews and discussions are interdisciplinary, drawing from sociology, ethology, and psychology. References.

Friendships in Normal and Handicapped Children. (1984). Edited by Tiffany Field, Jaipaul L. Roopnarine, Marilyn Segal. Norwood, NJ: Ablex.

The initial section of the book describes basic methodological issues in studying children's friendships. The second section consists of chapters presenting research studies on various facets of normal children's friendships. The last section contains chapters describing research on patterns of friendship among normal and handicapped children. One chapter addresses how to facilitate friendships among handicapped children. References.

The Political Life of Children. (1986). Robert Coles. NY and Boston: Atlantic Monthly.

Robert Coles, a child psychiatrist, recounts in this book the results of over twenty-five years of studying children and their families regarding political beliefs. Work on this book was done in the United States, South America, Northern Ireland, England, Nicaragua, Canada, Poland, Cambodia and Thailand, and Brazil. More space is devoted to Northern Ireland and South America than other national settings. References.

Sex Role and Pupil Role in Early Childhood Education. (1977). Patrick C. Lee, Gita K. Vouiodas. In *Current Topics in Early Childhood Education*, Vol. 1, edited by Lilian Katz. Norwood, NJ: Ablex.

The chapter looks at the origins of pupil role and its relationship to sex role in early childhood settings from nursery school through second grade. Through analysis of studies, the authors contend that what is termed "pupil role" places emphasis on conformity and receptivity as the proper stance for school-based learning. In so doing, the educators are ignoring theory and research which hold that learning is facilitated by activity. They also point out that "student role" victimizes both boys and girls with more long-term negative effects being felt by girls than boys. References.

Social Comparison and the Young Child: Current Research Issues. (1985). Judith A. Chafel. In *Early Child Development and Care*, 21 (1 - 3), pp. 35 - 59.

A synthesis of literature on social comparison in young children. Several theories are reviewed providing a conceptual framework for study of social comparison. Overviews of research on the following issues are given: what motivates children to engage in social comparison; with whom do children seek to compare; at what age does social comparison appear; does it follow a developmental progression; what are the effects upon subsequent behavior; and are there sex-related differences in the activity. References.

Social Learning Theory and the Development of Prosocial Behavior: A System for Research Integration. (1981). Rosemary A. Rosser. In *Parent-Child Interaction, Research and Prospects Theory*, edited by Ronald Henderson. NY: Academic. (Educational Psychology).

The purpose of the chapter is to examine the psychological debate as it relates to the development of prosocial behavior, to delineate the empirical evidence used to wage the debate, and to propose something of an integrative system for representing the content. Literature reviews of both the cognitive developmentalists and the learning approach are included. The last half of the chapter reviews the empirical work done in the area of prosocial development. References.

Reports of Research

Aspects of Social Development in Nursery School Children with Emphasis on Introduction to the Group. (1972). W. C. McGrew. In *Ethological Studies of Child Behavior*, edited by Blurton Jones. London: Cambridge Univ. Press.

This chapter reports a study of short-term changes in children's behavior immediately after introduction into an established group. Children ages three and four in an Edinburgh nursery school were observed to: (1) explore the possibility of short-term changes immediately after entry into the nursery and (2) compare these with long-term social changes. McGrew found that children's behavior at entry and the group's reaction to the newcomer were generally neutral curiosity. During the first day, the incoming child was subdued and exhibited signs of ambivalence. Conspicuous changes in the new child's behavior occurred within five days of entry. Nervous exploration decreased and social approaches, including agonistic ones, increased, but participation in quasi-agonistic "rough-and-tumble" play remained rare. Newcomers were behaviorally indistinguishable from the other children after approximately sixty-five days of nursery school experience. References.

Children and War: Political Socialization to International Conflict.   (1973). Howard Tolley. NY: Teachers College Press, Columbia Univ.

The volume reports a study made of four aspects of socialization to international conflict: (1) how and when children acquire attitudes toward war; (2) attitudes children have about a specific conflict--Vietnam--and how and when these were acquired; (3) how factual the knowledge is that children have; and (4) from what primary sources the children's information came. The book is well illustrated with tables showing data gathered. The volume concludes with an annotated bibliography as well as a sizeable reference.

Old and Young Together: Effects of an Educational Program on Preschoolers' Attitudes toward Older People.   (Jan/Feb 1986).   Mary Dellmann-Jenkins, Donna Lambert, Dorothy Fruit, Thomas Dinero. In *Childhood Education*, 62 (3), pp. 206 - 212.

A report of a study conducted with three- and four-year-olds using an intervention program to help the children develop realistic and positive attitudes about the aging process and the elderly. Study showed positive results with the experimental group of children. Seventeen citations.

Relating to Learning: Towards a Developmental Social Psychology of the Primary School.   (1983).   Peter Kutnick.   London: Allen & Unwin.   (Unwin Education Books).

Reports a study focusing on the underlying schemes of authority development. Parts of the study show children's behavioral interaction with school authority, understanding of authority, and schemes of adapting to the social/school context. The study also approaches theoretical issues of authority and moral development which intertwine with cognition and the social understanding of relationships. Ends with a summary of the study and recommends a restructuring of teaching style. References.

Toddler's Behaviors with Agemates: Issues and Interaction, Cognition, and Affect. (1981). Wanda C. Bronson. Norwood, NJ: Ablex. (Monographs on Infancy, Vol. 1).

This monograph presents a detailed report of a longitudinal study of peer interaction involving forty toddlers. Each toddler participated in ten 45 - 60 minute free play sessions spaced at roughly equal intervals between the ages of twelve and twenty-four months. Three or four children participated in each session. Reciprocal interaction was defined as mutual engagement involving some understanding of the other child's intent. Bronson finds reciprocal interaction to be rare throughout the second year, with the most prolonged peer contact consisting of struggles for the possession of toys. Bronson developed several innovative measures to assess the toddler's understanding of the peer's internal state. References.

Other References

Children's Friendships in School Settings. (1977).   Steven R. Asher, Sherri L. Oden, John M. Gottman.   In *Current Topics in Early Childhood Education*, Vol. 1, edited by Lilian Katz.   Norwood, NJ: Ablex.

Reviews research on children's friendships in nursery school and elementary school settings.   Most of the studies selected in the review have implications for educational practice.   General areas looked at are: stereotypes affecting children's friendships, influence of school environment on friendships, kinds of social skills important to achieving peer acceptance, and methods of teaching social skills to children lacking them.   References.

Observing Intelligence in Young Children: Eight Case Studies. (1976).   Jean V. Carew, Itty Chan, Christine Halfar.   Englewood Cliffs, NJ: Prentice-Hall.

Summarizes the environment and the development of eight children observed over the years from one to three according to the naturalistic research procedures of a study described in the 1973 book *Environment and Experience*.   Chapter 1 describes briefly the research.   Chapter 2 considers generally how the child experiences his environment.   Chapter 3 discusses ways mothers or principal care takers influence a child.   The roles considered are those of organizer, model, observer, facilitator, restrictor, and participator.   Pairs of case studies illustrate each particular issue.   The last two environments discussed are ones that are so deleterious that retardation in overall development results.   Persons looking for a book of case studies will find this resource useful.

One to One: The Story of the Big Brothers/Big Sisters Movement in America. (1985).   George L. Beiswinger.   Philadelphia, PA: Big Brothers/Big Sisters of America.

Chronicles the story of the Big Brothers and Big Sisters movement.   A description of the movement over an eight decade interval is given.   The first part of the book covers the growth of the volunteer movement.   The second part contains descriptions of leaders, examples of cases, and a commentary about the status of the movement today.   A list of affiliated agencies by year is provided in appendixes 1 - 3.   Footnoted.

10

Physical Development

DATABASES
TO CONSIDER

Embase
Medline   ERIC
Sport

HEALTH

Bibliographies

International Sport Sciences. Vol. 1 - . (April 1979 -). Philadelphia, PA: Franklin
    Research Center.

This is an interdisciplinary abstract of sport medicine, exercise, and sport
sciences. Entries are in numerical order under general categories such as:
injury, prophylaxis, diagnosis; case reports, exercise and rehabilitation;
surgery; pharmacotherapy; cardiovascular physiology; respiratory physiology;
nutrition and metabolism; biomechanics and kinesiology; etc. Book reviews
are included with each issue along with notices for conferences, symposiums
and meetings. Users will find an abundance of materials referencing
children.

Reviews of Literature

Behavioral Perspectives on Children's Accidents. (1984). Adam P. Matheny, Jane
    E. Fisher. In *Advances in Developmental and Behavioral Pediatrics*, Vol. 5,
    edited by Mark Walraich, Donald Routh. Greenwich, CT: JAI.

This chapter reviews the literature of accident proneness in children from
birth to fifteen years of age. A table of leading causes of death is given.
Historical explanations of accidents are included in the chapter. Pages 230 -
247 have a table of studies and noted findings regarding family characteristics
and accident-related behaviors. The last part of the chapter discusses
conceptual foundations of accident research and suggested research
directions. A lengthy bibliography of references is provided.

Beyond Separation: Further Studies of Children in Hospital. (1979). Edited by David Hall, Margaret Stacey. NY: Routledge & Kegan Paul.

This volume examines the effects of separation from home and family on hospitalized children. The book summarizes several studies carried out as part of a research project completed in the hospitals of Wales and includes research on a range of ages and conditions to be found among children admitted to the hospital. The book discusses the characteristics of children and their illnesses but also delves into the interaction of parental characteristics and aspects of the hospital environment and their effects on the child. After an introductory chapter, six chapters summarize data on these various influences. Included are discussions of an attachment theory, interpretation of the children's responses to the hospital experience, other family factors, children's perceptions and the meaning they attach to hospitalization, aspects of the hospital routine, and interactions among hospital staff. The final chapter summarizes the practical implications of this series of studies. Suggestions are made which include education and training of hospital staff, changes in the organization of children's wards, and suggestions for further research. References.

Child Health Psychology: Concepts and Issues. (1982). Paul Karoly, John J. Steffen, Donald J. O'Grady. NY: Pergamon. (Pergamon General Psychology Series).

This volume provides a basic outline of assumptions, theories, and issues underlying the practices of child health psychology. Chapter 1 delves into the realities and complexities of child psychology practices within a medical setting. Chapter 2 outlines an organizational framework for developmental pediatrics. Chapter 3 reviews the literature on children's understanding of their health and illness. Chapter 5 reviews methodological issues that are frequently neglected by pediatric researchers. Chapter 6 explains the basic tools of neuropsychological investigation, including a discussion of the Halstead-Reitan assessment procedure. Chapter 7 reviews what is known about pain. Chapter 8 by Tiffany Field explores the interaction between adults and high-risk infants. The final chapter discusses early mental health screening and intervention in public schools. Each chapter contains a bibliography of references.

Children and AIDS: The Challenge for Child Welfare. (1986). Gary R. Anderson. Washington, DC: Child Welfare League of America.

Concisely reviews what is known about the AIDS virus and children. CDC Guidelines for Foster Care of AIDS Children located in appendix. Forty-four references.

Chronic Illness and Disability through the Life Span. (1984). Edited by Myron G. Eisenberg, LaFaye C. Sutkin, Mary A. Jansen. NY: Springer-Verlag.

The thirteen chapters of the book are broken into six major sections according to life stages: infancy, children, adolescence, young adults, middle age, and old age. In the introduction the editors clearly define each of the life stages and give an overview of each within the chapter. Chapters are separately authored and contain bibliographies of pertinent research literature relevant to the chapter. Chapter 2 concerns psychological problems of infancy. Chapter 3 looks at birth and its effect on the family. Chapters 4 and 5 deal with implications of chronic illness or handicapping conditions in the family or during childhood.

Cigarette Smoking in Children and Young Adolescents: Causes and Prevention. (1981). Nancy R. Blaney. In *Advances in Behavioral Pediatrics*, Vol. 2, edited by Bonnie Camp. Greenwich, CT: JAI.

This chapter reviews the literature on youthful smoking and smoking prevention programs. The review suggests that methodological and conceptual problems limit both the validity and the practical application of the empirical data available. A lengthy bibliography is provided.

Discussion on Child Development: A Consideration of the Biological, Psychological, and Cultural Approaches to the Understanding of Human Development and Behavior. (1953 - 1956). Edited by J. M. Tanner, Barbera Inhelder. In the *Proceedings of the World Health Organization Study Group on Psychological Development of the Child*. NY: International Univ. Press.

Each of the four volumes in this series gives an account of the activities of the World Health Organization, the Research Study Group on the Psychobiological Development of the Child. The first volume covers general views of child development from various disciplines: psychological; medical; and cross cultural. Volume 2 bases its discussions on the broad theme of learning. Special attention is given to learning under stress and learning in the immature organism. Volume 3 focuses on the development of sex differences and the development of individuality or ego identity. Volume 4 is a synthesis of all the data presented at the previous meetings. References.

Early Developmental Hazards: Predictors and Precautions. (1978). Edited by Frances Degen Horowitz. Boulder, CO: Westview. (AAAS Selected Symposia Series No. 19).

This volume presents four papers followed by references. After a short review of the study of human development, Lewis Lipsitt reviews infant crib death. Trygg Engen discusses controlling food preferences in children. Leederman explores mother-infant bonding during the neonatal period. Arnold Sameroff discusses determinants in developmental deviancy. The last paper is by Sameroff and explores factors which influence IQ at age thirty months.

Infancy and Developmental Psychobiology. Vol. 2 of *Handbook of Child Psychology*. (1983). Edited by Marshall Haith, Joseph J. Campas. NY: John Wiley & Sons.

Provides a broad review of the historical, theoretical, and research domains of infancy and developmental psychology. Each of the thirteen chapters is written by a recognized authority in the field. Chapter 2 covers ethology and child development. Chapter 3 looks at perinatal brain development and behavior. Chapter 4 discusses normal and deviant development of functional lateralization of the brain. Chapter 5 covers neurobiology of cognitive development. Chapter 6 is entitled "Developmental Behavior Genetics." Chapter 7 looks at the visual perception of infants. Chapter 8 covers auditory development and speech perception in infancy. Chapter 9 discusses infant cognition. Socioemotional development is covered in Chapter 10. Chapter 11 covers early childhood programs. Chapter 12 examines attention, learning, and memory in infants. The last chapter looks at risk factors in development. References.

Pediatric Work Physiology. (1978). NY: S. Karger. (Medicine and Sport, Vol. 11.)

This volume provides a written documentation of research in the area of children's physiological work capacity, physical fitness, and growth and development. The papers are work of research teams and represent a multivariable, interdisciplinary perspective, reflecting present interest in physical activity. The organization of the present volume resulted in three chapter headings: Physiological Adaptations to Work; Clinical Pathology; and Growth and Development. References.

Progress in Child Health. Vol. 1 - . (1984 -). Edited by J. A. MacFarlane. NY: Churchill Livingstone. (Progress in Child Health).

A new series begun in 1984 which hopes to provide updates on current topics in the field including the areas of psychology and sociology as well as more medically-oriented topics. Topics will cover both the normal and the special child. Each chapter is written by a specialist and is a self-contained unit usually including a lengthy bibliography. This first volume contains twenty chapters and covers such divergent topics as: diagnosis of migraine in childhood; fetal alcohol syndrome; defective color vision in children; parent's recognition of the ill child; bonding; children and divorce; language development; Britain's National Cohort Studies; health services for children in school; and functions of child health clinics. Chapters in the volume vary in length and in the integration of empirical data, theory, and practical recommendations.

The State of the World's Children 1985. (1984). James P. Grant. Oxford, NY: UNICEF.

This UNICEF monograph reports on data gathered by the organization about the health, morality, life expectancy, birthweight, literacy, GPN, immunization programs, etc., of children around the world. The monograph is divided into three sections. The first, entitled State of the World's Children 1985, focuses on health-care programs such as oral rehydration, national vaccination days, and birth spacing; poverty, child-survival techniques; family planning; health-worker training; changing perception of families; and child development. Section II, entitled Lifelines, provides extracts and summaries from recent research and writing on cost-effective strategies for protecting the lives and normal development of the world's children. The last part is entitled Statistics and provides economic and social statistics on the nations of the world, with particular reference to children's well-being. References.

Reports of Research

The Family Life of Sick Children: A Study of Family Coping with Chronic Childhood Disease. (1975). Lindy Burton. London: Routledge & Kegan Paul.

This volume looks at the effect of chronic illness, particularly cystic fibrosis, on the child and the family. Fifty-three separate families in Northern Ireland were studied. Both parents were interviewed along with the child. The children were either in preschool or primary levels. Teachers were asked to assess the children's social maturation. The results of the study are presented within the book. A discussion of the effects of death on all family members and the way families cope with loss is included. The book is interestingly written and is enhanced by many case studies. There is a good review and citation of other studies relevant to the topic.

Other References

Child Health Policy in an Age of Fiscal Austerity: Critiques of the Select Panel Report. (1983). Edited by Ron Haskins. Norwood, NJ: Ablex. (Child and Family Policy).

The volume focuses on child health policy and in particular the policy issues raised by the publication Report of the Select Panel for Promotion of Child Health, a federal report concerned exclusively about children's health. Individual chapters look at state and federal relations; regulatory issues; government and family responsibilities; manpower needs in child health; cost-effective means of delivering health care services; budget cuts; and childhood mortality and morbidity; and the challenge to health programs posed by the New Right. Chapter 11 contains a table giving a summary of all the various federal commission reports from 1935 to present which affected or touched on children's health issues in any way. In the appendix a summary and classification of the Select Panel's recommendations is provided. Indexed.

Health in Day Care: A Manual for Health Professionals. (1987). Edited by Selma R. Deitch. Elk Grove Village, IL: American Academy of Pediatrics.

Addressed especially to community pediatricians, but also useful to other health workers, this manual discusses aspects of day care that require a physician's attention. Chapter 1 traces the positive effect of a nurturing environment upon the development of the infant and child, covering the period from the early 1900s to the present. Chapter 2 sets forth precise suggestions for program components advancing child health. Chapter 3 depicts the role of the pediatrician in advocating day care practices adopted to serve children with special needs. Chapter 4 addresses the issue of child abuse. Chapter 5 describes measures that retard the spread of contagious diseases in day care facilities and makes suggestions for the prevention of infection. Chapter 6 reviews factors that increase the risk of injury to children in the day care setting. Chapters 7 - 9 supply information intended to increase the health professional's ability to serve effectively as consultant. Many related materials are appended, such as sample letters, forms, and several checklists.

Health in Day Care: A Manual for Health Professionals. (1982). Committee on Early Childhood, Adoption and Dependent Care, American Academy of Pediatrics. Elk Grove Village, IL: American Academy of Pediatrics.

This manual is intended to assist physicians requiring information about health issues in child care facilities. Half the book is appendixes of sample letters, forms, and checklists of forms for child care personnel. The first four chapters address issues related to health promotion in child care. The remaining chapters address several aspects of health in child care: prevention and management of infectious diseases, reduction of injuries, and staff training concerning health and safety issues. This is a succinct, up-to-date review of health components for the day care professional as well as the physician.

MEDICINE

Bibliographies

Infant Feeding: An Annotated Bibliography. (1982). Compiled by Christine Marie Crowhurst, Bonnie Lee Kumer. Toronto, Ontario: Nutrition Information Service.

This selective bibliography is an annotated listing of over 700 publications related to infant feeding. Materials and articles are categorized into specific sections according to content: infant feeding, breast feeding, infant formula, solid foods, infant formula use in developing countries, and clinical concerns in infant feeding.

The Infant Formula Feeding Controversy: An Annotated Bibliography, 1970 - 1984. (1985). Edited by John A. Sparks. Dubuque, IA: Kendall/Hunt.

This annotated bibliography brings together general articles and studies as well as scientific articles and studies on the controversial question of infant formula feeding. In the introduction is a general overview of the controversy. The six subheadings used in the bibliography are: general articles and studies; scientific articles and studies; news articles; critic groups; church publications; and infant food industry publications. A publication index and author index conclude the monograph.

Reviews of Literature

Advances in International Maternal and Child Health. Vol. 1 - . (1981 -). Edited by D. B. Jelliffe, E. F. P. Jelliffe. Oxford and NY: Oxford Univ. Press. (Advances in International Maternal and Child Health).

This series brings together recent literature on major conditions affecting the health of mothers and young children from a global point of view. Topics such as breast feeding, infant formula, infant botulism, childhood autism, maternal and child health in various countries are typically covered in the annuals. Chapters conclude with bibliographies.

Childhood Encopresis and Enuresis: Causes and Therapy. (1979). Charles E. Schaefer. NY: Van Nostrand Reinhold.

This volume provides an overview of childhood encopresis and enuresis. The book is divided into two major parts. The first section deals with childhood encopresis and constipation and the second section with enuresis. The bibliography at the end of each section contains over 100 references to original and review articles published in English and foreign languages. Glossaries of terms are included with each section to assist the reader of the volume. The volume is written primarily for professionals.

Chronic Childhood Disorder: Promoting Patterns of Adjustment. (1975). Ivan B. Pless, Philip Pinkerton. Chicago, IL: Year Book Medical Publication.

This volume provides useful and readable surveys of the literature on various chronic disorders experienced during childhood. The book opens by advancing a model of adjustment which has "coping" and "self-esteem" as central concepts. One chapter surveys instruments for assessing adjustment, both on an individual basis and on a social basis (family, peers, and school). One chapter surveys the literature on the consequences of chronic childhood illness for later adolescence and adulthood. The most valuable chapter of the book reviews relationships between physical disability and psycho-social disability across a broad range of childhood chronic disorders. Groupings are made according to disorders of the central nervous system, special senses, cosmetic disorders, locomotor disorders, and systemic disorders. Citations to the literature are given for each of these conditions. The last chapter gives general principles of intervention which are useful but falls short of exploiting the wealth of implications raised by the book. The book gives an excellent introduction to the complex topic of chronic childhood disorders. References.

Conditioning and Enuresis. (1964). S. H. Lovibond. NY: Macmillan.

This classic provides an overview of the causes and effective treatment for enuresis. Part I generally reports treatment of enuresis by conditioning methods. Chapter 1 provides a review of historical studies of behaviors and treatments. Chapter 2 looks at the various theories of enuresis. Chapter 3 discusses the mechanisms of micturition. Chapter 4 sets forth the enuresis survey carried out by the author. Chapters 9 - 12 outline various treatment methods using conditioning. Chapter 13 gives general conclusions to Part I of the book. Part II generally covers studies done in the clinic using conditioning to treat enuresis. Nine small chapters make up this portion of the text covering: bed-wetting; enuresis; and conditioning. The appendixes contain information on the various instruments, scales, and surveys used in the studies described within the book. A lengthy bibliography is included at the end of the text. Indexed.

The Development of Cognitive Information Processing Strategies in Childhood. (1982). Lawrence V. Majovski, Lawrence C. Hartlage. In *Neuropsychology and Cognition*, Vol. 2, by Malateska, Hartlage. Boston: Martinus Nijhoff. (NATO Advanced Study Series, Series D: Behavioral and Social Sciences, No. 10).

The paper discusses ideas and concepts on how a child's brain develops and constructs internal representations of the real world via experiences. Twenty-four references.

The Development of Infants Born at Risk. (1984). Deborah L. Holmes, Jill Nagy Reich, Joseph F. Pasternak. Hillsdale, NJ: Lawrence Erlbaum.

This volume is a comprehensive yet compact review of factors which may bear on the medical condition of infants at birth and of possible relations between these prenatal conditions and developmental outcomes at later ages. The general categories of risk conditions in the newborn with which they deal are abnormal gestational age and abnormal fetal growth. For each of these risk conditions they discuss possible causes. These factors are then evaluated in light of research evidence as they may relate to developmental outcomes in later years, addressing in particular the problems of mental retardation, learning disabilities, behavioral disorders, and child abuse. One very important and interesting section, especially to the child development specialists and students of special education, describes and discusses the high-risk neonates after birth: their appearance and behavior, their nursery environment, and their parents' reactions and interactions. The chapters on early environment and intervention and remediation will also be of interest to scholars and researchers. References.

Human Developmental Neuropsychology. (1984). Otfried Spreen, David Tupper, Anthony Risser, Holly Tuokko, Dorothy Edgell. NY: Oxford Univ. Press.

This handbook is a readable overview of research on developmental neuropsychology. The first part of the book provides the background essential to an understanding of the growth of the nervous system. The second part reviews some conceptual and methodological issues deserving detailed treatment, such as the critical periods hypothesis, neural plasticity, and disconnection syndromes. The third part discusses the human fetus, embryo, or newborn and presents an overview of potentially damaging events and conditions that may affect normal growth. Part IV reviews the various functional disabilities frequently associated with damage to the nervous system: minimal brain dysfunction, motor disorders, attention deficit, visual disorders, auditory disorders, language disorders, cognitive disorders, learning disabilities, and emotional disorders. Eighty-one pages of references are provided.

The Hypnotic Treatment of Children in Pain. (1986). Lonnie Zeltzer, Samule LeBaron. In *Advances in Developmental and Behavioral Pediatrics*, Vol. 7, edited by Mark Walraich, Donald Routh. Greenwich, CT: JAI.

The chapter describes hypnosis as a pain mitigator with pediatric patients and summarizes the literature in this area. References.

Infants Born at Risk: Behavior and Development. (1979). Edited by Tiffany Sostek Field, Goldberg, Anita Susan, H. H. Shuman. NY: SP Medical and Scientific Books.

Presents research data on developmental follow-ups of infants born at risk: anoxia, low birthweight, prematurity, respiratory distress syndrome, metabolic disturbances, and central nervous system disorders. Most of the studies are collaborations between developmental psychologists and physicians. The chapters are divided among seven general sections: perinatal factors, neonatal evaluations, interactions of high-risk infants, intervention programs, and methodological issues. Individual chapters of particular interest include: Chapter 3, Prenatal Anoxia and Cognitive Development; Chapter 4, Relationship of Medical Events to Infant Development; Chapter 6, Assessment of Hearing; Chapter 7, Organization and Assessment of Crying in the Infant at Risk; and Chapter 11,

Development of Prematurely-Born Children through Middle Childhood. References.

Infectious Diseases in Day Care. (1987). Esther K. Sleator. Urbana, IL: Clearinghouse on Elementary and Early Childhood Education. (ED 269 151).

This monograph, written for the nonmedical reader, describes in detail the nature and severity of the many communicable diseases to which children who attend out-of-home care facilities have been known to be exposed and by which these children are sometimes afflicted. Studies from medical literature are cited.

Playing God in the Nursery. First edition. (1985). Jeff Lyon. NY: W. W. Norton.

Discusses the legal, social, moral, scientific, and economic implications of decisions to withhold treatment from severely handicapped newborns. References.

Principles of Pediatrics: Health Care of the Young. (1978). Edited by Robert A. Hoekelman. NY: McGraw-Hill.

This handbook provides a synthesis of pertinent information concerning the determinants of health and of disease in young children. The book is well-illustrated and gives suggested references along with further readings. A very comprehensive index enhances the volume.

Studies on Long-Term Outcome in Newborns with Birth Weights Under 1500 Grams. (1980). Beverly L. Koops, Robert J. Harmon. In *Behavioral Pediatrics*, Vol. 1, edited by Bonnie Camp. Greenwich, CT: JAI. (Advances in Behavioral Pediatrics).

The chapter reviews the historical development of concepts and technology of the intensive care nursery. Although the new technology improves the survival rates, studies show that there is a current incidence of twenty percent significant sensory, neurologic, or mental sequelae in survivors. Indications also are that the early separation from the parents may contribute to an increased incidence of child abuse and family disruption. A lengthy bibliography is provided.

Sudden Infant Death: Patterns, Puzzles and Problems. (1985). Jean Golding, Sylvia Limerick, Aidan Macfarlane. Somerset, England: Open Books.

This volume reports two major pieces of research and also gathers together essential research and comparative international data on the topic of sudden infant death. The book is a meticulous analysis of the various epidemiological factors involved. This volume is essential reading in studying the topic. References.

Variation in Body Stockiness among and within Ethnic Groups at Ages from Birth to Adulthood. (1987). Howard V. Meredith. In *Advances in Child Development and Behavior*, Vol. 20, edited by Hayne Reese. NY: Academic.

This is a lengthy international review of the literature on body form; for example, body build, body proportion, body configuration, physique, and body shape. Twenty tables introduce the statistics presented. A lengthy bibliography is included.

Reports of Research

Dry-Bed Training: Rapid Elimination of Childhood Enuresis. (1981). N. H. Azrin, T. J. Sneed, R. M. Foxx. In *Pediatric Behavioral Medicine*, edited by Ben Williams, John Foreyt, Ken Goodrick. NY: Praeger. (Praeger Special Studies).

A recognized classic in behavior therapy reprinted from *Behavior Research and Therapy*, 12 (1974): 147 - 156. This study reports the use of a urine alarm method along with training in inhibiting urination, positive reinforcement, training in rapid awakening, increased fluid intake, social motivation, self-correction of accidents, and practice in toileting with twenty-four children.

Neurological Development in Infancy. (1976). Bert Touwen. London: William Heinemann. (Clinics in Developmental Medicine, No. 58).

This monograph reports on a longitudinal descriptive investigation of fifty-one low-risk Dutch infants. They were examined every four weeks into their second year of life. There was a period of observation of spontaneous behaviors, as well as rating of reactions to particular fixed procedures, including most of the typical pediatric neurology assessment. Results from a large number of items, each scored on a several point scale, are presented and commented on in relation to other findings and neurological implications. The following were reported: age at first change in response, age at final change, interval between first and final change, and number of relapses in responding. Some items remained relatively constant or showed little appreciable interindividual variation; others showed intraindividual inconsistencies. The largest group of items did show gradual and consistent developmental change. On all items, eighty percent prediction bands are depicted for each score. A number of sex differences are set forth. Means and standard deviations on all the variables are included in appendixes, as well as interitem correlations. References.

Other References

Body Size of Infants and Children around the World in Relation to Socioeconomic Status. (1984). Howard V. Meredith. In *Advances in Child Development and Behavior*, Vol. 18, edited by Hayne Reese. NY: Academic. (Advances in Child Development and Behavior).

This chapter brings together international data on body size of infants and children and relates it to socioeconomic status of the child's family. Charts and tables abound in the chapter to illustrate some of the data collected. A lengthy bibliography follows the text.

The Development of the Infant and Young Child: Normal and Abnormal. Eighth edition. (1963). R. S. Illingworth. NY: Churchill Livingston.

This is a handbook of assessment procedures from infancy through the preschool period. The book is well-illustrated and chapters conclude with bibliographies. This latest edition contains rewritten chapters 1 and 2 as well as several new sections. The volume is intended for the health professional. References.

Hospital Care of Children and Youth. 1986 edition. (1986). Committee on Hospital Care, American Academy of Pediatrics. Elk Grove Village, IL: American Academy of Pediatrics.

Provides a general philosophy of child care, and general information concerning hospital medical care for children. Twenty-one chapters make up the volume. Topics covered include: community planning for hospital care, administration, quality assurance, delineation of privileges in the hospital, relationship between hospital-based and private practice physicians, admitting the child to the hospital, the general children's unit, hospitalization of emotionally disturbed children, pediatric intensive care unit, surgical service, and the dying child. Earlier edition of this handbook came out in 1978 with revisions in pamphlet form. The publisher expects a new edition in about five years (1992).

Manual of Physical Status and Performance in Childhood. 2 vols. (1983). Alex F. Roche, Robert M. Malina. NY: Plenum.

This two-volume set actually contains three volumes. Volume 1 is divided into 1A and 1B with the subtitle Physical Status. The volume includes data relating to body size and maturity. Volume 1A covers four measurement areas: stature and recumbent length; weight; height; and craniofacial measurement. Volume 1B covers six areas: trunk; lower and upper limb; physique; skeletal; maturation; and stature prediction. The index and annotated bibliography for both A and B are located in Volume 1B. Volume 2 contains data relating to performance, functional measurements, body composition, aspects of maturation, and a wide array of physiological variables. Volume 2 also contains an index and annotated bibliography. Both volumes contain numerous tables and charts of information. Anthropologists, physical educators, and health care professionals will find these references especially helpful with their research.

A Reference Manual of Growth and Development. (1979). J. M. H. Buckler. London: Blackwell Scientific.

This book provides quick access to information concerning the physical and mental characteristics of the developing child. Data are presented mainly in the form of charts and tables indicating normal development and ranges. Brief comments are included as explanation to aid in application. Little reference is made to causes or diagnosis of abnormal conditions and the manual does not include normal values for laboratory investigations. A brief bibliography is supplied.

The State of the World's Children. (1983). United Nations Children's Fund, UNICEF. Oxford: Oxford Univ. Press. (State of the World's Children).

An annual report put out by UNICEF, this year's report describes low-cost techniques which will reduce the mortality rate of children worldwide. Illustrations of countries or regions which have already achieved very low child death rates are provided. The report also shows how this change would help to slow down the rate of population growth. Part II describes the use of oral rehydration therapy, growth monitoring, expanded immunization, promotion of breastfeeding, family spacing, and food supplements as aids in lowering infant mortality. Part III provides graphs and charts of economic and social statistics on the nations of the world regarding children's well-being.

MOTOR DEVELOPMENT

Reviews of Literature

Acquisition of Motor Skills during Childhood. (1986). John Haubenstricker, Vern Seefeldt. In *Physical Activity and Well-Being*, edited by Vern Seefeldt, Chapter 2. Reston, VA: American Alliance for Health, Physical Education, Recreation and Dance.

The chapter summarizes what is known about development of motor skills and their relationship to the total welfare of the growing child. The first section provides an overview of motor development. The next section focuses on the development of motor behavior from early moments of life through the late childhood years. In the remaining sections the influence of biological age and the variability and stability of motor behavior is examined. The chapter ends with summary statements and a lengthy bibliography.

Advances in Pediatric Sport Sciences. Vol. 1, *Biological Issues.* (1984). Edited by Richard A. Boileau. Champaign, IL: Human Kinetics. (Advances in Pediatric Sport Sciences [APSS]).

This is the first of a projected series to be published every other year. Odd numbered volumes will focus on biological issues and even numbered volumes on behavioral issues. Topics covered under the biological issues include physiological, biomechanical, medical, and some topics within motor control and development as they pertain to pediatric sport sciences. Behavioral issues will draw upon other topics within motor control and development, sport and exercise psychology, sociology of sport, and anthropology of sport and play. The series is intended to help advance the understanding of children and their health and well-being as they participate in physical activities. References.

Age Changes in Motor Skills during Childhood and Adolescence. (1984). Crystal Branta, John Haubenstricker, Vern Seefeldt. In *Exercise and Sport Sciences Review*, Vol. 12, edited by Ronald Terjung. Lexington, MA: Collamore. (D. C. Heath).

The authors state that the review begins with a discussion of developmental sequences and the controversy surrounding the qualitative description of movement via total body configuration versus components analysis. It continues with an overview of age changes in motor skills assessed longitudinally on a resident group of children, followed by a compilation and comparison of motor achievements by children and youth from various regions of the world. The report concludes with a review of stability in selected movement skills during childhood and adolescence. References.

Cognition and Motor Process. (1984). W. Prinz, A. F. Sanders. New York: Springer-Verlag.

The volume brings together research and theory, regarding the relationship between cognition and motor processes, developed from papers presented at a conference at the Center for Interdisciplinary Research. The first section of the book encompasses motor control and action planning. The second section contains chapters on motor contributions to perception and cognition. Section III chapters cover mediating structures and operations between cognition and action. Section IV contains three chapters covering attention, cognition, and skill performance. Section V has three chapters which look at various aspects of interactions between cognition and action in development. References.

The Development of Movement Control and Coordination. (1982). Edited by J. A. Kelso, Scott and Jane Clark. NY: John Wiley & Sons. (Wiley Series in Developmental Psychology).

This is a collection of papers whose approach to motor skill development is "process oriented." The book is divided into four main topics. The first, entitled Information Coordination, and Control in Motor Skill Development, contains three papers. Part II is entitled Development of Schemas, Plans, and Programs and contains four papers. Part III has two papers and is entitled Timing Behavior in Development. The last part is entitled From Description to Explanation: An Emerging View and includes four papers. References.

The Human Infant as Focus in Theories of Handedness: Some Lessons from the Past. (1982). Lauren Julius Harris. In *Neuropsychology and Cognition*, Vol. 2, edited by Malatesha, Hartlage. Boston, MA: Martinus Nijhoff. (NATO Advanced Study Series, Series D: Behavioral and Social Sciences, No. 10).

A review of the early theories about handedness in infants proposed or theorized during the nineteenth century and before. References.

Life Span Motor Development. (1986). Kathleen M. Haywood. Champaign, IL: Human Kinetics.

This highly readable book gives a description of motor development from infancy to older adulthood. The author's chapters on early motor development and motor development during childhood are very well-written. In each, a thorough review of the literature is given. One excellent chapter describes the integration of visual, auditory, and kinesthetic development as correlates of motor development. References.

Motor Development: Current Selected Research. (1985). J. E. Clark, James H. Humphrey. Princeton, NJ: Princeton Book.

This first volume of a projected set presents original research and reviews on contemporary problems of interest to motor development specialists. Papers investigating motor control, motor skills, sociocultural considerations, and developmental delay make up the volume. With the exception of the "Reviews" section, all the papers are original research. Of the thirteen original research papers included in the book, five describe gross motor skills and/or fitness, six investigate motor-control-learning questions using traditional laboratory tasks. One evaluates play patterns and one applies a statistical technique to a test of motor proficiency. Three of the papers focus on the mentally retarded and approaches to studying motor skills acquisition, issues in memory for movement research, and timing-precision variables in motor performance. References.

Perceptual and Motor Development in Infants and Children. Third edition. (1986). Bryant J. Cratty. Englewood Cliffs, NJ: Prentice-Hall.

The text provides a well-written overview and introduction to current research on the topic. The fourteen chapters into which the book is broken cover early sensory-motor behavior and developmental theories; neurological beginnings of movement capacities; physical growth and changing body image; variables influencing motor development; beginnings of movement in the newborn; action sequences and skills exhibited by the larger muscle group in infancy and early childhood; motor performance in five- to twelve-year-olds; hand abilities in infancy and childhood; visual-perceptual development; and effects of exercise. References.

Physical Activity and Growth. (1982). Roy J. Shephard. Chicago, IL: Year Book Medical.

This volume containing thirteen chapters discusses various aspects of the interactions between physical activity and growth in both normal and disabled children. After a brief review of normal growth, assessment of maturity, regional growth, and regulating mechanisms, secular trends toward an increase in stature are discussed. The next topic addressed is physical fitness in young children. Motor skill development is also discussed. Two chapters explore the relative contributions of nature and nurture to the physical abilities of the child. The book includes a section on daily activity, physical performance, cardiorespiratory fitness, and obesity. One chapter reviews available literature on exercise and disease. A substantial bibliography is included.

Physical Activity and Well-Being. (1986). Edited by Vern Seefeldt. Reston, VA: American Alliance for Health, Physical Education, Recreation and Dance.

This volume reviews evidence in the biological and behavioral sciences relating physical activity to human well-being. Extensive bibliographies follow each chapter. Four of the chapters in Section I entitled Growth and Motor Function, will be of particular interest to child development specialists. Chapters 12 and 13 in Section III cover the topics of social and moral development in children. In Section V both chapters deal with children. Chapter 17 looks at the relationship of movement to cognition and Chapter 18 discusses the effects of physical education programs on children. References.

A Reanalysis of the Evidence for the Genetic Nature of Early Motor Development. (1985). Micha Razel. In *Advances in Applied Developmental Psychology*, Vol. 1, edited by Irving Sigel. Norwood, NJ: Ablex.

The chapter is a reanalysis of the empirical evidence most frequently cited as supporting the genetic theory of motor development. The analysis indicates that motor development can be accelerated by training and decelerated by conditions of deprivation. There is also evidence that there is a dependence of motor development on learning opportunities. The significance of the reanalysis shows strong evidence that those responsible for early child development must teach the child to sit, stand, and walk. Furthermore, the reanalysis indicates the importance of learning and instruction in human development over using lack of maturation as a convenient excuse. References.

Special Considerations of Exercise in Children and Adolescents. (1986). Oded Bar-Or. In *Nutrition and Exercise*, edited by Myron Winick. NY: John Wiley & Sons. (Current Concepts in Nutrition).

This chapter presents a select topic on pediatric exercise physiology. Some areas discussed include methodology of exercise testing, effects of training, and exercise prescription for the sick child. Fifty-eight references.

NUTRITION

Reports of Research

Children's Food Preferences: Developmental Patterns and Environmental Influences. (1987). Leann Lipps Birch. In *Annals of Child Development*, Vol. 4, edited by Ross Vasta. Greenwich, CT: JAI.

The focus of this paper is on the acquisition of food preferences and aversion to others. The author suggests that children learn which of the multiplicity of physiological, social, and psychological cues assist in controlling their food intake. Substantial references.

Malnutrition and Intellectual Development. (1976). Edited by John D. Lloyd-Still. Littleton, MA: Publishing Sciences Group.

A collection of five papers of empirical studies on the topic. Chase summarizes the data on alterations in brain cells, myelin lipid, and bran protein as the development of the brain is affected by malnutrition. Stein and Susser describe their studies of the effects of the Dutch famine of 1944 - 1945 on birth weight and subsequent mental development. Hurwitz's chapter on psychological testing is quite general and does not deal with the problems of assessment in societies where malnutrition is most severe. Chapter 5 on clinical studies of the effect of malnutrition on subsequent physical and mental development is an excellent summary of design problems and major findings of field studies.   The final chapter, on the social ecology of malnutrition, is general and speculative. This is a highly useful book for those who may be seeking a perspective on the worldwide problem of malnutrition and intellectual development. References.

Maternal Nutrition and Child Health. (1979). Douglas R. Shanklin, Jay Hodin. Springfield, IL: Charles C. Thomas.

This book deals with the relationship between nutrition in the prenatal period and the mental and physical health of the growing child. The initial chapter deals with the effect of starvation on reproduction and emphasizes the experiences in Holland and Russia during wartime. A discussion of influence of prenatal nutrition on birth weight, brain development, and the outcome of pregnancy is followed by an extensive discussion of the adverse consequences of sodium restriction during pregnancy and the nature and course of toxemia of pregnancy. The detailed chapter with the association between low birth weight and neuropsychiatric and physical disorders is followed by one relating the complications of pregnancy and low birth weight to conditions such as cerebral palsy, autism, hearing, reading and behavioral disorder, and mental deficiency. The final chapter looks at studies of the relationship of maternal diet and weight gain to infant health, and the influence of nutrition during infancy and early childhood on development. Substantial bibliography.

Other References

Nutrition in Infancy and Childhood. Third edition. (1985). Peggy L. Pipes. St. Louis, MO: Times Mirror/Mosby College.

A good beginning textbook with nutrition information about infants and children. Each chapter ends with lengthy references and suggested additional readings which will lead to research studies on the particular topic covered.

Pediatric Nutrition: Infant Feedings-Deficiencies-Diseases. (1982). Edited by Fima Lifshitz. NY: Marcel Dekker. (Clinical Disorders in Pediatric Nutrition).

This volume focuses on concepts in infant feeding as well as pathophysiology and management of frequently encountered disorders. The book is divided into three sections: (1) infant feedings; (2) nutritional deficiencies; and (3) nutrition and disease. Each of the thirty chapters is well referenced.

Pediatric Nutrition Handbook. Second edition. (1985). Committee on Nutrition, American Academy of Pediatrics. Elk Grove Village, IL: American Academy of Pediatrics.

This handbook summarizes knowledge concerning infant nutrition. The volume is divided into four sections. The first section, Feeding Normal Infants and Children, includes seven chapters. The next section is comprised of twelve chapters and is entitled Basic Nutrition Information. The third section covers Nutrition in Disease and contains thirteen chapters. Included in this section are chapters on obesity, nutrition and infection, hyperglycemia, iron deficiency, and chronic diarrhea. The last section includes chapters under the general heading of Dietary Modification. References.

Roberts' Nutrition Work with Children. Fourth edition. (1978). Ethel Austin Mortin, Virginia A. Beal. Chicago, IL: Univ. of Chicago Press.

This text reviews principles and procedures for attaining better nutritional health for children. The book assumes a basic knowledge of the science of nutrition. Of particular interest is Chapter 8 which summarizes worldwide nutrition programs. Also users might be interested in Appendix 5 which provides in outline form the milestones in history of the U.S. school lunch program from 1900 to 1975. The bibliographies found at the ends of each chapter are quite good.

SPORTS

General

Excerpta Medica Rehabilitation and Physical Medicine. Section 19. (1958 -). Amsterdam: Elsevier Science.

This is one of forty-four *Excerpta Medica* journals that are published ten times per year with a cumulative subject index in the final yearly issue (no. 10). The abstracts in each issue are arranged according to subject and may be scanned for current awareness on general topics. To help with more specific questions, each issue contains a detailed Table of Contents, author index, and subject index. These are accumulated in the last issue of each volume. This reference may be computer searched through the database called EMBASE which contains one and one-half to two times as many references as are announced in the abstract. Subject terms of interest include: child development, child psychiatry, child abuse, child behavior, child care, child health care, childhood cancer, handicapped child, learning, language, motor coordination, reading, sport, etc. This is one of the best databases of scholars or researchers doing work in the field of physical education.

Health, Physical Education, and Recreation Microform Publications. (1949 -). Eugene, OR: Univ. of Oregon, College of Health, Physical Education and Recreation.

A special type of reference consisting of indexes and the documents on microfiche. Presently there are five cumulative indexes, all on microfiche, to the collection of documents on microfiche. Materials included in this unique collection include doctoral dissertations and master's theses with some scholarly books and journals. Selection of the materials included is made by the College of Health, Physical Education and Recreation at the University of Oregon. A list of institutions subscribing to the collection is included in the indexes. Categories used in the indexing include: physical education, physiology of exercise, recreation and camping, health education, and psychology. An extremely fruitful resource of research in all areas of sport, physical education, health, and education.

Physical Education Index. Vol. 1 - . (1978 -). Cape Girardeau, MO: Ben Oak.

A subject index to domestic and foreign physical education and health professional journals. First published in March 1978, it is published quarterly with cumulative bound hardcover yearly index.

Physical Fitness/Sports Medicine. Vol 1 - . (1978 -). Washington, DC: Government Printing Office.

An index to 2,000 selected periodicals, including foreign language journals and papers. Subject coverage is sports medicine.

Sociobiology of Leisure and Sport Abstracts: A Review of Social Science Literature. Vol. 1 - . (1980 -). Amsterdam: Elsevier Scientific.

The content of the abstract is taken from the SIRLS database. Current journals, conference proceedings, unpublished papers, theses, monographs, and government documents are systematically searched for appropriate materials. SIRLS collects items pertaining to sport and other leisure activities including art, cultural development, play, games, and dance from the perspective of the social sciences, including anthropology, economics, social psychology, sociology, political science, and history. Foreign language materials are included. Their abstract is in English. Each quarterly is indexed by author and subject with a cumulative index appearing in the last issue each year. Indexes are straight-forward and easy to use. A list of the journals indexed appears at the beginning of each issue. All journals covered by current contents--social and behavioral sciences are checked for relevant articles. Subject index terms: childhood; child-development; elementary school; handicapped; motor-skill; perception; play; recreation; and youth-sport. A thesaurus of index terms does exist. This abstract is searchable by computer through the University of Waterloo, Waterloo, Ontario, Canada mainframe. Users should check with their librarians to see whether they have a password to search the SIRLS database.

Sport and Recreation Index. Vol. 1 - . (1973 -). Ottawa, Ontario: Sport Information Resource Centre.

Published twelve times a year, this index to sport and recreation journals is also a database searchable online through BRS. A letter preceding each item indicates for the user whether the article is basic reading material, intermediate level material, or advanced research material.

Sports and Physical Education: A Guide to the Reference Resources. (1983). B. Gratch, J. Lingenfelter. Westport, CT: Greenwood.

Part I covers popular reference materials useful in public libraries. Part II covers basic resources in sport and physical education. The guide has limited usefulness to scholars and graduate students.

SportSearch: The Contents of Current Sport Journals from throughout the World. Champaign, IL: Human Kinetics.

SportSearch monitors nearly 250 periodicals in sport and physical education over the world, mostly published in the English language. Published monthly, SportSearch is divided into four sections: Section I contains the sport specific journal contents, divided into categories such as aeronautical sports, basketball, etc.; Section II lists the contents for sport medicine and science periodicals, which are also divided into subcategories such as biomechanics, physiology, psychology, etc.; Section III is the professional section, listing periodicals for the professions of physical education, coaching, and officiating; Section IV includes abstracts which SIRC selected from recently received sport-related journals published within the last six to eight months. The abstracts are organized in subcategories concerning specific sport issues, sport medicine and science, as well as issues of concern to sport professionals. Different topics and journals appear in the abstracts each month.

Bibliographies

Bibliography of References for Intramural and Recreational Sports. (1975). R. McGuire, P. Mueller. Cornwall, NY: Leisure.

Lists and indexes 1,596 articles under thirty-two terms related to the administration of intramural and recreational sports' programs including information on elementary schools and play days. The bibliography is current through August 1975.

Reviews of Literature

AAHPER Research Consortium Symposium Papers: Socio-Psychological Dimensions, Research Design and Safety. Vol. 2. Book 3. (1979). R. H. Cox. Washington, DC: American Alliance for Health, Physical Education, Recreation, and Dance. (ED 171 717).

The symposium papers provide the reader with a synthesis of research in physical education and sports. In this particular volume multivariate considerations in children's physical education is covered as well as a discussion of planning children's physical education programs to enhance self-esteem.

Cardiorespiratory Exercise Training in Children. (July 1986). Stanley P. Sady. In *Clinics in Sports Medicine*, Vol. 5, No. 3.

Reviews longitudinal studies involving children in aerobic physical activity. The author divides the studies into short-term aerobic training (less than six months' duration) and long-term training studies (longer than six months' duration). Fifty-four citations are included.

Children and Exercise XII. (1986). Edited by Joseph Rutenfranz, Rolf Mocellin, Ferdinand Klimt. Champaign, IL: Human Kinetics. (International Series on Sport Science, Vol. 17).

Papers are divided under nine parts. The three papers in Part I discuss aerobic and anaerobic energy output in children, nutritional concerns of young athletes, and indicators and risk factors of cardiovascular diseases during childhood. Part II contains three papers on age-related metabolic processes. The four papers included under Part III discuss anaerobic thresholds for different types of exercise. Part IV contains twelve papers on physical activity, training, and cardiovascular risk indicators. Part V contains nine papers, three of which are longitudinal studies, covering various aspects of circulation. Part VI has two papers on respiration. Locomotor apparatus is the topic of the four papers in Part VII. The four papers in Part VIII cover physical performance and motor learning. The final section of the volume contains three papers. The first paper is entitled, "Electrical Impedance Cardiography as a Noninvasive Technique for Exercise Testing of Children." The second paper is entitled, "Dynamic Exercise Echocardiography in Children." And the final paper in the section is entitled, "Heat-Stress Reactions of the Growing Child." References.

Children in Sport: A Contemporary Anthology. (1978). Edited by Richard A. Magill, Michael Ash, Frank Smoll. Champaign, IL: Human Kinetics.

This anthology provides insight into what researchers consider important issues regarding competitive sport and children. The book is a compilation of eighteen papers grouped under six headings; namely, Historical Perspective, Readiness for Participation, Anatomical and Physiological Concerns, Psychological Issues, Moral Development, and Socialization Processes, with each section preceded by a short introduction by the editors giving an overview of the section. Within respective sections, some of the following topics were addressed: The Rise of Highly Organized Sports for Preadolescent Boys, The Conceptual Readiness Applied to Motor Skill Acquisition, Physical Growth and Maturity Characteristics of Young Athletes, Some Detrimental Effects of Competitive Sports on Children's Behavior, Moral Behavior of Children Particularly in Competitive Sports, and The Child in Competitive Sport: Influence of the Social Milieu. The editors expressed the hope " . . . that this anthology will serve as a strong base from which much needed research will emanate." References.

Completed Research in Health, Physical Education, and Recreation Including International Sources. (1959 -). Washington, DC: American Alliance for Health, Physical Education, Recreation, and Dance.

Published yearly, the references are divided into three general sections. First is a subject index to all the references cited in the next two sections. The second section is a bibliography of published research for that year, citing articles published in the 177 or more periodicals reviewed by the committee. Section III is the listing of the master's theses and doctoral dissertations from 74 institutions offering graduate programs in health, physical education, recreation, and allied areas. Most of the entries are abstracted.

Critical Periods: Relation to Youth Sports. (1982). Richard A. Magill. In *Children in Sport*, Second edition, edited by Richard Magill, Michael Ash, Frank Small. Champaign, IL: Human Kinetics.

This chapter discusses the construct of critical learning periods in regard to the child and sport. Also discussed is the importance of identifying when a child is optimally ready to learn a skill. The author gives a brief overview of how critical periods have historically been viewed in the developmental literature. A model of readiness is suggested that can appropriately be applied to the sport skill learning situation. References.

Effects of Physical Activity on Children: A Special Tribute to Mabel Lee. (1986). Edited by G. Alan Stull, Helen M. Eckert. Champaign, IL: Human Kinetics. (American Academy of Physical Education Papers, No. 19).

This volume contains an overview of progress in the study of the moral, social, psychological, and physical effects of exercise on children. Five articles emphasize the importance of physical education in the development of self-esteem, moral and social behavior, and intellectual performance in children. Four articles present evidence that the quality, as well as quantity, of physical activity also is important for biological health. Findings on the effects of strenuous exercise on growth, development, and health are inconclusive. The authors highlight various difficulties in research on the effects of exercise on the health of children. The final article reviews findings of the few large-scale national surveys that have been conducted to ascertain the level of physical fitness of children in the United States. This is an important reference for physical educators. References.

Effects of Physical Education Programs on Children. (1986). Paul G. Vogel. In *Physical Activity and Well-Being*, edited by Vern Seefeldt, Chapter 18. Reston, VA: American Alliance for Health, Physical Education, Recreation, and Dance.

This chapter identifies the health or performance related effects of exercise in the school setting on academic achievement and related topics. Two major divisions of information and brief summaries are presented in the chapter. The first includes evidence on the effects of physical education programs on school children. The second discusses the implications of the review.

Health Education and Youth: A Review of Research and Development. (1984). Edited by G. Campbell. Philadelphia, PA: Falmer.

This review of research is a result of the National Conference on Research and Development in Health Education which met at the University of Southampton in September 1982. A wide range of areas is covered: health knowledge and beliefs; smoking; health education for exceptional children, primary and secondary schools;. and initial and in-service health education. References.

Pediatric and Adolescent Sports' Injuries: Recent Trends. (1986). Lyle J. Micheli. In *Exercise and Sport Science Reviews*, Vol. 14, edited by Kent Pandolf. NY: Macmillan. (Exercise and Sport Science Reviews).

The author, a doctor, discusses injuries resulting from various activities and reviews the literature. Forty-six references.

Preschool and Elementary School Children and Physical Activity. (1984). ICHPER World Congress. Jerusalem, Israel: Emmanuel Gill.

The volume presents eighteen studies dealing with young children. Topics covered include: content and methodology in activity programs; child-centered primary programs; psychomotor research and development of preschool children; evaluation of physical educators; movement education; self-assessment approach to P.E. on the perceptual-motor development of seven- to eight-year-old children; structured P.E. on scholastic progress of culturally disadvantaged first graders; impact of movement education on motor and intellectual behavior of children in primary school; intellectual structure of elementary school-age athletes; influences of group-oriented and individual-oriented physical education programs; motor activity of preschool children; children's learning of motor skills; and impact of daily exercise on the biological, motor, and psycho-social development of primary school children. References.

Psychological Aspects of Sports Participation in Young Children. (1981). Amy Bookman Livingood, Catherine Goldwater, B. KurzRonald. In *Advances in Behavioral Pediatrics*, Vol. 2, edited by Bonnie Camp. Greenwich, CT: JAI. (Advances in Behavioral Pediatrics).

The chapter reviews research dealing with several aspects of children's involvement with sports. First studies dealing with personality and socialization functions affecting sports' participation are reviewed. Next the chapter integrates the theory and empirical findings regarding children's readiness for sports' involvement, including motor development and psychological factors. The chapter concludes with suggestions for further research. References.

Psychological Perspectives in Youth Sports. (1978). Edited by Frank L. Smoll, Ronald E. Smith. Washington, DC: Hemisphere. (Series in Clinical and Community Psychology).

Book discusses the status and effects of sport participation on the physical and psychosocial development of children. The ten research reports that follow are divided into three major sections. The first section, entitled Participatory Patterns and Characteristics of Youth Athletes, contains two reports. The second section, The Impact of Sports on Psychosocial Development, contains six reports. The final section of the book, Sport and the Handicapped Child, contains two studies involving handicapped children. Indexed.

Psychology of Motor Behavior and Sports. 4 Vols. (1976 - 1980). North American Society for the Psychology of Sport and Physical Activity. Champaign, IL: Human Kinetics.

Proceedings of the North American Society for the Psychology of Sport and Physical Activity. Each volume is on one or more topics, such as motor behavior, motor development, sport psychology, motor learning and control, children in sport and physical activity, motivation, sex differences and sex roles. Ceased publication with the 1980 volume. References.

Social Development. (1986). George H. Sage. In *Physical Activity and Well-Being*, edited by Vern Seefeldt, Chapter 12. Reston, VA: American Alliance for Health, Physical Education, Recreation, and Dance.

This chapter summarizes what is known about the effects of involvement in physical activities on social development in children. No definitive answers seem to appear after searching the current research literature. References.

What Research Tells the Practitioner about the Effects of Exercise on Children. (1976). R. Bird. Birmingham, AL: Univ. of Alabama Press.

A survey of physical educators reveals that physical development, especially its more specific parts dealing with physical fitness, is thought to be the least important P.E. objective of K - 2. Research is available on physical fitness as it relates to (1) incidence of childhood obesity, (2) cardiovascular endurance, (3) differential treatment of the sexes, and (4) participation in contact sports by children.

Other References

Encyclopedia of Physical Education, Fitness, and Sport. 4 vols. (1977 - 1985). Menlo Park, CA: Addison-Wesley.

A four-volume encyclopedia sponsored by the American Alliance for Health, Physical Education and Recreation. Each volume focuses on a different aspect of physical education and was published over an eight-year span. Volumes 2 - 4 have materials of interest to the child development specialist. Volume 2 is subtitled, Training, Environment, Nutrition, and Fitness. Volume 3 is subtitled, Sports, Dance, and Related Activities. Volume 4 is titled, Human Fitness. Each volume contains an index.

Physical Education for Preschool and Primary Grades. (1985). Noeline Thompson Kelly, Brian John Kelly. Springfield, IL: Charles C. Thomas.

This book provides activities and games which the primary teacher may use with the young child. The activities included were chosen because they exercise young minds as well as young bodies. For each activity objectives, equipment and play method are provided. The book is well-illustrated with photographs and graphics. The book is divided into ten chapters each covering a broad subject area: activities to stretch the muscles, tumbling and gymnastics, dance activities; throwing, catching, aiming, striking activities; races, relays and contests; physical fitness; water play; and physical education for special populations, methods. Section III, entitled Dance Activities, also includes singing games. Scores are provided with the text. References.

Recreation Programming for Visually Impaired Children and Youth. (1981). Jerry D. Kelley. NY: American Foundation for the Blind.

This volume represents a unique resource for trainers or consultants in visually impaired programs. The text explores the problems of providing recreational activities to visually impaired children and youth. Chapter 1, besides supplying a history of services to the visually impaired, provides two charts, one listing legislation affecting education and recreation and a second chart giving a chronology of events leading to integration of the visually impaired child into the community. Chapter 7 provides a list of national organizations serving the visually impaired; state and regional resources; federal resources; national organizations related to the visually impaired; recreational resources including products and suppliers; and graded physical activities for the visually impaired by sport activity. References and index.

11

Atypical Development

DATABASES
TO CONSIDER

Embase
Exceptional Child
Educational Resources
Medline

ERIC
PsycINFO

GENERAL

Bibliographies

An Annotated Bibliography on Mainstreaming the Hearing Impaired, the Mentally Retarded and the Visually Impaired in the Regular Classroom. (1978). Ronald D. Hein, Milo E. Bishop. NY: National Technical Institute for the Deaf (Rochester).

This two-volume set focuses on the mainstreaming of the hearing impaired, the mentally retarded, and the visually impaired from 1966 to January 1977. Materials cited include books, journal articles, conference papers, ERIC documents, and other published and unpublished reports. Volume 1 is a listing by authors and Volume 2 is a listing by topic.

Child Welfare Training and Practice, an Annotated Bibliography. (1982). John Pardeck, Rebecca L. Hegar, Kathy Newton-Nance, Cynthia Christy-Baker. Westport, CT: Greenwood.

Includes books, journals, training manuals, and audio visual materials published after 1964. Entries are arranged in seven sections by field of child welfare specialization: abuse and neglect; law and the court; substitute care; in-home service and parent education; institutions and special needs children; minority clients; and training and interviewing methods. An author and a subject index is included.

Learning and Communication Disorders: An Abstracted Bibliography, 1971 - 1980. (1982). Washington, DC: American Psychological Association. (PsycINFO RETROSPECTIVE).

Covers the decade from 1971 to 1980. Included are journal articles, books, and monographs. Entries are divided into three broad subject areas: theories, research and assessment; treatment and rehabilitation; and education issues. Under each of these subject areas are ten categories: behavior disorders, dyslexia, hyperkinesis, learning disorders, reading disabilities, psychoneurological disorders, communication disorders, hearing disorders, language disorders, and speech disorders. The volume concludes with a separate subject and author index.

Reviews of Literature

Advances in Special Education. Vols. 1 - 5. (1980 - 1986). Edited by Barbara K. Keogh. Greenwich, CT: JAI.

These five volumes review research in the area of special education. A variety of topics is covered. Chapters in each volume end with bibliographies. Each volume also contains separate author and subject indexes.

Approaches to Child Treatment: Introduction to Theory, Research, and Practice. (1986). James H. Johnson, Wiley C. Rasbury, Lawrence J. Siegel. NY: Pergamon.

An overview to child treatment methods, and their applicability to various types of problems. Treatment methods covered include: drug therapies, play therapies, family therapies, and child behavior therapies. A lengthy bibliography follows each chapter.

Developmental Disabilities: Theory, Assessment, and Intervention. (1982). Edited by M. Lewis, L. T. Taft. NY and London: Spectrum.

This volume initiates an interdisciplinary approach to the study, assessment, and treatment of developmentally disabled preschool children. The volume contains twenty-five chapters on developmental disabilities in the preschool child. The book is divided into five sections representing different areas of preschool development: sensory development (eight chapters), motor development (three chapters), cognitive development (six chapters), language development (three chapters), and affective/temperament development (five chapters). References.

Developmental Problems in Infancy and Preschool Years. (1986). Edited by Barbara K. Keogh. Greenwich, CT: JAI. (Advances in Special Education, Vol. 5).

Nine papers make up the volume, all addressing different problems of development. Topics covered include developmental disabilities, language disorders, social and behavioral problems, motor development problems, developmentally delayed children, and at-risk infants. Lengthy bibliographies follow each chapter.

The Relationship of Preschool Behavior and Learning Patterns to Later School Functioning. (1981). Robert W. Chamberlin. In *Advances in Behavioral Pediatrics*, Vol. 2, edited by Bonnie Camp. Greenwich, CT: JAI.

The chapter reviews the research looking at data supporting early identification of mental and physical disorders which might affect normal development if not treated early. The review indicates that a child's functioning at any given point or time is a complex mix of interacting biological and environmental variables which makes prediction of future outcomes difficult. References.

The Year Book of Psychiatry and Applied Mental Health. (1970 -). Chicago, IL: Year Book Medical.

Gives an overview of recent findings and theories in the field. Chapters are footnoted. Several sections in each yearbook will be of interest to the child development specialists: Learning and Memory, Mental Retardation, and Child and Adolescent Psychiatry. At the conclusion of each yearbook a separate author and subject index is provided.

Other References

Childhood Disorders: Preschool and Early Elementary Years. (1984). Joseph N. Murray, Caven S. McLoughlin. Springfield, IL: Charles C. Thomas.

A concise look at both the etiological and the remedial aspects of the following major childhood disorders; asthma, cultural-familial retardation, epilepsy, autism, cerebral palsy, overactivity, social isolation, enuresis and encopresis, school phobia, and developmental communication disorders. References.

Counseling and Therapy for Children. (1984). Jim Gumaer. NY: Free Press.

Part I focuses on information that is essential to successful counseling of individual child clients. Nine chapters cover: child development and counseling; child-centered counseling; play therapy and play process;

developmental play; art therapy; music therapy; bibliotherapy; behavioral counseling; and relaxation and guided fantasy. In Part II ideas discussed in Part I are explored in relation to counseling children in groups. The four chapters encompass: child-centered group counseling; growth-centered group counseling; problem-centered group counseling; and family counseling. In Part III consultation procedures are discussed as an integral part of the overall counseling process. References, recommended readings, and some periodical titles are provided with each chapter.

Diagnostic and Statistical Manual of Mental Disorders: DSM-III-R. Third edition, revised. (1987). Washington, DC: American Psychiatric Association.

Provides a classification of mental disorders including: descriptions of the clinical features of the disorders, and identifiable behavioral signs or symptoms such as disorientation, mood disturbance, or psychomotor agitation. Everyone working in the area of atypical behavior in child development will find this an invaluable reference.

Dictionary of Special Education and Rehabilitation, Second edition. (1985). Leo J. Kelly, Glen A. Vergason. Denver, CO: Love.

This special dictionary for the field of special education represents a major expansion and improvement over the first edition. At the end of the volume Kelly provides a list of associations and national centers associated with fields of special education; sources of legal assistance; microcomputer and technical centers; and finally a list of clearinghouses.

Encyclopedia of Special Education: A Reference for the Education of the Handicapped and Other Exceptional Children and Adults. (1987). Edited by Cecil R. Reynolds and Lester Mann. NY: Wiley-Interscience.

This three-volume work is concerned with all types of special individuals, including the gifted. The set is broken into seven categories, among them descriptions of educational and psychological test, interventions and service delivery, handicapping conditions, services related to special education, and legal issues. Biographies of current and past key figures are included. Major professional associations and special education journals and related fields are included. The text of PL 94-142 is included in the appendix. Entries are signed and range in length from one paragraph to several pages.

Family Violence Prevention Resource Guide for Air Force Helping Professionals. 2 vols. (1987). Washington, DC: Air Force Family Matters Branch.

A guide to preventive programs in the areas of parenting, sexual abuse, child abuse, alcohol abuse, stress management, and growing up skills. Volume 1 covers program development issues. Volume 2 contains the course outlines for workshops. In Volume 1 users will find a list of national organizations involved in areas of interest to child development specialists. The workshops for parenting in Volume 2 will be of interest to those conducting parenting classes.

Resource Guide to Special Education: Terms/Laws/Assessment Procedures/ Organizations. Second edition. (1986). William E. Davis. Boston, MA: Allyn and Bacon.

The guide is divided into five sections: terminology of special education and related areas; acronyms and abbreviations used in the field; assessment procedures; federal legislation and litigation; and selected agencies and organizations concerned with exceptional persons. Where appropriate, references are provided.

EXCEPTIONAL CHILDREN

Bibliographies

Down's Syndrome: A Comprehensive Bibliography. (1980). Siegfried M. Pueschel. NY: Garland STPM.

Catalogues over 6,000 references under general topics such as: dental/orofacial conditions; education/early intervention; growth and development; otolaryngology; psychology; pharmacology; speech/language; therapy/management; and twins/triplets. Unfortunately the volume does not include a general index so entries must be located through subject categories.

Dyslexia: An Annotated Bibliography. (1982). Martha M. Evans. Westport, CT: Greenwood. (Contemporary Problems of Childhood, No. 5).

This annotated bibliography on dyslexia lists more than 2,400 English language items. Books, journal articles, conference reports, proceedings of symposia, government documents, dissertations, collections of papers, chapters or parts of books, and articles from popular presses are included. The bibliography concludes with a separate author and subject index.

The Hyperkinetic Child: An Annotated Bibliography, 1974 - 1979. (1981). Carol Ann Winchell. Westport, CT: Greenwood. (Contemporary Problems of Childhood: A Bibliographic Series, No. 4).

Identifies, collects, classifies, abstracts, and indexes relevant literature on the topic of the hyperkinetic child. There are approximately 2,000 entries.

Mental Retardation, an Abstracted Bibliography, 1971 - 1980. (1982). Washington, DC: American Psychological Association. (PsycINFO RETROSPECTIVE).

Covers journal articles, monographs, and books published during the decade. Entries are divided among three general sections: theories, research and assessment; treatment and rehabilitation; and educational issues. Under each of these three sections are seven categories of retardation: autism, mental retardation, Down's syndrome, institutionalized mentally retarded, mild mental retardation, moderate mental retardation, and severe mental retardation. A separate subject and author index concludes the volume. References.

The Physically Handicapped: an Annotated Bibliography of Empirical Research Studies, 1970 - 1979. (1981). William A. Pearman, Phillip Starr. NY: Garland.

Reports research dealing with physically handicapped from about 102 professional journals.

Social Behavior of Mentally Retarded, An Annotated Bibliography. (1984). Manny Sternlicht, George Windholz. NY: Garland.

Chapter 1 covers patterns of social development; Chapter 2, family interactions; Chapter 3, peer and other interactions; Chapter 4, social adjustment in the classroom; Chapter 5, emotional disturbances; Chapter 6, criminal and delinquent behavior; Chapter 7, social adjustment and institutional settings; Chapter 8, community adjustments; Chapter 9, vocational and occupational adjustment; Chapter 10, leisure time pursuits; and Chapter 11, independent living. Within each chapter, entries are alphabetical by author. Because of the lack of a general subject index, users must depend on the table of contents.

Reviews of Literature

Autism: A Reappraisal of Concepts and Treatment. (1978). Edited by Michael Rutter, Eric Schopler. NY: Plenum.

This volume provides information on research, educational practices, clinical practices, and present knowledge about autism from an international point of view. Chapters deal with individual topics. A detailed subject index is provided. References.

The Development of Mediated Behavior in Children: An Alternative View of Learning Disabilities. (1982). Craig R. Barclay, John W. Hagen. In *Theory and Research in Learning Disabilities*, edited by Das, Mulcahey, Wall. NY and London: Plenum.

Reviews research supporting the idea that the LD child's memory development results from a growing ability to (1) use a mnemonic device; and (2) become aware of the causative relationship between strategy use and improved performance. A lengthy bibliography is provided. References.

Hyperactivity in Children: Etiology, Measurement, and Treatment Implications. (1979). Edited by Ronald L. Trites. Baltimore, MD: Univ. Park Press.

Reviews child hyperactivity in a series of readable conference papers. Topics covered include: diagnosis and assessment, prevalence, early intervention, food allergies, medication, and behavior therapy. References.

Labeling the Mentally Retarded: Clinical and Social System Perspectives on Mental Retardation. (1973). Jane R. Mercer. Berkeley, CA: Univ. of California Press.

Describes the history, the outcomes, and the relevant conclusions of a research effort aimed at comprehending the nature and extent of mental retardation in an American community. The first two chapters contain a description of the conceptual framework of the book. A careful analysis of the research setting is reported in Chapter 3. Chapters 4 through 7, and 8 through 12, discuss social systems and epidemiology. The final five chapters and three appendixes contain the outcomes and the relevant data of the research. The book has to be read carefully and thoroughly in order to be appreciated. The report constitutes a landmark in the study of the nature of mental retardation. References.

Malformations of Development: Biological and Psychological Sources and Consequences. (1984). Edited by Eugene S. Gollin. NY: Academic. (Developmental Psychology Series).

This book contains a varied group of nine reviews. Gollin gives an overview of the diagnostic process. Haas describes the background of the present labeling practices and resulting confusion. Chapter 3 is an overview of results when children suffer developmental delay and are labeled mentally retarded. Chapter 4 considers the interplay between the characteristics of children and their environment. Chapter 5 discusses hyperactivity. Chapter 6 draws a clear distinction between linguistic competence and linguistic performance. Chapter 7 describes and reviews environmental effects on the nervous system. Chapter 8 directs attention to the difficulty of establishing cause-effect relationships for human beings. Finally, Chapter 9, Genetics, presents a rather brief account of what is known about the genetics of particular human disorders and a summary of concepts relative to the inheritance of intelligence. References.

Movement Education and Severely Subnormal Children: A Review of the Literature. (1985). Joan Lishman. In *Early Child Development and Care*, 21 (1 - 3).

This 91-page journal article is a comprehensive review of the literature on movement education and severely retarded children. Twenty-five pages of bibliography are appended to the review.

Neurobehavioral and Perceptual Dysfunction in Learning Disabled Children. (1985). D. C. Morrison. Lewiston, NY: C. J. Hogrefe.

Presents theory and research concerning children who, shortly after birth, present signs of subtle neurobehavioral deviations from normal development. Chapter 10 is a description of children's responses to failure to learn, and the concluding chapter is an evaluation of attempts to intervene with neurobehaviorally dysfunctional children. References.

Perceptual and Learning Disabilities in Children. Vol. 2: Research and Theory. (1975). Edited by William M. Cruickshank, Daniel P. Hallahan. Syracuse, NY: Syracuse Univ. Press.

The second volume of a two-volume set, this book is devoted to theory and research. There are chapters concerned with sociocultural and nutritional deprivation, selective attention, motor and perceptual pathology, and the effects of distractors, as well as chapters dealing with special education strategies, behavior modification, and pharmaceutical treatment. Hallahan's chapter on distractibility deserves special notice for its discussion of research which provides an empirical base for a concept that has traditionally been given importance but not much substance. References.

Symbolic Development in Atypical Children: New Directions for Child Development. No. 36. (Summer 1987). Edited by Dante Cicchetti, Marjorie Beeghly. San Francisco, CA: Jossey-Bass. (Jossey-Bass Quarterly Series).

The six chapters in this volume highlight the development of symbolic processes in atypical children. Beeghly and Cicchetti review the results of longitudinal studies with Downs syndrome. Sigman and Mundy discuss deficits in social understanding and symbolic representations of autistic children. Chapter 3 suggests that maltreatment experiences exert harmful effects on communicative development of youngsters. Chapter 4 presents evidence that biological and environmental factors play an important role in ontogenesis of symbolization. The chapter by Snyder presents her research on symbolization in language-impaired children. Chapter 6 covers the topic of symbolic development in deaf children. Each chapter contains a lengthy bibliography of cited sources. A subject index to the monograph is provided.

Vestibular Processing Dysfunction in Children. (1985). Edited by Kenneth J. Ottenbacher, Margaret A. Short. NY: Haworth.

Provides current information on the anatomy and clinical assessment of vestibular system, and reviews clinical research relevant to vestibular processing in handicapped infants and children. Physical and occupational therapists, social workers, psychologists, and other professionals interested in the education and treatment of handicapped infants and children will find this volume a reliable and helpful resource. References.

Reports of Research

Brothers and Sisters of Retarded Children: An Exploratory Study. (1972). Frances Kaplan Grossman. Syracuse, NY: Syracuse Univ. Press.

Reports results of a research program designed to determine if growing up with a retarded sibling influences normal children's curiosity, self-concept, or feelings toward their parents. Although both case study and group data are reported, the major evidence for the study was derived from interviews with 149 subjects recruited from an Ivy League college, a private women's college, and two community colleges. Both statistical summaries and rich extracts from the interviews are reported. The material is organized to permit the nonstatistically oriented to skip sections while losing neither the richness nor the thrust of the argument. For those interested, still greater statistical detail is presented in the appendixes. References.

The Children of Kauai: A Longitudinal Study from the Prenatal Period to Age Ten. (1971). Emmy E. Werner, Jesse M. Bierman, Fern E. French. Honolulu, HI: Univ. of Hawaii Press.

This classic summarizes the findings of a longitudinal study of 3,000 pregnancies on the island of Kauai and followed-up over 1,000 of the live-born children and their families. Chapters 1 - 4 describe the setting and population of the study along with a review of related empirical studies. Chapter 5 details the outcome of all the pregnancies occurring in the Kauai community. Chapters 6 and 7 delve into the short- and long-term effects of perinatal complications and environmental deprivation on the physical, cognitive, and social development of preschool and school age children. Chapter 9 deals with the predictive value of early pediatric and psychological examinations. Chapter 10 discusses variations in child development associated with cultural factors. Chapter 11 discusses sex differences in the rate of intellectual maturation and responsiveness to achievement demands at home. Later studies reported in *Kauai's Children Come of Age* and *Vulnerable but Invincible: A Longitudinal Study of Resilient Children and Youth*. References.

Kauai's Children Come of Age. (1977). Emmy E. Werner, Ruth S. Smith. Honolulu, HI: Univ. of Hawaii Press.

This classic reports the fourth phase of the Kauai longitudinal study. Gives the follow-up data on subjects after the age of ten who were originally part of the study reported in *The Children of Kauai*. Of the original sample, 614 subjects were available for the follow-up. "The objectives of this study were (a) to assess the long term consequences of the learning and behavior disorders diagnosed in childhood by age 10; (b) to identify additional behavior disorders developed in the interval between 10 and 18 years of age; (c) to evaluate the predictive validity of diagnostic signs from records at birth as well as psychological and pediatric examinations and family interviews at ages two and ten in forecasting later behavior and learning disorders; (d) to examine the effectiveness of the community agencies' responses to youth at risk; and (e) to isolate demographic, family, and interpersonal variables that contribute to improvement in diagnostic status." References.

Lives of the Mentally Retarded: A Forty-Year Follow-Up Study. (1985). Robert T. Ross, Michael J. Begab, Earnst H. Dondis, James S. Giampiccolo, Jr., Edward C. Meyers. Stanford, CA: Stanford Univ. Press.

Describes the results of a unique study of school children identified as mentally retarded in the 1920s and 1930s. A sample of former pupils of ungraded classes in San Francisco who had exhibited both difficulties in classroom learning and low scores on individual intelligence tests were located. All participants were interviewed and administered the Wechsler Adult Intelligence Scale and the California Psychological Inventory. Following detailed descriptions of these methodological aspects of the study, separate chapters are devoted to presenting statistical data comparing the four groups with respect to aspects of (1) childhood environment; (2) education; (3) intelligence, personality, and self-evaluation; (4) work; and (5) social milieu.   Many interesting findings are presented in concise and readable prose: for example, it was found that, as adults, these individuals lost their identity as mentally retarded persons and most of them were functioning as self-supporting members of the community. References.

Vulnerable but Invincible: A Longitudinal Study of Resilient Children and Youth. (1982). Emmy E. Werner, Ruth S. Smith. NY: McGraw-Hill.

A sequel to *The Children of Kauai* and *Kauai's Children Come of Age*. This report focuses on two groups of children of Kauai, those who developed serious behavior and those with learning problems. Data are given on vulnerability and resiliency from a variety of perspectives. Chapters look at the effects of care-giving environment, sex differences, and stressful life events. A few individual case studies are included. References.

Other References

Autistic States in Children. (1981). Frances Tustin. London: Routledge & Kegan Paul.

Outlines the author's theory of autism which borrows heavily from the psychoanalytic writings of Mahler and Winnicott. The book is divided into three major sections. The first two sections deal with the etiology and treatment of autistic disorders, while the third provides clinical descriptions of specific children. References.

Bilingual Special Education Resource Guide. (1982). Edited by Carol H. Thomas, James L. Thomas. Phoenix, AZ: Oryx.

A guide for individuals involved with educational programming of the bilingual special child. Articles in the first part discuss major concerns of bilingual special educators. Information sources in the second part include lists of agencies and centers involved with bilingual special education, teacher training programs, indexes, databases, and journals, and a directory of individuals with expertise in the field. The appendix lists procedures and distributors of bilingual special education materials. A bibliography concludes the volume.

Exceptional Infants. Vol. 3. Assessment and Intervention. (1975). B. Z. Friedlander, Graham M. Sterritt, Girven E. Kirk. NY: Brunner/Mazel. (Exceptional Infant).

The third volume of the series gives a practical overview of assessment and intervention techniques used with the exceptional infant. Part I focuses on problems of developmentally disabled children with readily identifiable special needs, concerns and programs for minority or disadvantaged children, and issues of developmental assessment in all aspects of children's growth. Part II addresses the issues of children from low-income families and minority groups. Part III addresses research and clinical findings in the areas of language development, interaction of environment and cognitive development, psychological assessment, and cultural influences. Part IV covers screening techniques. Although old, the reference will be of interest and value to researchers in the discipline. References.

The Use of Rationally Defined Subgroups in Research on Learning Disabilities. (1982). Joseph K. Torgenson. In *Theory and Research in Learning Disabilities*, edited by Das, Mulcahy, Wall. NY and London: Plenum.

Chapter sets forth, step-by-step, the goals an investigator needs to meet in investigating cognition of an LD subtype. The chapter is considered required reading by many experts in the field. References.

GIFTED

Bibliographies

Annotated Bibliography on Academically Talented Students. (1961). John Curtis Gowan. Washington, DC: National Education Association.

Volume provides a thorough review of published materials on the gifted during the 1950s. Emphasis was given to research, theoretical essays, and reference materials such as bibliographies. Entries are briefly annotated. Users wishing a bibliography of earlier literature should consult Paul Witty's *The Gifted Child.*

Annotated Bibliography on Creativity & Giftedness. (1965). John Curtis Gowan. Northridge, CA: San Fernando Valley State College Foundation.

This annotated bibliography includes writings on creativity and gifted children since 1960 to the date of publication. Citations are in alphabetical order by name of the principal author. The bibliographic index where these citations may be found by subject has been arranged in a numbering system. The general headings are: general; theory and objectives; characteristics; practice; curriculum; guidance; administration; and research.

The Gifted Child. (1951). Edited by Paul A. Witty. Boston, MA: D. C. Heath.

A classic in the area of gifted education that contains an annotated bibliography on the gifted, pp. 277 - 323, by Elise H. Martins. Along with John Gowan's *Annotated Bibliography on the Academically Talented Student*, it provides a complete bibliography on the gifted up to 1961.

The Gifted Student: An Annotated Bibliography. (1977). Jean Laubenfels. Westport, CT: Greenwood. (Contemporary Problems of Childhood; A Bibliographic Series, No. 1).

This bibliography covers the literature since 1961. Of the 1,300 references, a majority will be of interest to teachers, administrators, counselors, school psychologists, and others working in education. Entries were located through both extensive manual and computerized information sources. Included are books, chapters in books, conference reports, government documents, pamphlets, and dissertations. Items excluded are anthropological studies, unpublished papers, foreign language references, personal correspondence, newspaper articles, and speeches. Entries are grouped according to the major categories listed in the contents. The book includes an author and selective key word subject index.

Reviews of Literature

Beyond Universals in Cognitive Development. (1980). David Henry Feldman. Norwood, NJ: Ablex. (Publications for the Advancement of Theory and History in Psychology).

The author brings together theories and research on cognitive development moving from the idea of "universals" to recognition of many other realms of human activity. The individual chapters are arranged to take the reader from the basic theoretical realms to a set of topics illustrating these views. Chapter 4 discusses the creative thinking process. Chapters 5 and 6 deals with child prodigies and education. Chapter 6 looks at the relation of developmental theory to education. The book is meant to be read as a whole so may cause some frustration to readers interested only in certain sections. References.

Creativity, Theory and Research. (1973). Edited by Morton Bloomberg. New Haven, CT: College and University Press.

An anthology of theoretical and research papers on creativity. After a comprehensive introduction, the book is divided into seven chapters which represent the psychoanalytic, humanistic, environmental, associative, factorial, cognitive-developmental, and holistic approaches to creativity. Each chapter begins with a theoretical article followed by supportive research. The book ends with an epilogue chapter that contains papers exploring various cultural and conceptual problems involved in creativity. Each chapter is well referenced.

The Gifted and Talented, Developmental Perspectives. (1985). Frances Degen Horowitz, Marion O'Brien. Washington, DC: American Psychological Association.

The volume provides the reader with a summary of current knowledge about gifted and talented children. Fourteen chapters are divided among three parts. Part I covers the nature of giftedness and includes chapters delving into cognitive development, creativity tests, and cultural perspectives of development of talent. Part II, entitled Aspects of Giftedness, contains chapters on the psychosocial development of gifted children, programs, problems of programs for minority gifted, and sex differences. Part III contains five chapters which explore approaches to studying the development of the gifted. Chapters conclude with references. A separate author and subject index is provided.

Gifted, Talented, and Creative Young People: A Guide to Theory, Teaching and Research. (1987). Morris I. Stein. NY: Garland.

Summarizes and annotates a wide range of works representing the major issues, orientations, research results, curricular, and instructional programs. Classical studies in theory and research are included. Focus is mainly on the literature between 1970 and 1980.

Intellectual Talent: Research and Development. Proceedings of the Sixth Annual Hyman Blumberg Symposium on Research in Early Childhood Education. (1976). Edited by Daniel P. Keating. Baltimore, MD: Johns Hopkins Univ. Press.

Seventeen papers presented at the Sixth Annual Hyman Blumberg Symposium held on October 4, 1974 at Johns Hopkins University are included in this volume. The volume is divided into four major sections. Sections I - III are composed of five chapters each with the final section containing only three chapters. The first section addresses the issue of identification and measurement problems. The second section deals with educational research programs. The third section describes the psychological characteristics of highly gifted youth. The fourth section contains critiques and general discussion. References.

The Psychology of Gifted Children: Perspectives on Development and Education. (1985). Edited by Joan Freeman. Chichester, England: John Wiley & Sons.

This volume provides an international perspective of 25 contributors from eight countries from four continents, on the topic of giftedness. Some of the contributions are reviews of current research. Gruber's chapter concludes that high-level cognition is associated with special sleep patterns and that the rate of REM sleep is positively correlated with IQ and is particularly high in gifted children. The Gruber contribution suggests that "high occulomotor rates observed in gifted children . . . may indicate a superior ability to organize information, and thus an advanced maturity of processing." One research report by Zi-Xiu of the People's Republic of China describes an initial effort to examine the characteristics of supernormal (gifted) children. Abrom's chapter on social giftedness summarizes the research comparing intellectually and nonintellectually gifted children in terms of social cognition, prosocial behavior, moral reasoning, and leadership. The chapter by Lewis and Michalson briefly looks at the gifted infant. References.

Reports of Research

Gifted Children: Their Identification and Development in a Social Context. (1979). Joan Freeman. Baltimore, MD: Univ. Park Press.

Freeman's book presents the results of the first major investigation of gifted children within their social environment (Gulbenkian Research Project on Gifted Children). This research, which was conducted in England, complements and supports Terman's pioneering work in the United States. It found gifted children to be emotionally and physically at least as sound as other children while recognizing the clear relationship between their development and future success and the nature and quality of their social environments. The research findings are clearly presented, making appropriate use of relevant research studies (American and British).

MENTAL HEALTH

Bibliographies

Bibliography of Child Psychiatry and Child Mental Health. With a selected list of films. Second edition. (1976). Irving Norman Berlin. NY: Human Sciences.

Includes over 4,000 citations on infant, child, and adolescent studies arranged topically.

Early Childhood Psychosis, Annotated Bibliography 1964 - 1969. (1971). Carolyn Q. Bryson, Joseph N. Hingtgen. Rockwood, MD: National Institute of Mental Health.

Entries are divided among seven broad categories: syndrome, intellectual development, perceptual process, language, neurobiological correlates, treatment, and theory.

Reviews of Literature

Autism and Severe Psychopathology. (1982). Edited by John J. Steffen, Paul Karoly. Lexington, MA: Lexington Books. (Advances in Child Behavioral Analysis and Therapy, Vol. 2).

A comprehensive review of research in the field of child psychopathology. Included are chapters on diagnosis, symptomatology, language, behavior, and thinking processes in disturbed children. Most are rich in cited research and attempt to place the multitudinous findings into a manageable theoretical framework. Several chapters are noteworthy. Chapter 5 surveys work on the analysis of language systems of autistic children. Chapter 6 is a comprehensive review of self-stimulatory and self-injurious behavior. The last chapter reviews language training for autistic children. The volume is highly specialized and technical.

The Child in His Family: Children in Turmoil - Tomorrow's Parents. Vol. 7. (1982). Edited by E. James Anthony, Colette Chiland. NY: John Wiley & Sons. (The Child in His Family; Yearbook of the International Association for Child and Adolescent Psychiatry and Allied Professions).

Reports a wide variety of clinical research, all categorized under the general topic of how well the child of today will parent tomorrow. Investigations looked at Sweden, Nigeria, and Northern Ireland. Overall the volume attempts to answer three questions: (1) what kind of parents do disturbed children make; (2) what kinds of children do disturbed parents make; and (3) what kinds of disturbed parents and children do different cultures make. Stress, civil war, drug abuse, alcoholism, suicidal behavior, disruption of attachment, and adoption/fostering are all covered in various chapters. Each paper included in the volume provides a lengthy bibliography of cited sources.

The Child in His Family: Children at Psychiatric Risk. Vol. 3. (1974). Edited by E. James Anthony, Cyrille Koupernik. NY: John Wiley & Sons. (Child in His Family).

This volume is subdivided into four sections. The first section deals with the theory of at-risk and the vulnerability of children. The second section considers the basic risks involved in heredity, constitution, reproduction, and early life experience. The third section covers the topic of environmental risks concerned with growing up in rapidly developing societies (third world). The last section concerns the area of risk and vulnerability. Papers dealing with acute illness in childhood, effects of long term foster care, antisocial behavior disturbances in childhood, and effects of divorce are included in the volume. References.

Childhood Pathology and Later Adjustment. (1979). Loretta K. Cass, Carolyn B. Thomas. NY: John Wiley. (Wiley Series on Personality Process).

Volume discusses research dealing with the long-term effects of clinical diagnosis in childhood and social adjustment in adulthood. Briefly, the research shows that diagnoses of childhood psychosis and severe character disorders including sociopathy are associated with adult pathology. Few studies show that neurosis in childhood leads to serious adult maladjustment and some studies found neurotic children were not distinguishable as adults from "normals." References.

Childhood Psychosis in the First Four Years of Life. (1984). Henry N. Massie, Judith Rosenthal. NY: McGraw-Hill.

Surveys the historical development of the concept of childhood psychosis from a broad perspective, summarizing contemporary research in developmental psychology. The authors report their own research which made use of home movies of infants who were later diagnosed as manifesting autism, symbiotic psychosis of childhood, or mixed form of early childhood psychosis. Comparisons were made with normal children within a control group. A nine-point treatment guide is presented and illustrated with a detailed case history. The appendix contains the Massie-Campbell Scale of Mother-Infant Attachment Indicators During Stress, with directions for administrations and use. References.

Children of Depressed Parents: Risk, Identification, and Intervention. (1983). Edited by Helen L. Morrison. NY: Grune and Stratton.

Presents recent theoretical, clinical, research, and treatment issues of the effects of parental depression on the developing child. Two of the chapters present results from longitudinal studies of offspring of depressed parents. One chapter by Cohler, Gallant, Grunebaum, and Kaufman reports findings from a study of depressed, schizophrenic, and normal mothers and their children. The important function of the father in mediating the effects of maternal psychopathology is suggested in the chapter by Gamer, Grunebaum, and Cohler. These researchers find that, compared to the husbands of nondisturbed women, fathers play a significantly greater role in daily child care when the mother is suffering from affective psychosis. A chapter by Fisher and Kokes gives an excellent overview of research methods in the study of risk and vulnerability. The issue of preventive intervention is addressed in a chapter by Bemesdorfer and Cohler. They describe an innovative new program called Thresholds, designed for psychiatrically disturbed mothers and their young children. References.

Children of Parents with Major Affective Disorders. A Review. (1985). William R. Beardslee et al. In *Annual Progress in Child Psychiatry and Child Development*, 1984, edited by Stella Chess, Alexander Thomas. NY: Brunner/Mazel.

Review of pertinent published studies of children with parents affected by psychological disorders. Studies indicate that children of such parents are very much "at-risk" of developing similar disorders. References.

Clinical Treatment and Research in Child Psychopathology. (1979). A. J. Finch, Jr., Philip C. Kendall. NY: SP Medical and Scientific Books. (Child Behavior and Development, Vol. 3).

A collection of original papers giving contemporary examples of the interplay of research and treatment across a variety of topics in child psychopathology. Chapter 1 is an overview of research methods including strategies for research and for sequencing of the research methods. Chapter 2 examines children's responses to experiences of success and failure and accentuates both adaptive and maladaptive outcomes. Chapter 3 examines anxiety. Chapter 4 discusses the literature on locus of control and its implications for child personality. Chapter 5 discusses research on hyperactivity. Chapter 6 discusses a five-year sequence of studies investigating impulsivity. The first chapter in Section II delineates a program for training parents to be modifiers of the noncompliant behavior of their children. Chapters 8 and 9 look at childhood encopresis and enuresis. Chapter 10 contains an overview of learning disabilities. Chapter 11 presents an empirical approach to the treatment of autistic children. Chapters 12 and 13 deal with retarded and delinquent children. Chapter 14 discusses benefits and problems of drug treatment with children. References.

In Search of Love and Competence: Twenty-five Years of Service, Training, and Research at the Reiss-Davis Child Study Center. (1976). Edited by Rudolf Ekstein. NY: Reiss-Davis Child Study Center.

Volume emphasizes the philosophy of the Reiss-Davis Child Study Center in Los Angeles which is psychoanalytic and dedicated to long-term one-on-one therapy for schizophrenia and autism. The articles are grouped into six parts: Part I, The Reiss-Davis Child Study Center: Its History, Its Philosophy and Purpose, Its Scope; Part II, The Training of the Professional; Part III, The Diagnostic Process, Assessment, and Training; Part IV, Clinical Studies and Treatment; Part V, Research and Exploration; Part VI, Education and School. References.

Motherhood and Mental Illness. (1982). R. Kumar Brockington. London: Academic.

Summarizes present knowledge on the psychiatric hazards of motherhood and psychological development of young children. Chapters 6 and 7 cover attachment and mother-child relationship. Each chapter concludes with a sizeable bibliography.

Research on Child Group Therapy: Present Status and Future Directions. (1986). Robert R. Dies, Albert E. Reister.   In *Group Psychotherapy, Future Tense*, edited by Albert Riester, Irvin Kraft.   Madison, CT: International Universities Press.   (Monograph Series of the American Group Psychotherapy Association.)

Reviews research on the efficacy of group psychotherapy with children. The chapter also outlines several critical issues which the authors think must be addressed before significant progress can be made for future clinical practice and empirical investigation. At the end of the chapter there is an extensive bibliography.

Reports of Research

Ego Impaired Children Grow Up: Post Discharge Adjustment of Children in Residential Treatment. (1978).   John B. Mordock.   Rhinebeck, NY: Astor Home for Children.

Outlines the results of a 10-year follow-up study of children treated at the Astor Home for Children in New York. The home opened in 1953 and admitted children six to ten years old having severe intrapsychic pathology frequently characterized by acting-out behavior. After therapy the children were discharged to foster homes, their families, or one of the guidance clinics. Chapter 4 details the history and current functioning of the former patients. Chapter 5 presents the conclusions related to predictions about the children. A bibliography concludes the study.

Mental Health Programs for Preschool Children. (A field study).   (1974). Raymond M. Glasscote, Michael E. Fishman.   Washington, DC: American Psychiatric Association, Joint Information Service.

This book reports a joint information service field study (American Psychiatric Association and National Mental Health Association) conducted in 1972 - 1973 in eight centers. It focuses on services to children under six years of age, a target group that, according to NIMH studies, receives less than 1% of the direct services provided through mental health. Part I of the book includes a brief review of the literature available on needs and care of young children.   Part II presents an overview of seven of eight programs visited and studied: The Dubnoff Center, North Hollywood; a "quartet of programs" in Topeka; Project Enlightenment, Raleigh; Developmental Center for Autistic Children, Philadelphia; M. L. King Jr. Parent-Child Center, Baltimore; Division of Child Psychiatry, Cedars-Sinai Medical Center, Los Angeles; and the Pre-School Unit, Cambridge-Somerville Mental Health and Retardation Center, Massachusetts.   The appendix presents a simple and straightforward instrument for data collection. References.

Silent Screams and Hidden Cries: An Interpretation of Artwork by Children from Violent Homes. (1985). Agnes Wohl, Bobbie Kaufman. NY: Brunner/Mazel.

The book is an atlas with interpretive text. Fifty drawings of 18 emotionally disturbed children from five to ten years old are analyzed. Each child drew a human figure, families, a house, and trees. The repeated projections of the 18 elementary age children whose drawings are presented mirror feelings of helplessness, powerlessness, fragmentation, depression, anger, and anxiety. Of the 18, 21% revealed sexual abuse. In the appendixes users will find charts presenting background information about the 18 children studied. An excellent bibliography is provided.

Directory

Directory of Residential Treatment Facilities for Emotionally Disturbed Children. (1985). Barbara Smiley Sherman. Phoenix, AZ: Oryx.

Well organized guide with four indexes to assist in searching for an appropriate facility by age, type of placement, characteristics exhibited, and type of funding. Descriptions of facilities are thorough and provide information on educational, vocational, social, and rehabilitative programs. References.

12
Creativity

DATABASES
TO CONSIDER

Exceptional Child
Educational Resources

AHCI
ERIC
PsycINFO

GENERAL

Bibliographies

Creativity in Human Development: An Interpretive and Annotated Bibliography.
(1976). A. Reza Arasteh, Josephine D. Arasteh. NY: Schenkman.

Section I focuses specifically on the young child. Provides a review of studies
on all aspects of creativity and related processes. A substantial annotated
bibliography concludes the chapters.

The Index of Scientific Writings on Creativity: Creative Men and Women. (1974).
Albert Rothenberg. Hamden, CT: Shoe String.

A comprehensive bibliography of the world literature on personality study of
creative persons in the arts. It contains references to scientific writings about
major figures in the arts listed in major abstracting and indexing sources and
book catalogues. Arranged alphabetically according to last name of the
creative artist. Entries are not annotated. This volume plus *The Index of
Scientific Writings on Creativity. General: 1566 - 1994*, provides a
comprehensive bibliographic coverage on creativity from indexed world
literature.

The Index of Scientific Writings on Creativity. General: 1566 - 1974. (1976).
Albert Rothenberg, Bette Greenberg. Hamden, CT: Shoe String.

A comprehensive index covering scientific writings on creativity from world
literature. The eight chapters include all aspects of creativity. Chapter 3
focuses on developmental studies including children. Chapter 8 focuses on

nurturing creativity through education. This volume along with the previously published, *The Index of Scientific Writings on Creativity: Creative Men and Women*, provides a comprehensive coverage of scientific writings on creativity from indexed world literature.

Reviews of Literature

The Arts and Cognition. (1977). Edited by David Perkins, Barbara Leondar. Baltimore, MD: Johns Hopkins Univ. Press.

This volume is a collection of writings by participants in Harvard's Graduate School of Education, Project Zero, on education and the arts. Part I, theoretical and definitional, deals with art as representation, as symbolization, and as an encoding process. In Part II, dealing with symbolic processes, Howard Gardner defines two significant components of artistic production based on Piaget's notions of operation and figuration. Part III deals with how symbols are translated into meaning. Barbara Leondar's study of storytelling by young children takes essentially a structuralist position. In the stories of very young children there is an inherent form which appears to disintegrate somewhat in slightly older children. Diana Korzenik acknowledges that children's drawings reveal far less than they know and that it is well to encourage and capture the child's running commentary while drawing if one is to learn what the child's drawing truly tells about its knowledge. Part IV reports experiments with art forms not often addressed in psychological research. References.

Children's Aesthetics. (1984). Ellis D. Evans. In *Current Topics in Early Childhood Education*, Vol. 5, edited by Lilian Katz. Norwood, NJ: Ablex. (Current Topics in Early Childhood Education).

This chapter represents one of the few current reviews of children and aesthetics to be found in the literature. A very comprehensive bibliography concludes the chapter which will be quite helpful to individuals doing research in art, music and general aspects of aesthetics and children.

The Creative Vision: A Longitudinal Study of Problem Finding in Art. (1976). Jacob W. Getzels, Mihaly Csikszentmihaly. NY: John Wiley & Sons.

Appendix 3 is a review of literature on creativity. Substantial bibliography.

The Gifted and the Creative: A Fifty Year Perspective. (1977). Edited by Julian C. Stanley, William C. George, Cecilia H. Solana. Baltimore, MD: Johns Hopkins Univ. Press.

This book is a highly interesting and well-edited report of the proceedings of a symposium held at Johns Hopkins University. The contributors provide an excellent overview of the leading longitudinal studies of gifted children, beginning with the more than 55-year-old study initiated by Lewis Terman, including the Johns Hopkins Study of Mathematically Precocious Youth and the Intellectually Gifted Child Study Group, also of Johns Hopkins, as well as E. Paul Torrance's longitudinal study of students specifically selected for their creative potential. An important note arising in all the longitudinal study papers is the need for distinguishing intellectual giftedness in the sense of IQ or special aptitude measures from creative potential which not all high IQ children have. Papers additional to those on longitudinal studies per se extend the interest value of the book by providing information on family experiences, personality characteristics, and social background.

Invented Worlds: The Psychology of the Arts. (1982). Ellen Winner. Cambridge, MA: Harvard Univ. Press.

This volume summarizes most of the relevant theory and research regarding the psychology of artistic behavior. The thirteen chapters are divided among five parts: personality and intellect, painting, music, literature, art and abnormality. Within each broad topic, Winner determines the important issues and presents relevant research and theory. Secondary topics include theories of artistic expression, the development of aesthetic sensitivity to art, and the art of autistic children. An exhaustive list of references is included.

Research in Arts Education. (1978). Judith Murphy, Lorna Jones. Washington, DC: Department of Health, Education, and Welfare. (ED 157 816).

Provides an overview of art education research from 1965 - 1970. Chapter 1 offers a history of art education research. Chapters 2 - 4 cover various funding programs and conferences. Chapter 5 focuses on research into art classroom occurrences and practices. Topics covered include measurement and testing, teaching methods, art in the curriculum, music in the curriculum, educational laboratory theater, and curriculum development. References.

Research on Teaching Arts and Aesthetics. (1986). Beverly J. Jones, June King McFee. In *Handbook of Research on Teaching*, Third edition, edited by Merlin Wittrock. NY: Macmillan.

Article synthesizes research in the areas of aesthetic education, visual arts education, dance, and dance education. References.

Reports of Research

Arts in Education. The Use of Drama and Narrative: A Study of Outcomes. (1986). E. N. Wright, R. E. Young. Toronto: Ontario Ministry of Education.

Study looked at the achievement gains made when daily story-telling sessions or drama sessions were used with grade one inner-city Toronto children. Results showed significant achievement gains, including vocabulary, with the story groups but less gains with the drama groups. References. A brief summary of this study may be found in Rosemary E. Young's *Bringing the 'Bedtime' Story into Inner-City Classrooms*. (1986). Toronto: Ontario Ministry of Education.

Other References

Learning to Read and Write: The Role of Language Acquisition and Aesthetic Development. A Resource Book. (1986). Ellen J. Brooks. NY: Garland. (Garland Reference Library of Social Science, Vol. 278).

The focus of this volume is the acquisition of literacy and its relation to two major areas of child development: language development, and aesthetic growth.   Chapter 1 looks at the connection between learning to talk and reading.   Chapter 2 delves into the relationship between cognitive processes and artistic activity and those that occur in reading and writing.   Chapter 3 focuses on current theoretical and instructional perspectives regarding reading and writing.   Chapter 4 integrates curriculum and its extension outside the classroom.

ART

Bibliographies

Art Education: A Guide to Information Sources. (1978). Clarence Bunch. Detroit, MI: Gale Research. (Art and Architecture Information Guide Series, Vol. 6).

Bibliography of books and pamphlets about art or art methods with children. Included are general reference sources and serials along with information on publishers and organizations. Author, title, and subject indexes are included.

Reviews of Literature

Art Education. (1982). Kenneth R. Beittel.   In *Encyclopedia of Educational Research*, Fifth edition, Vol. 1. NY: Free Press.

Reviews the literature of art education and provides a lengthy bibliography of references.

Child Art: The Beginning of Self-Affirmation. (1966). Edited by Hilda Present Lewis. Berkeley, CA: Diablo.

This slim volume brings together reports, discussions, and exhibits from a conference held on the Berkeley campus of the University of California in 1965.   The conference brought together the world's most distinguished art educators.   The theme of the conference was understanding the child's artistic development and its significance for creative living.   Schaefer-Simmern sees in the child's perfect drawing of forms an outward sign of inner order, a sign that the child has mastered his universe. Arno Stern finds logic in children's art work and in changes that occur as children grow older. Frank Barrow sees the dialectics of the creative process as a conflict between the tendencies to structure and to disrupt structure. Rhoda Kellogg talks about the emergence of new forms through the destruction of old. Sir Herbert Read sees art as a language, free from limits of time or place. Ralph Arnheim relates a case history of an exceptional child overcoming his handicaps through art. August Heckscher and Victor D'Amico express concern over formless art and recommend that educational goals aimed at cultivation of sensibilities, the training of tastes, and the discipline of emotions be developed. References.

Children Drawing. (1977). Jacqueline Goodnow. Cambridge, MA: Harvard Univ. Press. (Developing Child).

This volume of the series looks at children's drawings from the viewpoint of cognitive development rather than as a key to the emotional state of the child. Goodnow brings together research findings from a diverse set of sources to alert readers to material that is not readily available. Chapter 1 discusses why we should study children's drawings. Chapter 2 shows how the child's drawings are made up of units which combine into patterns and how the choice of units and combinations gives information about how the child is progressing through developmental stages. Chapter 3 discusses the way in which children approach a drawing. Chapter 4 concentrates on the copying of simple shapes and the implications of such tasks for problem-solving skills and applications to academic performance. Chapter 5 discusses how the child develops conventions so that others might understand his drawings. Chapter 6 discusses how children break away from the conventional equivalents that they learn and develop new representations. Chapter 7 is a summary of findings and some suggested directions for further study. Substantial references.

The Child's Representation of the World. (1977). Edited by George Butterworth. NY: Plenum.

This book is a collection of papers reporting experimental studies of children's drawings and art work. The first part consists of papers on children's drawing. The papers in the second section are concerned with the relation between action, perception, and the spatial field. The third part contains only a paper by Liam Hudson on the concept of representation in the tradition of Bartlett. The fourth part, containing four papers, generally covers the philosophical and cross-cultural aspects of representation. Butterworth's book is considered a classic in the area of children's art. References.

Developing Cognitive Skills through Art. (1982). Rawley A. Silver. In *Current Topics in Early Childhood Education*, Vol. 4, edited by Lilian Katz. Norwood, NJ: Ablex.

This chapter provides pertinent literature, rationale, and a summary of six studies which have used the Silver Test of Cognitive and Creative Skills. Implications of the test's uses for the educational practitioner are discussed. Twenty-one references.

Drawing and Cognition: Descriptive and Experimental Studies of Graphic Production Processes. (1984). Peter Van Sommers. Cambridge: Cambridge Univ. Press.

This book is a comprehensive study of drawing behavior, encompassing work by adults and children in semi-experimental settings and covering virtually all aspects of graphic work, from stroke making through controlled life and form, to drawing from models, with attention to the perception of planes and solids, to handedness, and to sequentiality and directionality in drawing. The investigator's approach is primarily observational and empirical. He uses data based on both groups and individual examples to support his conjectures and conclusions. While he stops short of a formal statement of theory, he does draw parallels with language and communication theories. Discussions concern the geometric, semantic, and pragmatic aspects of drawing, plus some consideration of personal style, and interrelation among these dimensions. He stresses the great diversity in drawing behavior, even within the procedures and strategies of one subject, this despite his extrapolations from single examples. References.

Educating Artistically Talented Students. (1984). Gilbert Clark, Enid Zimmerman. NY: Syracuse Univ. Press.

This volume addresses the many facets of educating children who have superior abilities in the visual arts. Chapter 1 provides a summary of the history of gifted students and presents a program structure for artistically talented students. Chapter 2 provides a review of literature dealing with identifying gifted students. Chapter 3 summarizes the research and inquiry into teacher characteristics and teaching strategies. Chapter 4 summarizes what is known about curriculum content and makes recommendations. Chapter 5 lists educational settings and arrangements for talented students. Chapter 6 is a summary of major issues and findings regarding the educating of artistically talented students. References.

Relating Art and Humanities to the Classroom. (1977). Robert J. Saunders. Dubuque, IA: William C. Brown.

This book raises fundamental questions about what constitutes an adequate art education for children in our culture. The discussions are comprehensive and knowledgeable, with useful surveys of the literature on each topic provided. The author draws his observations from a wide range of sources including the Owatonna Art Education Project (1934 - 1938) and the art objectives of the National Assessment Program of 1971. References.

Review of Recent Literature on Figure Drawing Tests as Related to Research Problems in Art Education. (1971). Harold J. McWhinnie. In *Review of Education Research*, 41 (2).

This paper reviews experimental research and its implications for the use of figure drawings as assessment instruments in art ability. Thirty-six references.

Young Children and Their Drawings. (1970). Joseph H. DiLeo. NY: Brunner/Mazel.

This monograph is in two parts. The first part explores and provides examples of art produced by normal young children. The second part investigates the art of children with unusual and deviant cognitive patterns. References.

Reports of Research

Children's Human Figure Drawings: Development, Sex Differences, and Relation to Psychological Theories. 2 vols. (1984). Karen Vibeke Mortensen. Denmark: Dansk Psykologisk Forlag.

This study analyzed and described children's drawings of human figures. The author used data collected from 180 children, ten boys and ten girls at each age level from five to thirteen years, drawn from kindergartens and schools. The study concentrated on sex differences in the children's drawings as well as projective features of the drawings. Findings indicate notable differences in the ways boys and girls draw same and opposite sex figures. The author concludes that these differences reside in part in basic psychological differences, not explained fully by socialization or training. The literature review in Volume 1 is comprehensive, critical, and insightful. These two volumes represent a landmark in the use of children's drawings for clinical psychological purposes. References.

Heidi's Horse. (1976). Text by Sylvia Fein. Pleasant Hill, CA: Exelrod.

Fein assembled an unusual developmental study of a single child's drawings. The earliest drawing is Heidi's scribbling at two years. By the time she is four, the horse emerges as a seven-legged stick figure with a happy human face. The sequence terminates with a horse drawn with mature artistic sensitivity when Heidi is sixteen years old. The sequence illustrates both the often observed lag between perception and performance and the rather cyclic character of developing maturity. The format and style of the book are attractive, and Fein has judiciously avoided interpretive comments, letting the horse, for the most part, do the talking.

How Preschool Children View Mythological Hybrid Figures. (1982). Harvey Nash. Washington, DC: University Press of America.

This book compares the responses of young children with those of adults confronted with mythological hybrid figures. The questions raised by Nash's findings are motivational as well as cognitive. He found that most preschoolers called the mythological hybrids "animals." References.

Les Deux Personages: L'être Humain Dessinè par les Garçons et les Filles de 6 à 18 Ans. (1977). Paul A. Osterrieth, Anne Cambier. Paris: Presses Universitaires de France.

This study supplies a remarkably objective taxonomy for classifying many of the features of children's drawings presently used "projectively" (many as used by Machover), such as movement, shading, quality of line, position of drawing on the page, use of space, dress, demeanor, and actions of the figure, etc. Written only in French.

Six Children Draw. (1981). Edited by Sheila Paine. London: Academic.

This small volume contains five essays and one interview concerning the drawings of children. The volume is illustrated with examples of 368 children's art. The juvenile work of two accomplished artists appears. The drawings of four contemporary children are also included, one a young man presently enrolled in art school and the other a child artistic as a youngster but normal in adulthood. With one exception, the essays lack the kinds of observations and accessory information desired by the child development researcher. However, the book still is of value to researchers in that it suggests a kind of research long needed to complement the growing number of quantitative studies of children's drawings based on collection obtained experimentally from samples of children. The systematic case study is promising as a source of information about how a complex skill, drawing, and artistic production generally develop.

What Children Scribble and Why. (1955, 1959). Rhoda Kellogg. Palo Alto, CA: National Press Book.

This book is based on a study of over 100,000 drawings and paintings by children two to four years old who attended the Golden Gate Nursery Schools in San Francisco. The stated purpose of the study was to draw attention to certain sequential, developmental aspects found in the work of children. The author collected more than 75,000 drawings of children over a five-year period. The twelve chapters break the drawings into types, such as radials and the sun, human figures, combinations, basic scribbles, etc. Each chapter begins with a discussion of that type of art followed by examples of children's work. Chapter 12 is a classification system for analyzing and filing drawings. Anyone interested in analysis of children's drawings will be fascinated by this classic.

Young Children's Sculpture and Drawings: A Study in Representational Development. (1974). Claire Golomb. Cambridge, MA: Harvard Univ. Press.

This book is concerned with a study made of two- to seven-year-olds and their representations of the human figure in Playdough, paper, and crayon drawings. The study was conducted in Israel and the United States and involved 300 children. The results of the study indicate that a child's representation of a person varies as a function of the specific task and the medium employed. References.

Other References

Resources for Educating Artistically Talented Students. (1987). Gilbert A. Clark, Enid D. Zimmerman. Bloomington, IN: Syracuse Univ. Press.

This book describes and evaluates a variety of resources for teaching artistically talented students. The volume is organized into four chapters. Chapter 1 reviews state policies about education of the gifted and talented. Chapter 2 gives suggestions for people beginning new programs. Chapter 3 reviews current methods used to identify gifted students. Chapter 4 outlines criteria for selecting instructional materials and evaluates an extensive list of available materials. Appendixes contain forms used by the Indiana University Summer Arts Institute, instructional materials, checklists, testing instruments, graded guides, and samples of student test responses. Listings of organizations and other resources available to administrators and teachers are included. References.

DANCE

Bibliographies

Dance: An Annotated Bibliography, 1965 - 1982. (1986). Fred R. Forbes, Jr. NY: Garland.

Lists references on dance in the areas of aesthetics, anthropology, education, history, literature, physiology, and sociology. About 187 entries in the chapter entitled Education directly relate to children ages five to thirteen. Entries are briefly annotated. Volume contains subject and author index.

DRAMA

General

Creative Drama in the Classroom. (1984). Nellie McCaslin. NY: Longman.

The new edition of this classic gives practical help for the nonprofessional. Each chapter includes lists of activities and resources. A lengthy bibliography is included.

The Dramatic Curriculum. (1980). Richard Courtney. NY: Drama Book Specialist.

Discusses drama education in schools and presents suggestions for including drama into the curriculum. Extensive bibliography.

Bibliographies

Child Drama: A Selected and Annotated Bibliography, 1974 - 1979. (1981). Carol Jean Kennedy. Washington, DC: Children's Theater Association of America.

This bibliography focuses on drama for children in preschool through ninth grade. Includes doctoral dissertations and some journal articles.

Children's Theater and Creative Dramatics: An Annotated Bibliography of Critical Works. (1985). Rachel Fordyce. Boston, MA: G. K. Hall.

Lists about 2,270 source materials relating to drama for children. Emphasis is on critical and instructional work. Entries are annotated.

Reviews of Literature

Drama: Educational Programs. (1985). R. B. Shuman. In *The International Encyclopedia of Education, Research and Studies*, Vol. 3. NY: Pergamon.

This brief article traces the history of drama in the schools. Short paragraphs cover the role of the teacher, mime, role playing, student generated improvisation, and educational outcomes. Sixteen references.

Dramatic Arts Education. (1982). John Stewig. In *Encyclopedia of Educational Research*, Fifth edition, Vol. 1. NY: Free Press.

Synthesis of research on creative drama in education. Substantial references.

Other References

Putting on the School Play: A Complete Handbook. (1980). Adrienne Holtze, Grace A. Mayr. NY: Prentice-Hall.

This book offers ideas on coaching methods, costumes, special effects, fiscal problems, and play selection for the drama coach or teacher in charge of the school play.

MUSIC
by Marian Ritter

Bibliographies

The Children's Jubilee. A Biliographical Survey of Hymnals for Infants, Youth, and Sunday Schools Published in Britain and America, 1655 - 1900. (1983). Compiled by Samuel J. Rogal. Westport, CT: Greenwood.

The entries in this annotated bibliography of hymnals for children is divided into two major groupings, American and British. Within each group the entries are arranged alphabetically by author or editor. Four indexes are included in the monograph. Index A is entitled Sponsoring Denominations, Organizations, Institutions and Societies. Index B is entitled Sponsoring Churches and Schools. Index C is entitled Authors, Compilers, Editors and Contributors. Index D is entitled Printers and Publishers. Users will find that not all entries are annotated.

Early Childhood Musical Development: A Bibliography of Research Abstracts, 1960 - 1975. With Implications and Recommendations for Teaching and Research. (1978). Gene M. Simons. Reston, VA: Music Educators National Conference.

Contains one- or two-page abstracts of virtually all the published research in early childhood music education from 1960 to 1975. This book deals with music responses and development of infants and young children from prenatal period to age seven. Indexed.

General

Ability Development from Age Zero. (1981). Shinichi Suzuki. Translated by Mary Louise Nagata. Athens, OH: Ability Development Association.

Discusses a basic understanding of his philosophy that he formulated almost forty years ago. He surrounded children with musical sounds from birth and started them on violin at a young age. The author believes that every child has a "sprout" of talent and it is the parents' responsibility to create an environment where that talent can be nurtured and developed. Indexed.

Children and Music. A Handbook for parents, teachers and others interested in the musical welfare of children. (1979). Atarah Ben-Tovim. London: A & C Black.

This book outlines benefits of learning to play a musical instrument and techniques of learning and practicing. Includes interviews with children. Indexed.

Children Create Music. A new approach to the musical education of small children. (Kinder gestalten Musik. Ein neuer Weg zur Musikerziehung bei Kleinkindern). (1982) Christine Gauster. Wien: Osterreichischer Bundesverlag.

Book discusses music as a form of self-expression similar to play activities. References.

Concerts for Children. (1977). Diethard Wucher. Regensburg: Bosse.

Describes how to organize concerts for children.

Council for Research in Music Education. Bulletin 59. (Summer 1979). Urbana, IL: School of Music, Univ. of Illinois Press.

Seven articles from this issue discuss developing musical ability in young children. Authors discuss rhythmic tasks and rhythmic forms. One interesting article discusses development of pitch concepts with children. References.

Council for Research in Music Education. Bulletin 66 - 67. (Spring/Summer 1981). Urbana, IL: School of Music, Univ. of Illinois Press.

Issue features eleven articles on the child's musical education and development. Rhythmic abilities of preschool-aged children are discussed. References.

Grundriss der Musik pädagogik. (1985). Sigrid Abel-Struth. Mainz: Verlag B. Schott's Sohne.

This thorough discussion by a respected German authority considers all aspects of the question of music pedagogy, its status as a discipline, and its relationship to other modern disciplines. The book contains an extensive bibliography of titles which includes items not only from the literature on music pedagogy itself, but relevant titles in other disciplines, including many English language titles.

Music--Part of the Child. (1980). Estrid Heerup. Kobenhavn: Gyldendal Paedagogiske Bibliotek.

The book discusses the musical development of children. It stresses the view that music should not be forced upon the child. References.

Musical Prodigies: Masters at an Early Age. (1973). Renee Fisher. NY: Association.

Description and analysis of over 300 musical personalities who were child prodigies. There are some omissions of prodigies and the author has included some questionable prodigies. The book is informative. References.

The Young Child and Music: Contemporary Principles in Child Development and Music Education. (1985). Edited by Jacquelyn Boswell. In *Proceedings of the Music in Early Childhood Conference*, Brigham Young University, June 28 - 30, 1984, Provo, UT. Reston, VA: Music Educators National Conference.

Included in this monograph are papers authored by specialists, music educators, learning theorists, and researchers discussing topics related to early childhood and music education. References.

Your Children Need Music: A Guide for Parents and Teachers of Young Children. (1979). Marvin Greenberg. Englewood Cliffs, NJ: Prentice-Hall. (A Spectrum book).

This book discusses the musical development of a child from birth to five years. In the second part, there is a wealth of "how-to-do-it" material. The book takes a practical approach based on current theories of child development, psychology, and music education. The emphasis is on how to carry out musical activities, but the theory behind those activities is revealed also. References.

Reviews of Literature

Council for Research in Music Education. Bulletin 86. (Winter 1986). Urbana, IL: School of Music, Univ. of Illinois Press.

Articles in this issue review research dealing with music development in early and middle childhood. Musical aptitude, rhythmic abilities, singing, and music reading are included. References.

Documentary Report of the Ann Arbor Symposium on the Applications of Psychology to the Teaching and Learning of Music. Session III: Motivation and Creativity. (1983). Music Educators. Reston, VA: Music Educators National Conference.

Summarizes current knowledge and theory in motivation and creativity. The results are then applied to teaching and learning music at all levels. Nine papers are included in the monograph which were presented at the Ann Arbor Symposium third session. Of particular interest to child development specialists might be the paper by Jacquelynee Eccles (Parsons) on motivating children to study music. Another interesting paper is one by Donald J. Treffinger entitled, Fostering Creativity and Problem Solving. References.

Music and Child Development. (1987). Craig Peery, Irene Weiss Peery, Thomas W. Draper. Holland: Springer-Verlag.

Provides an overview of research in the field. Summaries of thirteen separate research projects are included. Most chapters contain literature reviews in specific areas. Gaps in research are noted. Bibliographies conclude each chapter. An author and subject index is provided.

Music Education. (1982). J. David Bayle, Rudolf E. Radocy. In *Encyclopedia of Educational Research*, Fifth edition, Vol. 3.

Article synthesizes music research, teaching and learning, and curricular movements. References.

Research in Music in Early Childhood Education: A Survey with Recommendations. (1976). Marvin Greenberg. In *Council Research Music Education Bulletin*, XLV. Honolulu, HI: Univ. of Hawaii Press.

Reviews research through 1975 in music education for children up to the age of five. Summarizes findings on infants and musical response, singing skills, rhythmic response, music for disadvantaged preschoolers, listening to music, conceptual learning in music, aural discrimination, the role of the environment in music learning, evaluation tools, and teacher training.

Reports of Research

Challenges in Piano Teaching: One-to-One Lessons for the Handicapped. (1978). Sidney J. Lawrence. Hewlett, NY: Workshop Music Teaching Publications.

Using eleven case histories, Lawrence explains techniques he uses in teaching piano to children with perceptual dysfunctions or are hyperkinetic, hyperactive, retarded, or physically handicapped. References.

The Musical Experience of the Preschool Child. (1976). Helmut Moog, translated by Claudia Clarke. Mainz: B. Schott.

Reports a study of nearly 500 children and evaluation of material from some 1,000 parents. The tests included nursery songs, rhythmic patterns, instrumental excerpts, cacophonies and non-musical sounds. He played the same tests to children at ten different age levels, from six months to five and one-half years. The author attempts to relate his findings to what is known about the general development of the child. References.

Teaching Methods

Clinically Adapted Instruments for the Multiply Handicapped. (1979).   Cynthia
Clark, Donna Chadwick. Westford, MA: Modulations.

This sourcebook includes 100 adapted and original instrument descriptions
and designs. Each listing includes a diagram of the instrument, a description,
and instructions for use. Percussion, wind instruments, stringed instruments,
and melodic instruments are included. References.

Creative Music Education: A Handbook for the Modern Music Teacher. (1976).
R. Murray Schafer. NY: Schirmer Books.

This book describes involving students in creating music, ear training, the
acoustic environment, words and music, and music in relation to the other
arts. There are exercises for teachers to try in their classrooms. This book is
very valuable in teaching the students to understand the basic components.
References.

Creative Teaching of Music in the Elementary School. (1974).   Dorothy Hickok,
James A. Smith. Boston, MA: Allyn & Bacon.

Book explores ways of integrating music into the total school curriculum and
how to apply the principles of creative development to classroom teaching.
References.

Didactics of Elementary Education in Music and Movement. (1979).   Ursula
Gebhard, Michael Kugler. Munchen: Don Bosco.

This book explains Carl Orff practices of a musical education. A sequence of
two-year curriculum schemes and twenty-two detailed lesson plans are
included. References and glossary.

Eurhythmics, Art, and Education. (1930, reprinted 1972). Emile Jaques-Dalcroze.
Translated by F. Rothwell. Edited by Cynthia Cox. NY: Benjamin Bloom.

This book explains his theories and systems. It is a tool for guiding the young
to a better understanding of music and dance.

For the Love of Music: A Guide for Parents of Young Musicians. (1978). R.
Wilson. North Vancouver, BC: Douglas and McIntyre.

This book is a well-researched guide for parents whose children are already
musicians. It offers support for parents.

Hearts and Hands and Voices: Music in the Education of Slow Learners. (1976). David Ward. London: Oxford Univ. Press.

First chapter covers the development of musical skills in early childhood. In the following chapters music activity suggestions are listed in three different age groups; below age nine, nine to twelve years, and older than twelve years of age.

The Kodaly Context: Creating an Environment for Musical Learning. (1981). Lois Choksy. Englewood Cliffs, NJ: Prentice-Hall.

Summarizes the principles of the "Kodaly method" with emphasis on songs and new material. References.

MMCP Interaction: Early Childhood Curriculum. Second edition. (1971). Americole Biasini et al. Bardonia, NY: Media Materials.

This book is a comprehensive plan for early childhood music learning produced by the Manhattanville Music Curriculum Program and sponsored by the Arts and Humanities Program of the Office of Education. References.

Mostly Movement. Book I. (1979). Edith Wax, Sydell Roth. NY: Mostly Movement.

The activities outlined here are appropriate for groups of children aged three to eight and are based on the Dalcroze Philosophy of eurhythmics (body movement to music). Rhythm instruments are necessary for the majority of the activities, and the teacher must be able to sing.

Music. Basic Books in Education: Schooling in the Middle Years. (1974). Marjorie Lilian Glynne-Jones. London: Macmillan.

Book describes techniques for teaching music to eight- to thirteen-year-old children. References.

Music Experiences in Early Childhood. (1980). Barbara Andress. NY: Holt, Rinehart and Winston.

Book is devoted to singing and playing with sound-making objects for use with three- to five-year-old children. Includes ideas for music activities. Appendix contains definitions, a resource list, guitar chords, songs to use throughout the day, and a bibliography. Includes music and index. References.

Music Therapy for the Autistic Child. (1978). Juliette Alvin. NY: Oxford Univ. Press.

Presents various techniques used in helping autistic children achieve a degree of self-expression and communication through music.   Case histories included. References.

The Music Therapy Sourcebook: A Collection of Activities Categorized and Analyzed. (1981). Cecilia Schulberg. NY: Human Sciences.

This volume has a broad spectrum of activities related to music therapy adaptable to any age and category of client.   The sixteen chapters are arranged by the type of activity such as Music and Dance, and Music and Games. Each activity has the following subtopics: purpose of the activity; procedure for action; rules governing action; number of required participants; roles of participants; results or payoff; abilities and skills required for action; interaction patterns; physical setting and environmental requirements; and required equipment.   Four short chapters describe developmental music therapy, music therapy and music education, musical productions, and psychiatric musicology. These chapters are followed by appendixes of films, recordings, organizations, and books.

Oregon Calls the Tune. (1977). Delmer W. Aebischer. Salem, OR: Oregon ASCD Curriculum Bulletin.

Explores of what a total school music program, K - 12, consists. Chapter 1 gives indicators of quality programs. Chapter 2 outlines a general program. Chapter 3 gives illustrations of five mini courses for fifth through seventh grades. Chapter 5 talks about string programs. Chapter 7 reports the 1975 survey of music education in Oregon.   The appendix provides a self-evaluation checklist for school programs.

Orff and Kodaly Adapted for the Elementary School. (1985). Lawrence Wheeler, Lois Raebeck. Third edition. Dubuque, IA: William C. Brown.

This book describes the Orff and Kodaly teaching methods. References.

The Orff Music Therapy: Active Furthering of the Development of the Child. (1980). Gertrud Orff. London: B. Schott.

This English translation by Margaret Murray of the 1974 edition examines the relationship of Orff music therapy to Orff-Schulwerk. Also discussed is its use with different handicaps, including sensory, hearing and speech, physical, mental, and behavioral. Case histories are presented, along with suggestions for treatment and individual therapy. References.

Sing a Rainbow: Musical Activities with Mentally Handicapped Children. (1979).
   David Ward. London: Oxford Univ. Press.

   This is a valuable book which emphasizes methods to work with mentally
   handicapped of all ages.

Teaching Music in the Twentieth Century. (1986).   Lois Choksy, Robert M.
   Abramson, Avon E. Gillespie, David Woods.   Englewood Cliffs, NJ:
   Prentice-Hall.

   The four most commonly used approaches in North American public school
   general music teaching are discussed in this book: Jaques-Dalcroze, Kodaly,
   Orff and comprehensive musicianship.

Teaching Music to the Exceptional Child: A Handbook for Mainstreaming. (1980).
   Alice S. Beer, Richard Graham. Englewood Cliffs, NJ: Prentice-Hall.

   This book gives examples of goals and the music for meeting an instructional
   plan. Singing, moving activities, and playing are recommended. References.

They Can Make Music. (1973). Philip Bailey. London: Oxford Univ. Press.

   Provides step-by-step instruction for the classroom teacher.   There is an
   extensive appendix with a list of collections of devices on music-making aids
   usable with physically handicapped children. References.

Author Index

Title Index

Subject Index

About the Contributors

Enid E. Haag is Education Librarian and Associate Professor at Western Washington University, Bellingham, WA. She is the author of several articles appearing in the *Delta Kappa Gamma Bulletin*, and the *Journal of Physical Education, Recreation, and Dance* among others. She contributed to *Teaching Reading, Thinking, and Study Skills in Content Classrooms*.

Dana Johnson is the Online Reference Services Coordinator and Assistant Professor at Western Washington University Libraries. She is a graduate of Lewis and Clark College (B.S., 1981) and the University of Washington Graduate School of Library and Information Science (M. Libr., 1986). Her experience includes management of both a retail store and a computer laboratory for graduate students. She is actively involved in evaluation and application of computer technologies in her present position.

Marian Ritter is Music Librarian and Assistant Professor at Western Washington University, Bellingham, Washington. She received her B.M.E. in 1967 from the University of Portland in Portland, Oregon, and her M.L.S. in 1969 from the University of Portland. She taught music in the Portland Public Schools and Clackamas School District in Oregon before coming to Western in 1969.